Courbet

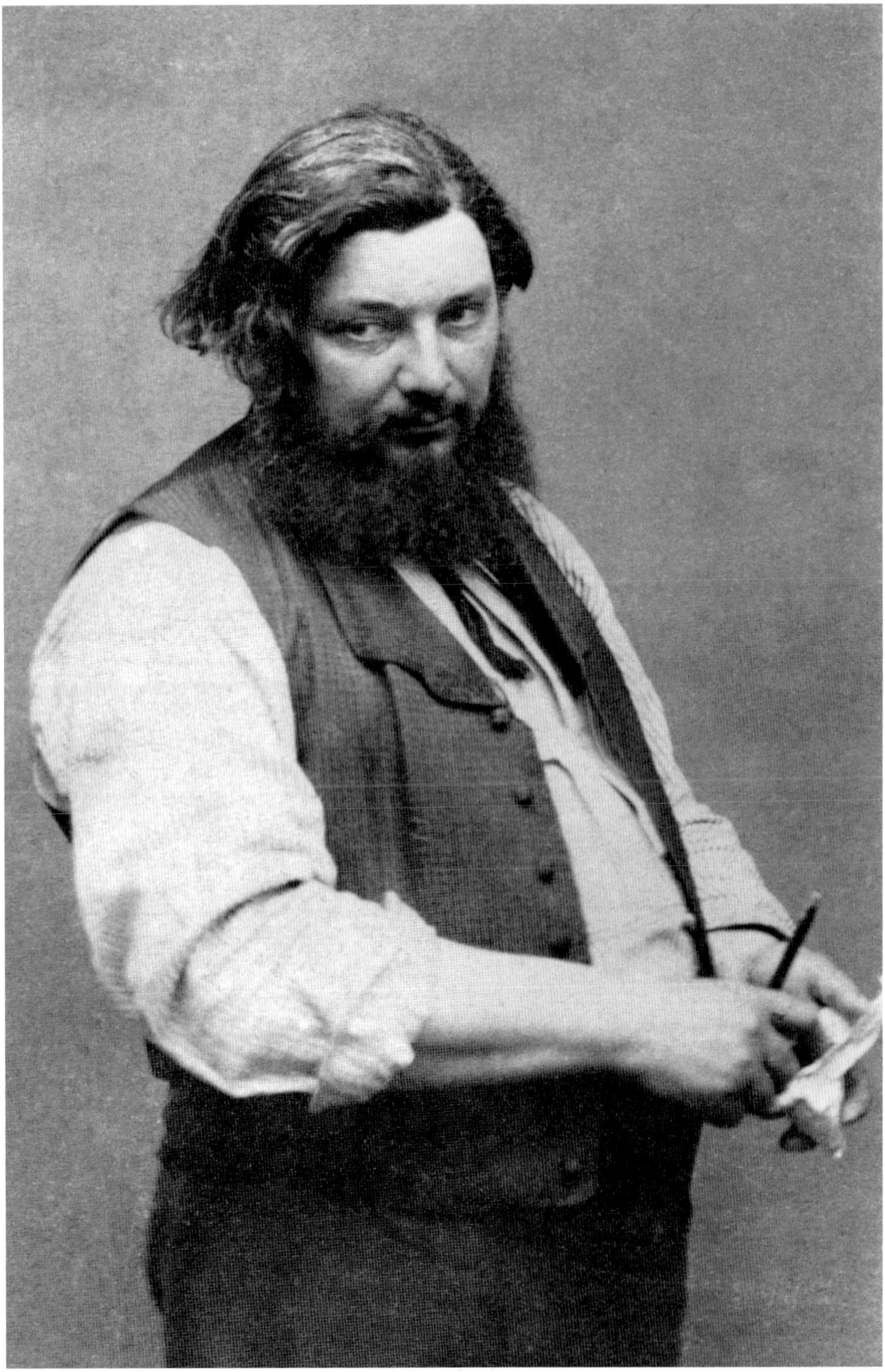

Courbet

Linda Nochlin

With 109 illustrations, 14 in colour

Thames & Hudson

To Nikos Stangos, in loving memory

I would like to thank the participants in my Fall 2006 graduate seminar on Courbet at the New York University Institute of Fine Arts for their help in preparing this book. Special thanks go to my two assistants, Camille Mathieu and Nate Donahue, and to Nicole Myers and Jodi Roberts, for their considerable efforts in the preparation of this manuscript. The other friends and colleagues who assisted me in my Courbet studies over the years are mentioned in the Introduction and in the relevant chapters. I am grateful to those at Thames & Hudson who advised and edited, especially my editors, Andrew Brown and Julia MacKenzie.

Frontispiece: Etienne Carjat, *Gustave Courbet*, after 1860

First published in the United Kingdom in 2007 by
Thames & Hudson Ltd
181A High Holborn
London WC1V 7QX

www.thamesandhudson.com

British Library Cataloguing-in-Publication Data
A catalogue record for this book is available from the British Library

ISBN 978-0-500-28676-0

Printed and bound in Singapore by CS Graphics

Contents

Introduction: Courbet, the Real Allegory

This book, like Courbet's famous *The Painter's Studio* [pl.11, pp.138–39], is a real allegory. Unlike Courbet's vast canvas, however, which is an "allegory summing up seven years of my artistic and moral life," it is an allegory of almost half a century of my life as an art historian. For the articles, written over a period of years extending from the early 1960s to 2006, not only inscribe the subjects in Courbet's life and production that interested me at the time they were written, but they register the changes in my own methodology, outlook, and style of scholarship. What has really not changed over the years is my sense of intellectual and emotional engagement with ideas and objects. I have never been, and never will be, a dry, objective scholar of Courbet, or any other artist or issue. I believe, to borrow the often cited but rarely followed dictum of the French nineteenth-century poet and critic Baudelaire, that art criticism, and to a lesser degree, its history, should be "partial, passionate, political, that is to say, written from an exclusive point of view, but a point of view that opens up the widest horizons."[1]

Courbet, as his self-portrait on the cover of this book so tellingly reveals, was and is, an immensely seductive artist. By this, I do not mean that his persona was physically engaging, as it obviously was at the early stages of his career, but rather that his work, despite its surface immediacy, and its apparent ease of availability, has often seemed, paradoxically, to hide a secret, or produced an effect of the occulted and suggested an alluring mystery of withheld meaning rather than the clear legibility one might expect of a realist artist. This effect of hiddenness makes the viewer, especially if that viewer is him or herself an artist, want to go further in the pursuit of the painting: it is psychological or even hermeneutic seduction that is at stake. If meaning is not immediately apparent, then the devices of allegory must come into play, calling forth a construction of meaning based on the ambiguous clues provided by the artist. Almost half a century ago, Hélène Toussaint suggested the presence of a secret code of Masonic signs as well as a cast of hidden political figures as a subtext in Courbet's *Studio*.[2] Other interpreters have unpacked simple or complex socio-political readings from scenes of village life or provincial landscape. More recently, the interpretive seductions lie in the realm of the psychosexual or erotic meanings to be drawn from Courbet's overtly sensual nudes, or less overtly, his landscapes, sexual or erotic, either in terms of unconscious content or references to a tradition of erotica or pornography.

Perhaps Courbet's admirers, artists most prominently among them, are seduced into reading their own obsessions or at the very least intense feelings into Courbet's mysterious imagery, whether it be that of a nude or a landscape or a funeral. "I little knew why I liked the great tree by Courbet [*The Oak of Flagey*, pl.13, pp.142–43], standing alone in a smallish canvas, and the only object there, but it is one of the pictures most vividly remembered," declared the Philadelphia-born portraitist Cecilia Beaux in the later nineteenth century.[3] More recently, painters as different as Balthus, John Currin and Kathleen Gilje, of whom more later, have been drawn to the example of Courbet. Marcel Duchamp drew heavily on the inspiration of the master, most overtly in his construction, *Etant données*, at the Philadelphia Museum of Art, and a few years ago, the installation artist Tony Oursler was commissioned to produce his own version of *The Studio in situ*, as it were, right next to the giant canvas at the Musée d'Orsay.

As for myself, as a graduate student at the Institute of Fine Arts of New York University, I was first seduced by the clearly political resonance of Courbet's works of the late 1840s and 1850s. This seduction was doubly re-enforced: on the one hand, by my study of the effects of the 1848 Revolution on art and artists in a term paper for a class on nineteenth-century art taught by H. W. Janson; on the other, by my contemporary and personal engagement with the vicious persecutions and drastic curtailment of civil rights brought on by the ideological witch hunt of so-called subversives led by Senator Joseph McCarthy and the House Un-American Activities Committee in the 1950s. The essays on the *Burial at Ornans*, on Courbet's *The Meeting*, Courbet and the Commune and the de-politicization of Courbet are clearly related to this political impulsion, if by no means completely defined by it. The essay on the image of the working woman, while still involved with the politics and class struggles of the nineteenth and early twentieth centuries, is deeply implicated with a new kind of political and social engagement: that of feminism, which was to assume a larger and larger role in my art-historical thinking. A major essay such as "Courbet's Real Allegory," which includes a lengthy feminist rereading of the multiply mysterious *Painter's Studio*, my *jeu d'esprit* with the then unrecovered *Origin of the World*, as well as my interpretation of the implications of the hotly contested iconography of the *Toilette de la mariée*, certainly are unthinkable without the dominating feminist component of my art-historical agenda, which continues, in ever-changing form, to this day.

It is because these essays are very much part of their times that I have made no attempt to "correct" or amend them, although I shall attempt, briefly, to place them in their historical and personal context. An attempt to bring them up to date would be deceptive and incorrect in terms of the context – the historical moment – in which they originated. Changing a text implies that if you keep digging away, you will finally get at the truth. Certainly, new material, new documents and new discoveries about individual paintings have come to light; new and fruitful interpretations have been made of all the works and issues I have written about. But the value of a particular piece of writing lies in the art-historical situation as it appeared at the time it was written, not some purportedly "better" relation to the facts. Indeed, some of the more controversial pieces, such as the one on the *Toilette de la mariée,* about which scholars have made well-supported counterarguments about the subject matter, and the *Studio,* a work that I have deliberately read in depth as an allegory, at times against the grain of the purported "meaning" of Courbet's own iconographic program, are important at least in part because they are, either intentionally or not, provocative readings. I may say, additionally, that I can think of nothing more boring and fruitless than revising an already completed text long after the fact. Writing a completely new article about an individual work or issue involving Courbet from a different point of view – certainly (I provide an example in the present volume with two articles on *A Burial at Ornans*); tinkering much later with an earlier text – never.

I shall begin at the beginning with a contextualization of the first piece in this volume, "Innovation and Tradition in Courbet's *A Burial at Ornans*." Some of the material for this article had appeared in my 1963 doctoral dissertation, "Gustave Courbet: A Study of Style and Society," written for the Institute of Fine Arts, New York University.[4] I wrote the article itself for a volume titled *Essays in Honor of Walter Friedlaender,* a supplementary issue of the Institute's publication, *Marsyas,* in 1965.

This is the place to acknowledge the enormous impact of the work of Meyer Schapiro on this article, and much of my subsequent work on Courbet in the 1960s and 1970s. Schapiro's magisterial article, "Courbet and Popular Imagery," which had appeared in the *Journal of the Warburg and Courtauld Institutes* as early as 1941, lay at the heart of my synthesis of iconography and form in analyzing the *Burial,* and my understanding of the painting's importance as a social, as well as an artistic document. When I had started out on my dissertation, I was confronted by a serious dichotomy in the ranks of Courbet scholars. To paraphrase my introduction to the work: on the one hand, there were those who found Courbet's social and political beliefs and activities either at odds with or at least irrelevant to the art of the master. On the other, were those who felt that Courbet's social and political outlook seemed to be the very foundation on which his art was based. Meyer Schapiro provided the missing but necessary link between these two views of Courbet, in pointing to the artist's consistent reference in the subject matter and style of the major works of the late 1840s and early 1850s – the *Burial* [pl.2, pp.66–67], *The Stonebreakers* [pl.7, p.71],

The Peasants of Flagey [54, p.122], the *Firemen* [15, p.33], and *The Meeting* [pl.6, p.71] – to popular imagery, specifically to the anonymous woodcuts produced for an untutored audience of peasants and workers, naïve in style and traditional in subject matter, known as *imagerie d'Epinal.* It was not that Courbet was unaware of more sophisticated styles and sources, far from it. He certainly references the Dutch, Spanish, and French seventeenth century in a work such as the *Burial.* But in the stiffness, the simple compositions, the unarticulated human figures, and the time-honored tropes characteristic of popular imagery, he found an art which was, he believed, at one with the democratic impulse of 1848, an art of the common people.

My engagement with the impact of *imagerie d'Epinal* continued and expanded in "Gustave Courbet's *Meeting:* A Portrait of the Artist as a Wandering Jew," which appeared in the *Art Bulletin* in 1967 and won the 1968 Arthur Kingsley Porter Prize for the best article published in the *Art Bulletin* in 1967 by a scholar under forty. The writing of this piece was especially propitious in that I actually found a direct source for the composition of the famous painting in a specific popular image: a representation of the Wandering Jew meeting two burghers of the town. The relationship was clear and undeniable. Nothing in my career as an art historian could possibly match the heady excitement of the moment when, sitting in my obscure desk in the Print Room of the Bibliothèque Nationale, leafing through box after box of dusty *images,* under the inspiration of Meyer Shapiro, I finally came upon The One: unquestionable and bright as the day when Courbet looked at it, or one just like it. I had found the Source! I must admit that I had had a particular interest in folk art long before I studied Courbet, and still have. Folk music was a hobby in high school and college. I listened, collected, and sang folk songs of all nationalities and types, leafing through volumes of English Child Ballads and their American equivalents from the Appalachians, collected by Alan Lomax and available through the Library of Congress; listening to Blues and sea chanties, Scottish and Irish ballads, memorizing, phonetically, Spanish Civil War songs and folk music, learning wonderful lyrics in Basque and Catalan as well as French. I loved the words and music, often modal, Aeolian or Dorian, or otherwise offbeat, but, as a young American leftist growing up in New York in the 1930s, 1940s and 1950s, I knew this was my music – our music, actually – for I was not alone in my folk-song cult, just more extreme than some. There were whole groups of us, often accompanied by a guitarist, or five-string banjo player, gathered in Washington Square over the weekends, singing "Viva la Quince Brigada" or "Pretty Polly." Courbet and his *imagerie d'Epinal* seemed from this point of view like an old friend, not a dry, long-dead scholarly subject.

The next piece I embarked on was also indebted to folklore, this time, the folkloric scenario relating to marriage and bridal customs in rural France, specifically in Courbet's native region of the Franche-Comté. The article, "Gustave Courbet's *Toilette de la mariée,*" certainly marked by its feminist viewpoint, was heavily indebted to a previous account of the nuptial scenario in the French provinces by

Jean Seznec, reprinted in "La Mariée en voyage: Smith's Courbet Abroad," *Bulletin of the Smith College Museum of Art*, where the painting resides to this day. Alas, it was not to be known as the *Toilette de la mariée* for long. In 1977, in the pages of the catalogue in which she shed so much new light on Courbet's iconography and intentions, Hélène Toussaint maintained that the painting was, in fact, originally intended by Courbet to represent the "Toilet of a Dead Woman," a picture of funeral preparations rather than bridal ones, transformed at a later date either by Courbet or by another hand in the interest of better saleability. Toussaint backed her claims with considerable evidence, both documentary and pictorial. In fact, Smith College itself has retitled its property, transforming it from bride to dead body with the flick of a label. But I am far from convinced, nor are several other scholars of the situation, most notably Marie-Hélène Huet, who, in a brilliant and well-argued article of 1995, questioning Toussaint's evidence point by point, proposes that the subject is indeed a bride, but a bride with a difference, a bride whose existence conjures up the image of death rather than celebration.[5] The mystery and ambiguity of meaning now enshrouding Courbet's *Toilette of the Bride/Dead Girl* adds depth and complexity to the scenario. Indeed, as Elizabeth Bronfen has pointed out in the pages of her provocative text, *Over Her Dead Body: Death, Femininity and the Aesthetic*, "Courbet's canvas brings the interchangeability of bridal and death ritual into focus in a complex way .... In this palimpsest the bride is only uncannily animate, with the dead body shining through its beautified disguise to disclose not only once again that beauty hides death, but also that inanimation is inherent in all representation."[6]

Equally feminist in its inspiration was my piece on the representation of the nineteenth-century working woman, centered on Courbet's monumental *Grain Sifters* of 1854 [pl.5, p.70], now in the Museé des Beaux-Arts of Nantes. In "The *Cribleuses de blé*: Courbet, Millet, Breton, Kollwitz, and the Image of the Working Woman," given as a paper in Frankfurt at the Courbet Colloquium in 1979, and subsequently published through the good offices of my friend and fellow Courbet scholar, Klaus Herding, I was interested in the difference between the powerful central figure who holds the sieve in her muscular, outstretched arms and the usual representation of the peasant woman as passive and resigned, as she so often appears in the work of Millet, or rosy-cheeked and alluring, as in the work of Jules Breton. It was Käthe Kollwitz, I felt, who picked up on the image of the powerful peasant woman early in the twentieth century, under the inspiration of August Bebel's *Woman and Socialism*, in her figure of Black Anna summoning her fellow peasants to revolt. *The Grain Sifters*, like so many of Courbet's canvases of the period, remains mysterious and provocative. It is painted with great subtlety and a seductive richness and variety of paint texture and depicted surface. The rich drapery of the orangey skirt, the furry cat curled up behind the bowl to the left, the scattered nubs of chaff on the floor, the lattice of light on the wall – all make the viewer want to reach out and touch them. The mystery, though, enhanced by the very material specificity of the painted details, remains. Just what are these people doing, I ask myself? In the article, I propose a little allegory of agricultural progress, moving from left to right; perhaps I am on the right track.

Also enabled by Klaus Herding was the article "Courbet, the Commune, and the Visual Arts," published in German in his volume *Realismus als Widerspruch: Die Wirklichkeit in Courbets Malerei* in 1978.[7] I had become deeply interested in the Commune, that short-lived radical government, or anti-government, established by the Parisian proletariat, leftists, and intellectuals for a few months in 1871. A great deal of new research on both the Commune and the visual arts, especially caricatures and photographs produced in conjunction with it, appeared on the anniversary of the event, including an exhibition in the working-class quarter of Saint-Denis. I spent a long time doing research on the Commune material, both old and new, in the years following the centenary of the event, my interest continuing as late as 1985, as evidenced by an interview by Jon Wiener in that year in the *Radical History Review*.[8] Herding's publication provided the ideal venue for an article examining Courbet's activities within an overview of the Commune and the visual arts more generally.

"The De-Politicization of Gustave Courbet: Transformation and Rehabilitation under the Third Republic" was originally presented as a talk in the late Kirk Varnedoe's session at the 1982 meetings of the College Art Association. The session was titled "French Art and Politics in the Third Republic"; the essay was originally published in the journal *October* that year and later in *Art Criticism and Its Institutions in Nineteenth-Century France,* a collection of essays edited by Michael Orwicz.[9] It is basically a piece of critical historiography, demonstrating how Courbet was interpreted to serve varying purposes by critics and supporters with different social and political agendas. What is interesting in Courbet's case is how transparent so many of these interpretive strategies now seem today, the would-be purely "artistic" ones as much as the overtly political texts.

My piece centered on Francisco Oller and his relation to Courbet was again prepared for a conference, this one in Ponce, Puerto Rico, in celebration of the one hundredth anniversary of the birth of the Puerto Rican master. "Courbet, Oller, and a Sense of Place: The Regional, the Provincial, and the Picturesque in Nineteenth-Century Art" deals with a topic I have been involved with often in recent years: that of national identity and its expression in art. Certainly, it has arisen recently in at least two quite different projects: the first is the article on "Courbet and his Territory," which is the final piece in this volume of essays. But the issue of national or ethnic self-awareness also appears, heavily intertwined with the dominating one of gender identity, in the exhibition and catalogue, *Global Feminisms,* that I curated with Maura Riley for the Brooklyn Museum in 2007. In the case of Oller, it was a question of how to be modern, of one's own times, by finding a language and a subject matter that at once referenced the style of the French vanguard and yet remained in some way faithful to his national roots, his identity as a Puerto Rican, albeit a member of the elite, and a cosmopolitan figure as well. The question of creating an American art, at once authentically national yet undeniably contemporary, whether Northern, Central or Southern, has continued as a major topic for artists through the twentieth century and beyond, in the work of such artists as Rivera, Kahlo, both Orozcos, Wifredo Lam, and many others too numerous to mention in Latin America; Emily Carr or "The Seven" in Canada; the Regionalists and Georgia O'Keeffe in her New Mexican paintings. Also, but more problematically, the work of the American Abstract Expressionists and Pop artists bears witness to the ubiquity of this particular dimension of modern production.

Courbet's "*L'Origine du monde*: The Origin without an Original" was first presented as a paper in Rosalind Krauss's session, a symposium on "Originality as Repetition," at the College Art Association meetings in 1986.[10] It made quite a sensation, as I remember, with members of the audience giving little shrieks or laughing nervously as slide after slide, blurry, underdeveloped or hand tinted, of Courbet's virtuoso rendition of the same indiscreet subject, the female sex-organ, or cunt, as I more conveniently call it, appeared on the screen accompanied by a properly scholarly and objective lecture. Of course, the whole point of the piece has been somewhat lost now that the canvas, prepared for private delectation by its commissioner, Khalil Bey, and a select group of male guests, hangs in public on the wall of the Musée d'Orsay, accompanied by postcards and a slew of enticing and often highly informative publications.[11] Still, it makes its point on a theoretical level if not on a material one, now that the original *Origin* is available to the view of a wide and generally receptive public. I must admit I have always felt rather put off by *The Origin*. Certainly, it doesn't arouse me; it embarrasses me. It doesn't produce any of that lovely, momentary goosey feeling that really good literary porn does, and even a third-rate adult video can probably raise my blood pressure higher at least momentarily. On the other hand, I never get used to it. I don't feel capable of accepting it as merely another nude in Courbet's repertory, as some art historians, especially male, would have me do. It certainly has nothing of intimacy; its closeness is that of the gynecological examination, not that of the lover admiring his partner's aroused body. Perhaps I would respond to *The Origin* more positively if Courbet had made it one of a pair of paintings, the putative pendant delineating similarly, "con amore," as an outraged Maxime du Camp would have it, a *man's* lower body and penis. Certainly, it takes two to make an origin! It is, perhaps, most accurately described as a beautifully painted "beaver shot," produced with an accuracy that borders on that of the medical illustration – or the hand-tinted photo. Courbet I believe is once again in competition with a relatively new rival medium – photography – from which he most probably derived the basic material of his image, greatly improving on it in terms of texture, color and startling close-up viewpoint. In effect, in *The Origin* he is asserting that his image is more realistic than the one captured by the new medium and made the greater claim to indexicality. Valérie Bajou is entirely correct in her assertion that by adopting pornographic photographs as a source for both the iconography and composition of *The Origin* Courbet was demonstrating both his technical prowess and modernity.[12]

In "Courbet's Real Allegory: Rereading *The Painter's Studio*," a catalogue essay written for the major exhibition of Courbet's work, "Courbet Reconsidered," curated by Sarah Faunce and myself in 1988, I appropriated Courbet's vast cast of characters for a feminist replay of his scenario, a creative rather than a scholarly maneuver, and as such, a highly transgressive, as well as enormously satisfying move. That is not all I do in this long, two-part essay. I also attempt to unpack the implications of the allegorical mode in *The Studio*, looking back to the work of Walter Benjamin, Angus Fletcher, Paul de Man, Klaus Herding and many others for inspiration. In addition, I try to plumb the depths of the notion of the Unfinished in art: the cloudy, suggestive and always open-ended status of the work that has never been completed and never will be. Once more, Courbet is mysterious in this vast summarizing canvas: both because he wants to be – "guess who can," he exasperatingly remarks to a friend in a letter purportedly explaining the meaning of the work – and because the canvas, as an unfinished and at least partially unreadable text, offers, in fact, a challenge to art-historical interpretation. I see this essay as a summarizing, ambitious, and inevitably open-ended – never finished – climax to my study of Courbet's major paintings of the 1850s, in many ways invoking the qualities of the painting to which it is devoted.

My most recent essay, "Courbet and his Territory: How Landscape Means" was originally presented as a lecture at the Getty Museum in Los Angeles, on the occasion of their exhibition "Courbet and the Modern Landscape," curated by Mary Morton and Charlotte Eyerman in 2006. In the essay I have amalgamated two very different approaches to the issue of landscape and meaning. The first is a long – sixty-five pages – intensely scholarly article I wrote in the late 1970s on Courbet's *Oak of Flagey*, then in the Pennsylvania Academy of the Fine Arts. The second is a more general and personal account of Courbet's involvement with "nature" and its representation, on his home turf and by the sea in Normandy. To contextualize Courbet's landscape approach, I draw on Cézanne and the contemporary landscape photographer Robert Adams, and inevitably become embroiled in contemporary ecological issues. These are now of great concern to me and many others, especially contemporary landscape photographers and video artists like those assembled in the remarkable exhibition "Ecotopia" at the International Center for Photography in New York in 2006–7. Future work on Courbet's landscapes would certainly reflect these contemporary concerns as my earlier work incorporated the political concerns of that day.

What might I have added to this volume, had I "but world enough, and time"? Certainly, an essay on the portraits, especially the extraordinary *Portrait of P.-J. Proudhon in 1853* [1], painted posthumously in 1865, based on memory, a photograph, and a death mask, one of the greatest portraits of the century and unique in its oddness and veracity. I might have wished Courbet had chosen a more sympathetic socialist thinker and activist, someone like Herzen or Bakunin, for his masterpiece,

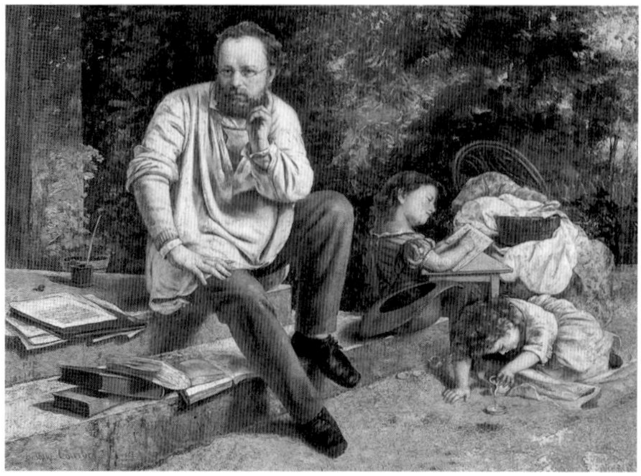

1 *Portrait of P.-J. Proudhon in 1853*, 1865. Oil on canvas, 147 x 198 cm, 57⅞ x 78 in.

but of course it was Proudhon, his long-time friend and fellow Franc-Comtois whom he decided to commemorate after the anarchist philosopher's death.[13] Perhaps there is a semi-satirical homage to David's neo-classical *The Lictors Returning to Brutus the Bodies of his Sons* [2] embedded in the pensive, even brooding, classical thinker's pose of the protagonist, and in the slight suggestion of classical drapery in the folds of the peasant smock Proudhon wears in solidarity with the working class; David's impress appears also in the strict division of the canvas into masculine and feminine zones, the ball of yarn indicating the absent feminine presence. But Courbet, unlike David, makes the space of commemoration domestic rather than public, including two peacefully playing little daughters in the tranquil little garden, rather than the distraught, dramatically grief-stricken young daughters in the *Brutus*. Equally significantly, he removed the image of the wife of his protagonist after the picture was first shown, substituting the metonymic ball of yarn for her redundant persona, still visible in x-ray. No doubt Mme. Proudhon detracted too much from the dominating presence of her misogynistic husband, the hero of the piece. It is not just the iconography of the painting, personal and political at once, but how it is painted that seduces, its combination of the ordinary, the downright pedestrian even abject details, and the loving way they are painted: each element caressingly differentiated as shape and substance – shoes, sweater, blouse, steps – yet equalized in their degree of accuracy. The seduction of the real, however, is not the only thing that draws us to the *Portrait of P.-J. Proudhon in 1853* today, but a proto-postmodernist allure in the composition's assiduous additive-ness, its refusal to amalgamate all the parts into a slick, satisfyingly harmonious whole. It strikes the contemporary viewer as something new, something different from any other portrait of its time and place, uncannily, if perhaps not intentionally, awkward and unresolved, despite its high degree of finish.

Most of all, I should like to devote some time to the study of Courbet and modernity: the artist's fascinating and problematic relationship to twentieth-century and contemporary art. I am not so interested in direct takeovers of Courbetian motifs,

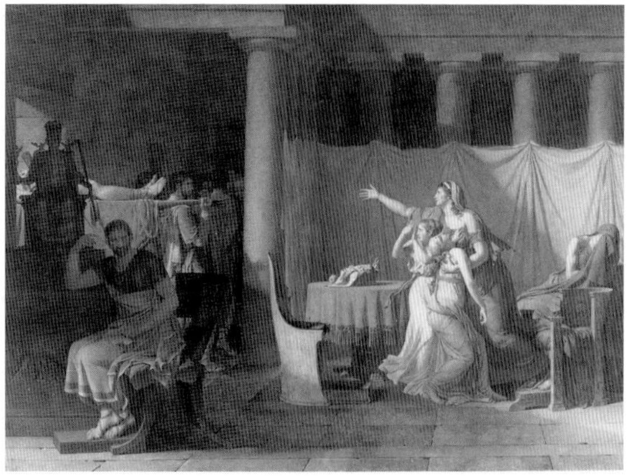

2 **Jacques-Louis David**, *The Lictors Returning to Brutus the Bodies of his Sons*, 1789. Oil on canvas, 323 x 422 cm, 127⅛ x 166⅛ in.

such as Picasso's variation on the theme of *The Young Ladies of the Banks of the Seine* [74, p.176], nor even a work as grotesquely provocative as Renoir's blubbery *Bathers* of 1918, which I have elsewhere characterized as "the postcoital sequel to Courbet's scandalous lesbian *Sleepers* of 1866 [36, p.58], the two lovers now satiated and languorously awake, the blonde woman lying back in the traditionally seductive hands-behind-the-head pose, the dark haired 'dominant' nude apparently meditating in the classical 'thinker' pose, if one can associate anything as coherent as thinking with this monstrously corporeal creature."[14] Renoir, in his old age, has created a scene of pastoral innocence out of Courbet's torrid nude couple. Nor am I really concerned with the various contemporary artistic progeny of *The Origin*, works such as Marcus Harvey's *Julie from Hull*, which overlays gold de Kooning style Ab Ex facture with the contours of Courbet's lower-belly study.[15] Duchamp's multi-layered and volatile appropriations and manipulations of Courbet *topoi* have been noted and analyzed in the case of the peep-hole installation in the Philadelphia Museum, but not until recently has a wholesale rapport between the two artists been established, as in the case of *The Large Glass (Bride and her Bachelors)* and the *Toilette de la mariée*, or *The Woman with a Parrot*. These are seen as providing natural analogues for Duchamp's more arcane enterprises, at least according to such diligent investigators as Nicholas Lowie and Sheridan Lowrey, both connected to the Museum for Jurassic Technology in Los Angeles, in their unpublished essay, "Combes de Jura, cols alité coucher de la mariée," and who have published some of their findings relating Courbet and Duchamp, among other things, in a fairly incomprehensible, if invigorating pamphlet titled *Jura-L.A [A] Rrose is an apple* ....[16]

What really interests me, however, is Courbet's unquestionable impact on the current of what I might call "perverse realism" in modern and contemporary art. I am thinking particularly of Balthus, and, today, of John Currin and, though with a feminist edge of wry humor, Kathleen Gilje. Balthus, who avowedly loved Courbet, is really the key figure in "making strange" motifs and figures from the master.[17] (In this way, he almost functions as a link between Courbet and that contemporary connoisseur of strangely sexualized bodies and disturbing poses, John Currin.) *The Mountain,* a major work of the 1930s by Balthus, obviously references Courbet's *Young Ladies of the Village* [pl.4, p.70], a connection made palpable by the typical Franc-Comtois cliffs behind the figures, which are strangely disconnected and, in the case of the reclining female, overtly seductive, in contrast to the primness and propriety of Courbet's three sisters decked out in their Sunday best. In *The Children* (there are actually several versions) of 1937, the little girl in the foreground is appropriated from the innocent – but to Balthus, suggestive – figure of Proudhon's little daughter reading in the garden in Courbet's portrait. Balthus's version is far from innocent, however. To a post-Freudian, associated with the Surrealists, childhood is rife with forbidden, scarcely contained desire, and the young girl, especially, is ripe for perverse experience. Did Balthus seek out Courbet because he found in him a streak of hidden, almost surreal *unfreundlichkeit* in his work; or was he simply projecting his own bizarre fixations onto the relatively neutral territory offered by Courbet's canvases? Who can say? And what constitutes "neutrality" in a work of art, especially in work as full of ambiguities, contradictions and dissonances as Courbet's?

In John Currin's work, all creatures and human relations are conceived under the aegis of the Uncanny. A kind of withered exquisite grotesquery marks the human body, especially as it ages, transforming women especially into startlingly fashionable yet horrific crones. You don't know whether you are meant to laugh or cry. References

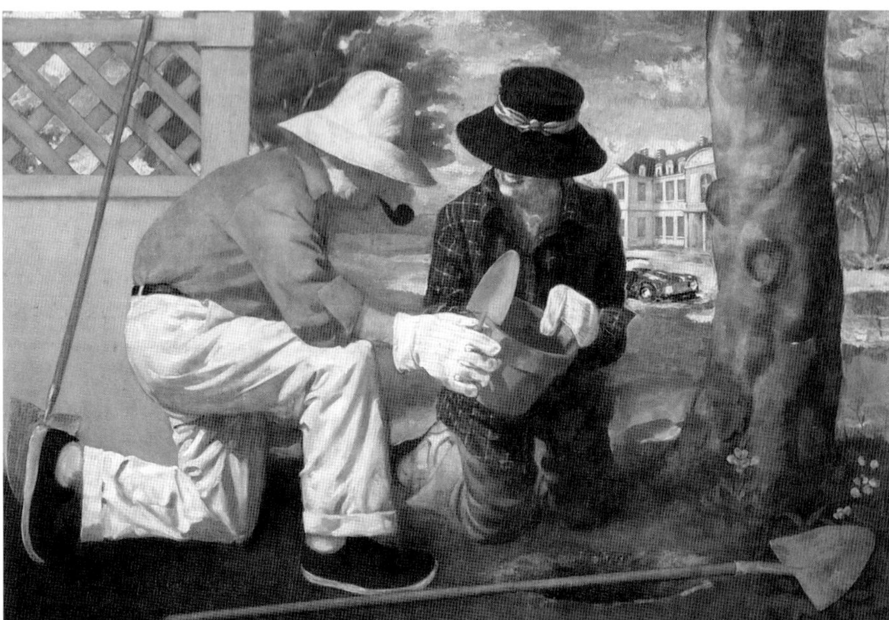

3 **John Currin**, *The Gardeners*, 2001. Oil on canvas, 132 x 190.5 cm, 52 x 75 in.

to the history of art, oddly skewed, abound. Courbet is an obvious touchstone, but a Courbet mysteriously sinister, made strange and more than strange by odd alterations of mood and detail, or exaggerations of potential weirdness already existing in the prototype. In *The Gardeners* of 2001 [3], clearly a re-conception of Courbet's monumental *Stonebreakers* [pl.7, p.71], Courbet's anonymous representatives of the oppressed proletariat have been transformed into a sinister upper-class middle-aged couple, apparently re-potting a plant, or perhaps up to something more devious. The pose of the male figure, with its carefully, realistically wrinkled trousers and big protective hat, blatantly mimics Courbet's old man with the hammer, but his hands, like his partner's, are protected by big, white gardening gloves. And instead of the desolate stony road and mountain foiling the stonebreakers in Courbet's picture, Currin has sardonically substituted an enormous mansion and a meticulously painted sports car in the background. Why does this feel as though a little of the *Burial* has crept into the scene in the foreground, implications of death or even murder? I wonder if Currin actually read what Proudhon later wrote in praise of Courbet's directness in his depiction of poverty in *The Stonebreakers*: "If Courbet … was as fond of antithesis as Victor Hugo, nothing would have been easier than to create a contrast in his picture; he would have placed the stonebreakers next to the gate of a mansion; behind that gate, in perspective, a large and elegant garden; … Courbet preferred the bare, open road with all its aridity and monotony."[18] Currin, like Courbet, rejects contrast between rich and poor in his recasting of a socially critical work of the nineteenth century, only he does it tongue in cheek: his "workers" and his setting are both incontrovertibly rich!

In Currin's *Kissers* of 2006, it is the voluptuous and full-bodied figures of Courbet's *Sleep*, another Khalil Bey commission, that are the obvious source. It is as though he has zoomed in on the original painting for a close-up. But Currin imbues Courbet's motif with his own brand of slick, sickly perversity – Courbet *via* Balthus – steeping the refined surfaces in a self-consciously contemporaneity relishing the open-mouthed kiss and the aura of mock-decadence, re-enforced by the seductiveness of the blonde and brunette flesh painting and the sexual intensification of the interlocking curves of arms, heads, and drapery. Perhaps referencing *The Origin* in its square, close-up format, and certainly mindful of the eighteenth century, Boucher perhaps, in the tiny, tantalizingly erect nipple in the foreground, *The Kissers* puts a new spin on the idea of decadence in art. And it certainly is sexy, with touch and taste called into play as much as vision.

Kathleen Gilje's project is a different one: a feminist debunking of the "greatness" of male representations of naked women by means of realism itself. In the case of her line-for-line version [4] of Courbet's *The Woman with a Parrot* in the Metropolitan Museum, a totally convincing full-scale copy (Gilje has practiced as a conservator), she has added what she claims to be an x-ray of the canvas – convincingly painted in black, white, and gray, revealing that beneath the parrot's perch once stood a nude

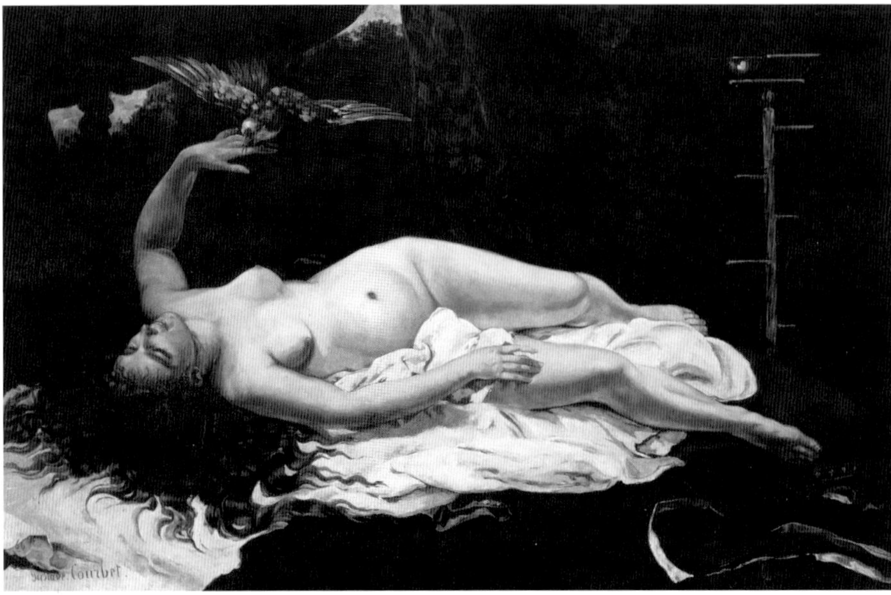

4 **Kathleen Gilje**, *Courbet's Woman with a Parrot, Restored*, 2001.
Oil on linen, 129.5 x 195.6 cm, 51 x 77 in.

figure of the artist himself, fully erect, looking down at the model. In the interests of saleability, he removed his naked presence and substituted the present perch and the parrot. So convincing were both the painting and the "x-ray" that several gallery goers who should have known better were completely taken in by the spoof: Courbet hoisted on the petard of his own realist reality – or rather, reality effect! This is what art is about, say the images: male desire for and power over the female body.

Finally, I would like to recognize the work of two authors not yet mentioned, but who along with Valérie Bajou, Petra Chu, James Rubin, and Klaus Herding, have been a source of information, stimulation, and provocation. T. J. Clark and Michael Fried, both in different ways, revised and re-invigorated Courbet scholarship and interpretation in ways too numerous to mention. I often think that intelligent disagreement, minor or vehement, is a more potent stimulant to thought and illumination than mere acceptance, goading one into a writerly rather than a merely passive readerly response to the material, to borrow Roland Barthes's terms. In any case, I would like to reiterate the fact that I believe art history to be a cooperative rather than a solitary endeavor. Whatever I have produced of value is based on the thought and research of many others, past and present. This of course includes my students, especially those in my 2006 seminar on Courbet at the Institute of Fine Arts. Like me, my predecessors and peers, it would seem that a future generation of art historians has been seduced by the example of Gustave Courbet.

1 | Innovation and Tradition in Courbet's *A Burial at Ornans*

While Gustave Courbet's *A Burial at Ornans* [pl.2, pp.66–67] is generally held to constitute a landmark in the art of the nineteenth century, its revolutionary quality is usually considered a function of the artist's choice of subject rather than a result of pictorial innovation. Yet a careful examination of the painting both reveals the extent to which it is formally as well as thematically advanced, and brings out the connection of Courbet's innovations with the whole climate of progressive thought surrounding the 1848 Revolution.

From the vantage point of the present, it is perhaps difficult to see exactly why the *Burial at Ornans* created such a furor among Parisian critics and public when it first appeared in the 1850–51 Salon.[1] It is only when one examines the work in the context of the accepted standards for a major Salon piece at the time that the reasons for the scandal created by Courbet's painting become clear.[2] If, for example, one confronts the artist's "tableau historique,"[3] begun a year after the Revolution of 1848,[4] with the most highly praised history painting of the Salon of the year preceding the uprising, Thomas Couture's *Romans of the Decadence* of 1847 [5], a work which had in fact found favor in the eyes of such progressives as the left-wing critic, Théophile Thoré, and the anarchist philosopher, P.-J. Proudhon,[5] the gap which separates the traditional painting of the period from Courbet's Realism becomes immediately apparent.

Despite Couture's intention to create a timely commentary on the corruption of Louis-Philippe's government in *The Romans of the Decadence*,[6] his painting, in comparison with Courbet's, is an anachronism, not merely because he has conveyed his message in the outmoded language of the past, but in the very fact that his painting contains any explicit message at all. In clothing a social meaning in classical garb, Couture was of course merely following a time-honored precedent. In a similar way, David had criticized the government of Louis XVI in *The Oath of the Horatii* at the end of the eighteenth century, and Delacroix had found it necessary to elevate the actuality of the 1830 Revolution to the realm of acceptable art by the addition of a classically

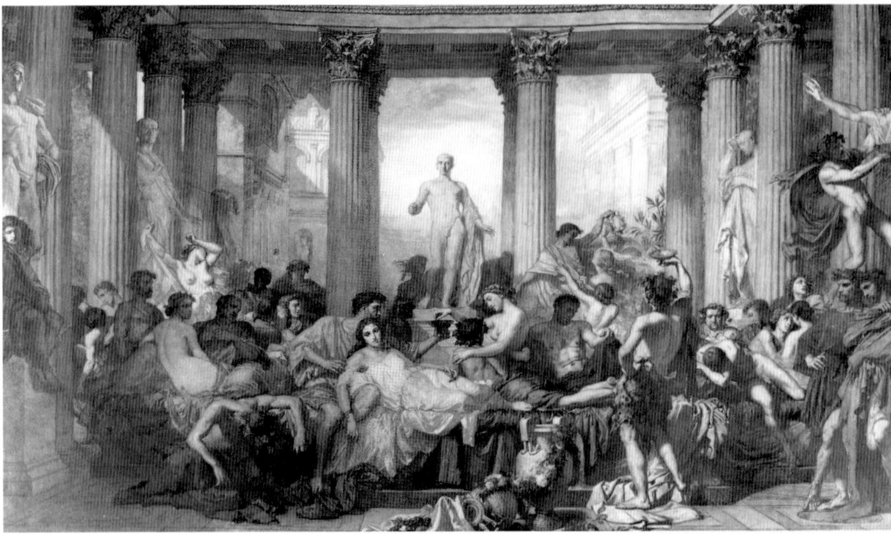

5 **Thomas Couture,** *The Romans of the Decadence,* 1847. Oil on canvas, 466 x 773 cm, 181 x 304 in.

draped, allegorical figure of Liberty, which in a sense, became the "meaning" of the picture[7] as opposed to the mere representation of a specific event from that revolution. It was thus not the message as such, but the very lack of the customary narrative meaning or implication in a painting of its scale and pretentions which scandalized the public in Courbet's *Burial*, and this meaninglessness was seen as a function of a total lack of ordered composition in the traditional sense of the term.

It is certainly obvious that Couture's dependence on tradition and his essential conservatism as an artist, in opposition to Courbet, goes far deeper than togas and classical columns, and penetrates into the basic formal configuration of his painting. One might even go so far as to say that if the arrangement of the elements in Couture's painting can be characterized as a "composition," then that of Courbet's must be termed an "anti-composition," so devoid is the *Burial at Ornans* of the leading principles characteristic of traditional art.[8]

In Couture's *Romans of the Decadence*, one is immediately made aware of a central psychological focus which is also the formal focus of the composition, to which the other elements lead, as directions of movement, and to which they are in turn subordinated. The figures themselves are arranged in groups, each member of which is related to the other members and to the total formal and narrative structure of the picture. Since each figure is constructed to perform his role adequately in terms of the whole composition, no one figure is individuated and specified as a unique entity, but becomes, in a sense, an actor in the overall pictorial drama. Moreover, the figural groups are manipulated so that they occupy and define a clearly articulated spatial stage; at the same time, a sense of psychological "depth," of multiple layers of significance and implication which the informed spectator could share with the erudite artist, is created by the misty vista of fading classical grandeur behind the world of the figures, with aerial perspective functioning to suggest the past-within-the-past, a kind of pictorial pluperfect. Furthermore, Couture has given added authority and more universal significance to his message of mid-nineteenth-century decadence not merely by placing it in the historical past by means of antique costumes, architecture, and statues, but also by composing his vast tableau vivant on the basis of the artistic past as well, introducing motifs and poses from such approved predecessors as Raphael, Michelangelo, Poussin, Veronese, and Tiepolo.

To all this, Courbet's *Burial at Ornans* offers the most striking contrast, a contrast which goes far beyond the mere fact that one artist has represented a scene from ancient Rome and the other an event from mid-nineteenth-century Ornans. In Courbet's painting, there is no question of being led beyond the concrete, individuated aspect of contemporary reality. There is, in fact, nothing especially significant for the composition to lead one towards as an emotional or intellectual focus of significance. This is, of course, even more apparent in Courbet's first conception of the scene, the charcoal drawing of 1849 now in the Musée des Beaux-Arts, Besançon, [6] where the movement of the procession simply proceeds uninterrupted across the surface of the paper, without even the minor hiatus of the group around the grave provided in the finished painting. Yet even this group is hardly emphasized in any consistent fashion by pose, position, color or amount of detail and density of paint from the rest of the figures; or rather, one might say that attention is immediately distracted from this group by the insistent and diverting concreteness of the rest of the cortege. There seems to be no particular reason, in terms of an ulterior meaning or message, for the way the figures are grouped. On the contrary, the arrangement seems casual and fortuitous, without beginning, middle or end. One finds that there is no real reason for the boundaries of the picture being precisely where they are, since they are not implied by closing elements as they are in Couture's painting. Despite the fact that Courbet has turned inward the heads of the three female mourners at the far right, one feels that the procession and the landscape background could have been extended or contracted, the present limits of the painting having been determined simply by the number of individuals portrayed. Nor has Courbet attempted, as did Couture, to

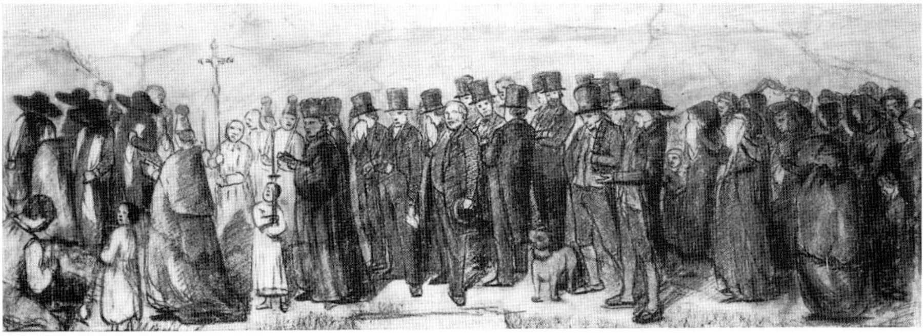

6 Study for *A Burial at Ornans*, 1849. Charcoal on bluish paper, 37 x 95 cm, 14⅝ x 37⅜ in.

make deep spatial recession function as the pictorial equivalent of psychological depth and metaphysical profundity in his painting. The figures in the *Burial at Ornans* are not manipulated so as to occupy a spatial stage, and foreshortening is generally reduced to a minimum, as is aerial perspective. Because of the relatively unmodulated richness of the paint texture and the starkness of the individual color areas, as opposed to the suavely-orchestrated, muted tonality of Couture's painting, Courbet's figures seem flat and restricted to the surface of the canvas, rather than existing within and reinforcing a pictorial space. And whereas Couture has drained his figures of their detailed individuality so as to enable them to play their roles in the compositional drama, Courbet has, on the contrary, emphasized the specific character and idiosyncratic lineaments of each individual at the expense of generalization and universality of meaning. The richness of the pictorial detail tends to give an almost equal emphasis to all areas of the canvas, a pictorial "democracy," which, along with the vast scale of the canvas, seemed most apalling to conservative critics at the same time that it appeared most sympathetic to the more progressive ones.

It was precisely because of this compositional *égalitarisme*, this lack of the customary hierarchy of values, of generalization, of selectivity and hence, of conventional emotional or dramatic significance, that one of the more intelligent conservative critics found fault with Courbet, not for the artist's choice of subject:

> L'*Enterrement à Ornus* [*sic*] constitue en effet l'œuvre capitale, le tableau d'histoire de M. Courbet. Si M. Courbet avait daigné élaborer sa pensée, ajuster les diverses parties en élaguant où dissimulant celles qui déplaisent au profit des motifs heureux qui pouvaient se recontrer, il eût produit un bon tableau. Le sujet en lui-même s'y prêtait: il n'est pas nécessaire, pour émouvoir, d'aller chercher bien loin; les funerailles d'un paysan ne sont pas pour nous moins touchantes que le convoi de Phocion. Il ne s'agissait d'abord que de ne pas localiser le sujet, et ensuite de mettre en lumière les portions intéressantes d'une telle scène .... Si ce sont des portraits de famille, laissez-les à Ornus [*sic*]. Pour nous, qui ne sommes pas d'Ornus [*sic*] nous avons besoin de quelque chose de plus qui nous attache. Ce qu'il fallait éveiller chez le spectateur, c'était le sentiment naturel qui accompagne une pareille scène.[9]

Louis de Geofroy's demand for the "natural sentiment which accompanies such a scene" would, for example, have been amply fulfilled by a very different painting of precisely the same subject as Courbet's *Burial*, Augustin Roger's *A Village Burial* [7], which had figured in the Salon of 1822.[10]

In Roger's painting, emphasis on the moral and religious significance of the event, rather than its mere concrete actuality tends to bring this minor artist's representation of contemporary life in the provinces far closer in spirit to Couture's

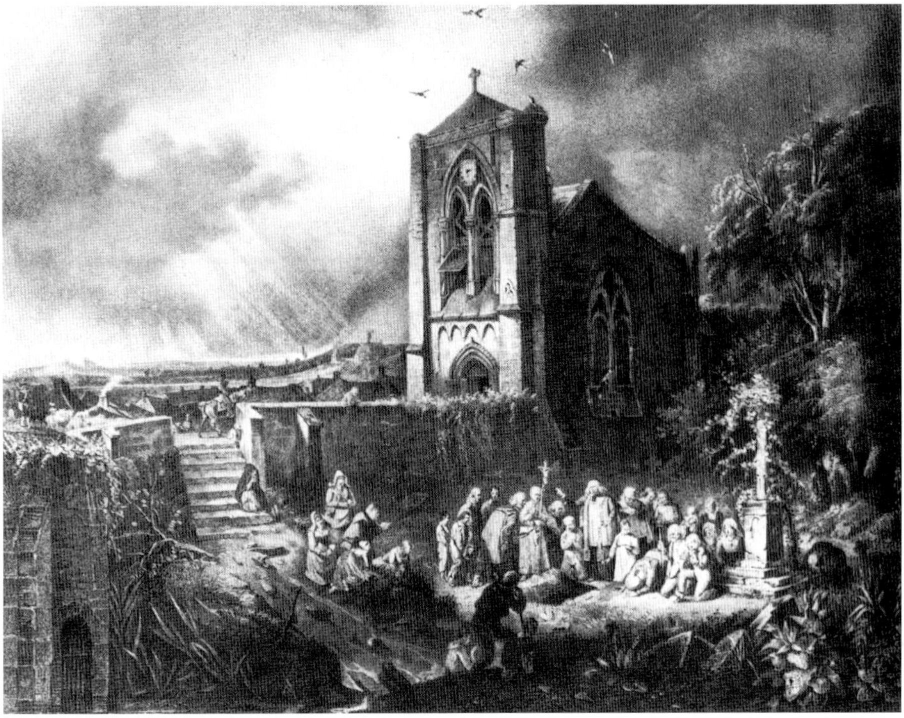

7 **After Augustin Roger**, *A Village Burial*, 1822. Lithograph by Bellay

Romans of the Decadence than to Courbet's *Burial at Ornans*. This emphasis is clearly indicated by the compositional focus on the open grave, accentuated by the dominating church with its cross and clock above it, the rankly overgrown foliage, and the suitably anguished and pious attitudes of the picturesquely generalized villagers. That de Geofroy had nothing against the representation of the lower classes in art is further indicated by his praise of more conventional works with such subjects, works like Bonvin's *Intérieur d'un orphelinat*, Chaplin's *Intérieur* (*Basse-Auvergne*), or Luminais's *Braconniers* and *Pilleurs de mer*;[11] what the critic of the *Revue des Deux Mondes* objected to was the fact that Courbet had, in his view, simply limited himself to the recording of reality at its crudest and hence had failed to produce a work of art: "C'est grande pitié qu'en l'an 1851 on soit réduit à faire démonstration des principes les plus élémentaires, à répéter que l'art n'est pas la réproduction indifférente de l'objet le premier passant, mais le choix delicat d'une intelligence raffinée par l'étude, et que sa mission est, au contraire, de hausser sans cesse au-dessus d'elle-même notre nature infirme et disgraciée."[12]

De Geofroy is quick to point out the connection between Courbet's regrettable lack of spiritual elevation and his formal innovations (or retrogressions, as this critic sees them). "Par suite de ce système de peindre les objets tels qu'on les rencontre, et d'écarter tout ce qui pourrait avoir l'air d'une combinaison, les tableaux de

M. Courbet ne présentent ni jour ni l'ombre, et ont un aspect extrèmement plat. La perspective n'y est pas plus soignée que l'effet."[13] As the critic implies, Courbet's composition, or lack of it in the traditional sense, is determined by his primary interest in individual elements, objects or figures, and in the creation of their material equivalent on the canvas.

Yet while conservative critics found this method of composition banal and awkward, it was precisely for this daring formal unorthodoxy that Courbet's artistically and politically progressive supporters praised him. Said Courbet's foremost champion and ringleader of the "bataille réaliste," the author and critic Champfleury: "Par la *composition* et l'*arrangement* des groupes, Courbet rompait déjà avec la tradition. Sans connaître les admirables toiles de Velasquez, il se trouve d'accord avec l'illustre maître qui a placé des personnages les uns à côté des autres, et ne s'est pas inquiété des lois posées par des esprits pedants et médiocres."[14] Courbet's democracy of vision, his additive, egalitarian composition, were seen as the concommitants of a democratic social outlook. The relation of the *Burial at Ornans* to the ideas of 1848 went far deeper than any overt socialist message, as Champfleury correctly observed.[15] The connection of the painting with the progressive social thought of the mid-nineteenth century lies not merely in Courbet's momentous decision to paint such a subject life-size, which immediately raised it to the category of history painting,[16] but also in the fact that by giving equal emphasis to all elements, by breaking with traditional methods of constructing a painting, a work such as the *Burial* could be connected in its simplicity, awkwardness and lack of rhetoric both with the art of the people and with the very haphazard, random structure of everyday, down-to-earth reality itself. Truth and democracy were both seen as functions of the same naïve, stalwart confrontation of actuality. For instance, one of Courbet's most sympathetic and intelligent critics, the Fourierist François Sabatier-Ungher,[17] finds that Courbet has created a new style appropriate to the nature of modern life. In the *Burial at Ornans*, far from being trivial, "il est vrai .... Voilà la démocratie dans l'art."[18]

In the same way, Courbet's style could be seen as directly related to the simplicity and naïveté of popular art itself. Champfleury likened the *Burial* to the art of the popular image-maker: "De loin, en entrant, l'*Enterrement* apparaît comme encadré par une porte; chacun est surpris par cette peinture simple, comme à la vue de ces naïves images sur bois, taillées par un couteau maladroit, en tête des assassinats imprimés rue Git-le-Coeur. L'effet est le même, parce que l'exécution est aussi simple. L'art savant trouve le mème *accent* que l'art naïf."[19] The reminiscence of popular imagery in this painting must have indeed been striking, since the hostile de Geofroy remarked on it as well: "Evidemment, M. Courbet est un homme qui se figure avoir tenté une grande renovation, et ne s'aperçoit pas qu'il ramène l'art tout simplement à son point de départ, à la grossière industrie des maîtres imagiers [*sic*]."[20]

While it is impossible to find a specific source for the *Burial* in popular imagery, or to maintain that Courbet was merely trying to repeat the conventions of the *image d'Epinal*, his painting, nevertheless, in both the iconography and the angular line-up

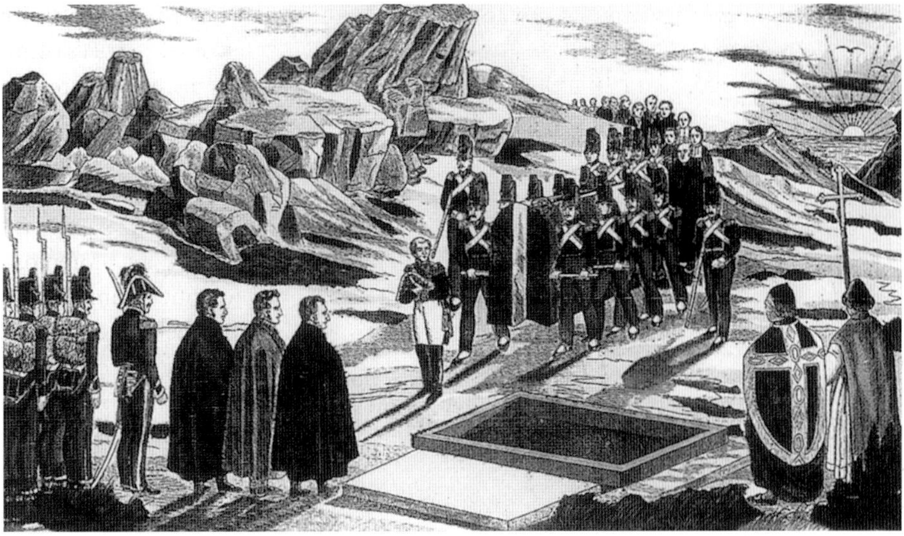

8 *Napoleon's Funeral Procession, 1821*, 1835. Woodcut, 41.2 x 60.1 cm, 16¼ x 23⅝ in.

of stiff, awkward figures, may be related to such nineteenth-century *images* as the *Degrés des âges*,[21] or, even more specifically, to *Napoleon's Funeral Procession* [8], which was created at the time of the July monarchy, and also represents a funeral procession in a rocky landscape.[22] Courbet, in turning to the revivifying source of popular art is thus at once the first major artist to look toward the primitive in the nineteenth century,[23] and is, at the same time, asserting his own feeling of identification with and sympathy for his own highly publicized "popular" background. By daring to turn to popular imagery as a source and by creating a history painting which reminded contemporary critics of one, Courbet was making a statement which was both politically and aesthetically radical.

Social and artistic factors are again inextricably mingled in the case of the relationship of Courbet's painting to that of the Le Nains, "ouvriers peintres"[24] and painters of the people, interest in whose work was crystallized into a revival by the political occurrences of 1848 in Courbet's own circle mainly by Courbet's major defender, Champfleury.[25] The elements which Champfleury found admirable in the Le Nains' manner of composition are precisely those which have been remarked on in Courbet's *Burial at Ornans*. Said Champfleury of the Le Nains: "Leur façon de composer est anti-académique; elle échappe aux plus simples lois, ils ne s'inquiètent pas de grouper leurs personnages .... Ils ont cherché la réalité jusque dans leur inhabilité à placer des figures isolées au milieu de la toile; par là, ils sont les pères des tentatives actuelles, et leur réputation ne peut que s'accroître."[26] Thus, in the case of the Le Nains', as in the case of Courbet's painting, the representation of reality is equated with a lack of composition and a lack of skill or facility, both of which are considered artificial, academic, and, by implication, a kind of imposition of the preconceptions of the Establishment on the raw material of common, everyday experience. The psychological and pictorial disassociation of the figures from each other in Courbet's *Burial*, an aspect of Courbet's basically undramatic approach to painting, can finally be perceived as a virtue, as a stalwart refusal to employ the hierarchical schemata of high art to embellish, and hence distort, the brute facts of what exists here and now for the honest observer.

Yet Courbet also drew on more conventional sources from the art of the past in constructing his vast canvas, though it was a sector of that past which had been relatively neglected in paintings of such scale and pretentions: the art of the Dutch and the Spanish masters of the seventeenth century. Sabatier-Ungher points out the relation of Courbet's *Burial* to the work of Rembrandt, Velázquez, and Zurbarán, all of whom, he feels, raised everyday life above the level of the commonplace.[27] Certainly, the stark, unmodulated contrasts of black, white, and red on which the painting is constructed, the solidity of the shadows and the very subject of a burial itself may owe something to Zurbarán's so-called *Funeral of a Bishop*, then in the Soult Collection in Paris.[28] An even more specific relation exists between Courbet's canvas and a prototype from the art of seventeenth-century Holland; the *Burial* is, in fact, based on a well-known group-portrait by Bartholomeus van der Helst, *The Company of Captain Bicker* of 1643 [9], which Courbet must have seen and admired in Amsterdam in 1847.[29] Van der Helst was often considered the rival of Rembrandt at the time, and an illustrated article on the Dutch artist had appeared in the *Magasin pittoresque* in 1848, in which he was praised for "un sentiment puissant de la vérité."[30] Certainly, the scale and format of van der Helst's work and the poses of some of the figures, especially of the kneeling burgher and of the little boy on the far left have been taken over by Courbet. Yet despite the general similarities, Courbet's painting remains less "composed" and less rhetorical: there is less suggestion of depth and space through movement and foreshortening, and certainly less sense of an arbitrarily imposed, active relation among the figures in the *Burial at Ornans*. What is important is the

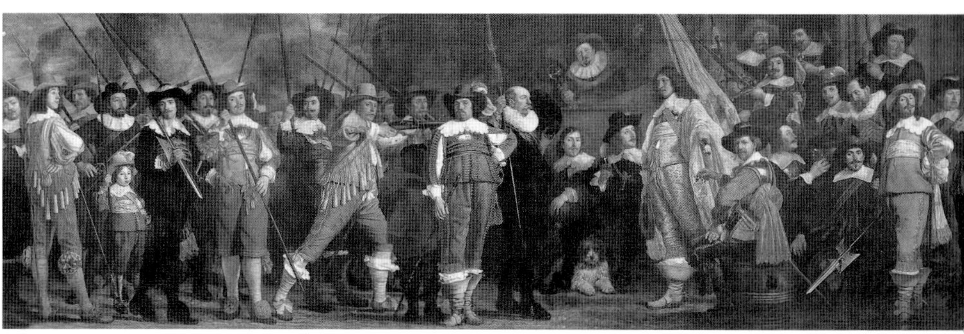

9 **Bartholomeus van der Helst,** *The Company of Captain Roelof Bicker and Lieutenant Jan Michielsz Blaeuw*, 1643. Oil on canvas, 235 x 750 cm, 92½ x 295¼ in.

fact that Courbet should have turned for inspiration to a painting based on the simple observation of rather ordinary people in the milieu in which they lived when he felt he needed some traditional support for his own large-scale history painting.

For the *Burial at Ornans* is, among other things, a group portrait; or perhaps one should say it is the portrait of a community, Courbet's own community, gathered around the grave of one of its members. The artist himself actually tended to look on the creation of his painting as a communal enterprise. Evidently the whole town of Ornans was anxious to participate. Wrote Courbet to Champfleury: "ici les modèles sont à bon marché, tout le monde voudrait être dans l'*Enterrement*; jamais je ne les satisferai tous, je me ferai bien des ennemis; ont déjà posé le maire qui pèse 400, le curé, le juge de paix, le porte-croix."[31] Indeed, part of the two-dimensional, additive quality of the work is due to the fact that the *Burial* was created as a series of individual portraits. Courbet worked on his canvas in a studio which was only sixteen inches longer than the canvas itself and about fourteen feet wide, so that while he was painting he was never able to get far enough back to view the work as a whole.[32]

Yet the painting does not owe its originality and power to the fortuitous difficulties attending its creation: its lack of physical depth and conventional metaphysical implication are functions of factors far more profound and significant than the narrowness of Courbet's studio. It is the artist's involvement with the concrete, discrete fact which keeps one riveted to the surface here, in both the physical and the psychological sense. Mary Cassatt was wrong when she likened the *Burial at Ornans* to a Greek frieze,[33] although one can of course see what she meant. In actuality, there can be nothing less classical than this painting, just as there can be nothing less Christian than the attitude conveyed by the funeral represented, a fact which conservative critics immediately realized and which they found impious and offensive, a part of the generally "socialist" flavor of the work as a whole.[34] Despite his general obtuseness in the face of a work of art, Courbet's friend, the philosopher P.-J. Proudhon, suggests something of importance when he observes of the *Burial at Ornans*: "Nous avons perdu la religion des morts; nous ne comprenons plus cette poésie sublime dont le christianisme d'accord avec lui-même, l'entourait."[35] It is not that Courbet is overtly anti-religious in this painting, but simply that for him the transcendent meaning of funerals in general is completely unimportant in comparison to the concrete existence of *this* funeral at Ornans. It is this particular event which has been recorded, not with photographic minuteness and literalism, but with fidelity and a lack of preconception. This lack of preconception is particularly evident in the handling of color in the *Burial at Ornans*: the red of the beadles' robes, like that of their noses, is nothing more than a local phenomenon; the merging of the dresses of the black-clad women to the right and the consequent unity created by the rhythmic succession of their white-framed heads is more the result of a simple statement of fact – they all wore black to the funeral – than of abstract contrivance on Courbet's part; the earth around the grave has been painted with an amazing degree of richness and substantial detail; the brilliant turquoise-striped stockings of the old veteran, Secrétan, and the rich texture of his greenish-gray velveteen breeches stand out as strong, harsh, unharmonized notes rather than tactfully submitting to the demands of a generalized significance.

"La plus profonde faculté picturale de Courbet, le ressort essential de son tempérament, c'est un sentiment prononcé de la vitalité de la matière."[36] Here, in the *Burial at Ornans*, this faculty is given free expression in a completely contemporary kind of history painting; history itself, formerly thought to occur in the elevated realm of kings, nobles, and heroes was now perceived as dependent upon the concrete actions and reactions of ordinary people.[37] And just as the content no longer needed to be elevated and generalized to be significant, so too the formal means by which this content was expressed no longer needed to be embellished and idealized; on the contrary, such tampering with the facts must now be considered to lie in the realm of falsehood. As Ernest Renan had pointed out in *L'Avenir de la science*: "l'humanité cesse de croire à des chimériques beautés pour arriver à découvrir les merveilles de la réalité."[38] Courbet, in the *Burial at Ornans*, has expressed the progressive spirit of his time by representing an event in the lives of "le peuple" in a style which is itself a metaphor of the specificity, the concreteness and the randomness of ordinary life, on a scale hitherto reserved for the representation of elevated or distant events in a suitably idealized style. In this fact lies the revolutionary nature of the painting, and of Realism itself.

2 Gustave Courbet's *Meeting*: A Portrait of the Artist as a Wandering Jew

In his own day, Gustave Courbet was generally considered a painter of reality: his compositions were held to be records of sheer, unmediated observation and were praised or criticized as such by contemporary observers.[1] In more recent years, Courbet's dependence upon traditional art and upon popular imagery in particular has been recognized: such works as the *After Dinner at Ornans* [10], the *Burial at Ornans* [pl.2, pp.66–67], *The Wrestlers* [66, p.156], and *The Painter's Studio* [pl.11, pp.138–39], have been clearly related to specific pictorial antecedents.[2] Yet one of his major paintings of the 1850s, *The Meeting* [pl.6, p.71] of 1854, has continued to be viewed as nothing more than the faithful, if typically egotistical, recording of a specific event in a particular locale: the artist's meeting with his patron, Alfred Bruyas, and the latter's servant and dog on the road to Sète just outside the town of Montpellier.[3] The painting was criticized by Roger Fry for sacrificing "plastic significance for a crude and meaningless verisimilitude to actual objects,"[4] and a purposeful rejection of traditional principles of composition has been considered its most striking characteristic.[5] Indeed, the artist's fidelity to

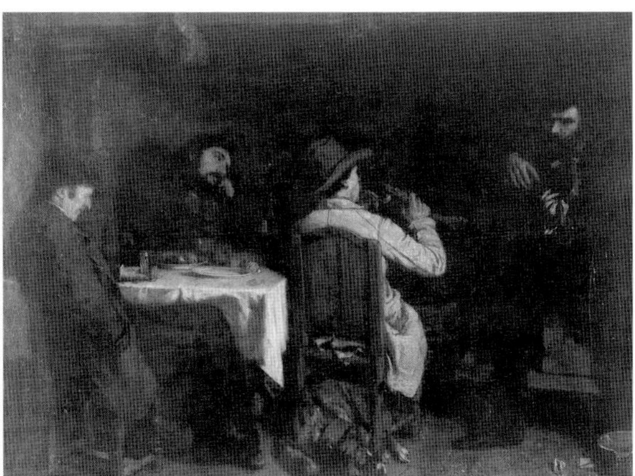

10 *After Dinner at Ornans*, 1848–49.
Oil on canvas, 195 x 257 cm, 76¾ x 101¼ in.

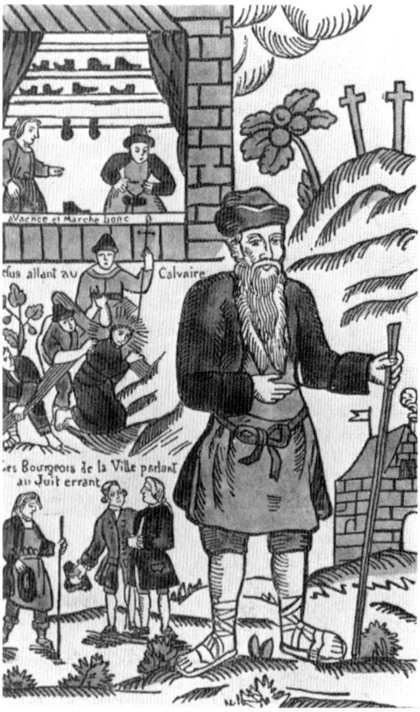

11 *The Wandering Jew*, frontispiece from Champfleury's *Histoire de l'imagerie populaire*, 1869

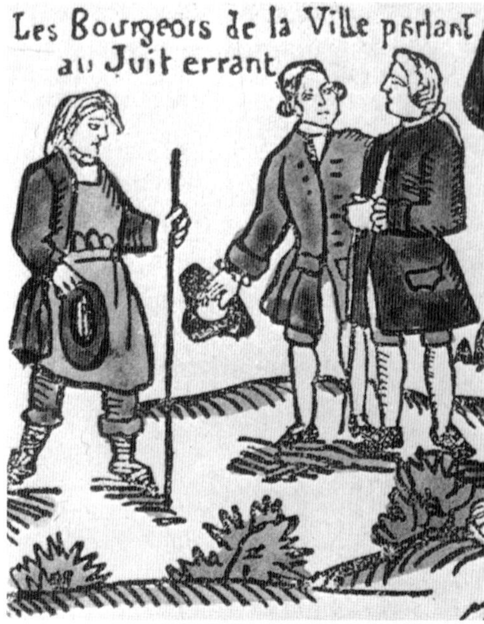

12 *The Burghers of the Town Speaking to the Wandering Jew*, detail of fig. 11

the sheer data of experience has seemed so uncompromising, his procedure in this work has been likened to that of the lens of a camera;[6] any minor deviations from perceptual objectivity which the painting may seem to exhibit have generally been laid to the artist's notorious self-adulation.[7] Yet *The Meeting* is a document neither of sheer narcissism nor of pure observation, although there is more than a measure of both in it; its composition is unequivocally based upon a source in popular imagery: a portion of a broadside of the Wandering Jew, representing the encounter of the Jew with two burghers of the town, which was later to serve as the frontispiece of Champfleury's *Histoire de l'imagerie populaire* [11, 12].[8] While the artist has completely transformed his schematic prototype, the implications arising from its use are of great significance, both in interpreting the work in question and in reexamining Courbet's artistic position as a whole during the crucial years of the "Realist battle," the decade of the 1850s.

Courbet and his supporters generally tended to minimize the role played by pictorial prototypes in his œuvre, at times even going so far as to deny any familiarity on the artist's part with traditional painting at all. "As an instrument of education and study, Courbet never had anything but his magnificent eye, and that was certainly enough," declared his friend and champion Max Buchon.[9] Yet despite the artist's disdainful dismissal of "M'ssieu Raphaël" and "M'ssieu Michelangelo,"[10] his condemnation of Titian and Leonardo as "petty thieves,"[11] and his manifest distaste for the "slaves" of Raphael and Phidias in his own century,[12] Courbet's own statements, the reports of his friends, and his works themselves bear witness to the fact that, while he may have rejected that portion of artistic tradition which he considered academic, idealized, artificial, or rhetorical – the art of the Establishment, in short – he was certainly familiar with and admired a certain segment of the art of the past. The Dutch, the Spaniards, and the French "painters of reality," all those who seemed to him faithfully to reproduce the life and appearance of their own times, were much to his taste. "I am already enchanted with everything I have seen in Holland, and it is truly indispensable for an artist," he wrote in 1847. "A trip like this teaches you more than three years of work."[13] He expressed admiration for "Ribera, Zurbarán [and] Velázquez above all"[14] and coupled the latter with Rembrandt in a typically self-aggrandizing aphorism.[15] He executed copies after works by Rembrandt [13], Hals [14], and Velázquez.[16]

While in the case of popular imagery, Courbet never specifically acknowledged his debt, both his critics and his supporters immediately likened his paintings of the 1850s to the work of the anonymous image-makers.[17] Aside from the internal evidence provided by the paintings themselves, one can be sure that Courbet was familiar with such images, which were currently admired by members of his coterie: the study of folklore, in fact, constituted an integral part of the primitivizing, popularizing strain of social thought and historical research in advanced circles immediately preceding and following the 1848 Revolution.[18] In this connection, one thinks, of course, of George Sand and the worker-poet movement, or of Michelet and his quasi-mystical adulation of "le peuple," but within Courbet's more intimate

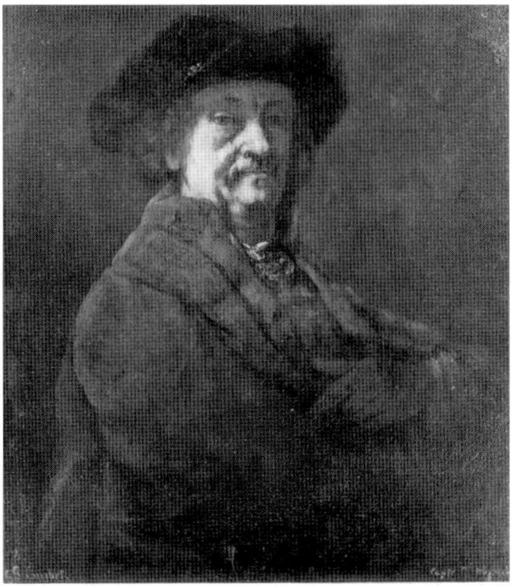

13 Copy of Rembrandt's *Self-Portrait*, 1869. Oil on canvas, 87 x 73 cm, 34¼ x 28¾ in.

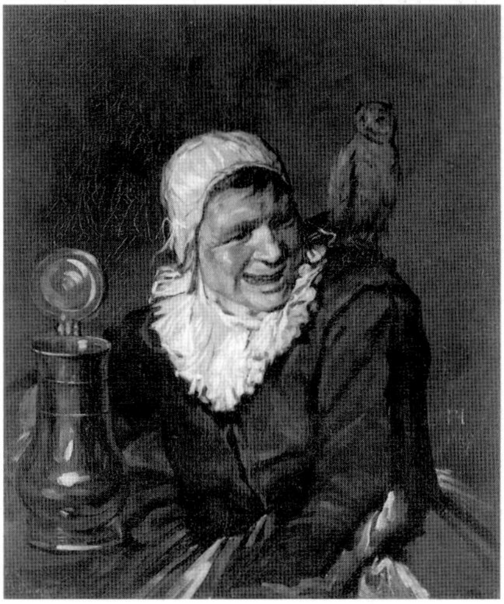

14 Copy of Frans Hals's *Malle Babbe*, 1869. Oil on canvas, 85 x 71 cm, 33½ x 28 in.

group of friends, the Franc-Comtois poet and critic Max Buchon was one of the leading figures in the upsurge of interest in folk art and literature of the mid-nineteenth century. "The most inexorable protest against professors and pastiches is popular art," proclaimed Buchon in 1856. "To approach our popular literature is to ascend once more to our authentic origins, is to get back into possession of our spontaneity, the only creator of lasting productions."[19] Courbet's close friend, the anarchist philosopher P.-J. Proudhon was equally optimistic about the creative potential of the popular classes: "No more confidence in the heights of society! Let the worker go forward on the same footing as the scholar and the artist .... There is no one in reality more a scholar and more an artist than the people," he maintained.[20] But it must have been through his chief supporter, the Realist writer and critic, Champfleury, author of the first important study of popular imagery,[21] that Courbet became acquainted with a wide range of examples of this genre, and, in addition, infected with his friend's unbounded enthusiasm for the works of the popular artists. Champfleury praised the works of the *imagiers* for their naïve charm and unerring revelation of the innermost nature of the people. "There are no bad *images* for interested eyes," he stated. "For a long time the people have been interested in these prints; we become acquainted with their intimate feelings by penetrating these illustrations."[22]

During the 1850s, the period when he created most of his major figural compositions and when the Realist impulse was at its height, many of Courbet's works were based on prototypes deriving either from that segment of the art of the past which was meaningful to him as a Realist, or from popular images or illustrations, or, at times, upon a combination of both. An examination of the relation of some of these paintings to their sources reveals little haphazard borrowing, but rather, a clear connection with the underlying social impulse that motivated Courbet's works themselves at the time.

References to Dutch and Spanish painting as well as to popular imagery give added resonance and authority to the powerful series of portraits which constitutes the basic substance of the *Burial at Ornans* of 1849–1850, transforming observed reality into what might accurately be termed a history painting of contemporary life.[23] For the underlying disposition of the figures, Courbet turned to a work which was at the time considered one of the great masterpieces of Dutch seventeenth-century group portraiture, a monumental, friezelike representation of ordinary people in their customary outdoor milieu: Bartholomeus van der Helst's *Company of Captain Bicker* of 1643 [9, p.26].[24] Courbet had probably seen this work, considered to be the rival of Rembrandt's *Night Watch*, during his trip to Amsterdam in 1847, and it had been praised for "un sentiment puissant de la vérité" in an illustrated article about its author which had appeared in the *Magasin pittoresque* in 1848.[25] The Spanish painter Zurbarán is probably responsible for the stark, unmodulated contrasts of black, white, and red, as well as the solidity of the shadows, which characterize the *Burial*, and perhaps provided partial inspiration for the very subject of the work itself.[26] Zurbarán was another artist of the past, who, in the opinion of the nineteenth-century Realists, had treated everyday life with brutal honesty, thereby raising it above the level of the commonplace.[27] In addition, a popular image, such as the *Degrés des âges*, may be responsible, as Meyer Schapiro has suggested, for the change in the composition of the *Burial* from the one indicated in the original drawing for the work [6, p.21] to that of the finished painting.[28]

A masterpiece of Dutch art, popular inspiration, and personal observation of reality entered into the creation of another of Courbet's epics of modern life, perhaps intended as the urban counterpart of the *Burial at Ornans*, the unfinished *Firemen Running to a Fire* of 1851 [15], now in the Petit Palais in Paris. Whether or not the subject was actually suggested to Courbet by Proudhon, and whether or not, as legend would have it, the republican chief of the fire brigade of the Rue St.-Victor obligingly turned in a false alarm in order to provide Courbet with authentic documentation,[29] the composition of this enormous canvas is clearly inspired by Rembrandt's so-called *Night Watch*, admired by Courbet on his trip to Holland in 1847, a work which, like Courbet's *Firemen*, might well have been considered a representation of "men … accomplishing their civic and domestic functions, with their present-day appearance."[30] Yet, as in the case of the relation of the *Burial at Ornans* to van der Helst's *Company of Captain Bicker*, the seventeenth-century Dutch prototype has been completely recast to meet the demands of a subject taken from contemporary life, as well as those of Courbet's stylistic predilections. The décor and the cast of characters of the

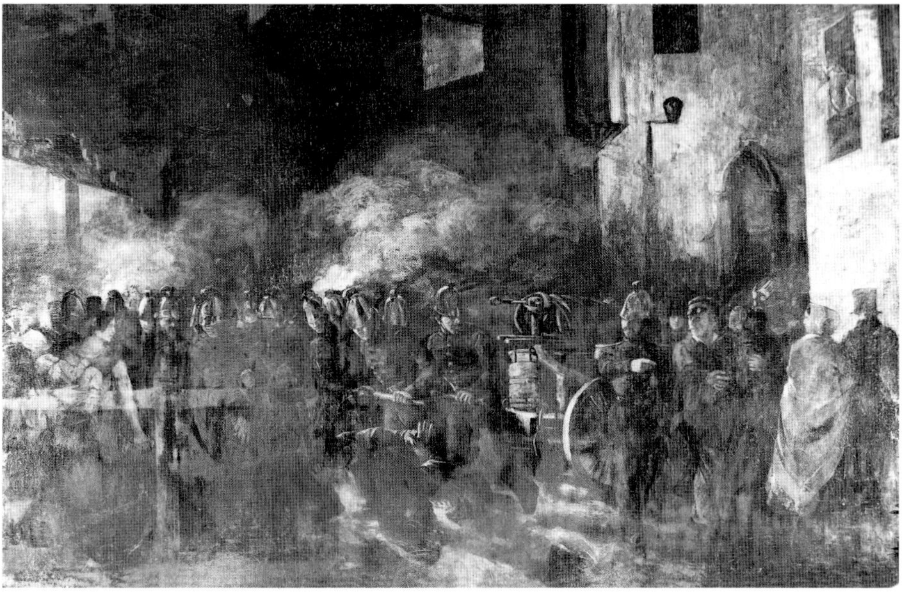

15 *Firemen Running to a Fire*, 1851. Oil on canvas, 388 x 580 cm, 152¾ x 228¾ in.

Firemen are, of course, those of nineteenth-century Paris, and, as in the case of the relation of the composition of the *Burial* to its seventeenth-century Dutch prototype, Courbet has reduced and simplified the formal and expressive complexity of Rembrandt's group portrait, lining up his figures across the surface of the canvas rather than having them emerge from an evocative, shadow-filled background.

The reductive tendency of the composition, as well as the iconography of the *Firemen*, may be due to the intervention of popular, or more accurately, semi-popular, art. The theme of fires and firemen, while hardly touched upon by major artists, had long been a favorite of their more popular counterparts, especially of the *canardiers*, those creators of broadsides consisting of crude woodcuts accompanied by simple commentaries, dealing with crimes of passion, disasters, and other "épouvantables catastrophes";[31] on a more elevated level, publications like *L'Illustration* or the *Magasin pittoresque* used more accurate, circumstantial, and realistic wood engravings, often with nocturnal settings, to document their accounts of such topical events as fires and explosions. It is certainly conceivable that when seeking documentation for his painting, Courbet turned to such wood engravings, for example, the one used to illustrate the account of the fire in Saint Peter's Church in Hamburg in the *Magasin pittoresque* [16],[32] or that of the great fire in the Bazar Bonne-Nouvelle in *L'Illustration*.[33] In addition, *L'Illustration* had published a long article, "Le Sapeur-Pompier," investigating the duties of firemen and the most advanced techniques of fire-fighting, amply documented with wood engravings, one of which, *Sapeurs-Pompiers – Le sinistre* [17], comes quite close in subject and composition to the *Firemen Running to a Fire*.[34] Courbet's friend, the *chansonnier* Pierre Dupont, may have provided still another source of inspiration, popular and contemporary, for the iconography of the *Firemen*, in his song entitled "L'incendie," where the firemen are called "soldats pacifiques" and the description of a fire by night seems to correspond closely to the action of Courbet's painting.[35] Like Dupont, Courbet has emphasized the social significance of the scene, not merely by giving a major role to the proletarian figure in *blouse* and cap who assists the fire

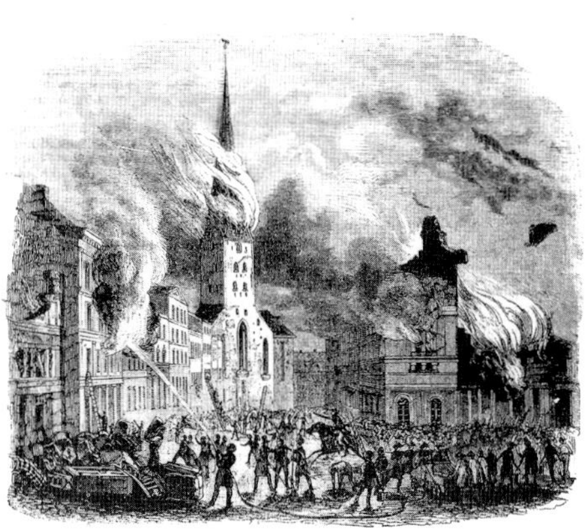

16 *Fire in Saint Peter's Church, Hamburg, May 7 1842*. Wood engraving, *Magasin pittoresque*, 1842

18 *Vélasquez faisant le portrait d'une infante*, engraving after Velázquez, from Réveil, *Musée de peinture*

19 *Fabrique de tapisseries* (*The Spinners*), engraving after Velázquez, from Réveil, *Musée de peinture*

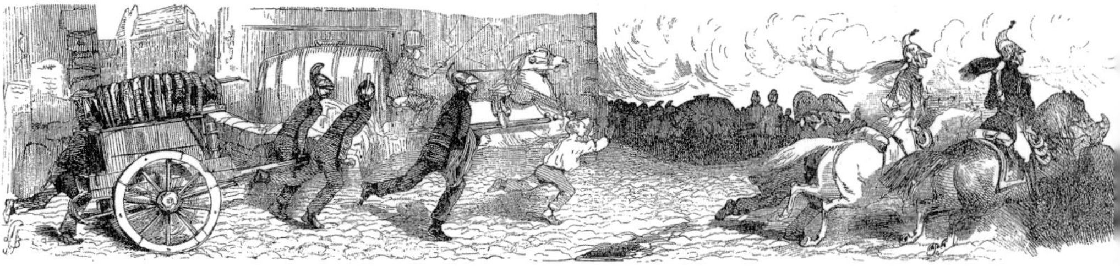

17 *Sapeurs-Pompiers – Le sinistre.* Wood engraving, *L'Illustration*, 1843

captain, in the right foreground, but also by the rather obvious opposition that he has established between the woman of the people, dressed in rusty brown, clutching her baby to her breast and leading a little boy by the hand on the left, and the well-dressed couple on the right, obviously representatives of the bourgeoisie, who are set off from the rest of the painting by their isolated position, their costume, and their color harmony, as observers rather than participants in the active scene.[36]

In two other major works of the 1850s, Courbet turned to the art of the past – that of seventeenth-century Spain – and to popular imagery: *The Grain Sifters* [pl.5, p.70] of 1854, now in the Musée des Beaux-Arts of Nantes, and the unfinished *Toilette de la mariée* [pl.8, p.72] of about 1858,[37] in the collection of the Smith College Museum of Art. These canvases may be related to paintings by Velázquez, *The Spinners* in the first case, *The Maids of Honor* in the second, both of which Courbet probably knew through engravings, such as those published in Réveil's popular *Musée de peinture* [18, 19].[38] Although less well known than his compatriot Zurbarán, Velázquez had already provided a source of inspiration for Millet[39] and was admired in the 1850s as a recorder of the ordinary, or even the seamy side of life, as a painter of realistic scenes, cripples, and dwarfs.[40] To Courbet, naturally unaware of the complex iconography of *The Spinners*, Velázquez's painting must have seemed a forthright work-scene, rather

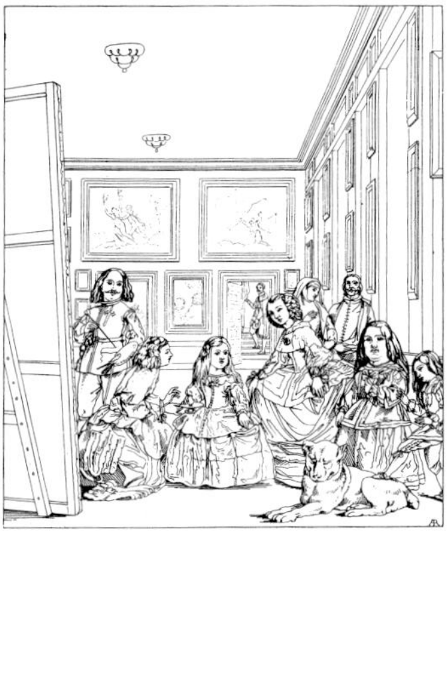

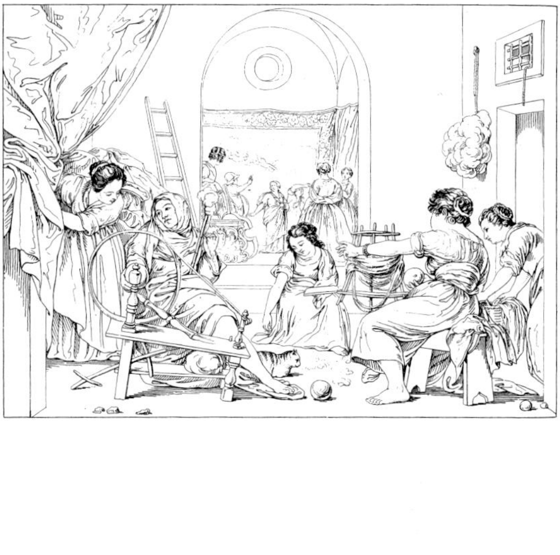

like the one he himself envisaged in *The Grain Sifters*, and it is even possible that he sensed a certain underlying social significance in the Spanish painting, with its apparent contrast between the industrious working women in the foreground and the idle courtiers in the rear. The gesture of the central figure of the woman holding the sieve in Courbet's painting repeats, with modifications, that of the wool winder with her back to us in Velázquez's work, and both the pose of the woman picking through the grain in a dish and that of the boy to the right seem to have been loosely derived from those of figures in the Spanish prototype. Even the background element of the sacks of grain to the left in Courbet's painting seems like a free adaptation of the piled-up skeins of wool or cloth to the left in *The Spinners*. In the case of the relation of the unfinished *Toilette de la mariée* to Velázquez's *Maids of Honor*, a relationship, incidentally, first suggested by Roger Fry,[41] both the general spatial divisions of the composition and some of the individual figures, such as the girl kneeling in the foreground to put the shoe on the bride, seem to have been derived from the Spanish work. Yet here again, as would only seem natural in the case of a painting the theme of which, as Jean Seznec has pointed out, was taken from Franc-Comtois folk tradition, and is itself, in his words, "almost a document of folklore,"[42] popular imagery played a significant role. An *image* such as the *Coucher de la mariée* [20], from Paris, *chez* Codoni, is close to the *Toilette de la mariée* in its general configuration, and, more specifically, seems to have inspired the pose of the figure holding the sheet to the left of the painting.

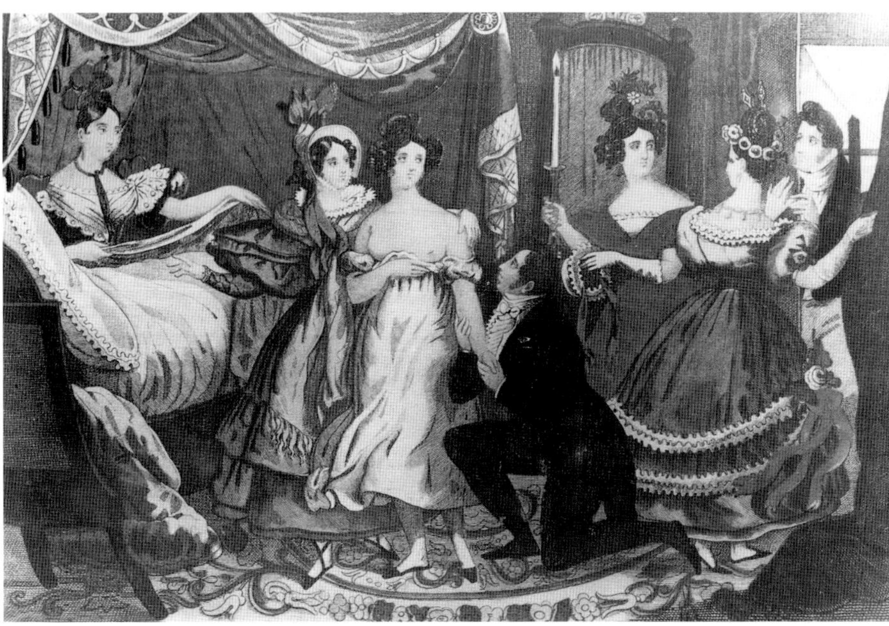

20 *Le Coucher de la mariée*, popular image from Paris, *chez* Codoni

What is important in all these cases is not merely the fact that Courbet has made use of prototypes taken from the art of the past and from popular imagery or illustration in many of his major figural compositions of the 1850s, but that in almost every instance, the borrowings are meaningfully related to Courbet's conception of realism, both in terms of the actual themes of these sources or of their provenance: from the realistic painters of seventeenth-century Holland and Spain and the naïve productions of the popular image-makers or the wood-engravers of the contemporary press, proletarian by definition, as it were. In none of these cases would it be correct to say of Courbet that "almost any form of visual representation would seem to have served as a stimulus to his own conceptions":[43] such a characterization would perhaps be more appropriate for Courbet's work during the 1860s, when, in the words of Meyer Schapiro, the artist moved "toward a more personal, aestheticized view."[44] It would be as ridiculous to seek a social motivation behind Courbet's use of an engraving after a work by Landseer [21] for his *Stag Taking to the Water* [22] of 1861, now in the Musée des Beaux-Arts at Marseilles,[45] or that of a figure from Delacroix's *Massacre of Chios* for the mounted hunter in *The Hunting Horn* of 1867[46] as it would be to read a social significance into these works themselves. Yet even some of the seemingly neutral landscape themes of the 1860s were in fact the products of an underlying social impulse, as Heinrich Schwarz has pointed out in the case of the *Landscape with a Mill near Ornans* of 1869;[47] and what may appear on the surface to be nothing more than an objective rendering of a tree, may actually be a forceful expression of Courbet's regional pride and identification with Franc-Comtois tradition. *The Oak of Flagey* [pl.13, pp.142–43] of 1864, in the Pennsylvania Academy of the Fine Arts, Philadelphia, exhibited in 1867 with the more significant title the *Chêne de Flagey, appelé chêne de Vercingétorix. Camp de César, près d'Alésia, Franche-Comté,*[48] was probably inspired by a series of articles on "remarkable trees" of all the regions of France which had run in the *Magasin pittoresque* in the 1850s. More specifically, Courbet was trying to vie with the "chêne gigantesque de Montravail aux environs de Saintes," the subject of an article with a strikingly similar illustration [23] which had appeared in this publication in 1850.[49] In any case, during the 1850s, Courbet was highly selective in his use of pictorial prototypes, his choices controlled by his stated desire to translate the customs, the ideas, and the aspect of his times;[50] controlled, in short, by his intention to create an epic art of everyday reality much as, in his view, had the Dutch and Spanish painters of the seventeenth century, a contemporary art at the same time made enduring by reference to the instinctive veracity and naïve grandeur of popular imagery and vivified by his own bold assault on perceived reality. Courbet's decision to base his important commemorative portrait, *The Meeting*, on a popular image of the Wandering Jew was thus in no way fortuitous, but determined by the implications of the proposed painting itself.

There seems little doubt that Courbet had conceived of the general scheme of *The Meeting* even before he left for Montpellier in May 1854. At this time, he was deeply

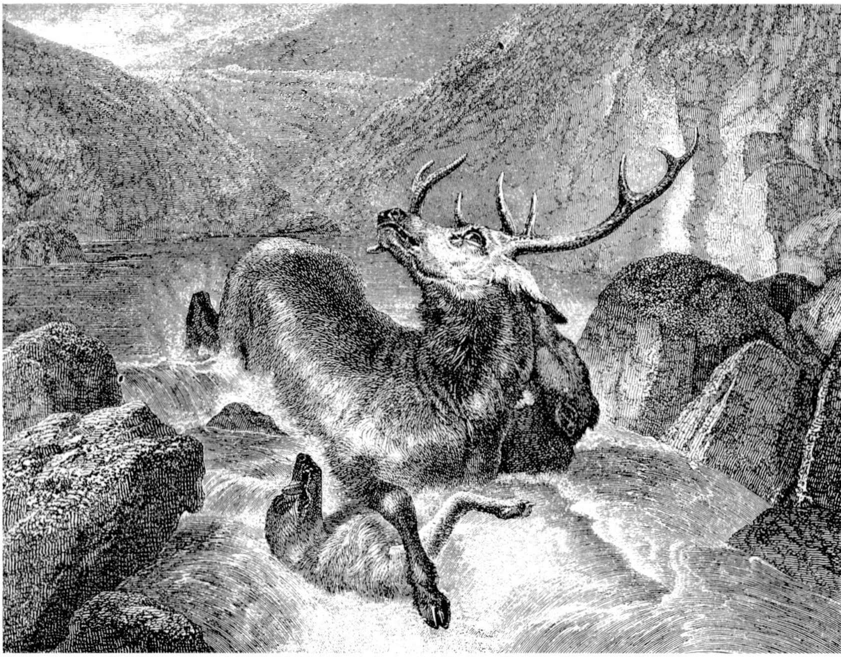

21 **After Landseer**, *The Death of the Stag*. Wood engraving, *Magasin pittoresque,* 1851

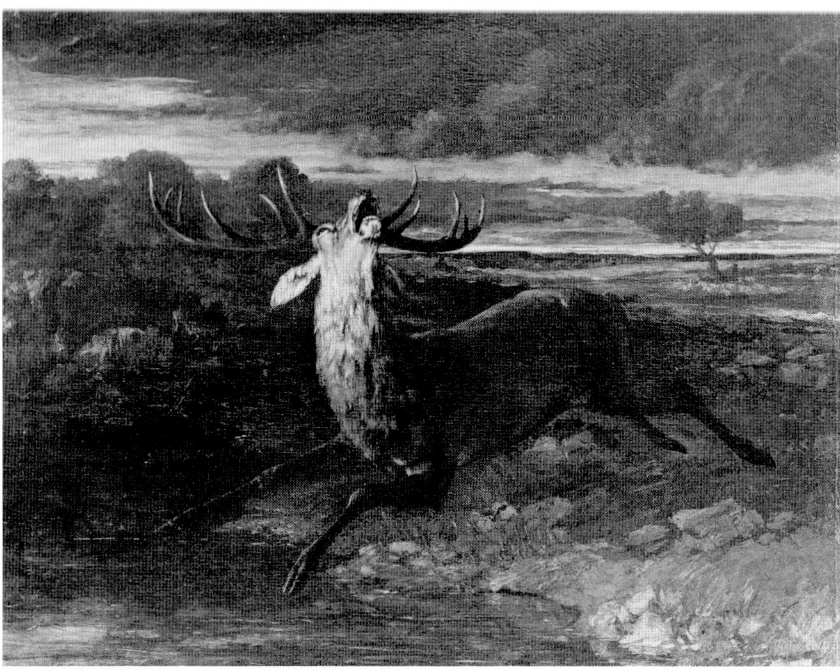

22 *Stag Taking to the Water*, 1861. Oil on canvas, 220 x 275 cm, 86⅝ x 108¼ in.

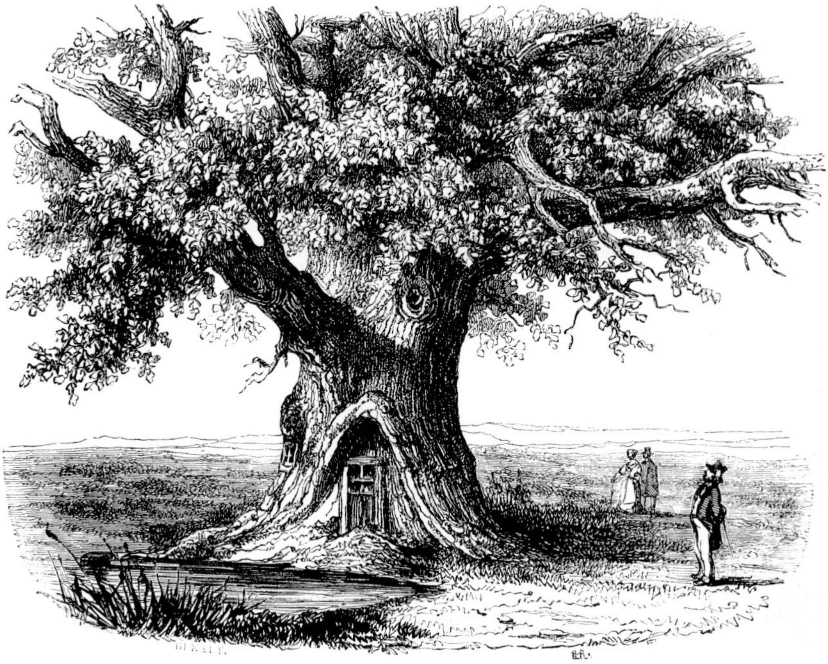

23 *Giant Oak of Montravail.* Wood engraving, *Magasin pittoresque*, 1850

preoccupied with what he termed the "Realist solution" and was already contemplating a joint Realist enterprise with his friend and patron, Alfred Bruyas: an independent exhibition of his own works in conjunction with those of the Galerie Bruyas.[51] In a letter written to his patron shortly before his departure for Montpellier, Courbet stressed the unusual importance of their relatively recent first encounter: "I met you. It was inevitable, for it was not we who met each other, it was our solutions."[52] As far as the compositional prototype of *The Meeting* is concerned, it too must have been familiar to Courbet prior to his sojourn in Montpellier. The main figure of the Wandering Jew from the very broadside in which the meeting of the Jew with the two burghers acts as a subsidiary incident had already provided the prototype for his portrait of Jean Journet in 1850.[53] There is thus every reason to believe that the conception of *The Meeting* antedated the occurrence of the incident upon which it was supposedly based.

It was no doubt through Champfleury that Courbet had become acquainted with the broadside of the Wandering Jew in question, as well as its many variants.[54] Champfleury was, in fact, to use it as the frontispiece of both editions of his important work on popular imagery, so much of which was devoted to investigation of the legend of the Wandering Jew; and while his *Histoire de l'imagerie populaire* was not published until 1869, Champfleury had, according to his own admission,[55] embarked on his research into Wandering Jew material at least twenty years prior to its publication, and by the 1850s, was certainly one of the leading authorities on the subject in France. His essay, "Le Juif-errant," is even today considered one of the major contributions to research in the field.[56] Closely allied to Champfleury, Courbet would have had ample opportunity to familiarize himself with both written and pictorial representations of the Wandering Jew legend at the time he painted *The Meeting.*

The implications of the Wandering Jew theme were themselves extremely rich and complex, as Champfleury indicates in his study. By the middle of the nineteenth century, the legend of the Wandering Jew had undergone many metamorphoses in the course of its long and cosmopolitan existence, and had evolved from a simple, apocryphal story of sin, retribution, and eternal wandering, into a socially conscious morality tale, often providing the scaffolding, or more accurately, the pretext, for elaborate left-wing literary productions. "The Jew," says Champfleury, "served for ... social compositions in which all modern aspirations were heaped together."[57] Best known of these "social compositions" is of course Eugène Süe's *roman feuilleton, Le Juif errant,* Fourierist and Saint-Simonian in inspiration, and dedicated to the "mystique ouvrieriste," in which the Jew and the Jewess, symbols of unceasing persecution, represent the two chief victims of contemporary society: the worker and woman.[58] While Champfleury considered that the literary versions of the story suffered in comparison with "the sharpness of outline, the simplicity of the account"[59] provided by those of the anonymous authors, he nevertheless praised one of the less ambitious attempts to rework the old *complainte,* a socially conscious song, "Le Juif errant," written by the *chansonnier* and poet Pierre-Jean de Béranger, in which the author, "taking up the idea and not the details, sings about humanity and fraternity in relation to the Wandering Jew."[60] At approximately the same time that Courbet painted *The Meeting,* his friend, the *chansonnier* Pierre Dupont, was working on still another, far more ambitious socially oriented variant on the Wandering Jew theme, the *Légende du juif errant,* criticized by Champfleury as an example of "the poverty of didactic art,"[61] in which the ballad itself was followed by a lengthy epilogue in limping alexandrines, setting forth a vision of the future in which the newly discovered forces of science and industry would unite all humanity in a modern paradise on earth.[62]

The importance of the theme for Courbet, in both its traditional and its contemporary interpretations, is indicated by the fact that he turned to it in at least two other works besides *The Meeting.* He himself had created one of the topical "socialist" variants on the Wandering Jew theme in 1850, in the form of a lithographed "popular image," accompanied, like the anonymous broadsides, with a *complainte* to be sung to a traditional air.[63] This work, *The Apostle, Jean Journet, Setting Off for the Conquest of Universal Harmony* [24], represents a well-known radical evangelist, a Fourierist missionary, as he goes off to convert the world, staff in hand. The pose of Jean Journet in Courbet's lithograph is clearly related to the traditional imagery of the Wandering

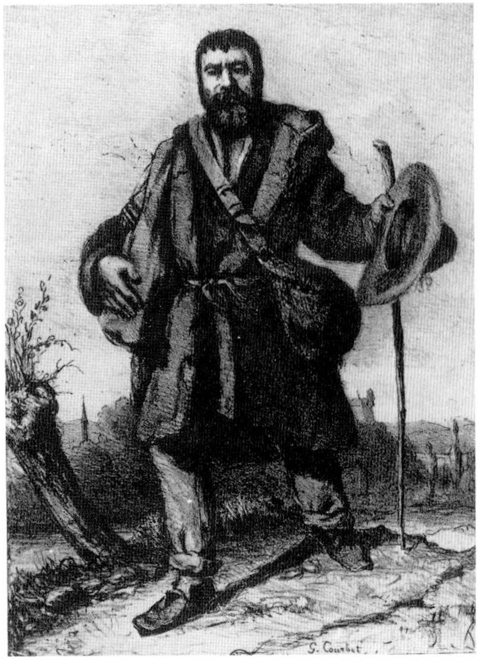

24 *The Apostle, Jean Journet, Setting Off for the Conquest of Universal Harmony*, 1850. Lithograph

Jew,[64] and, as we have already indicated, might well have been derived from the main figure in the same broadside, later published as the frontispiece of Champfleury's book, in which the Jew meeting two burghers of the town acts as a secondary image.[65] The Wandering Jew in Courbet's lithograph has been transformed, as in so many of the contemporary variants of the legend, from a helpless victim into an active witness to a new social order. The accompanying verses, similar in their narrative content and crude style to those of the anonymous Wandering Jew *complainte*, stress the humanitarian mission of this wanderer:

Bientôt, apôtre intrépide,
　Je me guide
Au flambeau de vérité;
Dans le bourbier je m'allonge,
　Je me plonge,
Pour sauver l'humanité![66]

In later years, Courbet was to turn once more to the theme of the Wandering Jew, in *A Beggar's Alms* [25], signed and dated 1868, "his last large protest canvas against the injustices of the world," according to Benedict Nicolson, painted at a time when such

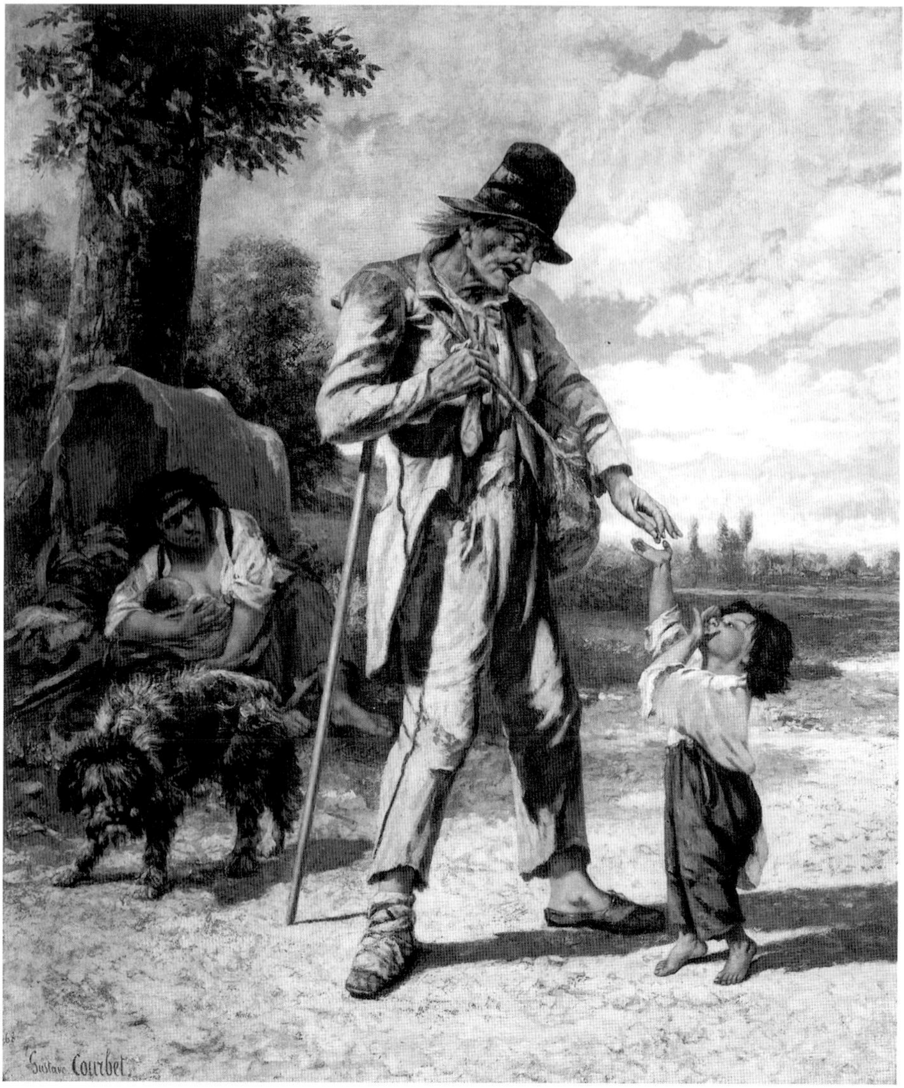

25 *A Beggar's Alms,* 1868. Oil on canvas, 221 x 175.3 cm, 82½ x 69 in.

socially motivated themes were rare in his work.[67] While the painting is certainly not one of Courbet's greatest triumphs, as Nicolson points out, it is, nevertheless, as he maintains, "a fascinating document in the later history of realism,"[68] and reverts, in its genesis, to 1854, the very year of the creation of *The Meeting*, when Courbet was contemplating a painting of a gypsy family.[69] Specific motifs in this work are also related to those in paintings of the mid-1850s: the ragged woman with her baby in the background of *A Beggar's Alms* is probably derived from the same drawing in Courbet's Louvre Sketchbook which provided the source of the mother and child, described by

Courbet as "an Irishwoman suckling a child," in the left foreground of *The Painter's Studio* of 1855 [pl.12, pp.140–41];[70] the "gypsy" boy who receives the coin in the Glasgow painting bears a striking resemblance to the admiring youth who stands to the left of Courbet in the earlier work. Yet the central incident of the old mendicant presenting a coin to a ragged urchin, depicted in *A Beggar's Alms*, owes its inception once more to the legend of the Wandering Jew, in one of its later and more socially oriented metamorphoses: a broadside consisting of the customary *image* and *complainte*, published by Wentzel in Wissembourg in 1860, and discussed at considerable length by Champfleury in his essay. According to Champfleury, the basic essence of the legend of the Wandering Jew, its "allegory of charity," had finally been revealed in the Wissembourg broadside, where, in a cartouche interrupting the ornamental border at the base, the Jew is represented dropping a coin into the hat held out to him by a poor man.[71] "For the first time," concludes Champfleury, "the print has shown the Wandering Jew as human. His role is finished. He is saved. Punished for his lack of charity, he is uplifted by charity."[72]

It is certainly likely that Courbet had in mind this variant of the Wandering Jew legend, dwelt upon in great detail by Champfleury, when he created *A Beggar's Alms*. The protagonist of this painting should not be considered a simple beggar at all, but rather the footsore Wandering Jew as he was depicted in the Wissembourg broadside, charitably offering one of his traditional five *sous* to a creature even less fortunate than himself; the awkward figure is represented in not entirely successful combination with the gypsy family painting Courbet had contemplated in 1854 as one of a series of roadside scenes along with *The Stonebreakers*[73] [pl.7, p.71] and, possibly, *The Meeting*, which could, in a sense, be considered an epic of the open road. All three of these works, *Jean Journet, The Meeting*, and *A Beggar's Alms*, are later examples of that transformation of traditional Christian or classical iconography into the idiom of the secular and the contemporary so typical of the first half of the nineteenth century, effected, for example, in the transformation of a Christian martyr or the Christ of the Deposition into a dead revolutionary hero in David's *Death of Marat* [68, p.163], or that of the enthroned Zeus into a contemporary political leader in Ingres's *Napoleon I on the Imperial Throne*. This transformation was to achieve its apotheosis in Manet's half-ironic, half-serious updating of traditional sources in the *Déjeuner sur l'herbe* and the *Olympia* in the 1860s. It is obvious, then, that the *image* of the Wandering Jew meeting two burghers of the town was not a mere compositional convenience for Courbet when he set about painting *The Meeting*, but was rather considered by him to be a meaningful framework, rich in associative values, for his own conceptions at this period.

The image of the artist as a wanderer, manifested by Courbet's identification with the Wandering Jew from the popular woodcut was, of course, not a new one when Courbet embodied it in *The Meeting*. On the metaphorical level, many romantic artists and writers had envisioned themselves as marginal creatures, restless voyagers at home nowhere on the face of the earth. Balzac, for example, had denominated himself "the Wandering Jew of thought ... always afoot, forever on the move, with no rest, with no emotional satisfaction."[74] In the realm of more concrete existence, many of the creative figures of Courbet's own time, particularly the young Realists, acted out their roles as wanderers in the form of extended walking trips – voyages of discovery and self-discovery – in which informal attire, casual manners, and freedom of behavior were of the essence in the enterprise. In 1849, the Goncourt brothers undertook an extensive journey through France, "le sac au dos et le bâton à la main," dressed and equipped like the poor art students of the time in smocks and caps with packs and parasols on their backs.[75] Two years earlier, in the summer of 1847, Gustave Flaubert had undertaken a similar voyage with Maxime du Camp in the wilds of Brittany, which the former describes in the following terms: "Packs on our backs and hobnailed boots on our feet, we have done about 160 leagues on foot along the coast, sometimes sleeping completely dressed, due to lack of sheets and bed, and eating scarcely anything but eggs and bread." Flaubert goes on to praise the virtues of the trip: "The sea ... the open air, the fields, the freedom – I mean true freedom: that which consists in saying what you want ... and in walking at random."[76] In 1854, Courbet's friend, the *chansonnier* Pierre Dupont, published his hymn to the joys of the open road in the form of a song, "Le voyageur à pied," provided with an appropriate illustration of the traveller, "Guêtre, lavé, la tête fraîche,/L'œil limpide comme un miroir,/Le sac au dos."[77] Courbet himself was even more explicit about the liberating qualities of vagabondage. In a letter of 1850 to his friend Francis Wey, he declared: "In our overcivilized society, I must lead the life of a savage; I must even free myself from governments .... I have, therefore, just started out on the great, wandering, and independent life of the gypsy."[78]

In *The Meeting*, Courbet has represented himself not merely in the image of the wanderer, but as a voyager with a cause, conceiving of himself as the traveling apostle of Realism in much the same way that he had depicted Jean Journet as the traveling apostle of Fourierism four years earlier.[79] Courbet was certainly not devoid of messianic impulses; it is to this aspect of his character that Baudelaire scornfully referred when, in 1855, he summed up Realism as "Courbet sauvant le monde."[80] Courbet himself made the high aim of his enterprise explicit in a letter of 1855 to Alfred Bruyas, written shortly before the opening of the Realist Exhibition which the latter did so much to bring into being: "And you may be sure that you are thereby serving a holy and sacred cause, which is the cause of Liberty and Independence, cause to which I have consecrated my entire life."[81] Yet once again, it is important to realize that such a magisterial concept of the role of the artist was not simply a personal idiosyncrasy of Courbet's, but was part of a more general notion about the function of the artist in society. Earlier in the century, the Saint-Simonians had evolved a semi-mystical idea of the artist as a priest or messiah who was to exercise "un véritable sacérdoce";[82] one of the Saint-Simonian writers had even gone so far as to assert that *only* the artist, under proper Saint-Simonian auspices, needless to say, was worthy of leading humanity.[83] These notions about the messianic function of the artist found their climactic expression in Victor Hugo, who literally envisioned the poet as a prophet leading mankind onward to a Utopian future:

Le poète en des jours impies
Vient préparer des jours meilleurs.
Il est l'homme des utopies,
Les pieds ici, les yeux ailleurs.
C'est lui qui sur toutes les têtes,
En tout temps, pareil aux prophètes,
Dans sa main, où tout peut tenir,
Doit, qu'on l'insulte ou qu'on le loue,
Comme une torche qu'il secoue,
Faire flamboyer l'avenir![84]

Courbet, as a Realist, holds a more prosaic staff, rather than a torch, in *The Meeting*, but such ideas as those expressed in "La fonction du poète" may well have been sympathetic to him at the time.[85] While the basic outlines of his pose in *The Meeting* may have been determined by those of the Wandering Jew in the popular image, a high sense of confidence and conviction of the importance of his mission as a Realist is conveyed by striking deviations from the popular prototype; by the assertive upward tilt of the artist's head, by the forceful turn of his body into the spatial setting, by his aggressive domination of the pictorial environment, by his surefooted stance, emphasized by the emphatic contact of his staff with the earth.

Still another significant alteration of the popular prototype is Courbet's substitution of the figure of Bruyas's servant, Calas, for the second burgher in the popular image. Since the painting was probably planned before Courbet's departure for Montpellier, and since, furthermore, it is extremely doubtful whether the incident presumably recorded in *The Meeting* actually took place at all, this substitution could hardly have been effected in the interests of accurate *reportage*.[86] It should rather be considered an expression of Courbet's own sense of solidarity and identification with the people. He himself took pride in being provincial and plebeian: his rustic manners, his large appetite, his hearty handshake, his accentuated *patois*, his pride in his physical strength, even his technique of painting with his hands, a rag, or the palette knife, using the cheapest colors disposed in ordinary jars[87] – all were consciously popular and, as such, belligerently opposed to the characteristics of aristocrat, bourgeois, and post-romantic dandy alike in Paris. He intensely disliked being referred to as an artist: "Les artistes, je les méprise";[88] he refused what he considered the false distinction of a decoration, saying "this aristocracy does not seem enviable to me."[89] Like his friends Buchon and Proudhon, he felt that the people were not only the truest sources of inspiration for an artist, but also his most comprehensive public as well: "The people enjoy my sympathies. I must address myself to them directly, so that I may draw my knowledge from them, so that they may make me live."[90] In *The Meeting*, it is the simple, peasant-like servant, as much as his master, who "recognizes" genius, and, in formal terms, offers the apparently fortuitous but nonetheless significant counterbalance for the figure of the artist himself. Edmond About's sarcastic comment that the servant looks as though he were serving in the Mass[91] is not so wide of the mark: he is, in fact, acknowledging the advent of the messiah of Realism.

The *image* of the Wandering Jew also provided a meaningful compositional and iconographic framework for Courbet's conception of his relation to his patron. Since the time that *The Meeting* first appeared in the 1855 Exposition Universelle, critics have been struck by the extreme diffidence of Bruyas's gesture, and the painting was immediately subtitled "Bonjour, M. Courbet" or "La Fortune s'inclinant devant le Génie." "His admirer and friend comes to meet him and salutes him most politely," remarked Edmond About in his Salon account of this work. "Fortunio, I mean, M. Courbet, doffs his hat to him with a lordly gesture."[92] More recently, Klaus Berger has remarked on Bruyas's "old-fashioned ceremonious gesture."[93] This gesture is, in fact, determined almost completely by that of the corresponding figure in the popular image; and, even more important, the verses of the traditional *complainte* accompanying the *image*, describing the Wandering Jew's meeting with the two burghers, habitually emphasized, as Champfleury points out,[94] the cordiality of their reception of the wanderer. The burghers are almost invariably characterized as "fort docile" and their invitation to the Jew is always couched in language of an extreme courtesy:

> On lui dit: bonjour, maître,
> De grace accordez-nous
> La satisfaction d'être
> Un moment avec vous ...[95]

Neither the artist's arrogance nor the Wandering Jew prototype, however, completely determined Courbet's conception of his relation to Bruyas, as he depicted it in *The Meeting*. On a personal level, Courbet seems to have felt genuine respect and warm affection for his unconventional and generous patron, despite his usual violent hostility toward anyone or anything that represented authority, and in his letters as well as his portraits he gives the impression of regarding his maecenas as a partner in the Realist enterprise, rather than as a mere financial supporter. "With your antecedents, your intelligence, your courage, and your pecuniary means, you can save us during our lifetime and make us skip over a century," he wrote to Bruyas in 1854.[96] In addition to representing him in *The Meeting* and in the right-hand group of figures in *The Painter's Studio*, Courbet painted three portraits of Bruyas, two during the summer of his visit in 1854 [26],[97] and one in 1853 [27], in which the sensitive and sickly Bruyas is shown with his blue-veined hand resting on a green book imprinted with the words: "Etude sur l'art moderne. Solution: A. Bruyas,"[98] certainly an expression of confidence and esteem on the artist's part. And while one might suspect somewhat mixed motives in some of the artist's more effusive encomiums of Bruyas, passages of his letters to his patron certainly convey a sense of deep attachment. "When I have decided to love someone, it is for life," he wrote to Bruyas in 1854. "You are my friend; you cannot doubt it."[99] Bruyas, on his part, was no doubt charmed by Courbet's vitality and sheer productivity, qualities that he felt sorely lacking in himself, and he gave evidence of his admiration for the painter by constant encouragement and support, purchasing his paintings, lending him money, most significantly for the construction of Courbet's Pavilion of Realism in 1855, and even sending him photographs when requested to do so.[100] Certainly, the affection and friendship that bound the two men, commemorated by *The Meeting* and expressed in the work by Bruyas's grave gesture of welcome and Courbet's more open acknowledgment of pleasure, was mutual.

This sense of the equality of artist and patron, or even of the superiority of the former, suggested by *The Meeting* was not unique to Courbet's painting. Sentimental,

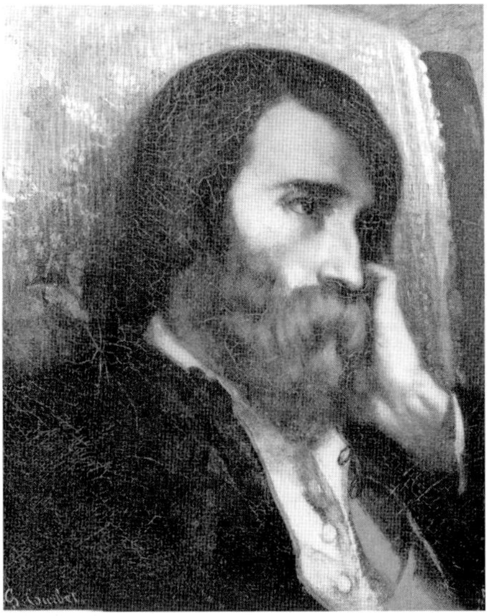

26 *Portrait of Alfred Bruyas*, 1854. Oil on canvas, 45 x 39 cm, 17¾ x 15⅜ in.

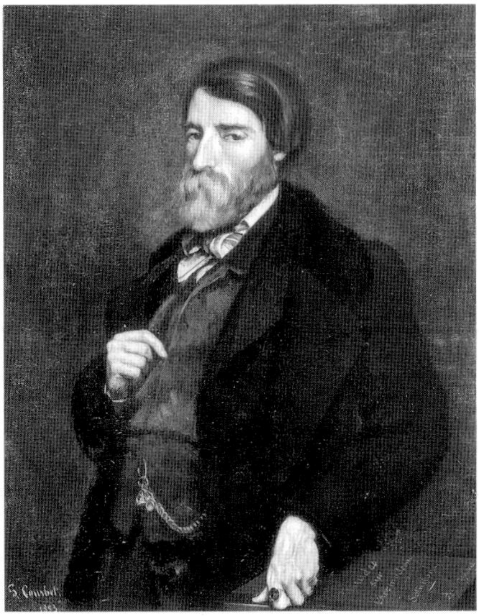

27 *Portrait of Alfred Bruyas*, 1853. Oil on canvas, 91 x 72 cm, 35¾ x 28⅜ in.

anecdotal, pictorial representations of the elevation of the artist vis-à-vis the patron, such as Ingres's *Death of Leonardo da Vinci*,[101] where the dying artist is tenderly supported in the arms of Francis I, or Robert-Fleury's *Charles V Picking up Titian's Paint Brush*,[102] in which the monarch stoops down to assist the aged painter, are simply superficial symptoms of a more serious nineteenth-century phenomenon. The drastic change that occurred during this period in the relative status of patron and protégé was, of course, a natural concomitant of both the more general social revolution of the times and the notion of the magisterial function of the artist himself. Romantic artists, alienated from the middle class that was nevertheless their source of livelihood, had long attempted to replace the aristocracy of birth with one of talent. Chateaubriand, for example, had written in a letter to Mme. Récamier in 1823: "Talent ought to have privileges. It is the oldest aristocracy and the most certain, that I know,"[103] and Alfred de Vigny noted in his journal in 1848: "David d'Angers, when he sculpted my bust wanted to write on it, in spite of me, the *count of Vigny*. I insisted that my name stand alone, saying that if two or three members of Posterity remembered my name, it would be that of the Poet and not that of the Noble."[104] A graphic illustration, rather similar in form to the incident represented in *The Meeting*, of the tendency of the aristocracy of art to replace that of birth or money is presented in an amusing, and perhaps apocryphal, incident presumably reported by Beethoven concerning his and Goethe's encounter with nobility: "Yesterday, as we were walking back, we met all the imperial family, we saw them coming from afar, and Goethe let go my arm to get out of their way onto the side of the road .... For myself, I pulled my hat down over my eyes and bore down on to the very centre of the company, hands crossed behind my back! Princes and courtiers parted and stood aside, the Archduke Rudolph took off his hat to me, the Empress was the first to salute me; their lordships *know* me."[105] The same recalcitrant spirit toward authority is exhibited in Courbet's own dramatic refusal of the Comte de Nieuwerkerke's cordial offer of government patronage: "You can imagine," Courbet relates in a letter to Bruyas, "how furious I became after such an overture; I replied that I understood absolutely nothing of all that he had just said to me, first of all because he assured me that he was a government and that I felt myself in no way included in that government, that I, too, was a government, and that I defied his to do anything at all for mine that would make me accept."[106] While in *The Meeting*, Courbet, like his counterpart in the popular image, may take his hat off to return his patron's salutation, the implications of the gestures are clear: by the middle of the nineteenth century, the independent, self-respecting artist feels that he has every right to be saluted by fortune.

Coming at a climactic point in the painter's career, and as the end term in a whole series of self-portraits, *The Meeting* is both a mature expression of Courbet's conception of himself as an artist, and, at the same time, an important example of his style and viewpoint as a Realist. Courbet's earlier self-portraits reveal the artist as a rather

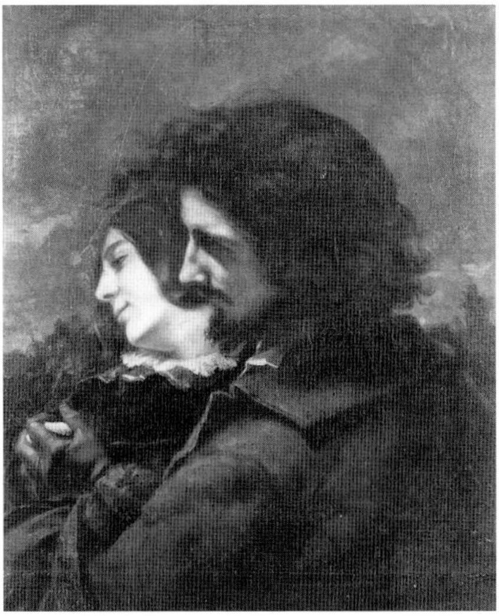

28 *Lovers in the Countryside*, 1844. Oil on canvas, 77 x 60 cm, 30¼ x 23⅝ in.

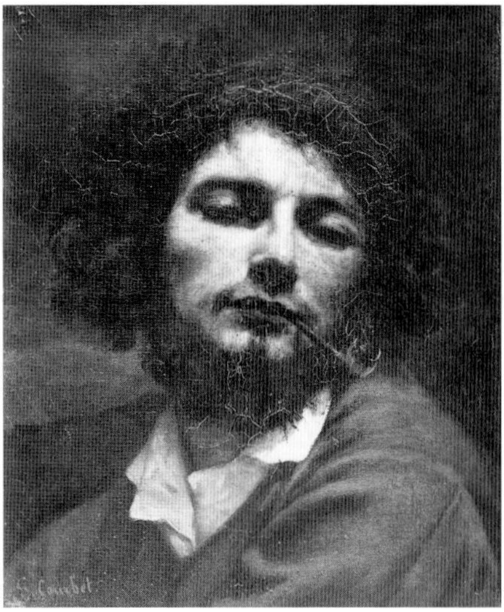

29 *Self-Portrait: Man with Pipe*, c.1848–49. Oil on canvas, 45 x 37 cm, 18⅛ x 15 in.

narcissistic, self-conscious if extremely gifted young man, whose good looks are emphasized by the dark shadows and mannered gestures of the current romantic school. In 1844, he had represented himself as a wounded hero [pl.9, p.72], in the manner of Dumas or Byron,[107] basing his pose on that of Delacroix's wounded St. Sebastian,[108] or, at about the same time, as a romantic lover [28], against the backdrop of a turbulent sky, under the inspiration of George Sand.[109] In the later forties, he had depicted himself as a young bohemian, peering out languidly through half-closed eyelids, puffing on a pipe [29], rather in the manner of Brouwer's *Smoker* in the Louvre;[110] or he had conceived of himself as a modern rival of the great portraitists of the past, such as Titian, whose *Man with the Glove* in the Louvre was certainly the source of the old-masterly sobriety, if not the romantic self-adulation, of *The Man in the Leather Belt* [30].[111]

Within this series of self-portraits, *The Meeting* constitutes a decisive turning point, a rejection of romanticism and eclecticism on both the stylistic and psychological levels. In May, 1854, Courbet had written to Bruyas: "I have made many portraits of myself during my life, corresponding with the changes in my state of mind – I have written the story of my life, in short .... There remains one more of them for me to do, that is the man firm in his principles: the free man."[112] It would certainly seem as though Courbet had *The Meeting* in mind when he made this statement, and that the work must be regarded not only as a portrait of the artist as a Wandering Jew, but as a portrait of Courbet as a free man, in the sense implied by the letter. Within the context of Courbet's series of self-portraits, *The Painter's Studio:*

A Real Allegory Summing Up Seven Years of My Artistic and Moral Life, the centerpiece of Courbet's Realist Exhibition of 1855, may be seen as a monumental aftermath, the Wandering Jew come home, as it were, home to a world that is at once that of created art and observed reality. In it Courbet has depicted himself, his painting materials, the rejected studio properties of romanticism and classicism, with a nude, unidealized "inspiring muse" at his side, his variegated proletarian sources of inspiration to his left, his literary and artistic friends to his right, engaged in the very act of creation itself. "Here," as Harry Levin has put it, "the real allegory is that of the self-portraying artist, whose world is the studio and whose studio is the world, whose symbols are actualities and whose ideology is his art."[113]

The Meeting, then, must be considered one of the major statements of Courbet's Realist undertaking. In its formal qualities, as well as in its thematic implications, it is a forceful pictorial paradigm of Courbet's creative outlook at its height, embodying a viewpoint toward, rather than a mere reproduction of, reality. While the composition may have been based on that offered by the popular image, and the latter may account for certain of its expressive qualities, like the dignified stiffness and restraint of the poses of Bruyas and his servant, there is little of the naïve schematization or simplification of popular imagery in the actual appearance of the work.[114] On the contrary, the idiosyncratic lineaments of each of the observed, individual elements of the painting have been exploited by Courbet to their fullest. The forcefully modeled

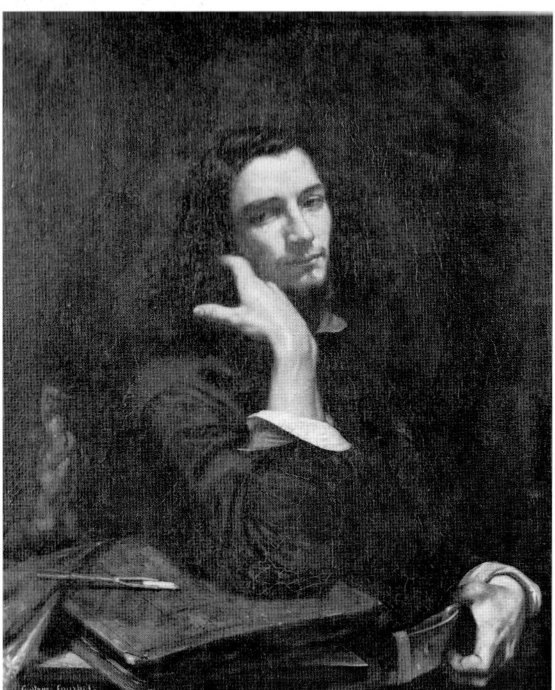

30 *Self-Portrait: The Man in the Leather Belt*, 1846. Oil on canvas, 100 x 82 cm, 39⅜ x 32¼ in.

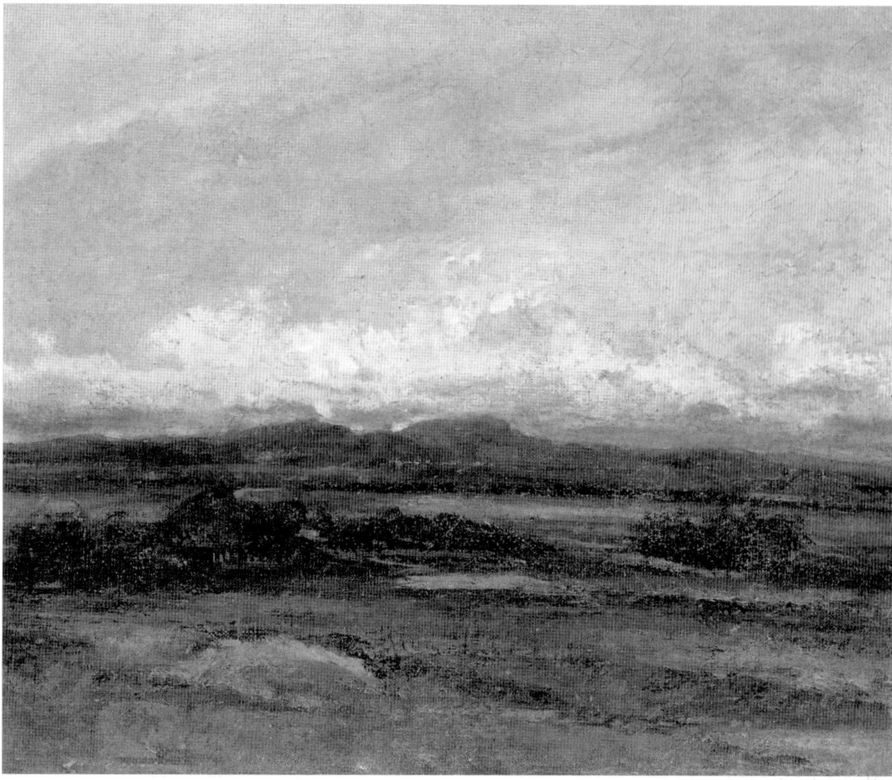

31 *Ponds at Palavas*, 1857. Oil on canvas, 38 x 46 cm, 14⅞ x 18⅛ in.

silhouettes of Calas, Bruyas, the black-and-white dog, and of the artist himself, stand out as discrete, densely painted units against the glowing turquoise sky. The artist's delighted response to the light-filled, brightly colored atmosphere of the Midi seems to have anticipated van Gogh's: the whole tonality of this work is far lighter and more intensely saturated than that of his previous paintings, and he has accurately recorded the characteristic details of the foliage of the region around Montpellier in the foreground.[115] The landscape background is obviously based on a painted sketch "sur le motif," probably one similar to the later *Ponds at Palavas* [31], now in the Musée Fabre,[116] while his own head and that of his patron are modeled after portraits [26, 32] that he created during the course of his visit.[117]

Characteristically, Courbet has made no attempt to unite the figures by means of an underlying color orchestration, nor has he suggested the interrelation of figures and atmosphere through blurred contours or loose, open brushwork. From the formal point of view, *The Meeting* is indeed the sum of its various individual units, a work in which traditional principles of composition have been resolutely rejected in favor of an additive pictorial organization,[118] an organization which, in its informality,

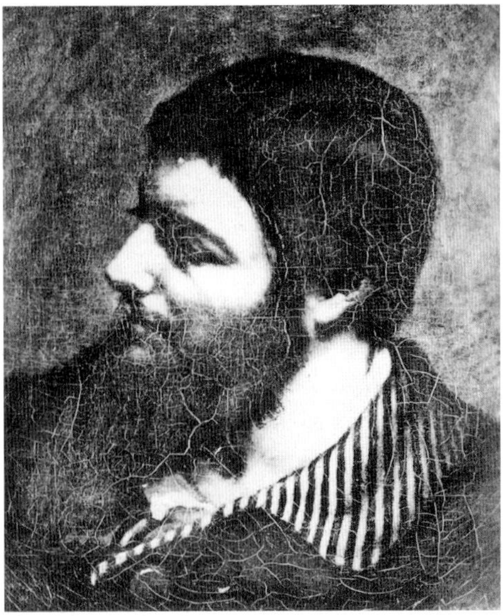

32 *Self-Portrait with Striped Collar*, 1854.
Oil on canvas, 46 x 38 cm, 18⅛ x 15 in.

its lack of accentuation, of suave transitions from part to part, or of externally imposed coherence, seemed to Courbet the embodiment of the very nature of experienced reality itself.[119] As a visual entity, the work is spontaneous, direct and fresh in its handling, objective yet intensely personal in its impact: one can see why Salon visitors in 1855 may have found it unconventional or even offensive on the stylistic level as well as on the thematic one.

Viewed within the context of nineteenth-century painting as a whole, however, *The Meeting* is truly a work lying midway between the past and the future. Adventurous in his choice of themes, his rejection of *poncif* and preconception, innovating in the random, additive quality of his compositions, the deliberate stiffness and awkwardness of his forms and his insistence on the materiality and density of the pigmented surface, unconventional in his choice of sources and subjects, Courbet, in *The Meeting*, as in the other major Realist masterpieces of the 1850s, is nevertheless still connected to the great tradition of Western picturemaking. He reveals this by the very fact that he feels it necessary to turn to preexisting imagery at all, in order to provide a basis for his new vision of the contemporary. The grandiosity of conception of these paintings and the monumentality of their scale imply a new and more suitable kind of history painting, rather than a complete rejection of this time-honored genre and all that it implied. His very manner of working was traditional: his major masterpieces were always carefully built up in the studio on a dark underpainting, generally on the basis of sketches or previously existing works, rather than completed in one or two sessions in the open air.

Although it would be a ridiculous oversimplification to consider Courbet's Realist paintings of the 1850s mere propaganda, or to insist too strongly on the connections between his art and his political beliefs or his popular and provincial background, Courbet's sense of reality was nevertheless conditioned by these values. The word "realism" obviously had a special connotation for Courbet, which he summed up, awkwardly it is true, by stating that the basis of realism was the negation of the ideal and of all that followed from it; and that it was in this way that he had achieved the emancipation of reason, the emancipation of the individual and, finally, democracy. In short, for Courbet, realism and democracy were inseparably linked. "Realism," he affirmed, "is in essence the democratic art."[120]

While a work like *The Meeting* establishes an image of reality that is vividly contemporary, specifically localized, and egregiously personal, yet it is a reality conceived of in terms quite different from those more adventurously disengaged ones that were to inspire the Impressionists' attempt to capture the ever-changing, ephemeral surface of appearance on their canvases. It was Monet and Degas who were to struggle to achieve liberation from all pre-existing or predetermined modes of perception and notation in order to create a stylistic paradigm for a reality that was *nothing but* appearance at a given moment, a reality freed from the last vestiges of extra-pictorial value, to achieve a realism, in short, which accepted completely the world of appearance as reality and as the *only* reality for the artist. A comparison of *The Meeting* with a similar composition by Degas, such as the *Place de la Concorde (Viscomte Lepic and his Daughters)*, of about 1875,[121] with its cutoff view of the main figures, its tangential spatial organization, its deliberately casual unbalances, its sophisticated denial of expressive or compositional focus, its exaggerated jump from foreground to background, suggesting, but not necessarily imitating the indifferent yet accurate recording of a passing event by the instantaneous photograph, and with its poignant suggestion of the necessarily transient nature of all such events or encounters, brings Courbet's relatively traditional approach to reality, and its pictorial concomitant, into sharp relief. "Je ne peins pas l'être, je peins le passage":[122] Montaigne's dictum might well apply to the Impressionist's enterprise, never to Courbet's. A painting of human figures in a landscape, like Monet's *Wild Poppies* of 1873,[123] where figures, setting, and atmosphere are regarded as a single, indissoluble if impermanent, visual entity, reveals the extent to which, for Courbet, the picture is still considered a *subject* to be developed in the studio on the basis of sketches and prototypes and with a unifying theme, no matter how richly endowed with perceptual veracity, rather than an evanescent *motif*, to be seized on the spot, all at once, in the open air, with the more conventional human attitudes willfully subordinated to the imperatives of immediate sensation.

Yet it was Courbet who, in paintings like *The Meeting*, opened the way for the Impressionist revolution. His realism did not imply a finicky verisimilitude nor a painstaking reduplication of minute detail; it was rather that courageous confrontation of reality, that sounding of the hollowness of rhetoric, outworn traditions, and formal conventions, which is the Realist's mission. Like the great Realist novelists, Stendhal and Flaubert, who found their themes in the most trivial *faits divers* of the popular press, in the actions and lives of the most ordinary people, rather than those of the grand, the exotic, or the mighty, so Courbet could turn for his subjects to the lives of his friends and contemporaries, seeing them neither as symbols of elevated ideals, nor as personifications of some higher level of value. And, as in the case of the novels of the great Realist writers, just because of this refusal of transcendence, beyondness, or shopworn idealism, just because of this insistence on the intractable opacity of things and the intransigent presentness of human beings, Courbet's paintings crystallize the spirit of the age and expand to assume their own, new epic dimensions. While *The Meeting* is not merely the representation of an isolated incident, it could be, and is, among other things; its meaning is not contained in some super-erogated message or in an underlying symbolic content, but rather is openly revealed by the pictorial structure itself. The inspiring motif of the Wandering Jew is an element in this structure, expanding but in no way explaining it, and as such, is directly related to Courbet's conception of realism. The motivations that led him to assimilate his meeting with Bruyas and his servant to that of the Wandering Jew with two burghers, or even to conceive of a popular image as a suitable pictorial prototype at all, are the same as those that led him to choose a contemporary, personal event like that depicted in *The Meeting* as the subject for a major painting.

3 Gustave Courbet's *Toilette de la mariée*

Courbet's *Toilette de la mariée* [pl.8, p.72] has been justly praised by art historians and critics ever since it was first published by Guy Eglington in the *International Studio* in 1924.[1] Yet despite its grandeur of scale – it measures 188 × 251.5 cm (74 × 99 in.) – and conception, the major problems surrounding the painting have been little investigated: Courbet's intentions in undertaking the work; the nature of its sources; the iconography of the painting; the question of its date; the reason for its obvious and intriguing spatial ambiguities; and why it remained unfinished.[2] In the course of this essay I hope to grapple with some of these problems: to situate the *Toilette* in the context of Courbet's œuvre in terms of its theme and its date, and within the broader framework of French Realism generally; to examine its pictorial sources and prototypes; to investigate the iconography of the painting as a whole and in detail; to speculate about the reasons for Courbet's alterations of the composition and spatial setting; and finally to connect Courbet's figure-space dilemma and its implications to nineteenth-century art generally and to the Realist enterprise specifically. Viewed within the context of visual representations of weddings and brides generally – a theme which has been treated from antique times to the epoch of Dada – Courbet's *Toilette de la mariée* is neither a complex moral allegory like Bruegel's *Peasant Wedding Feast*, nor a simple genre scene like Sir David Wilkie's *Bride at her Toilet* [33], but occupies a ground somewhere in between, the ground of Realism as a self-conscious movement, established by Courbet and his followers and supporters in the 1850s.

Date and context

In situating the painting within the context of Courbet's work and that of French Realism, it is necessary to deal with the problem of the date of the *Toilette*. This is often given as *c.*1865–70, for no apparent reason – Eglington quite correctly asserted

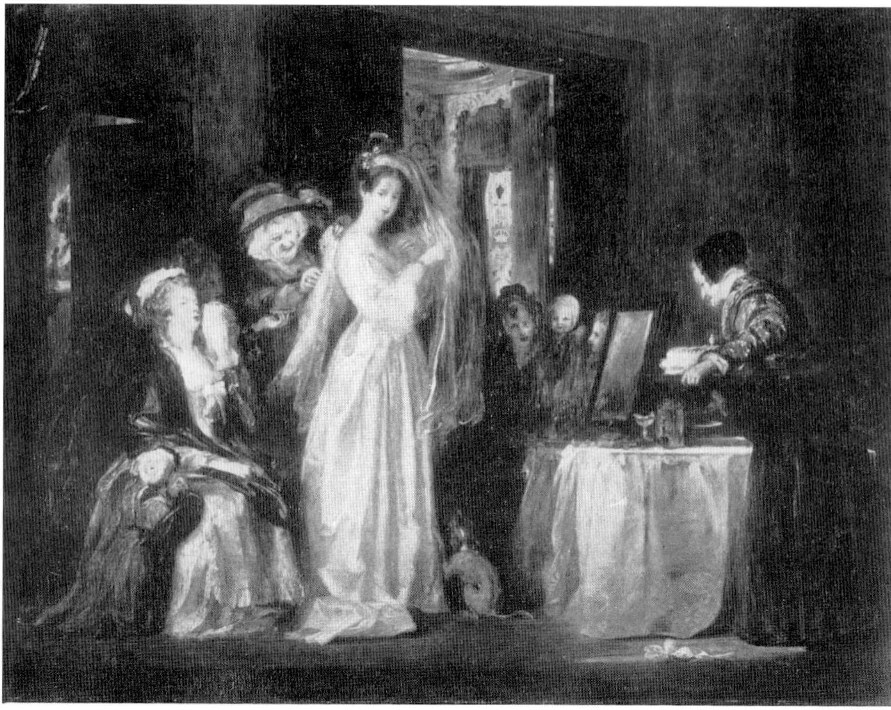

33 **David Wilkie**, *The Bride at her Toilet on the Day of her Wedding*, 1837. Oil on canvas, 97.1 x 122.5 cm, 38¼ x 48¼ in.

that it could hardly be later than 1855,[3] and Douglas Cooper in 1960 sensibly suggested 1858–60.[4] While its composition obviously relates it to *The Painter's Studio* of 1855 [pl.11, p.138–39], the *Toilette* clearly belongs at the same time to the ambitious cycle of large-scale paintings of major events in rural life – the rural life of his own province, the Franche-Comté – which Courbet undertook during his Realist period *par excellence*, the decade of the 1850s: such works as the *Burial at Ornans* of 1850 [pl.2, pp.66–67], *The Peasants of Flagey Returning from the Fair*, exhibited in the Salon of 1850–51 [54, p.122], or *The Grain Sifters* of 1854 [pl.5, p.70], which also resembles the *Toilette* in being an interior scene in which light entering through lattice-work is compressed into a rich pattern of criss-crossed *pâte* on the upper left-hand wall in the background. Like them, the *Toilette* embodies Courbet's intention, explicitly stated in the introduction to the catalogue of his private Realist Exhibition in 1855, "to represent the customs, the ideas, the appearance of my own era according to my own understanding of them." In their grandeur of scale and seriousness of intention, these works of the 1850s indeed constitute Courbet's attempt to create a history painting of modern life or, more specifically, an aspect of modern life that was actually fast disappearing, and perhaps all the more precious for this very reason: the life and customs of the provincial peasantry and petty bourgeoisie.

The 1850s and 1860s were a period of intensive study of the language, songs, and art of the people, and they saw the publication of collections like those of J.-M. Garnier, C. Nisard, or Courbet's friends Max Buchon and Champfleury.[5] In 1852, a government directive requested all teachers in the French provinces to collect local folk-songs.[6] George Sand, in the interests of more idiomatic locution for her peasant characters, collected over six hundred local Berrichon expressions.[7] Folk art, viewed as the collective, spontaneous expression of the deepest feelings and creative impulses of the people, folk customs seen as the time-consecrated, formalized re-enactments of their basic beliefs and social organization, were felt to have an interest and a vitality lacking to the arts and *mores* of their educated superiors.[8] So it is no accident that the Realists, especially in the earlier stages of their enterprise, concentrated their attention on the reality of lower class, or petty bourgeois, often provincial life, instead of on that of the more sophisticated urban upper classes. The uneventful, often monotonous life of the rural Folk seemed to be more deeply enmeshed in the dense texture of "reality" than that of their betters.[9]

The specific theme of the wedding made its appearance more than once in the annals of realist literature. The iconography of the provincial wedding was described at great length by George Sand, a writer much admired by Courbet, in a long appendix to *La Mare au diable*, of 1846, called "Les Noces de campagne": here, the author records all the details of the wedding customs of her native Berry, customs which were already falling into disuse at the time.[10] Wedding ceremonies, interestingly enough, were the subjects of at least two imaginary "realist paintings" which figured in realist novels: in the Goncourts' *Manette Salomon* (1865) the hero, the painter Coriolis, prepares *Un Mariage à l'eglise* and its pendant, *The Recruit's Medical Examination*, as major offerings to the Exposition Universelle of 1855;[11] in Zola's *L'Œuvre*, of 1885–86, the great realist painter Bongrand, a character based at least partly on Courbet, is supposed to have achieved his first notoriety with *La Noce de village*, "a wedding procession spreading out through a wheatfield, the peasants studied very closely and very accurately, with the epic appearance of Homer's heroes."[12] The work is acclaimed as the cornerstone of a whole new school, and the fact that Bongrand is supposed to have later painted, as a pendant, an *Enterrement au village* makes the relation of the character to Courbet even more striking.[13]

Motifs and sources

If we turn to Courbet's *Toilette* for a more detailed examination, it immediately becomes apparent that realism, for Courbet, did not imply photographic verisimilitude or anecdotal picturesqueness, nor did it imply the capturing of an ephemeral visual incident, as it would later to the Impressionists, but, rather, a temporally weighty structure appropriate to the dignity and importance of his subject: the recording of the customs, the ideas, the appearance of his own era and, he might

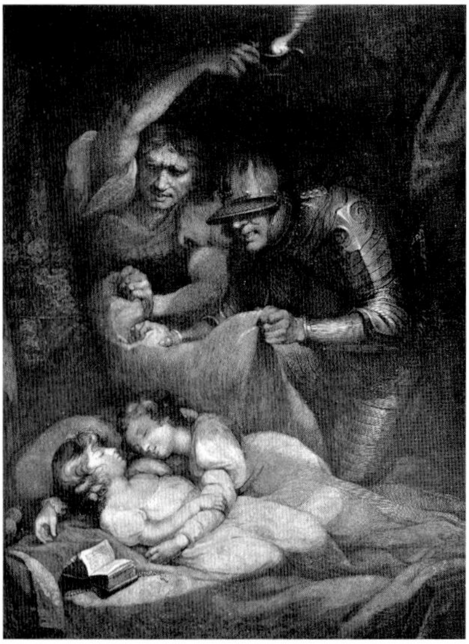

34 **After James Northcote**, *The Death of Edward V and his Brother*. Engraving

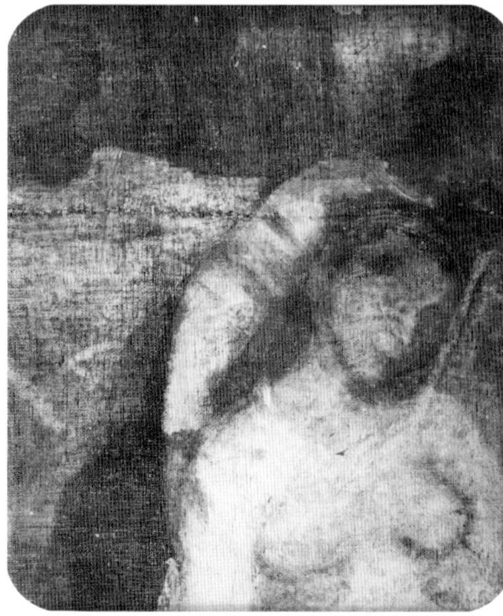

35 X-ray detail of Plate 8, *Toilette de la mariée*

36 *Sleep*, 1866. Oil on canvas, 135 x 200 cm, 53⅛ x 78¾ in.

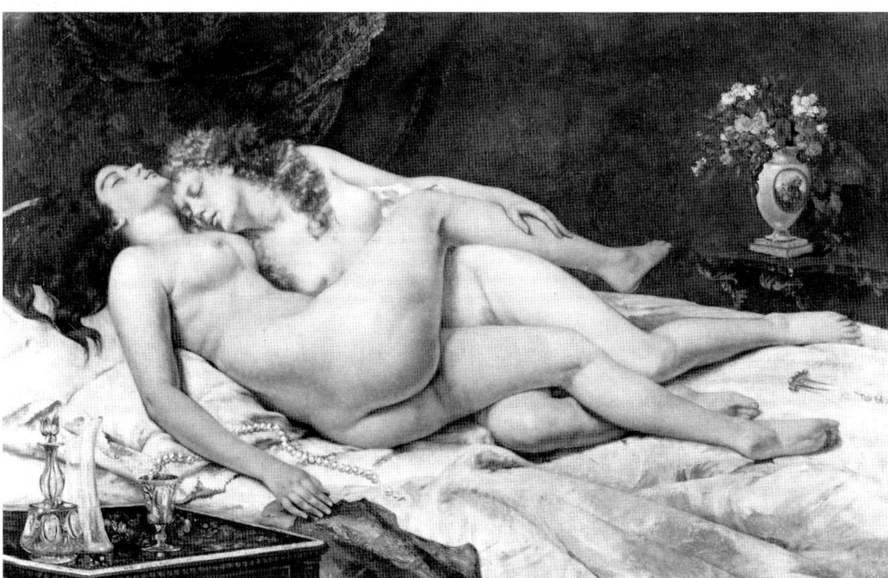

have added, of his own region. For Courbet, such communal celebrations were indeed secular rites of deep significance, and, as we shall see, in the *Toilette* he has compiled an anthology of the wedding customs of the Franche-Comté,[14] customs which in actuality formed a temporal sequence, within a single, grand image on a single, if ambiguous, spatial stage. While the toilet of the bride is the central event depicted,[15] it by no means accounts for the iconography of the painting as a whole, as it does in genre paintings of the theme of the bride's toilet preceding Courbet's in the nineteenth century – such works (which may or may not have been known to the artist) as the younger Fragonard's *La Toilette de la mariée* of *c.*1828, P. R. Vigneron's *Les Apprêts d'un mariage* (before 1830), or Wilkie's *The Bride at her Toilet on the Day of her Wedding* [33].[16]

In attempting to investigate sources and prototypes for Courbet's *Toilette*, the painting may be divided into two halves: a left-hand portion, containing the "toilet" proper, close to the foreground and large in scale, enclosed by a large, canopy-like structure; and a right-hand portion, implying a deeper space with smaller-scale figures farther away from the spectator.

It may be said of the painting as a whole, and certainly of the left-hand portion containing the bride at her toilet, that Guy Eglington was on the right track when he asserted that Courbet's painting was a nineteenth-century reply to the court painters of the eighteenth century.[17] The suggestion of the derivation of the motifs, if not the whole composition of the *Toilette*, from the art of the eighteenth century is a good one; although it must be admitted that while the theme of the wedding was popular in that epoch and that of the toilet even more so, to my knowledge there exist no eighteenth-century representations of *toilets* of *brides*. That Courbet had a great relish for, as well as an ability to transform or enlarge, themes of the eighteenth century can be readily seen in the relation of his 1858 *Hunt Picnic*, now in the Wallraf-Richartz Museum, to Carle van Loo's *Hunting Breakfast* in the Louvre; or, more amusingly, in his tongue-in-cheek transformation of an engraving after James Northcote representing the *Death of Edward V and his Brother* [34][18] into the far-from-innocent *Sleep* (also known as *Paresse et luxure*) [36] representing two voluptuous nude women locked in a passionate, if somnolent, embrace.[19] The ultimate source of the left-hand portion of Courbet's *Toilette* would seem to go back to the minor art of the eighteenth century, or to the eighteenth century as revived in the engravings or lithographs of the *petits maîtres* of the nineteenth century, and to a combination or variation of three motifs which were specialities of eighteenth-century minor art: the toilet; its subcategory, the *lever*; and the *coucher de la mariée*.

The relation of the figure of the bride and her attendants to the toilet scenes of the eighteenth century becomes even more striking when we realize that Courbet had originally intended to depict his bride nude [35] and only later altered her figure to the semi-clothed condition in which she now appears.[20] In her original nakedness the bride, fussed over by her attendants, looks remarkably like such readily available,

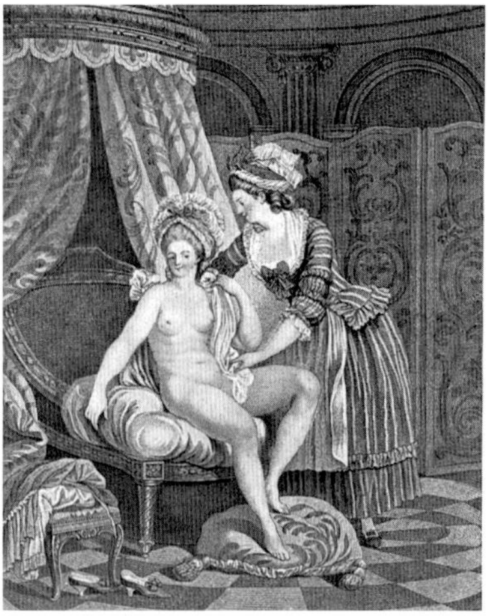

37 **After N. R. Jollain**, *The Bath*. Engraving

38 **Rembrandt van Rijn**, *Bathsheba*, 1654. Oil on canvas, 142 x 142 cm, 56 x 56 in.

39 *Bather Sleeping by a Brook*, 1845. Oil on canvas, 81.3 x 64.8 cm, 32 x 25½ in.

mildly titillating eighteenth-century color engravings as *The Bath* [37] or the *Toilette* after N. R. Jollain, Regnault's *Lever*, or his engraving after the *Bath* by Baudouin.[21] The same conjunction of a naked feminine protagonist decked out by clothed attendants, and the sexual overtones it could imply is, of course, present in one of the great toilet scenes of the seventeenth century, Rembrandt's *Bathsheba* [38] in the Louvre, similar to Courbet's original, nude bride (as well as to his earlier *Bather Sleeping by a Brook* [39]), in the pose of the servant at the woman's feet and the rather pensive, introspective attitude and expression of the main figure.[22] Why did Courbet decide to change his bride from nude to clothed? Perhaps in the interests of greater specificity, of truth to the period and the locale.[23] Or perhaps, although this is mere speculation, Courbet came to feel that a clothed bride was both more modest and more appropriate to the theme of a country wedding. Or (although this is more speculative still) he may have been urged to dress his bride by his friend and fellow Franc-Comtois, the anarchist philosopher P.-J. Proudhon, prude and anti-feminist *extraordinaire*, author of that

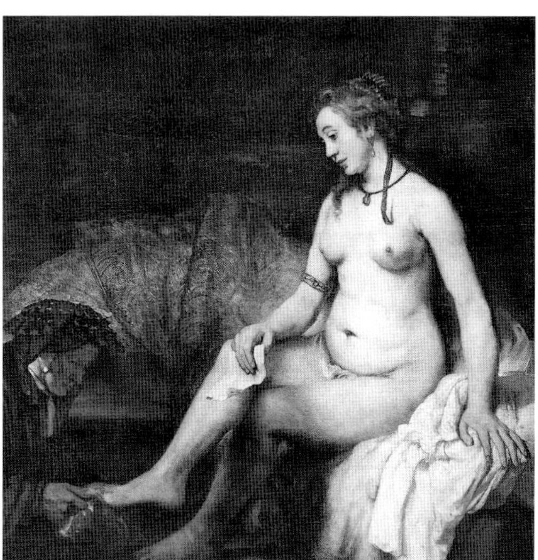

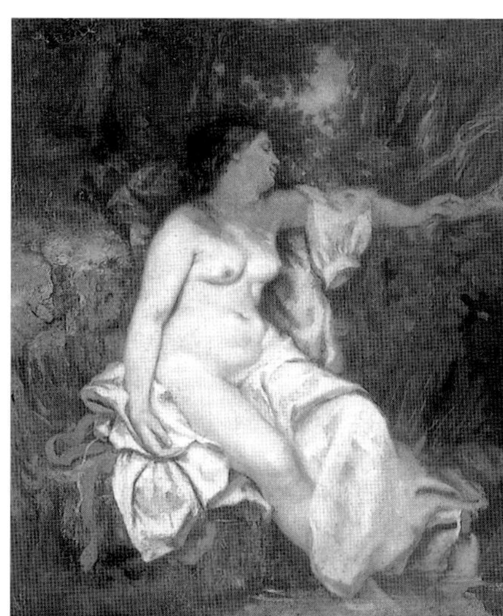

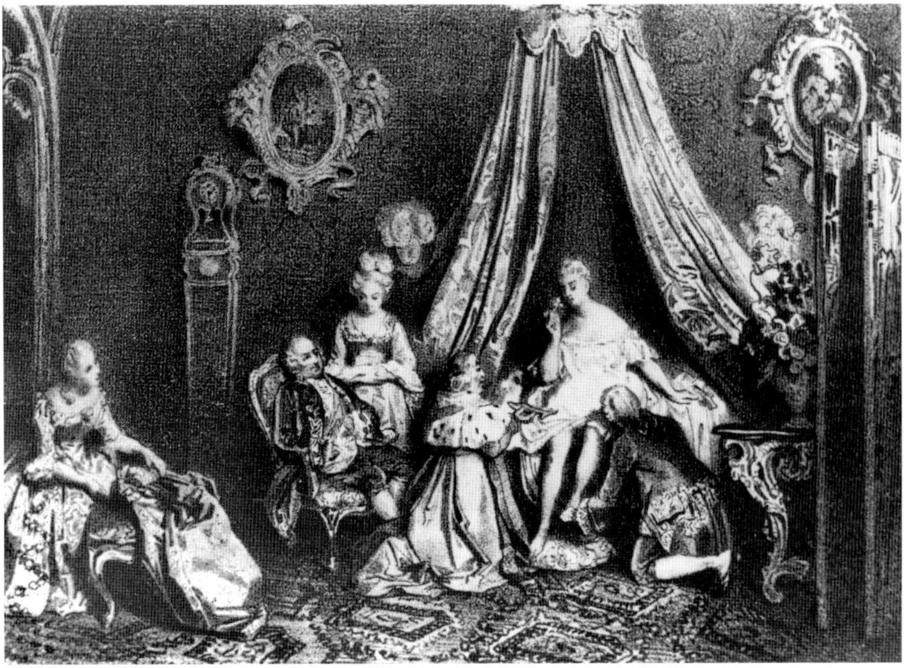

40 **After Jean Gigoux**, *Madame du Barry and Louis XV.* Lithograph

milestone in the history of misogyny, *La Pornocratie ou les femmes dans les temps modernes*,[24] who in his posthumously published *Du Principe de l'art et de sa destination sociale* (written largely about, and in consultation with, Courbet), severely criticized the disparity between moral intentions and salacious actualization in pictorial treatments of the theme of Susannah at the Bath.[25]

Even closer in the grouping of the figures and to the partially clothed condition of Courbet's final version of the bride is a work by a countryman of his (he came from Besançon) and a friend who was well known as a reviver of eighteenth-century motifs, Jean Gigoux. Gigoux's *lever* scene, *Mme du Barry et Louis XV* [40], exhibited in the Salon of 1833 and reproduced in *L'Artiste*, was itself based, no doubt, on an eighteenth-century prototype; in any case his composition is similar to Courbet's in the motif, if not the sex and status, of the kneeling figure offering the shoe, the presence of the bed, and the clothing heaped up at the left.[26]

Yet as far as the conjunction of bride, attendants, and meaningful bed – the theme of the left-hand portion of Courbet's painting – is concerned, the major source of inspiration would seem to be that offered by the traditional representation of the Bridal Night or the *coucher de la mariée*, widely disseminated in France in the form of prints, most of which could trace their ultimate ancestry to the version created by the eighteenth-century artist Pierre Antoine Baudouin [41] for

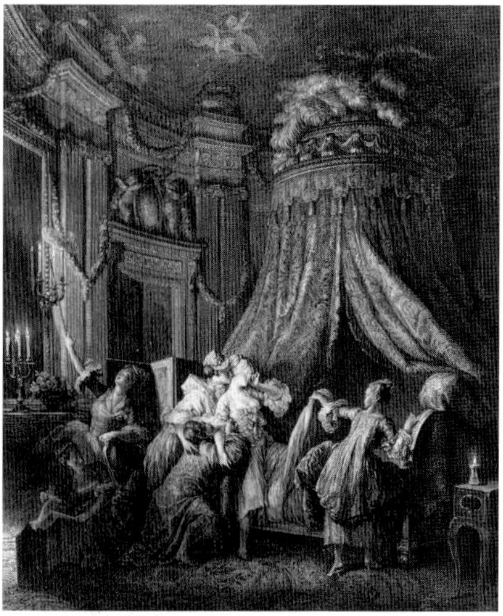

41 **After Pierre Antoine Baudoin,** *Le Coucher de la mariée.* Engraving by Moreau le jeune

the Salon of 1767, where it was roundly condemned by Diderot for lasciviousness and *invraisemblance.*[27] The popularity of Baudouin's composition, engraved by Moreau le jeune, was attested to by the sheer number of variants based upon it, like the anonymous Empire print of about 1818 [42], brought up to date in its neo-classical costume and décor and brought down to its audience in the general *embourgeoisement* of its cast of characters. The theme of the *coucher de la mariée* descended the ladder to popular imagery, and to the costume and décor of the 1830s or 1840s, in an *image populaire* from Paris, *chez* Codoni [20, p.36], which may well have been familiar to Courbet[28] and bears a certain general resemblance to the composition of his *Toilette*, especially in the motif on the left of the girls lifting the bed sheets; the theme appeared in popular lithographs as well, like those of Eugène Devéria [43] or N.-E. Maurin, also from the 1830s.

While the number of variants on the theme of the *coucher de la mariée* reveal the possible precedents available to Courbet, they make clear at the same time the distance which separates his *Toilette* from the frivolous and banal raw material offered to him by his eighteenth- and nineteenth-century predecessors in the field. For while the painting is ostensibly a toilet and the toilet of the bride indeed occupies a central position in the composition, the painting as a whole might better be entitled "Les Noces à la campagne," or, more explicitly viewed within the context of Courbet's work, "The Wedding at Ornans," a pendant to the *Burial at Ornans.*[29] Support for this interpretation is offered by Courbet's announced intention to go even farther in recording the communal celebrations of his region in a grisly sequel to the *Toilette*, a *Wake*, which he described to his friend and biographer Gros-Kost[30] in the most detailed and enthusiastic terms. The painting was to have represented the corpse of a young girl lying in state, surrounded by the hubbub of funeral festivities, with groups of merrymakers eating and drinking around the already greenish body – "a very realist subject" Courbet pronounced it, stating that he was in the process of brushing in the underpainting.[31] While no trace of a *Wake* by Courbet now remains, aside from a reference to a *Toilette de la morte* in a sale catalogue of 1882,[32] Courbet's intention to depict rural funeral customs was fulfilled in *The Wake* [56, p.130] painted in 1893 by his disciple and pupil, the Puerto Rican Realist Francisco Oller, in a gigantic canvas representing the funeral of a new-born girl among the hill people of Puerto Rico.[33]

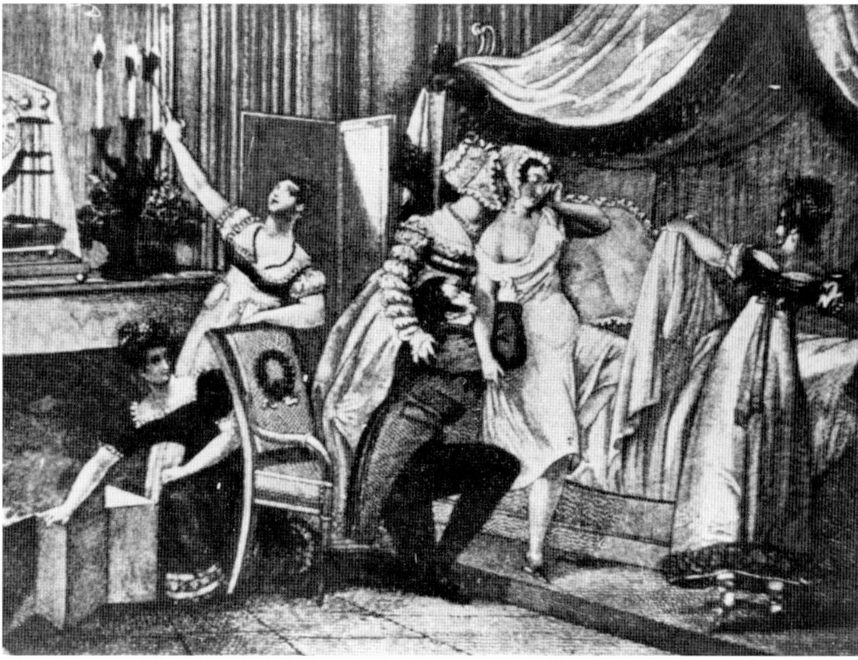

42 *Le Coucher de la mariée.* Anonymous engraving after fig. 41

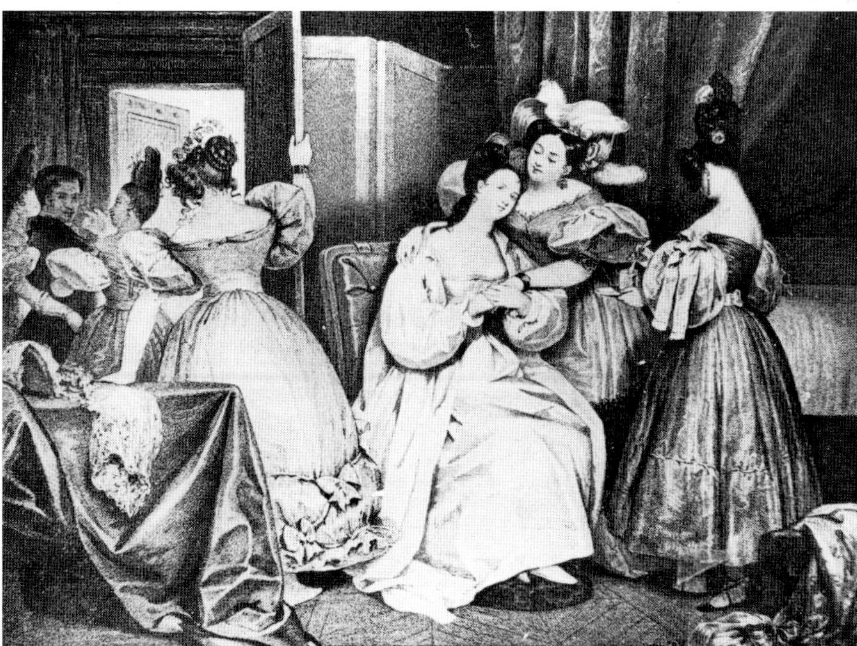

43 **Eugène Devéria,** *Le Coucher de la mariée.* Lithograph

As a representation of the marriage practices of the peasantry, Courbet's *Toilette* belongs to a long tradition, going back as far as Bruegel and his peasant wedding pictures,[34] continued in the genre painting of seventeenth-century Holland, notably in the works of Jan Steen (an artist much admired by the Realists), and carried on by such nineteenth-century followers of the Dutch little masters as David Wilkie in his *Bride at her Toilet*, mentioned above, or *The Penny Wedding*;[35] or by the Austrian Ferdinand Waldmüller (*The Perchtolsdorf Peasant Wedding*, 1843, or *The Departure of the Bride*, 1860 and 1863); or the Norwegian artist Adolf Tidemand in *Dressing the Bride*, of 1867.[36] Yet in representing the customs of the Franche-Comté, it is significant that Courbet did not choose the more popular, livelier, and more colorful subject of the wedding feast or dance, but rather chose to depict all the stages of the wedding ritual in a quieter, less picturesque pictorial context.

While the left-hand side of the painting may in fact have been shaped by pictorial prototypes, the right-hand side is determined by the demands of Courbet's iconography, which, as Jean Seznec has pointed out, is based upon the "nuptial scenario" of his region, a scenario repeated, with local variations, throughout all of France.[37] Many of the details of the meaning of the various elements of the wedding ceremony were supplied by local folk songs, made familiar to Courbet either through the intermediary of his close friend Max Buchon, who published his *Noëls et chants populaires de la Franche-Comté* in 1863, or simply through the personal experience of the artist himself, who composed several popular songs of his own and illustrated some of the *Chansons populaires des provinces de France*, introduced by his friend Champfleury in 1860.[38]

Within the framework of the marriage ritual, the very dressing of the bride had symbolic significance, the headdress and the shoes being of particular importance. The former, made of large artificial flowers, was placed on the bride's head by a particularly privileged young girl, and the shoes – shades of Cinderella! – were a gift from the fiancé.[39] Courbet has represented precisely the moment of putting the shoes on the bride's feet and has placed a girl weaving the headdress of flowers directly to the right of the central group. In one Franc-Comtois bridal song, a group of guests entering the house of the bride offers her gifts of apples, pears, and nuts, and in addition:

> . . . un peigne pour la belle peigner
> Et une tresse pour la belle tresser
> Un miroir pour la belle coiffer . . .[40]

Opposite: Plate 1, *A Burial at Ornans* (detail)

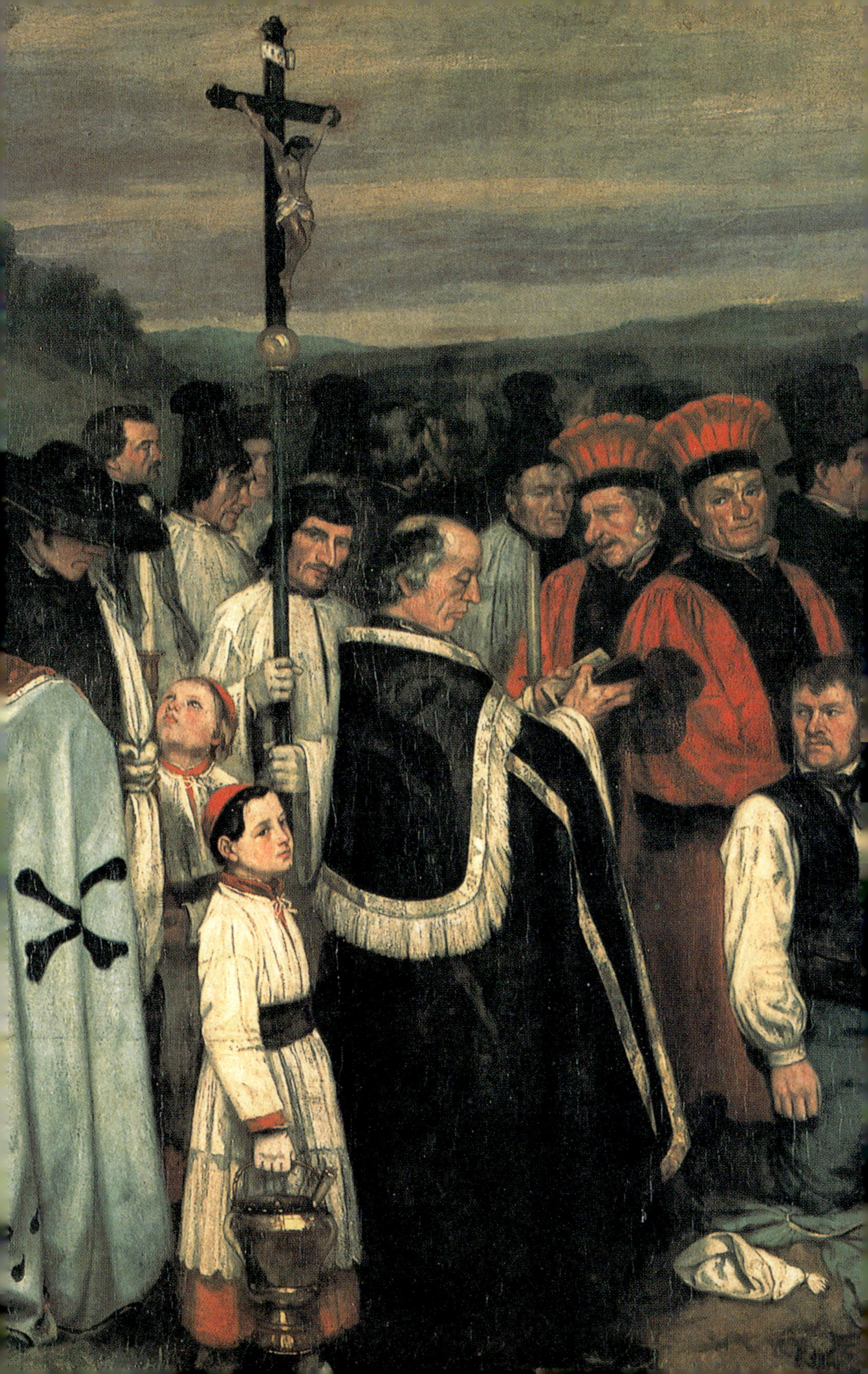

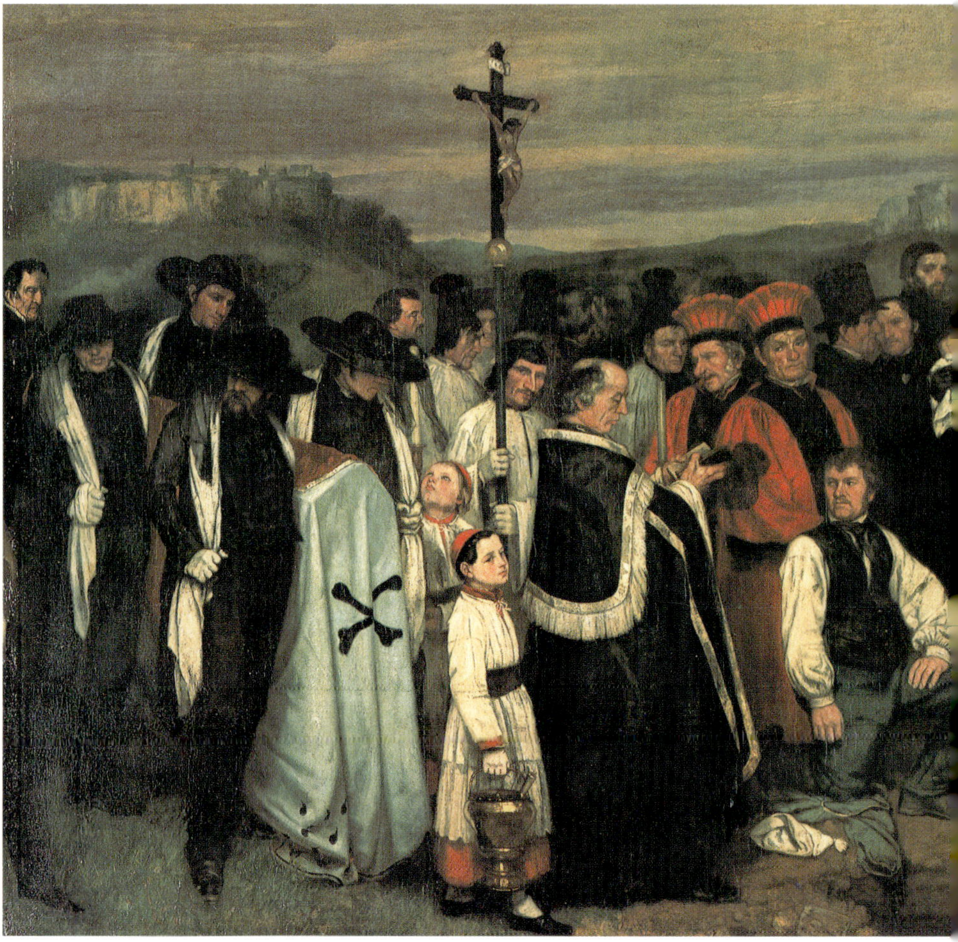

PLATES 2 AND 3 (detail, overleaf) *A Burial at Ornans*, 1850.
Oil on canvas, 315 x 668 cm, 124½ x 263¾ in.

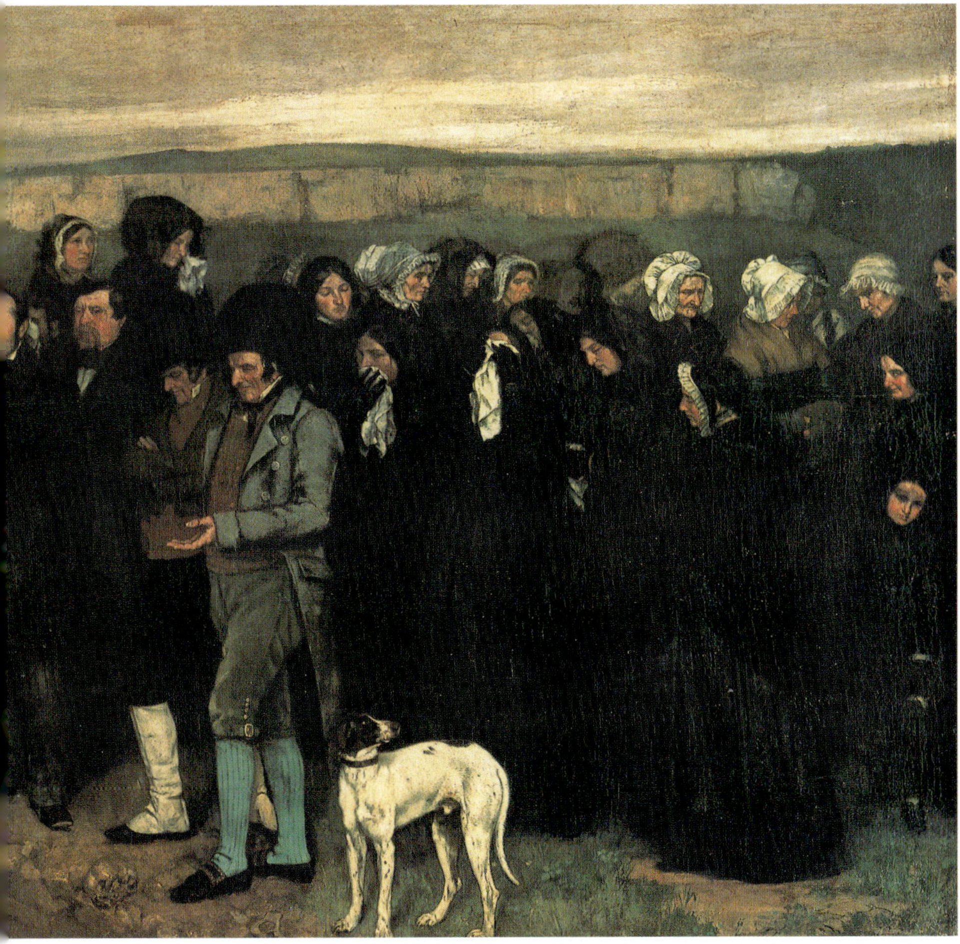

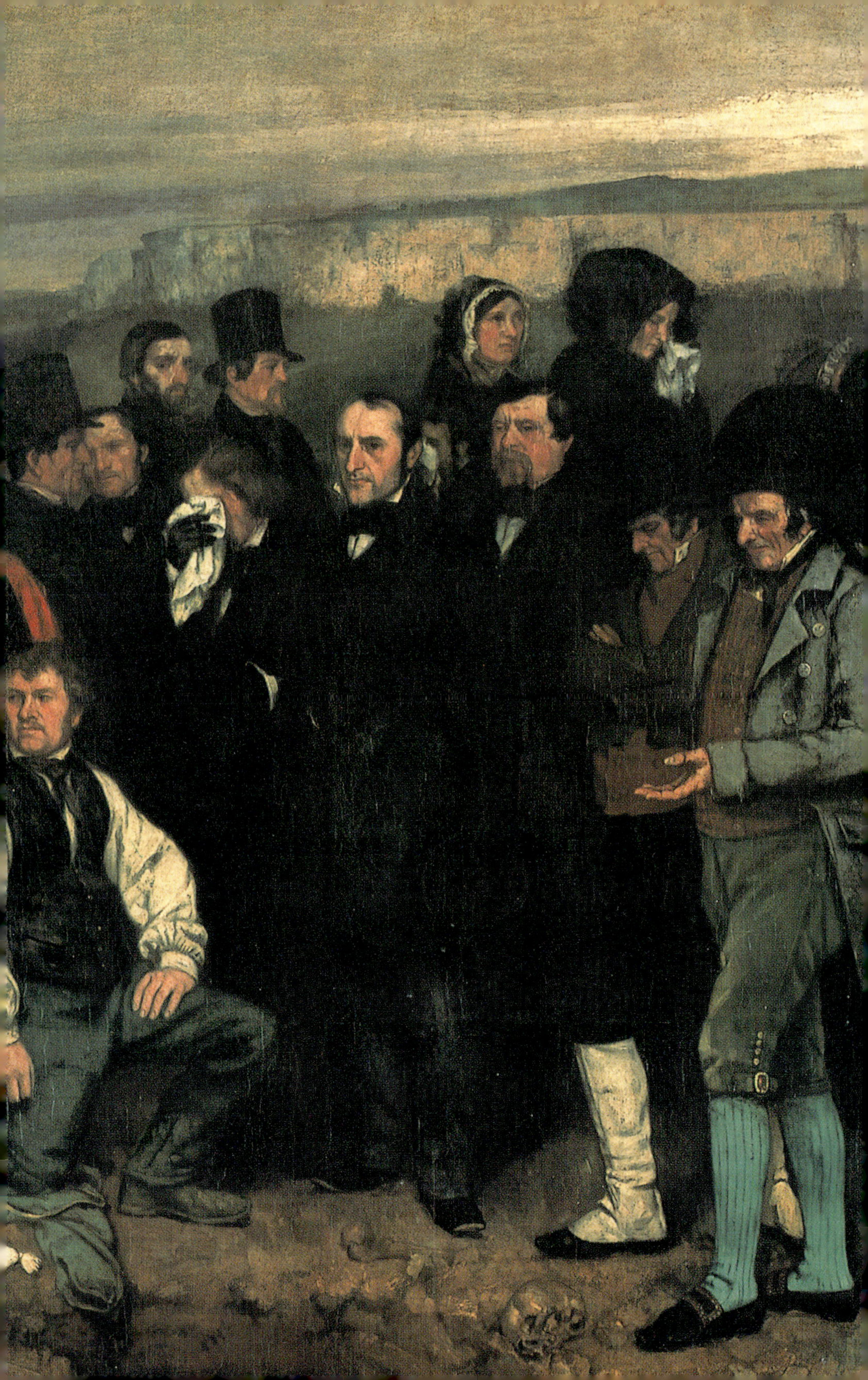

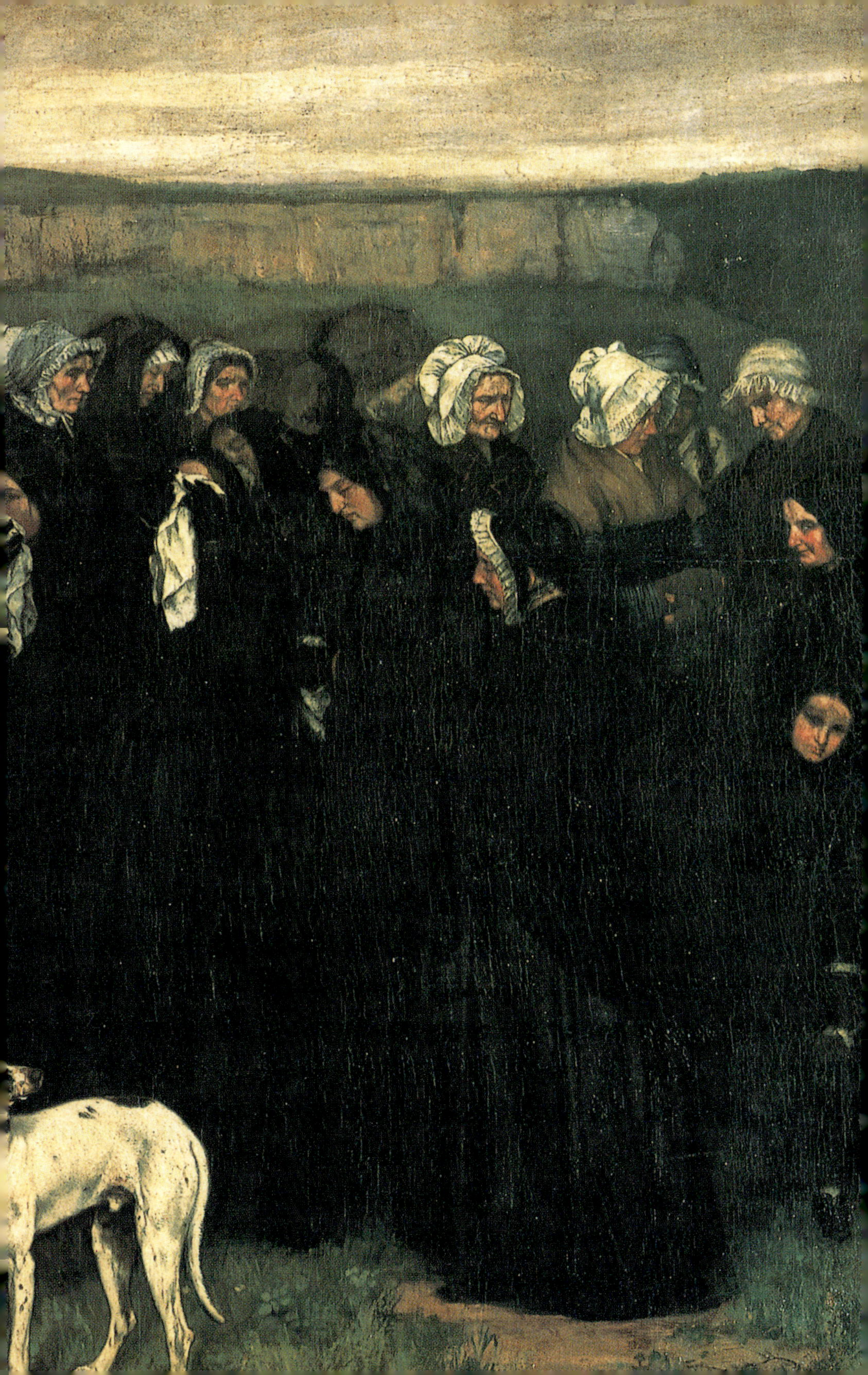

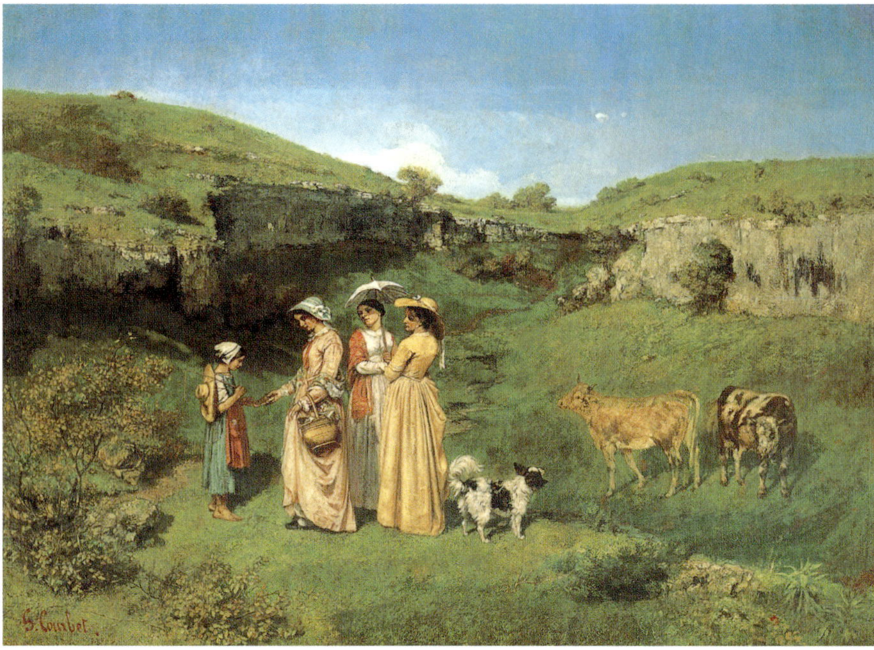

PLATE 4 *The Young Ladies of the Village*, 1852.
Oil on canvas, 194.9 x 261 cm, 76¾ x 102¾ in.

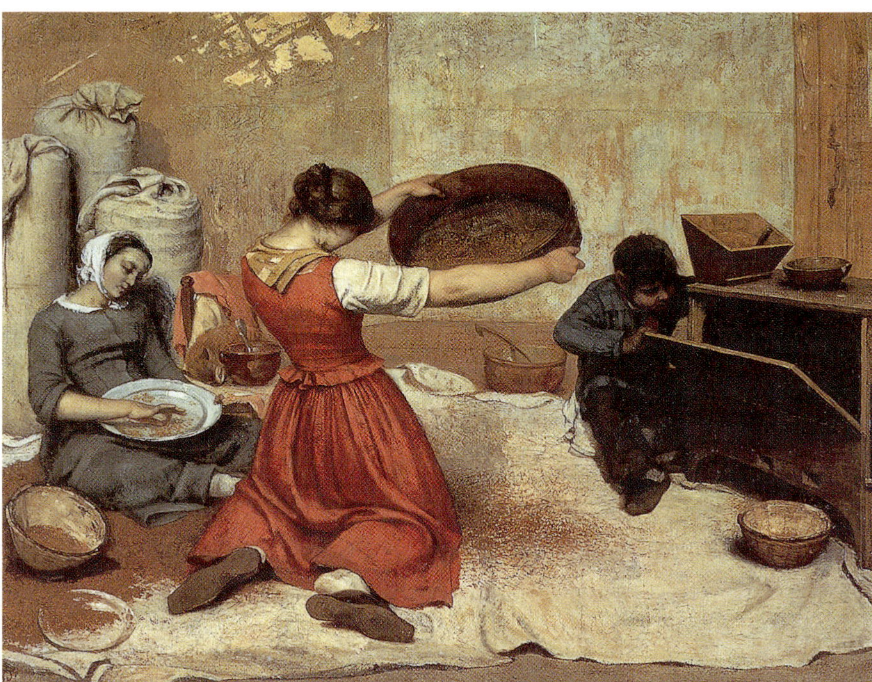

PLATE 5 *The Grain Sifters* (*Cribleuses de blé*), 1854.
Oil on canvas, 131 x 167 cm, 51¼ x 66 in.

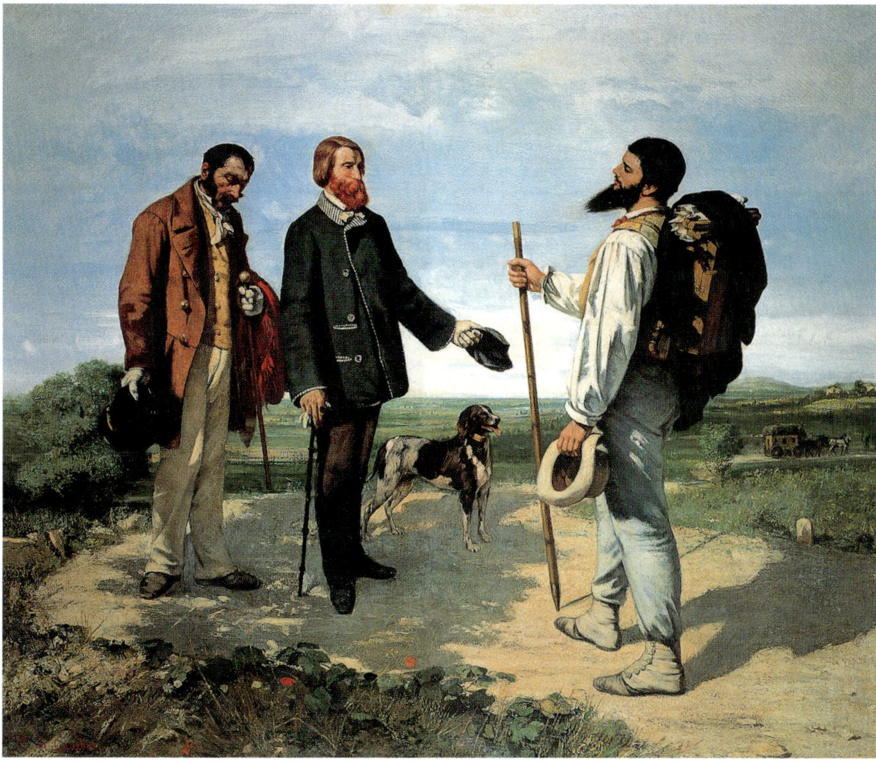

PLATE 6 *The Meeting*, 1854.
Oil on canvas, 129 x 149 cm, $50\frac{3}{4}$ x $58\frac{5}{8}$ in.

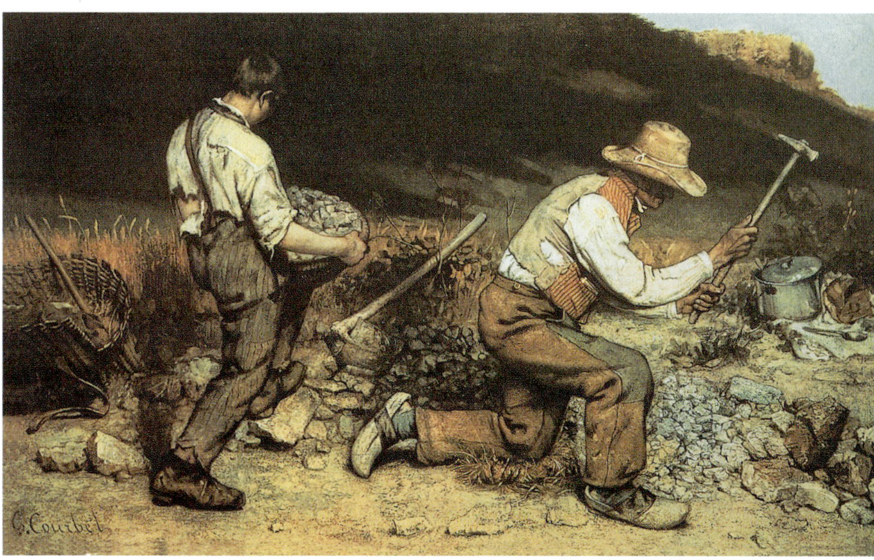

PLATE 7 *The Stonebreakers*, 1849–50.
Oil on canvas, 190 x 300 cm, $74\frac{3}{4}$ x $118\frac{1}{8}$ in. (Destroyed)

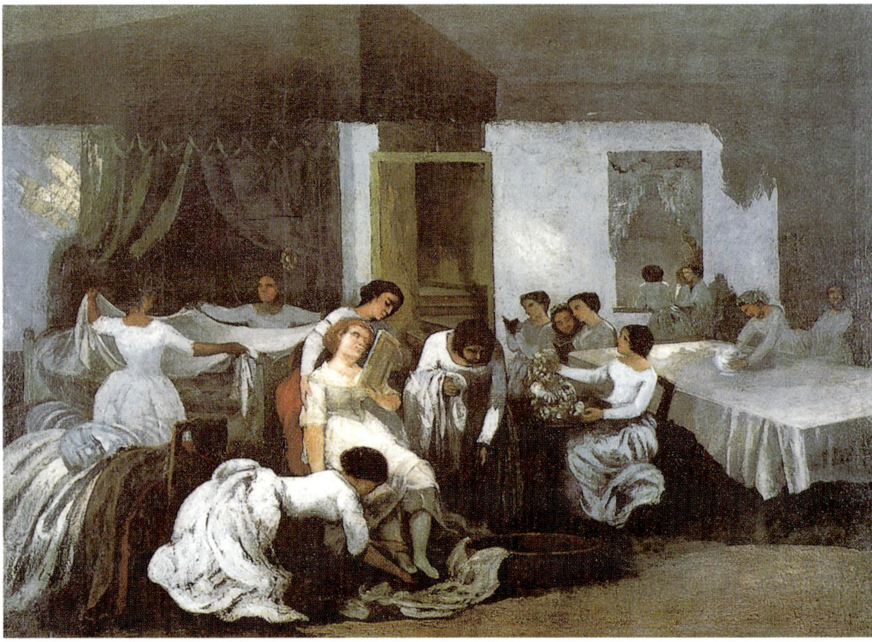

PLATE 8 *Toilette de la mariée/Toilette de la morte* (*The Preparation of the Bride/Dead Girl*), *c.*1858.
Oil on canvas, 188 x 251.5 cm, 74 x 99 in.

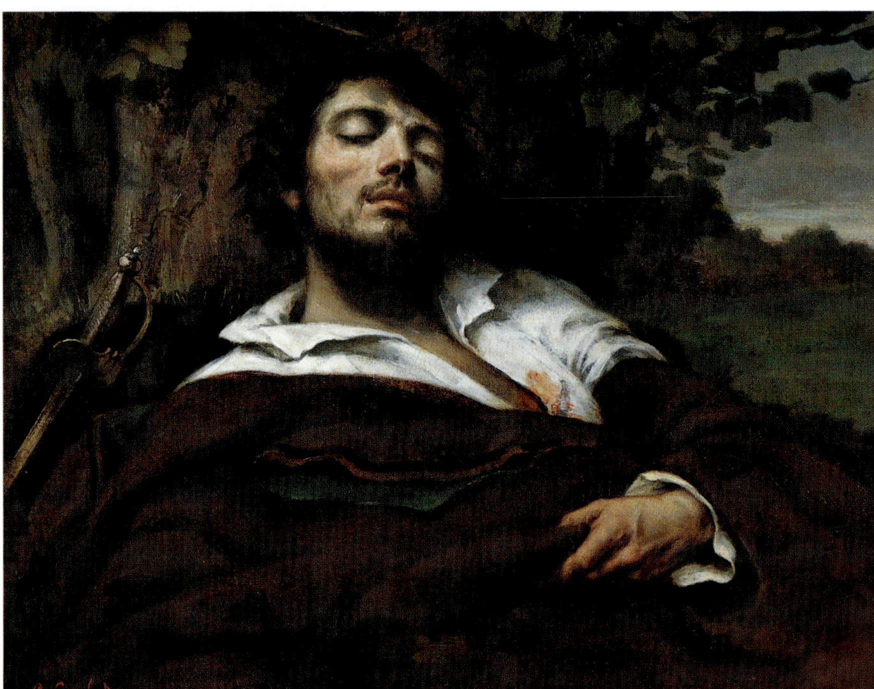

PLATE 9 *Self-Portrait: The Wounded Man*, 1844–54.
Oil on canvas, 81 x 97 cm, 31⅞ x 38¼ in.

Significantly enough, Courbet has chosen to emphasize the combing of the bride's hair and the mirror which she holds in front of her face. The importance of both the hair and the holding of the mirror are features of the later, clothed version of the bride's toilet rather than the original, nude version, which leads one to believe that Courbet wished to give additional emphasis to the *folklorique* aspects of his work when he revised it.

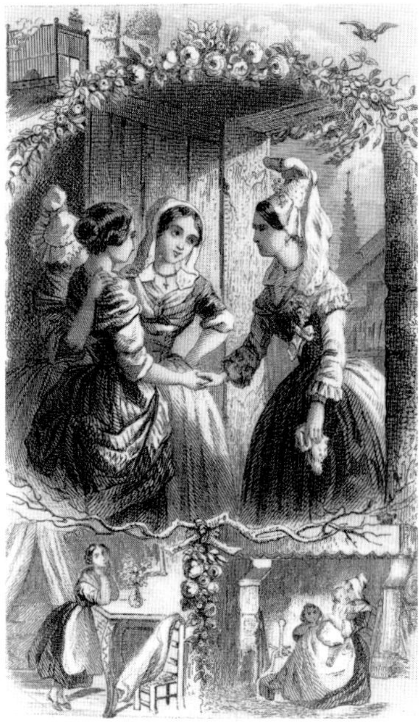

44 **Colin Jorel**, *Adieux de la mariée.* Engraving in Pierre Dupont, *Chants et chansons*, III, Paris, 1855

Behind the girl weaving the headdress is a group of three young girls holding books. These young women doubtlessly constitute a reference to the custom of the "adieux," or the Bride's Song. The young girls of the neighborhood would arrive at the bride's house, sometimes bringing a symbolic bouquet and a cake, to sing the half-melancholy, half-satirical farewell to youth and freedom, reminding the young bride-to-be that she must now cast aside the pleasures and liberties of maidenhood and assume the onerous responsibilities of the married state. It was the almost universal existence of this melancholy song, at times indistinguishable from a dirge, in French marriage rituals, that led the brilliant Marxist critic and sociologist Paul Lafargue, one of the first students of the deeper social significance of folklore, to maintain as early as 1886, in his *Chansons et cérémonies populaires du mariage*, that study of popular folk songs such as this revealed the basic contradictions within traditional social institutions, in this case those of marriage and the family. For the farewell songs to the bride bore witness to the striking contrast between the official manifestations of joy in marriage – the Church and State proclaiming its sanctity and its protective, positive role in the life of the young bride – and the very different image projected by popular folklore, an image far more cynical, pessimistic, and bitter, emphasizing the future misery of the victim/heroine and envisaging the bride "as a condemned prisoner," to use the words of Lafargue.[41] While this cynicism is somewhat mitigated in the more sentimental version of the "adieux" created by Courbet's friend, the popular *chansonnier* Pierre Dupont [44], even here the bride admits that she is "moitié triste, moitié contente" as she asks her "chères compagnons de mes jeux" to accompany her departure with songs. She bids farewell to her virginal bed, to flowers and birds, to strawberries and nuts, to dancing, fine shoes, and dainty scissors – to the tokens of carefree adolescence – since from the morrow on she is to be a farmer's wife (indeed, an overwhelmingly demanding burden in the days before mechanization) and perhaps, in time, a mother.[42] A version from Poitou, published by Courbet's friend and champion, Champfleury, reminds the young bride:

Vous n'irez plus au bal,
Ma très-chèr' camarade;
Vous n'irez plus au bal,
Au bal, ni aux ballades;
Vous gard'rez la maison
Tandis que nous irons.

Rossignolet des bois,
Qui chante au vert bocage,
Quand il a des petits
Il change de langage;
Avant qu'il soit un an,
Belle, en ferez autant.[43]

Still another version of the song, popular in the western regions of France and known to Balzac, reminds the bride that she can no longer go to dances but must stay at home with her baby, that she will be obliged to obey her (not necessarily sympathetic) husband and must care for the farm animals without respite. The hazards of the married state for women are graphically and touchingly outlined:

Vous n'irez plus au bal,
Madame la mariée,
Danser sous le fanal,
Dans les jeux d'assemblée:
Vous garderez la maison,
A bercer le poupon.

Avez-vous écouté,
Ce que vous dit le prêtre:
A dit la vérité
Et comme il vous faut être:
Fidèle à votre époux
Et l'aimer comme vous.

Quand on dit son époux,
On dit souvent son maître:
Il ne sont pas si doux,
Comme ils ont promis d'être.
Il faut leur conseiller
De mieux se rappeler.

Si vous avez, Bretons,
De bœufs dans vos herbages,
Des brebis, des moutons,
Des oisillons sauvages,
Songez soir et matin,
Qu'à leur tour ils ont faim.

At this point, the bride's visitors hand her the symbolic cake to remind her that she must work and suffer for her daily bread, and then offer her a bouquet to remind her that all false honors wither like flowers:

Recevez ce gâteau
Que ma main vous présente,
Il est fait de façon
A vous faire comprendre
Qu'il faut pour se nourrir
Travailler et souffrir.

Recevez ce bouquet
Que nous venons vous tendre:
Il est fait de gênet
Pour vous faire comprendre
Que tous les vains honneurs
Passent comme les fleurs.[44]

In a Franc-Comtois version of the bridal song, in this case supposedly sung by the bride herself, the last verse actually ends with the bride in tears, when she sees the carefree lot of the unmarried girls:

Lorsque je vois ces fill's à table
A rire, à boire et à chanter,
De temps en temps je les regarde,
Des larmes m'y coulent des yeux.[45]

To the right of the three young girls in Courbet's painting, a woman places a flowered soup tureen on the table. According to Seznec and Léger,[46] this contains the traditional *soupe au fromage* of the region, which formed part of a meal served to the wedding party in the morning, before the departure for the church; yet it is also possible that Courbet, by isolating the soup tureen and placing it on a line almost horizontal with the portentous bed-sheet to the left, was implying another stage of the marriage ritual. According to Tiersot, a nineteenth-century student of French folkways, folksongs, and customs, the traditional marriage ceremony ended in the evening of the wedding-day in the nuptial chamber, with the burlesque and often quite suggestive custom of the "*soupe au lait.*" When the young couple went to bed, the wedding party would bring them a milk soup containing slices of bread tied together with a string, which they were obliged to eat with a spoon with a hole in the bottom. The new husband and wife were forced to swallow the soup down to the last drop, urged on by lively songs and indelicate jibes from the whole wedding party.[47]

There still remain some unexplained elements in the *Toilette de la mariée*: the doorway with its staircase, prominent in the center of the composition, and the two young girls in the background looking out the window. Since all the other motifs of the painting play a role in the "nuptial scenario," as Seznec calls it, we should be able to find a similar significance for these figures. Still unaccounted for in the iconography of the painting is one wedding custom, almost universally observed in the French provinces in the nineteenth century: that of the so-called livrées or livraison, a mock battle on the morning of the marriage between the family and friends of the young bride-to-be, barricaded within the house, and the party of the groom outside, who besiege it. This custom, the history and implications of which are discussed at great length by Lafargue, was endemic, with local variants throughout France, Europe, and even, in somewhat altered form, among primitive peoples as well. In general, in the French ceremonies, a lengthy dialogue would ensue between the two groups, or their spokesmen, often in the form of a set piece, followed by a song of as many as twenty verses, during the course of which the groom's party urged the bride's family to open the door:

Ouvrez vos portes,
Abaissez vos ponts

begins the wedding song from the Franche-Comté.[48] In general, the groom's family offered more and more presents as an incentive to the bride and her family, sometimes even going so far as to mention the bridal price paid for the girl, and these mounting offers were answered by constant refusal on the part of the besieged bride's family. Finally, in one version of the "livraison," as recounted by George Sand in her somewhat romanticized account of *berrichon* wedding customs in *La Mare au diable*, it is the groom himself who is offered to the bride:

> Ouvrez la porte, ouvrez,
> Marie, ma mignonne,
> C'est un beau mari qui vient vous chercher
> Allons, ma mie, laissons-les entrer.[49]

At this point the besieged family of the bride would unlatch the door and the groom would enter the house either alone or accompanied by members of his family.

I would like to suggest that the two young girls looking out the window constitute a reference to this essential act of the "nuptial scenario" and that they are in fact on the look-out for the groom's party. The prominent doorway is, of course, a reference to the entry of the bridegroom – the other, and absent, protagonist of the occasion.[50] Courbet may actually have thought of adding the figure of the groom himself; certainly, an appropriate prototype for such a figure standing on a staircase framed by a doorway in the background would have been offered by Velázquez's *Las Meninas*, a work whose composition has been compared to that of the *Toilette*, notably by Roger Fry.[51] The relation to Velázquez is further supported by the obvious kinship of the central, bending bridal attendant to the analogously placed figure in the Spanish artist's *Las Hilanderas*, better known to mid-century Realists as *La Fabrique de tapisseries* [19, p.35].[52]

If these elements in the rear section of the painting actually constitute a reference to the marriage custom of the *livraison*, then Courbet's painting is indeed a pictorial compendium of the customs and traditions of his region, ethnology writ large and transformed through grandeur of scale and breadth of conception into a kind of contemporary history painting. While those critics who make pure form, whatever they may mean by it, the touchstone of pictorial value may find the *Toilette* all the better for being unfinished, those of us who conceive of pictorial structure as a complex totality involving all significant elements can only regret that Courbet never realized his ambitious project in the fullness and phenomenological exactitude characteristic of his finished works.

Pictorial construction

Why did Courbet leave such an important work unfinished? While of course one cannot discount the usual contingencies of life – sickness, departure, the pressure of other work – it seems to me more likely that Courbet left the *Toilette* unfinished simply because he couldn't finish it: that is, he was unable to cope with the problem of disposing his complex figural groups convincingly within the pictorial space. Laboratory examination as well as the naked eye reveal a number of major changes in the painting, the most radical of which took place when the painting was near completion – and a number of structural inconsistencies as well. For example: there are two distinct "vanishing areas" in the painting, one established by the vanishing point of the orthogonals of the canopy to the left, the other by the convergence of the edges of the table to the right, as well as other perspectival inconsistencies that are somewhat less disturbing. The disparities in the diminution of scale (or the size of the figures in relation to their putative spatial positions) in the two sides of the painting are fairly obvious. These inconsistencies are not due to a desire for a de Chirico-like perspectival ambiguity on Courbet's part but occur because the painting is actually a palimpsest of structural alternatives. The most obvious of the revisions are those of the canopy over the alcove and/or bed at the left and the addition of a heavy impasto of white lead to the left of the door and to either side of the window at the rear.

In part, these compositional-spatial problems are due to Courbet's basic view of his paintings as additive "patchworks" of separate, individually conceived elements.[53] This piecemeal approach to pictorial construction has been convincingly brought out by Bruce MacDonald in his recent analysis of Courbet's *Quarry* [85, p.195] in Boston. While the *Toilette* is not literally a stitching together of heterogeneous motifs, as are *The Quarry* and several others of his works,[54] Courbet's practice of putting together discrete motifs implies a number of separate viewpoints and directions of viewing for the several parts of his composition, as opposed to the single viewpoint and fixed direction of viewing essential to "correct" geometric perspective drawing. Courbet's spatial inconsistencies are, of course, by no means a flaw – on the contrary, they constitute a basic component of his style and his attitude towards reality. For the Realist, as Flaubert asserted, truth indeed lay in the particulars, not in an imposed general order. It was, for example, this tendency to see truth in the particulars, and hence to construct what might be considered a close-up, piece-by-piece view of landscape, which accounts for some of the compositional "flaws" of Courbet's *Young Ladies of the Village* [pl.4, p.70]. Antagonistic critics were quick to seize upon the faulty perspective construction of the work when it first appeared in the Salon of 1852: Edmond About compared the painting to Hogarth's caricature of perspective errors, and Gustave Planche maintained that the incorrect scale of the cows in the middle ground made them look like wooden toys.[55] In *The Painter's Studio*, where Courbet was coping with a problem similar to that in the *Toilette* – arranging a large group of figures, separately conceived, in a spacious indoor setting – the figure-space problem is more successfully resolved, partly because the spatial areas to either side of the central group are of the same depth and the figures diminish in scale at approximately the same rate to left and to right – that is, figures on the same vertical plane on either side are approximately the same size, which is not true of the figures in the *Toilette* – and partly because the underpainting has seeped through the thinly brushed figures in the rear, which are considerably too small in scale, veiling them in beneficent obscurity. Even so, Courbet felt obliged to add an additional strip to the top of his canvas in order to supply a more ample spatial setting to account for the rather sudden diminution of the background figures in *The Studio*.

Whatever changes Courbet made before he abandoned the *Toilette*, he was obviously trying to correct the discrepancy in scale between the large figures in the left-hand portion of the painting and the smaller ones at the right: the large canopy with its incorrect vanishing point may originally have been a way of accounting for the striking difference in scale between the left and right-hand figures on the same vertical planes, by suggesting that the left-hand group was farther forward than the right-hand one. But in the process, the right-hand group, with its iconographically important elements, must have been swallowed up in the pictorial depths, as it were, and the significant doorway must have seemed too distant from the group of the bride and her attendants.

It would have been at this point that Courbet added a heavy coat of white lead to the back wall, no doubt intending to bring the background forward and thereby condense and concentrate his composition. Yet why did Courbet continue this white overpainting only up to a level corresponding to the bottom of the canopy horizontally, and vertically on a line with the woman with the soup tureen at the right? It seems reasonable to suppose that Courbet was attempting to resolve his figure-space dilemma, and, at the same time, to mitigate the conflict between contradictory vanishing points by sacrificing the upper and right-hand portions of his painting, making it more of a close-up, as it appears in the masked photograph of the painting [45]. In this way, the left-hand and right-hand figural groups are more unified and compact, at least in the sense that both are contained in the same, shallower spatial stage, even if they are still inconsistent in scale. The meaningful door is now more prominent, and, at the same time, the distraction of the "horned" perspective of the corner of the table at the right has been eliminated. Perhaps Courbet then realized that there was no satisfactory solution to his dilemma of reconciling scale, readability, and pictorial unity – or perhaps he just grew tired of grappling with it – and abandoned his painting, much to the satisfaction of earlier twentieth-century critics like Roger Fry, Walter Pach, and Alfred Vance Churchill,[56] who preferred the *Toilette* as it is: unfinished, ambiguous, and relatively abstract.

Yet this problem of co-ordinating figures and space is not Courbet's alone but is shared by at least one other major innovator of the nineteenth century. The rules of

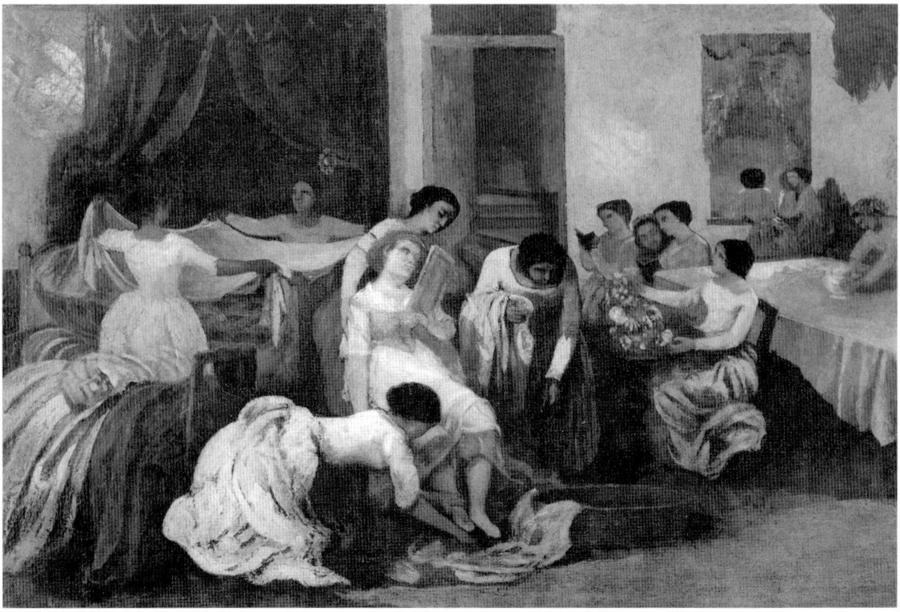

45 Masked photograph of *Toilette de la mariée*

46 **After P.-A.-J. Dagnan-Bouveret**, *Marriage Benediction in the Franche-Comté*, 1882. Lithograph

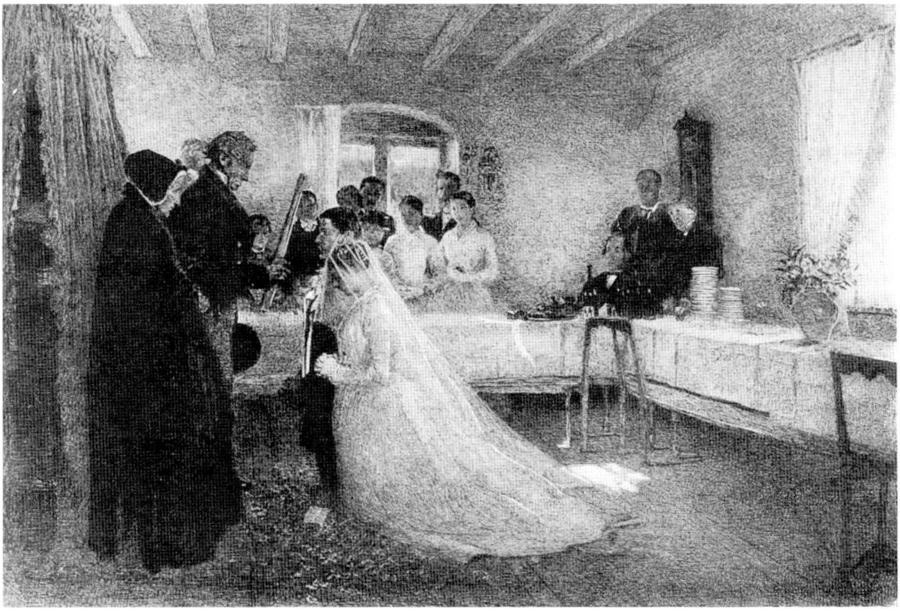

geometric perspective – a single vanishing point or a coherent system of co-ordinating orthogonals, a fixed viewpoint and direction of viewing, the regulation of diminution of scale, all this in concert with the imposition of complex iconographic schemes and meaningfully hierarchical figural groupings – had solved the problem of figure-space co-ordination in a rich variety of ways for creators of large-scale figural paintings from the Renaissance down through the middle of the nineteenth century. For more traditional painters of Courbet's own time the disposition of figures, meaningfully interrelated by action and expressive intention, within a large-scale setting would seem to have posed few problems, however "problematic" the representation of action and expression may have been in a painting like *The Romans of the Decadence* [5, p.20].[57] Even in a painting as poor and banal as Dagnan-Bouveret's *Marriage Benediction in the Franche-Comté*, of 1882 [46], so close to and yet so far from Courbet's *Toilette*, the convincing and anecdotally meaningful placement of figures in a setting seems to have created no difficulty.[58] Courbet, almost from the first, was accused of creating "meaningless" paintings as a result of "faulty" perspective or composition. His inability to create, or lack of interest in creating, traditionally "dramatic" or "meaningfully" expressive compositions may be seen as early as his *Lot and his Daughters*, of 1840, where these "faults" may be laid to the youthful inexperience of the artist, or later in *The Bathers* of 1853 [47]. Delacroix quite correctly remarked on the "vulgarity and *inutilité* of the idea" in this painting, adding: "What do these figures want [to express]? .... She – the figure on the left – makes a gesture which expresses nothing, and another woman ... is seated on the ground engaged in removing her stockings. Between these two figures there is an exchange of ideas impossible to understand."[59] Here, the lack of significant interrelation or dramatic *raison d'être* of the figures cannot be laid to mere lack of experience, but must stem rather from some more profound, if not consciously articulated, shift in the basic notion of what paintings, important paintings, were to be about.

A younger innovator, Manet, was faced with a very similar problem: indeed he often cut up his paintings, dissatisfied with their incongruities of organization, or – like Courbet, who tended rather to put separate motifs together in a single new composition – worked additively. A present-day art historian has even accused Manet of being unable to construct a satisfactory composition.[60] Yet Manet's paintings cannot, on this account, be considered bad paintings. By the second half of the nineteenth century the convincing disposition of three-dimensional figures in a co-ordinated illusionistic space to create a meaningful, dramatic-expressive unity is by no means synonymous with a "satisfactory" or "successful" pictorial structure. Whether or not Courbet or Manet could have achieved Raphael's or Rubens's rhetorical unity of design and expression is really aside from the point. The point is that by the middle of the nineteenth century the whole enterprise and ideology of advanced art positively militated against and precluded the achievement of such a goal. The very nature of

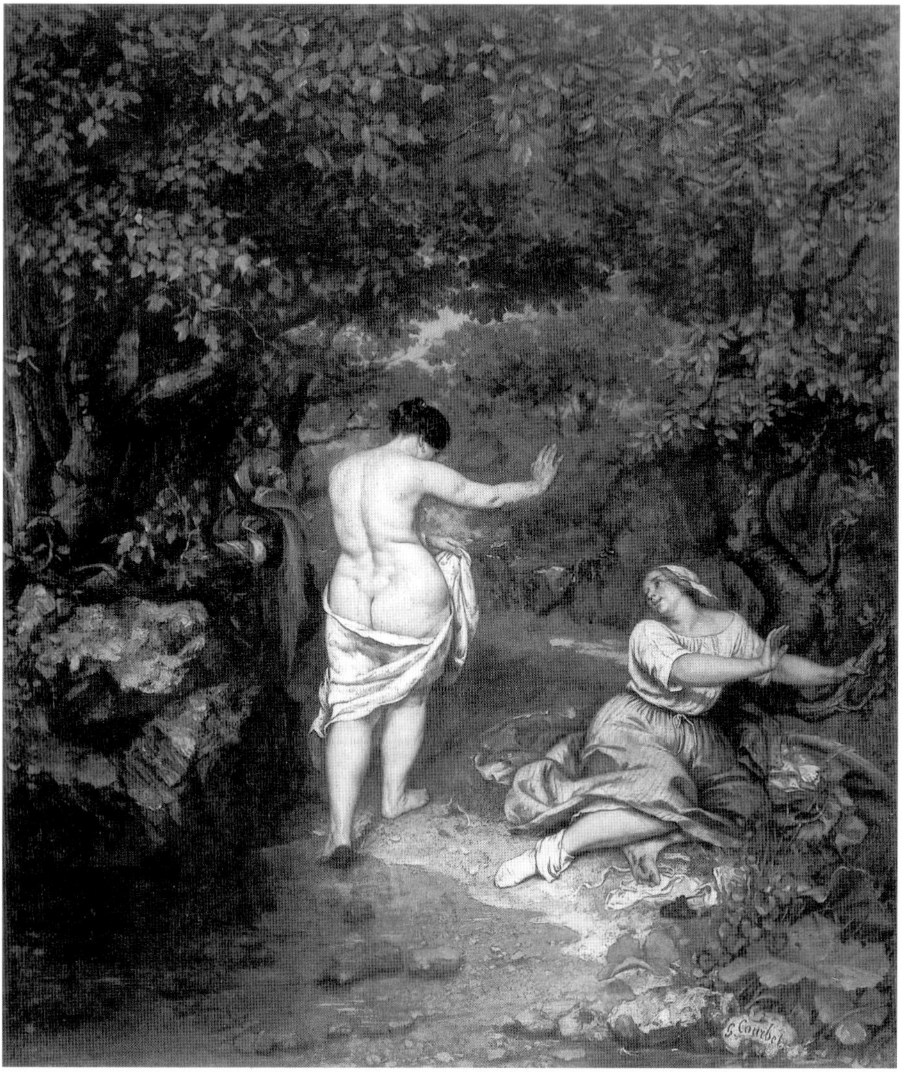

47 *The Bathers*, 1853. Oil on canvas, 227 x 193 cm, 89⅜ x 76 in.

the Realist and post-Realist enterprise implied the rejection of traditional, *a priori* methods of construction, the abandoning of the rule-determined, of the artifice of imposed compositional focus and consequently of dramatic or expressive "meaningfulness" in the normal sense. It is no accident that the key terms of Realism are "honesty," "sincerity," "naïveté," and "contemporaneity" – a determination to perceive and to formulate the subject matter of one's own times for oneself, without rules. The pictorial notation and construction of realist works (in the largest sense) are based on the notion of the moral, epistemological, and aesthetic primacy of the concrete particulars in experience.

Such a notion implies a sacrifice, as of course do all major stylistic innovations. Obviously, Courbet has not resolved his dilemma completely, and it bothered him in the *Toilette*, but acknowledging the existence of a dilemma in the work no more constitutes a judgment of it than would the observation of similar irresolutions in the work of Giotto or Jan van Eyck. It remained for *avant-garde* artists at the end of the century to resolve the problem – if one can call it a resolution – either by rejecting it like Gauguin or the Nabis, and accepting the primacy of the flatness of the pictorial surface itself as the artist's reality, or by accepting the inalterably problematic status of the figure-space situation as the very cornerstone of one's art, as did Cézanne, with his ever-repeated probings of the tension between three-dimensional fact and two-dimensional fiction. Courbet, then, stands midway between the past and the future of nineteenth-century art in the *Toilette*, rejecting *a priori* spatial construction and an artificially unified composition, yet still unwilling to give up the illusion of substantial human existence in a consistent three-dimensional space.

4 | Courbet, the Commune, and the Visual Arts

Courbet painted only one important picture directly related to his involvement with the Commune: the *Self-Portrait at Sainte-Pélagie* [48], probably created in about 1873–74.[1] In contrast to the dramatic immediacy of some of the charcoal sketches he created during his imprisonment,[2] Courbet's depiction of himself in captivity seems quite tranquil, almost idyllic: it is an image suggesting contemplation rather than suffering. If one compares the painting with the imagery of incarceration, specifically political incarceration, derived from the romantic tradition – Goya's heart-rending series of ink drawings of the victims of Spanish reaction, for instance, or Delacroix's energetically expressive *Prisoner of Chillon* (Louvre, 1834) – the lack of rhetorical emphasis or heroic overtones in Courbet's representation of himself after the fall of the Commune becomes even more apparent.

The painting is probably based in part on solid fact. It bears some resemblance in pose, gesture, and costume to a recently discovered self-portrait drawing made by the artist when he was in hiding from the Versaillais police.[3] If, in the drawing, Courbet has depicted himself as aging, bloated, and beardless, still, the youthful slenderness of his form in the *Self-Portrait at Sainte-Pélagie* may owe as much to factual reality – actual weight-loss due to the rigors of prison life – as to narcissistic self-idealization. The dark hair and beard, however, do seem anachronistically youthful.[4]

Whatever the relative roles of factual observation or personal vanity in the genesis of the *Self-Portrait*, it seems clear that the choice of motif, of pose, of formal arrangement in this, the only representation of his Commune experience has broader significance for its creator. Despite the fact that Courbet played an extremely active role in the political and artistic life of the Commune, he ultimately chose to depict a moment of stasis and withdrawal: a passive pose, an interior setting. If a little light, a bit of nature glimpsed through the bars and frame of the prison window testify to the

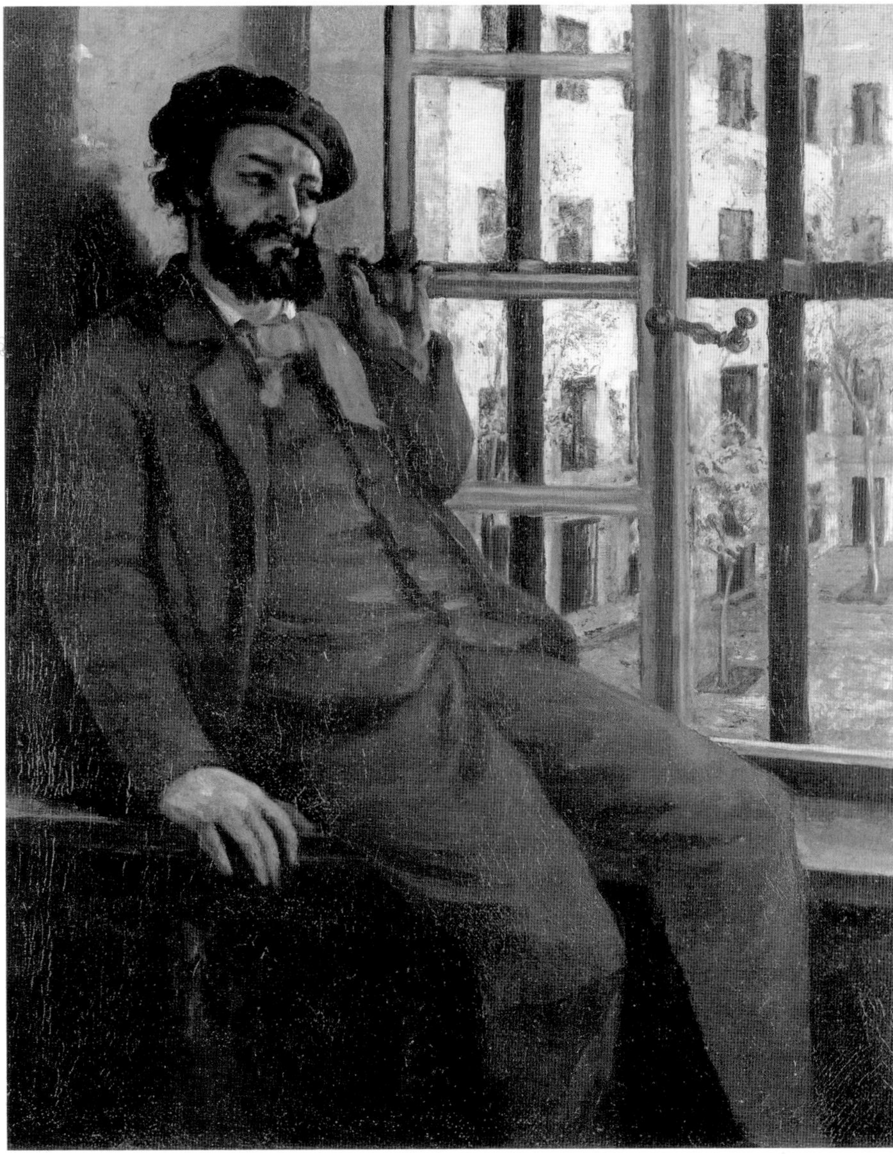

48 *Self-Portrait at Sainte-Pélagie*, *c.*1873–74. Oil on canvas, 92 x 72 cm, 36¼ x 28⅜ in.

existence of the external world, that world of nature from which Courbet had looked out so self-confidently in his early *Courbet with a Black Dog* (1844), there is nevertheless little sense of Courbet's customary pride, self-confidence, and vibrant unity with the natural order, characteristic of his earlier self-imagery, in this post-Commune self-portrait. It is as though Courbet's level of energy had fallen with the fall of the government with which he was so intensely and actively involved during most of its brief

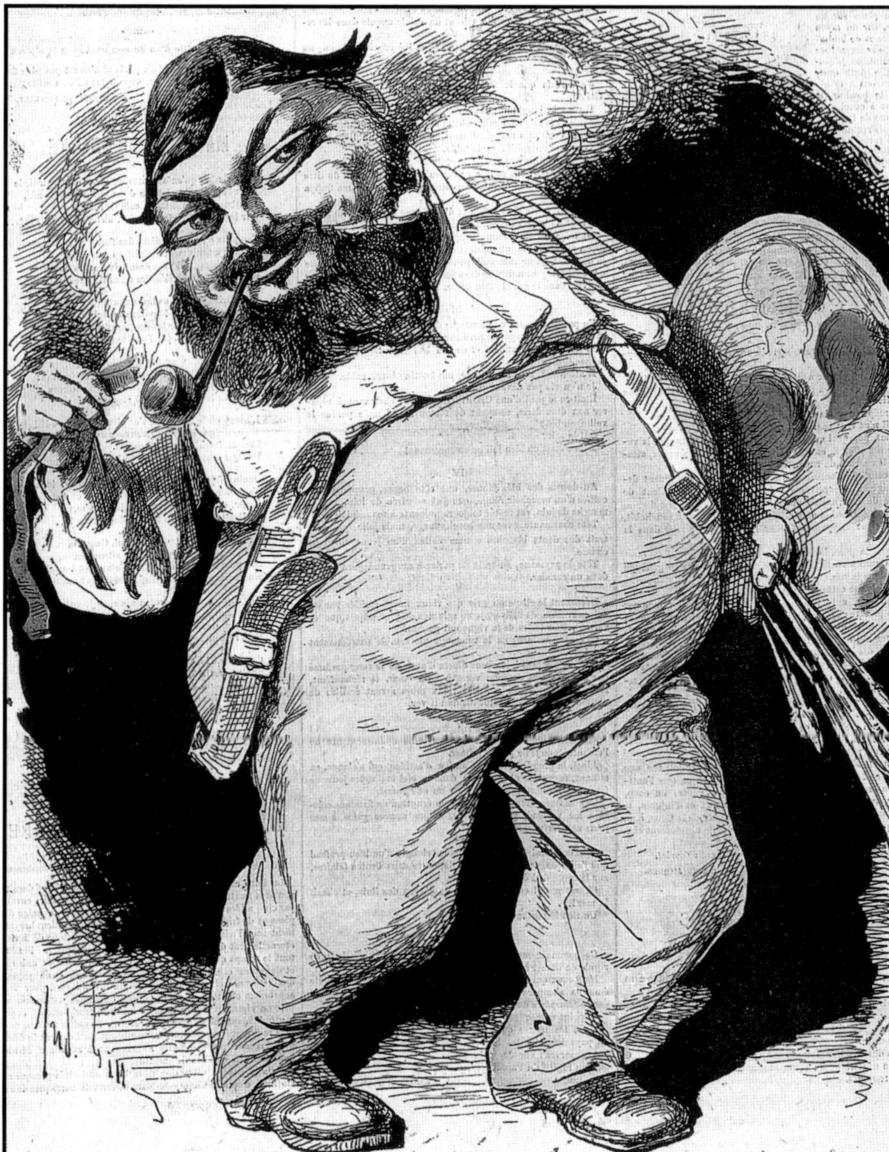

49 **Gill**, *Courbet avant la lettre.* Engraving, *L'Eclipse,* July 2, 1870

existence. Indeed, in the prison self-portrait Courbet projects, perhaps unconsciously, a certain sense of relief, as though its subject were more than a little content to take refuge behind the bars. The little room functions, in terms of pictorial metaphor, more as cosy interior than threatening dungeon. Or rather, one might say that the line between contentment and resignation is difficult to discern from the visual evidence offered by the artist himself. Prison indeed may have seemed a port in the storm after the terrible days following the entry of the Versaillais troops into Paris: the chase, the enforced underground life, the humiliation of the trial, the genuine terror experienced at the spectacle of the execution of friends and fellow communards.

How different is the Courbet, depicted less than a year before the artist's downfall, by his friend the caricaturist Gill, (also to be a supporter of the left-wing government), in *L'Eclipse* of July 2, 1870, *Courbet avant la lettre* [49]! Here the artist appears fat, feisty, and quite literally bursting with self-importance, wickedly lighting his pipe with what appears to be a piece of ribbon. Both the ribbon and the title no doubt allude to a notorious political-aesthetic incident in which Courbet had been implicated at this time: the artist's refusal of the Legion of Honor and the simultaneous publication of his letter to the Minister of Fine Arts in *Le Siècle*, explaining why he had rejected the coveted decoration. "L'honneur," he had declared in the famous letter to Maurice Richard of June 23, 1870, "n'est ni dans un titre ni dans un ruban, il est dans les actes et dans le mobile des actes. L'Etat," he continued, "est incompétent en matière d'art." And, he concluded: "Je décline l'honneur que vous avez cru me faire. J'ai cinquante ans et j'ai toujours vécu libre; laissez-moi terminer mon existence libre. Quand je serai mort, il faudra qu'on dise de moi: celui-là n'a jamais appartenu à aucune école, à aucune église, à aucune institution, à aucun adadémie, surtout à aucun régime, si ce n'est le régime de la liberté."[5] Courbet was shortly to play a most active and dedicated role in what he and many others believed to be the very embodiment of the "régime de la liberté," in his capacity as President of the Federation of Artists and elected Member, from the sixth arrondissement, of the Commune government itself. For Courbet, the Commune was, all too briefly, the fulfillment of his dreams of a government without opressive, domineering institutions, the Proudhonian Utopia of social justice come true. "Je suis dans l'enchantement," he wrote his parents on April 30, 1871; "*Paris est un vrai paradis*; point de police, point de sottise, point d'exaction d'aucune façon, point de dispute. Paris va tout seul, comme sur des roulettes. Il faudrait pouvoir rester toujours comme cela. En un mot c'est un vrai ravissement."[6]

Courbet's active involvement in governmental art affairs had begun before the actual proclamation of the Commune. As early as September 6, 1870, two days after the proclamation of a republic following the demise of the Second Empire, Courbet was elected head of a commission of artists. The main task confronting the commission was the protection and storage of monuments and works of art in museums and galleries in Paris and its environs. Almost immediately, the issue of the fate of one of these monuments, the Vendôme Column, symbol of Napoleonic tyranny, raised its head. Courbet's role in the destruction of the Column, which was pulled down on May 16, 1871, remains equivocal until this day; it seems clear, however, on the basis of the most recent research, that he hardly bore single-handed responsibility for the deed. Nevertheless, the issue was to plague him for the rest of his life and has, as an issue, unfortunately tended to overshadow the importance of his other activities during this period.[7] Indeed, the exaggerated attention paid to the question of whether and to what degree Courbet was implicated in the Vendôme Column incident, or the implications of his use of the term "déboulonner," have often functioned to divert art historians from paying attention to his other activities during this period, and to the whole interesting situation obtaining for the Commune and the arts as a whole.

In any case, on or about September 14, Courbet proposed that the Vendôme Column, a monument "dénué de toute valeur artistique, tendant à perpetuer ... les idées de guerres et de conquêtes" be dismantled – the term used was the ambiguous "déboulonner" – and that the materials be transported to the Mint.[8] In actuality, Courbet was at this very moment occupied with art-related activities at the opposite pole of destruction: that is to say with the preservation and protection of art works, a concern which was to continue not only through the period of the siege, but that of the Commune as well. Thus, what it seems important to emphasize is the larger issue at stake, for Courbet, and by extension, for all those in charge of art affairs during periods of turbulent political change: preservation versus destruction. Courbet seems to have been impaled on the horns of this dilemma, on the one hand, straining himself to the utmost to preserve the artistic heritage of Paris, often in the face of difficulty and opposition; and on the other hand, responding to widespread popular demand for the destruction of a hated symbol of tyranny and oppression. The issue has broad reverberations, relating it to what Henri Lefebvre, the great historian of the Commune, has termed "revolutionary urbanism" – in the words of Lefebvre, "reconaissant l'espace social en termes politiques et ne croyant pas qu'un monument puisse être innocent (démolition de la colonne Vendôme, occupation des églises par les clubs, etc.). Ceux qui ramènent de tels actes au nihilisme et à la barbarie doivent avouer qu'en contrepartie ils se disposent à conserver tout ce qu'ils considèrent comme 'positif,' c'est-à-dire tous les résultats de l'histoire, toutes les œuvres de la société dominante, toute les traditions."[9]

Primary among the achievements of the Commune in the realm of the visual arts, and of Courbet as the director of its art affairs, was giving artists themselves control over their own destinies and that of the artistic life of their nation through democratic organization. On April 6 and 7, 1871, Courbet, as president of the artists' association, called on his fellow artists to assemble at the Ecole de Médicine in order to discuss and take steps to organize the visual arts. The meeting, which took place on April 14, attracted more than 400 persons, according to the report which appeared in the *Journal officiel* of the Commune on the following day. Courbet presided, assisted by the sculptor Moulin, and the industrial artist Pottier, future author of the *Internationale.* The egalitarian thrust of the meeting, unusual for its time, is indicated by the fact that commercial as well as "fine" artists were invited to participate. Pottier initiated the proceedings by reading a detailed report giving some notion of the ambitious revisions in contemporary theory and practice envisioned by the leaders of the group. The major direction of the envisaged reforms could be summarized in one sentence: "Confier aux artistes seuls la gestion de leurs intérêts."[10] Nothing could have offered a more striking contrast to the authoritarian, hierarchical organization of the art institutions of the Second Empire than the very structure proposed by the newly constituted Federation of Artists. There was to be equality of rights among all members of the Federation, and the independence and dignity of each artist was to be watched over by a committee elected by universal suffrage of all artists. This committee would consist of 16 painters, 10 sculptors, 5 architects, 6 engravers and lithographers, and 10 members representing the decorative arts.[11] This democratic governing structure conceived of itself as having a three-part mission: the conservation of the treasures of the past; the implementation and revelation of all the elements of the present; and the regeneration of the future through teaching. Monuments and museums, collections and art libraries in the public domain were confided to the adminstrative overview of the committee. Exhibitions were to be organized by the committee on the most fair-minded basis possible, without commercial overtones and without distribution of awards; the committee was also to oversee the teaching of drawing and modelling in primary and professional schools, based on logical and sympathetic methods.[12] Publicity would by taken care of by a new journal, the *Officiel des arts*, which would publish information interesting and useful to artists and offer a wide range of artistic viewpoints for the consideration of various artistic communities. In addition, this democratically elected committee would arbitrate litigations in the art world; and finally, "par la parole, la plume, le crayon, par la réproduction populaire des chefs-d'œuvre" – in other words, through every instrument of mass diffusion available at the time – the committee of the Federation of Artists would attempt to disseminate art and knowledge of art throughout the Republic.[13] On May 2, the Federation of Artists suppressed the Academy, the Ecole des Beaux-Arts, and the Schools of Rome and of Athens. Although the immediate issue in this case may have been a financial one, the principle behind the suppression of these established institutions was clearly articulated in a report published in the *Journal officiel* of May 10: the radical rejection of the authoritarian principle which had been the very essence of the former administrations.[14] At the same time that the committee supervised the revision of the entire academic structure of art, it concerned itself with the equally important task of reopening the museums of Paris and its environs.

As elected president of the 47-member committee of artists, as well as participant (as elected member and member of the committee of public education) in the Commune government itself, Courbet obviously had little time for his own work during these momentous months. As a member of the Government, he was part of the minority opposition, which included many of the most open-minded members of the Commune: Jules Vallès, Varlin, Malon, and Longuet, among others. On May 1,

Courbet, along with 27 other members of the Government, voted against the formation of a committee of public safety.[15] Whether or not he actually resigned from the Assembly as early as May 11 – before the decisive action on the fate of the Vendôme Column – remains unclear.[16] Whatever his actual role in the decision-making about the Column's destruction on May 16, his name was securely tied to it both in the minds of his conservative enemies and in the popular imagination. When the Versaillais troops entered Paris, Courbet was evidently working at the Louvre, busily protecting the national collections from mishap:[17] the issues of protection versus destruction met head on right to the end of Courbet's career as a political activist.

Although the art history of the Commune is inevitably connected with Courbet, the actual art work relating to the Commune has nothing at all to do with him: indeed, it might be said that the most important manifestations of visual imagery relating to the Commune have little or nothing to do with what is generally considered to be "high" art at all. True, there were some relatively ambitious paintings on canvas devoted to Commune subjects, painted both during its brief existence and afterwards. Georges Clairin's *A Corner of the Palais de Justice, during the Semaine Sanglante*, represents, with academic picturesqueness and pathos, a desparate moment during the last days of the Commune; the Spanish painter Ignacio de Leon y Escosura (1834–1901), on the contrary, in his *Rue de Rivoli (mai 1871)*, represents a similar moment of the street-warfare of the period with the highest degree of photographic realism, including a representation of himself, in his smock, crouching in the foreground in front of a top-hatted gentleman, sketching the engagement as it takes place.[18] More visually innovative are interpretations of Commune atrocities, done long after the fact, it is true, by an artist most sympathetic with its ideals, the Neo-Impressionist Maximilien Luce: paintings like *La Mort d'Eugène Varlin* or *Une Rue de Paris sous la Commune* (1903–5), in which the horror of the motif – a group of slaughtered figures, including a woman – is heightened ironically by the clear pastel color, the measured pointillist technique, and the everyday banality of the Paris street setting.[19]

More revealing as a group, and more successful in conveying a sense of immediacy are the innumerable "eye-witness" sketches of various episodes and incidents of the Commune, reporter-like drawings, sometimes reproduced as prints, often rapid and summarizing in their technique although at times quite detailed, which purport to convey a sense of their authors' actual presence on the spot: works like Pilotell's moving drawing of *Raoul Rigault, fusillé*, in which the eye-witness veracity of the image is underlined by the inscription: "vu par l'auteur le 24 mai à 5 heures du soir rue Gay-Lussac";[20] Ernest Picchió's (or Pichio's) lithograph version of *Le Mur des fédérés*, with its scattered, haphazardly fallen corpses dominated by the roughly sketched, bullet-pocked wall, inscribed "Vive la Commune,"[21] one of many versions of this crucial subject, later to be treated, without the victims, on a more grandiose scale by the Russian artist Ilya Repin,[22] as well as by Steinlen and Vallotton; and, perhaps best known of all of these "eye-witness" sketches of summary executions, those by

Edouard Manet: the wash drawing *The Barricade* and its lithographed version; and his lithograph, presumably based on his own visual experience during the days of street fighting and repression in May, *The Civil War*, representing a dead soldier and the feet of another victim before a barricade.[23] In the context of the multitude of drawings of street fighting and summary executions which took place during the last days of the Commune, Manet's works can be seen in context as part of a whole series of similar visual responses to such atrocities, although perhaps marked off from the majority of them by their unique and laconic distillation of the subject. Still other interesting and impressive visual reports of aspects of Commune activity appeared in the form of wood-engraved drawings in mass-circulation periodicals like the *Graphic*; works like Boyd Houghton's *Womens' Club at the Boule Noire, Boulevard Rochechouart* or his extraordinary image of the *Commune Barricades*, no doubt a bit dramatized, with its gesticulating, flag-holding orator and rifle-bearing harridan viewed from the rear, but nevertheless remarkable for the sense of actuality created by a group of women and children dragging what appears to be a grand piano, partly cut off by the border, up the stones of the barricade in the foreground.[24]

If so-called high art failed for the most part to create a sense of the actuality or of the ideals of the Commune, then popular art – in the form of illustrations, cartoons, caricatures, and posters, as well as photographs – succeeded signally. By its very nature, the values and ideological commitments of a short-lived, popularly based political and social entity like the Commune could best be mediated through a very different kind of visual imagery than that of traditional history painting.

Political cartoons on both sides of the fence, Versaillais and Communard, were unrelentlingly savage and uniquely authentic in their bodying forth of basic issues. In the treatment of no other subject are the conflicting values of Communards and Versaillais more clearly revealed than in their dramatically opposing representations of women. Commune symbolism was, as Henri Lefebvre has pointed out, overwhelmingly feminine: "Dans l'imagerie populaire comme dans les chansons et poèmes … tout le symbolisme s'emprunte à la femininité."[25] While nature, in the form of the Tree of Liberty, still dominated in the revolutionary symbolism of 1848, in that of 1871, a mature woman, breasts often nude, could stand for, according to the context, either Liberty, the Nation, the Republic, the City of Paris, the Revolution, or the Commune itself. This symbolism of course had multiple significances: desireable and maternal at once, it suggests the idea of the birth of man from woman, or, in historical terms, the birth of a new order of society from the nourishing body of the Revolution.[26] Although the image of Revolution as woman still represented aspiration more than actuality in terms of revolutionary praxis, women were in fact more active both as actual participants and in organizing themselves to determine their needs *as* women than they ever had been before in revolutionary situations.[27] The imagery of the Commune bears witness to the presence of women in many aspects of its activity: illustrations like Boyd Houghton's, mentioned above, which stressed women's, more specifically, working-class women's activism, both in the fighting on the barricades and in the heated discussions at their own clubs; drawings like Moloch's *Barricade de la place Blanche, défendue par les femmes,*[28] in which women are obviously participating as an independent military force, side by side with their male comrades at arms; or Lix's far less sympathetic yet still relatively objective drawing for *Le Monde illustré* of a fiery woman orator speaking from the pulpit to a varied female audience at the Women's Club of Saint-Germain-l'Auxerrois.[29] The imagery of that exemplary communard heroine and leader, Louise Michel bears special study: Théodore Steinlen seems to have represented her on the barricades, at a later date, in a painting flooded with vivid color and wild drama;[30] two small paintings by Jules Girardet, on wood, now in the collection of the Musée de Saint-Denis, represent her in more realistic, if highly sympathetic, fashion: *Louise Michel Speaking to a Group of Communards* and *The Arrest of Louise Michel.*[31] In both of these works, reminiscences of earlier paintings of significant incidents in the lives of women saints or martyrs adds a certain touch of poignance. Louise Michel also figures, incorrectly, it must be noted, in one of the many "photographies truquées" purporting to represent actual moments in the history of the Commune: Appert's *Prison et chantiers à Versailles. Le 15 août 1871*, where she appears with crossed arms second from the right.[32]

Perhaps in no other realm was the virulence of anti-Communard imagery so exaggerated as in its representation of the women of the Commune. The whole mythology of the "pétroleuses" – working-class women accused by the Versailles government of setting fire to houses and public buildings – so viciously disseminated in caricature and writing – epitomizes the terror, sexual as much as political, aroused in the breasts of the patriarchal guardians of order when faced with women – above all, working-class women, the bourgeois male's "natural" prey – taking their destinies into their own hands. The visual imagery of the women of the Commune, identified with the "pétroleuse" by its opponents, brings to a climax that time-honored imagery of "Mad Meg" or the Dulle Griet: the peasant woman as an active force, symbol of terrifying anarchy, the very emblem of the world upside down, destroyer of property, and, in her very being, the unnatural woman, subverter of order and of "civilized" values. How different from the image of the humble, accepting peasant or working-class woman perpetuated by even such humanitarian artists as Millet or Daumier is that of the activist women of the Commune! And how offensive to bourgeois sensibilities! In one, anonymous, cartoon, the "pétroleuse" is represented as an ugly, snaggle-toothed virago standing malevolently with her bottle of fuel before a graffiti-covered wall;[33] in another, a hideous hag in working-class dress is represented under the sign of Scorpio in Nérac's series *Les Signes du zodiaque*, with the subtitle "Club de l'emancipation des femmes," probably a reference to the Union des Femmes, in the lower left-hand corner.[34] An anonymous cartoon pillories the Women's Clubs and the activities of women orators, as well as popular pronunciation, in *La Grande Orateuse*, in which the woman orator is shown sacrilegiously preaching from the pulpit of a church to the "grand Club des Amazones de la Commune."[35] Still another cartoon unites Courbet, the Column, and one of the "immoral" *cantinières* of the Commune: in Léonce Scherner's "L'Homme qui était un jour appelé à démolir la Colonne." Courbet is represented hacking away at a pile of stones, a reference to his *Casseurs de pierres*, as the Vendôme Column falls over in the background and a pert, short-skirted, bloomer-clad personification of feminine immodesty looks on to the right.[36]

No discussion of the visual arts and the Commune would be complete without some consideration, however brief, of the role of photography. The Commune was certainly the first major revolution which could avail itself fully of this miraculous, still relatively new medium; indeed, the Commune took place during what has been called the "golden age of photography" by scholars of the field.[37]

A thoroughgoing investigation of the role of photography in creating the imagery of the Commune would have to deal with the implications of the ubiquitous presence of stones – walls, barricades, finally ruins – in Commune and post-Commune iconography. During the Commune, the photograph of the barricade manned by its defenders functioned as an optimistic icon of neighborhood solidarity and working-class determination. After the defeat of the Commune, photographic images of very different kinds of walls – the ruins of Paris – served as pessimistic, graphic warnings against any repeat performances on the part of the defeated Left. Album after album reiterated the theme of disemboweled houses, mutilated façades, burned-out roofs: *Guide-récueil de Paris brûlé*; *Ruines de Paris en 1871*; *Ruines de l'Hôtel de Ville* – the list of such photographic warnings against defiance of the status quo is almost endless.[38] The very veracity of the photographic medium, or rather, its ability to instill credulity in the minds of a relatively naïve audience, made it an effective propaganda weapon. Altered photographs, collages, photomontages all were put to propagandistic use for perhaps the first time on a large scale by supporters of the Versailles government, thereby creating apparently authentic images of Commune atrocities to be swallowed whole by a public that had not yet learned that the camera could lie. Examples from the album of "photos truquées" prepared by E. Appert, entitled *Crimes de la Commune*, works obviously created with paste and scissors after the fact, and bearing such mendaciously explicit titles as "Massacre des Dominicains d'Arcueil ... 28 mai, 1871" or "Assassinat de 620 otages 26 mai, 1871 Rue Haxo" still turn up in history books as eye-witness records of actual events.[39]

On the Commune side, the most memorable of all photographic images, indeed, perhaps, the most memorable of all visual records of the Commune, is the terrible and mutely eloquent *Cadavres de Communards fusillés*, now ascribed to Disdéri,[40] in which the anonymous victims of the Repression, identified only by numbered tags at their breasts, are starkly presented to us lined up in their crude and narrow coffins. How different these, or similar Communards had looked, glancing out at us confidently in the series of barricade photographs by Braquehais or other, anonymous photographers! Similar in their sense of veracity are the series of photographic records of the Place Vendôme by the first photographic reporter of French history, Bruno Braquehais, mentioned above, in which the sequence of events involved in the demolition of the Column is objectively recorded, along with a whole, vivid cross-section of Communard society. In the summarizing shot of the series, the photographer has focused on the fallen statue of Napoleon, lying in the foreground amid the crumbled stones of his empty socle, while in the background, dim and blurred with movement, the crowd surges in dynamic abstraction behind the barrier.[41]

In short, to return to the stated subject of this investigation, one might say that Courbet, just because he was a politically active artist during the period of the Commune, contributed little to it in the way of actual imagery. Yet it would be wrong to maintain for this reason that he did not contribute to the general atmosphere of spontaneity and freedom; and, in more concrete terms, it would be impossible to deny that he did much to preserve artworks and monuments in Paris. His role in the destruction of the Vendôme Column, will, I believe, always remain unclear: no doubt it was considerably smaller than his enemies contended but somewhat larger than his friends maintained. Yet paradoxically, the one major painting of his Commune experiences, the *Self-Portrait at Sainte-Pélagie* may, in a certain sense be said to have relevance to the future direction of advanced art: its imagery conveys both a sense of withdrawal from the world of action, and, by extension, presents an image of the artist as a self-contained, isolated entity. Communal, politically integrated large-scale commitments on the part of artists did not occur again for many years. On the contrary, even so politically active and committed an artist as Paul Signac, later in the century, was to stress the individual and aesthetic, rather than the overtly political dimensions of his efforts, when he maintained that the anarchist artist was not the one who did anarchist pictures, but rather the one who fought selflessly with all his individuality against bourgeois conventions by means of a personal contribution.[42] The next time that art and the revolution were to meet on a truly grand scale and with considerable repercussions was to be neither in France nor in the nineteenth century, but rather in Russia in the twentieth.

5 The *Cribleuses de blé*: Courbet, Millet, Breton, Kollwitz, and the Image of the Working Woman

In the middle of the nineteenth century, two major artists, Courbet and Millet, painted representations of contemporary agricultural practice. Courbet's *Cribleuses de blé* (*Grain Sifters*) [pl.5, p.70] was first shown in the Salon of 1855; Millet's *Les Glaneuses* (*The Gleaners*) was exhibited in the Salon of 1857.[1] The two paintings, both relatively large in scale and ambitious in their intentions and achievement, are, of course, in many ways strikingly different. Millet's is an outdoor scene, organized in terms of vast spatial extension, whereas Courbet's is an indoor one, more compactly organized on an uptilted surface; Millet's *facture* is relatively neutral, the paint-strokes in most cases suavely blended together to create an effect of unity and continuity of forms, space, light, and setting, whereas Courbet uses a dense, aggressive impasto and a discrete, more additive composition to define the picture surface. The pictorial structure of Courbet's *Grain Sifters* is dominated by the aggressive energy of the central figure, whereas Millet's is a more relaxed, emptier structure, more lightly held together by the rhythmic repetition of similar forms. In addition, the interpretive histories of the two works are strikingly different: the *Gleaners* is so well known that it has become a kind of visual myth, a myth transparent to multiple interpretations accruing to it over the years and inseparable from it as an experienced phenomenon; Courbet's *Grain Sifters*, on the contrary, has been little discussed, is relatively unknown, and remains fresh and iconographically opaque. Nevertheless, both works are related in that both of these scenes of agricultural life represent the intersection of two of the most problematic issues of nineteenth-century social history: the issue of the status of the working classes and that of the position of women.

Although both works may be said to be realist, and both purport to – and in fact do – incorporate aspects of contemporary reality into their visual fabric, they are both, at the same time, historically conditioned mythic structures, replete with messages about sex, about nature, about work, about women's role, about the nature of history – both in short are documents of nineteenth-century ideology itself, mediated through the vision of particular artists.

What elements of ideology controlled that image of the woman worker in the mid-nineteenth century? First of all, the notion that sheer need – the threat of poverty for herself or her children – was the only acceptable reason for a woman to work outside of the domestic situation which defined her essential being.[2] Working women, like the one depicted in Daumier's famous *Laundress*, who were poor, who were fated by sheer necessity to work as part of their central nurturing function, were accorded serious, sympathetic treatment. In Daumier's painting, the humble nobility of the proletarian working mother is emphasized by the pose – the self-effacing bend of the laundress toward her child – and the praiseworthy altruism of this gesture is heightened further by the way it is silhouetted against the irregular urban halo in back of the laundress, whose double burden of laundry and maternity is picked up by the slant rhyme of the composition. The middle-class woman who worked, on the contrary, was mercilessly pilloried by Daumier in his caricatures. It was an almost unquestioned assumption of nineteenth-century thought that middle class women who worked – writers, for instance – only did so for specious and inappropriate self-fulfillment, and were therefore "unnatural" women and inadequate mothers. Daumier, for example, in a caricature like "Adieu, mon cher, je vais chez mes éditeurs" of 1844, depicted such a woman as a frivolous, self-indulgent creature who deserts her home, leaving her child to the care of her long-suffering husband. The trope of the neglectful, middle-class mother who ignores the needs of her family for "higher things" is a commonplace in the middle of the nineteenth century; both Daumier and De Beaumont depicted blue-stockings busily writing on the joys and duties of motherhood while the baby tumbles into the bathtub;[3] Dickens, in the character of Mrs. Jellyby in *Bleak House*, creates the archetypal image of the reprehensible "do-gooder" whose children suffer total neglect and whose housekeeping is chaotic, as she works for the good of African natives while oblivious to the pressing need of those who have the only rightful claim to her efforts: her long-suffering family.

Factory work for women was generally deemed a menace, not merely because the woman worker was frequently exploited, or because it might undermine her health, but, above all, because it took her away from her role as sustainer of the family and transformed her into a social being, a human creature potentially in touch with wider issues and capable of conscious activism. Jules Simon, for example, later to become Minister of Public Instruction and an important political figure in the Third Republic, in his humanitarian tract, *L'Ouvrière*, written in 1861, maintains that factory work for a woman is intrinsically bad even if it is physically easier for her than grinding domestic labor in field or farm because it impinges on woman's natural modesty and takes her away from her preordained role as guardian of the family. A woman worker is no longer a woman, Jules Simon claims, and he repeats with emphasis Michelet's striking phrase: "l'ouvrière, mot impie."[4] The woman factory worker was generally not deemed a serious subject for artists, at least not until later in the century,[5] although she was depicted as a part of the working process in articles about factory work in the popular illustrated journals of the time.

The rural woman worker, the peasant woman, on the contrary, insofar as she was poor, passive, natural, and understood to be content with her God-given role as mother and nurturer, served as an ideal vehicle not only for ideological definitions of feminity but for those of the good worker as well. Indeed, one might say that the female peasant, like her male counterpart, virtually embodied the positive image of the working class in the middle of the nineteenth century: the urban worker, male and female, was both more problematic as a moral being and ultimately far more suspect. As Robert Herbert has pointed out, in the case of male workers, the positive image of labor was primarily a rural one in the second half of the nineteenth century.[6] In the case of the imagery of women workers, urbanization often signified downfall: the lure of the city was visualized as constituting a concrete moral threat to the virtous female farmworker in a painting like Glaize's *Misery the Procuress* of 1860;[7] and, as Eunice Lipton has pointed out, a popular urban motif of the working-class woman, that of the laundress, was almost always viewed as an overtly erotic or, at the very least, as a sexually problematic one.[8]

The potent ideological association of the peasant-woman with a timeless, nurturing realm of Nature helped to defuse her potentiality, and, indeed, her actuality in France, where the memory of women armed with pitchforks was all too clear, as a real political threat. The assimilation of the peasant woman to the natural order also helped to rationalize rural poverty and the necessity for grinding, continuous labor, as well as serving to justify the peasant woman's subjugation to a tradition of male tyranny within peasant culture itself. Works like Millet's *Woman Feeding her Child* of 1861 or Segantini's *The Two Mothers* of 1889, the latter with its overt connection between the nurturing functions of cow and woman, make clear the presuppositions of a society which maintains motherhood as woman's "naturally" ordained work, and demonstrates, at the same time, that the *peasant* woman, as an elemental, untutored – hence eminently "natural" female – is the ideal signifier for the notion of beneficent maternity, replete with historical overtones of the Christian Madonna and Child. The Italian artist Teofilo Patini in *Mattock and Milk* of 1883 creates a modern, naturalistic secular Madonna of Humility, who sits and gives suck on the same ungrateful soil her husband tills so arduously. In an image like this one, the spiritual and the animal polarities of the concept of motherhood are effortlessly conjoined. Fritz Mackensen, a member of the Worpswede colony in Germany, towards the end of the century, depicts the peasant woman in a similar way in *Der Säugling* of 1892, in which the monumental nursing mother looms over the horizon, seated not on the ground this time, but on a wheelbarrow, a prop which effectively mediates between the reality of nature and the peasants' fate of obligatory toil.

The peasant woman also served as the natural vehicle for uplifting notions about religious faith. In works like Alphonse Legros's *The Ex-Voto* of 1860[9] or Wilhelm Leibl's *Three Peasant Women in a Church* of 1883, piety is viewed as a natural concomitant of edifying fatalism. The peasant woman served as the perfect visual embodiment of a conservative instinct to perpetuate age-old rituals, carrying them on by practice and precept from generation to generation.

Yet contradictorily – for ideology is, in effect, designed to absorb and rationalize self-contradiction – at the same time that the peasant woman was viewed as naturally nurturing and pious, her very naturalness, her proximity to instinct and animality could make her serve as the epitome of untramelled, unartificed, or "healthful" sexuality, as opposed to the more corrupt, damaged eroticism of the urban working-class girl. Sometimes this sexual force is veiled in idealization, as in the work of Jules Breton, who specialized in glamorizing the erotic charms of the peasant girl for the annual Salons and for the delectation of American Middle Western *nouveau riche* collectors. Sometimes it is served up more overtly and crudely, as in works like Antoine Vollon's *Chicken Woman of Dieppe* with its peasant protagonist's revealing décolletage. But in either case, the peasant woman's natural role as a signifier of earthy sexuality is as important an element in nineteenth-century visual ideology as her nurturant or religious roles.[10]

Breton, who specialized in sweetly provocative field workers, literally *saw* his subjects as naturally glamourous, as living, contemporary artworks, in fact. He felt that peasant girls' figures were improved by their wholesome activity in the open air, and that their daily work in the fields helped give them the well-proportioned bodies and the graceful, dignified posture of antique statues.[11] It is no wonder that rich American collectors in the nineteenth century were attracted to Breton's peasants: these charming young women were poor, they knew their place, they were not poor *American* working girls, which might have been unsettling, they were physically attractive, unlike many of Millet's peasant women – and, of course, Breton's repertory was almost exclusively feminine. A work like *The Song of the Lark*, bought by the Chicago collector Henry Field in 1885, became for a long time one of the most popular and frequently reproduced paintings in America.[12] One should not underestimate the role played by erotic attraction in the popularity of a work like *The Song of the Lark* and in the appeal of the image of the idealized peasant girl generally for collectors like Field. What could be a more appropriate combination for an American businessman than a sexy young body whose charms were justified by the virtue of labor and revealed by worn, coarse homespun or cotton? Ruddy peasant skin, when ladies were white; firm peasant muscles, when ladies were dainty; uncorseted peasant bodies when ladies were corseted and carapaced; bare feet and legs when women's ankles were always covered: these were sexually provocative in ways that are lost to us today.[13]

At times, sensual relish could be heightened by reference to the very virtue of the work contravened by the image in question, as is the case of Courbet's *Sleeping*

Spinner of 1853. The image of spinning is traditionally identified with female domestic virtue. It is considered the most womanly of the manual arts. Spinning was indeed so exclusively a female duty that the word "distaff" came to mean "woman." "She layeth her hands to the spindle, and her hands hold the distaff" says the Bible of the good woman.[14] A *sleeping* spinner, then, conveyed a sense of duty abandoned, womanly virtue along with it. A kind of slutishness, or at the very least, sexual availability has been thought of as a corallary of idleness in the moralizing imagery of Northern art since at least the sixteenth century. "Lady Dissolute" is the sobriquet of the neglectful spinner in a mid-sixteenth-century Flemish print, *Carefree Living*, published by the Hieronymous Cock shop;[15] sleeping spinners, lacemakers, and servant girls abound in the iconography of seventeenth-century Dutch painting, all with the same implication of weakness of moral fiber, a warning to women about the dangers of sensual abandonment.[16] The theme of the neglectful spinner can be found in the repertory of popular art as well, in a nineteenth-century *image d'Epinal, Bonne Sainte-Fainéante, protectrice des parasseuses*, in which the moral weakness of idleness, personified by the woman who sprawls seductively day-dreaming on her chaise longue is heightened by the abandoned distaff and unemptied chamber pot beneath her bed, and contrasted both with the industrious folk outside her window and the spider who virtuously spins *her* web on the neglected window frame.

Yet it would be a mistake, and an oversimplification, to see Courbet's *Sleeping Spinner* as simply a continuation of the moralizing tradition of the past. One has only to compare Courbet's sleeping woman with a seventeenth-century "moral emblem" like Vermeer's *Girl Asleep* in the Metropolitan Museum to see the world of difference that separates the two. This difference is constituted not only by the plethora of meaningful symbolic allusions to the vice of sloth personified by the sleeping girl surrounding the figure in the seventeenth-century painting, but to the assumptions on which such a moralizing allegory was based: the notion that, as Madlyn Kahr has put it, people have free will and must accept responsibility for their dreams and fantasies as well as for their actions; the notion that idleness, or sloth, leads to other vices.[17] Indeed, in the most literal sense, for the traditional moral imagist, "in dreams begin responsibilities." Nothing could have been further, I believe, from Courbet's intentions in this painting than to suggest an overt moral issue, despite the fact that remnants of seventeenth-century Dutch precedents linger on in the very motif he has chosen. In addition, it is important to realize for the nineteenth-century admirer of Dutch art, the moral content was scarcely perceptible. Sleeping spinners or sleeping servant girls were generally interpreted as simple realistic genre scenes, objective records or contemporary life, devoid of symbolic implications. Certainly, Vermeer's nineteenth-century discoverer, Courbet's friend Thoré-Bürger, was far from believing that Vermeer had emblematic intentions in a painting like *Girl Asleep*.[18] For Courbet, unlike his seventeenth-century counterparts, the sensual availability, the self-abandonment implied by the motif of work neglected in the image of a young woman who falls asleep at her spinning wheel, is a source of delight, not a cause for reproach. There is, indeed, as Werner Hofmann and Aaron Sheon have suggested, something both of the fairy tale and of romantic dreaminess in the mood and attitude of Courbet's figure: overtones of the Sleeping Beauty who pricked her finger with the spindle, of the wistful songs of Schubert and Béranger on the theme of the spinner, or of Charles Nodier's dream-ridden heroine from his novel, *Trilby*.[19] And even if P.-J. Proudhon later characterized the spinner as "une franche paysanne," contrasting her with the false and prettified versions of peasant girls more generally shown at the Salon,[20] other observers of the work, including the critic Champfleury, have found her to be too rosy, well-fed and charming to be a truly proletarian figure.[21] Certainly, the work which is probably the immediate pictorial source of the motif, a drawing of a sleeping spinner by Vidal which had appeared in the 1850–51 Salon, the Salon in which Courbet had exhibited his *Stonebreakers* [pl.7, p.71] and the *Burial at Ornans* [pl.2, pp.66–67], is decidedly Rococo and more related to the tale of the "Belle au Bois Dormant" than to the rigors of rural labor.[22] The overt setting forth of the pleasures of dreaminess, the frankly sensual, vaguely erotic aura that emanates from the richly, sensitively painted image pushed invitingly close to the spectator on the surface of the canvas is at any rate extraordinarily different from Millet's contemporary images of virtuous working women, quasi-religious icons of domesticity, depicted spinning, knitting, or sewing. Such an image is the Barbizon painter's *Woman Sewing by Candlelight*, in which the religious implications of selfless labor are made even more explicit through the juxtaposition of the sewing hands and the sleeping child in the background; it and the bent-over figure of the industrious mother are bound together by the luminous, spiritually significant vertical of the candle. The probity and self-forgetful humility suggested by Millet's depiction, as well as the alert concentration of his knitter's pose, are the very contrary of that sense of self-indulgent *disponibilité* created by Courbet in *The Sleeping Spinner*.[23]

Millet's *Gleaners* embodies a similar notion of the near-sanctity of rural labor. The painting is, at the same time, an effective visual rationalization of the role of the peasant woman within rural society. In *The Gleaners*, the genuinely problematic implications surrounding the issue of gleaning, though by no means completely erased, have been transformed into what might well be called a nineteenth-century realist "version of the pastoral."

The "droit de glanage" and gleaning itself, traditionally the way the poorest and weakest members of rural society were permitted to obtain their bread, had, since the Middle Ages, down through the nineteenth century, and particularly at the time of the 1848 Revolution, been fraught with controversy.[24] It was, furthermore, a controversial area in which women had played a relatively active role, participating in the recurrent disturbances connected with the rights of gleaning: in the eighteenth century, for example, three *glaneuses* of Etampes had been condemned by the

Parlement to be thrashed naked, branded with the letter "V" for *voleuse*, then forced to bear placards saying "voleuses de grains pendant la moisson sous prétexte de glaner," and finally banished.[25] In the years closer to the time of the painting of *The Gleaners*, around the time of the 1848 Revolution specifically, the last, widespread violent resistance by the traditional peasant community to the encroachment of capitalist agriculture on their traditional rights, among them, the "droit de glanage" had taken place.[26]

Yet if a few overwrought conservative critics of the time may have seen the specter of revolution hovering behind the three bent female figures in Millet's *Gleaners*,[27] a more objective reading of the pictorial text here reveals that Millet was, on the contrary, unwilling to emphasize the expression of genuine social conflict implied by the contrast between the richness of the harvest of the wealthy landowner in the background (an absentee landowner whose presence is effectively but minutely suggested by the mounted *garde champêtre* in the background to the right), and the poverty of the gleaning figures bending over the rough, depleted earth in the foreground.[28] On the contrary, Millet, like most of his contemporaries, it must be said, chose, by ennobling the poses and assimilating the figures to biblical and classical prototypes, to remove them from the politically charged context of contemporary history and to place them in the transhistoric context of high art. At the same time, through the strategies of his composition, Millet makes it clear that this particularly unrewarding labor must be read as ordained by the order of nature itself rather than brought about by specific conditions of historical injustice. Indeed, the very fact that the workers in question are *glaneuses* rather than *glaneurs* makes their position more acceptable: women are more effortlessly incorporated into the natural order. Millet emphasizes this woman-nature connection in a specific aspect of his composition: as Robert Herbert has pointed out, the bodies of the bending women are quite literally encompassed and limited by the boundaries of the earth itself:[29] it is as though the earth imprisons them and condemns them to this fate, not a specific economic system like feudalism or capitalism.

Millet's *glaneuses*, pastoralized as they are, look positively grim, their work harsh and repetitive, in contrast to the romanticized setting, rosy in the warm light of the setting sun, the poetically varied poses and the nostalgic atmosphere of Jules Breton's *Sarcleuses* of 1860.[30] Looking at Breton's healthy, lithe young weeders (who are actually gathering a food-crop rather than weeding in the usual sense of the term), it is hard to remember that the life of the female peasant in his day was grim, brutal and exhausting. Breton preferred his field workers young with reason. "There is not a woman who is recognizable at the end of three years of marriage," wrote an observer of peasant life in the Haute-Alpes in 1845. The peasant wife had to rise from childbirth almost immediately, take up the demanding household tasks, do fieldwork in July and August, baby at her breast, take care of the cattle and clean the cattle barn, do the milking, and participate in the harvest in the fall.

According to many witnesses, peasant women never sat down to table with their menfolk, but stood, ready to serve those who ate at the table. Nor was classical physical beauty of the type admired by Breton considered a particularly desirable quality in a peasant woman: it was simply not practical. Peasant proverbs of the period bear this out: "La beauté ne se mange pas à la cuillière" goes one; "Il vaut mieux dire: Laide, allons souper que lui demander: Belle, qu'avons nous à souper?" goes another.[31] There is not only no sense of the grimness of peasant women's lives in Breton's rosy vision of toil in the fields, there is not even a sense of the physical strain involved in bending, lifting or pulling. Breton, on the contrary, distanced his peasant-girl models from concrete effort by assimilating them to harmonious prototypes in classical antiquity, thereby reducing hard-working laborers to sentimentally sweet art-objects. A poet of sorts, he articulated his aestheticized vision of one of his *glaneuses* quite succinctly:

> C'est une enfant des champs, âpre, sauvage et fière
> Et son galbe fait bien sur ce simple décor . . .

In another poem, related to his painting *La Lavandière* of 1890, the sentimental classicism obfuscating his vision is made even more apparent:

> Phidias eut revé le chef d'œuvre que voile
> Cette jupe taillée à grands coups d'ébauchoir.[32]

Neither the bent poses and pathos of Millet nor the sweetness and romanticization characteristic of Breton's treatment of women workers is evident in Courbet's *Grain Sifters* of 1854. *The Grain Sifters* is indeed a "strange picture," as Courbet called it: strange from a purely pictorial point of view, that is, as well as an iconographic one. Although I do not agree with Mlle. Toussaint that the oddities of the composition and color scheme are attributable to the influence of Japanese art,[33] the painting does owe much of its originality to the radical premises of its structure. Pictorial coherence is achieved here in what one might call true realist fashion by a sort of additive unity, a piecemeal but effective coherence which tends to play down what would otherwise be the total domination of the central figure. One feels an underlying relationship to Chardin in the seemingly casual placement of objects of related shape and surface texture throughout the picture. Yet the distribution of Courbet's basins, bowls, and containers is actually far more random and more widely spread out across the surface of the canvas than that of the objects neatly related within a clearly receding space in a work like Chardin's *Pourvoyeuse* in the Louvre. As a result, in *The Grain Sifters*, the echoes are muted so that the resulting harmonies are harsher, often verging on or actually becoming assonance. Perhaps, though, it is the sheer vitality of matter itself which militates most convincingly against implications of the sentimental or the grandiose in the painting and makes it unique. Despite the fact that space is implied by the corner-view, and light by the reflection on the wall above the head of the girl with the sieve, in the absence of any softening atmosphere one is far more aware of the differentiated textures of the white-washed wall, the wooden door and moulding with its sliver of *image d'Epinal* affixed to it, the darker wood of the *tarare* or *blutoir* to the right, and the bulging, creamy beige sacks of grain than of their space-creating or space-occupying functions; light itself is transformed into a tangible pattern of creamy impasto, criss-crossed by a dense granular lattice-work of shadow. In its contrast to the effect of cosiness, the blurring of contour created by the atmospheric penumbra in a typical Millet interior, one can see what the critic Julius Meier-Graefe meant about *The Grain Sifters* when he referred to the "ruthless sincerity of its form."[34]

The pose of the central figure is, it is true, somewhat stylized, a little grandiose. The gesture of the sifter is assertive, the slightly over-contrived oval formed by her slender waist, the back of her straining neck, and the sieve, balanced by the firm orangey pyramid of the outspread skirt and set off against the calculated pathos of white-stockinged feet, half emerging from their rough slippers. But grandiose or not, this energetic, dominating central figure is an extremely compelling image of the woman agricultural worker. The subject of *The Grain Sifters* as a whole, however, is an extraordinarily opaque one. What, exactly, is going on here? No one has ever even defined the precise nature of the subject, much less its broader ramifications. Yet before knowing exactly what the iconography of the picture is, we can respond on the most immediate level to the sheer physical force of the central figure. Whatever Courbet meant by the picture, it would seem to have little to do with that mythology of resignation, piety or natural submission to the given order of things suggested by the paintings previously under discussion. Nor is the picture prettified, like Breton's, nor is it overtly erotic, although the voluptuous muscularity of the central figure, as well as various latent references to sexually charged motifs lying behind the manifest content may, as we shall see, contribute mightily to the sheer vitality of the painting.

Even the exact title of the subject is ambiguous. Although consistently entitled *Les Cribleuses de blé* in the plural when shown in the nineteenth century, the work actually represents only a single grain-sifter, the central figure: the two peripheral figures are engaged in quite different activities. In the letter Courbet wrote to his friend the critic Champfleury, in 1854, explaining *The Painter's Studio*, he ended by saying: "J'ai un tableau de mœurs de campagne qui est fait de cribleuses de blé qui entra dans la série des *Demoiselles de village*, tableau étrange aussi."[35] When the work was shown in Brussels in 1857, it was entitled *Les Cribleuses de blé, scene de mœurs agricoles, Franche-Comté*, and when it was shown in Besançon in 1860, *Les Cribleuses ou les enfants des cultivateurs du Doubs*.[36] Two facts emerge: that Courbet in some way saw his painting as "strange," which suggests that he intended some sort of hidden meaning or implication; and that he was intent on recording the customs of his native region of the Franche-Comté, as he had already done in *The Young Ladies of the Village* [pl.4, p.70] and the *Burial at Ornans* and was to do in *La Toilette de la morte* [pl.8, p.72] – customs that were already beginning to disappear. Indeed, with particular reference to the activities depicted in *The Grain Sifters*, it is significant that by the second half of the nineteenth century, with the advent of increasing mechanization, women were being driven out of the major operations of harvesting and winnowing on more progressive farms, as Eugen Weber has pointed out. With the adoption of reaper-binders, the heavy, compressed bales of hay and straw became too heavy for women to handle, and the change from sickles to scythes demanded more strength than most women could muster.[37]

I should like to suggest that in this painting Courbet is, among other things, creating an image of progress in the realm of agricultural operations: an image, on the one hand, personal – it may well be his sister Zöe with the *crible* and his sister Juliette to the left[38] – and on the other social. For by suggesting that methods of agricultural work do in fact change, Courbet is automatically taking the woman agricultural worker out of the realm of transcedent, unchanging nature and reinserting her into the realm of history – a realm in which there can be change and progress. On the left, one may hypothesize, we have lazy, retrograde and inefficient hand separation of wheat from chaff; in the center, the more progressive and energetic use of the *crible* or sieve. Millet's *Vanneur* (*Winnower*) of 1847–48 represents a more primitive stage of the same sort of implement, incidentally, the shell-shaped wicker *van*; one is tempted to see Courbet's figure as a kind of response to Millet's monumental *Winnower*, a work which had been sold to Ledru-Rollin almost immediately after its creation.[39] To the right, in Courbet's painting, would be the final stage of sifting, or milling progress – mechanization taking command, albeit on a rather simple level – with a device so simple a child can run it: the *tarare*, an implement into which grain is poured through a funnel at the top and falls through a series of graduated meshes which divide the grain from the heavier chaff.[40] If the notion that the theme of agricultural progress is embodied in the painting remains speculative, it does seem clear that Courbet intended to represent *three* different processes in this painting rather than merely the one, sifting.

The motif of the woman with the sieve, however, the dominant image of the picture, has a long tradition in art and text, and a tradition which tends to support the generally sexual interpretation of the painting advanced by Werner Hofmann and others.[41] Are there actually latent erotic implications in *The Grain Sifters?* Is the pose of the central figure actually "indecent," as one nineteenth-century observer called it?[42] What are the implications of the gesture of the little boy on the right who peers into the open door of the *tarare?* Are art historians like Hofmann simply reading twentieth-century Freudian meanings into a sexually innocent painting, or, on firmer ground, are they using modern psychoanalytic and psycho-historical techniques to reach deeper but nevertheless quite valid levels of meaning in the texts of the past when they see Courbet's grain sifters as a basically erotic subject?[43] In the case of the central figure with the sieve, the coincidence with a traditional sexual *topos* seems to make an erotic interpretation more justifiable, for the sieve-bearer recalls the antique story of Tuccia recounted by Pliny and Valerius Maximus, which tells the exemplary fate of a Vestal Virgin falsely accused of losing her virginity who proves herself against her accusers when water fails to pass through her sieve.[44] The story was often represented in traditional art: in France, for example, by a School of Fontainebleau artist.[45] Whether or not Courbet was aware of such traditional precedents in high art is of course debatable. Yet to what degree had associations of sieve and the female sexual organ become a more available topic by the nineteenth century, perhaps perpetuated in popular sayings or folklore? And to what extent is one justified in suggesting certain "natural" associations between circular forms and female sexuality? But here, I think, we get lost in the mists of archetypal speculation, similar to those surrounding the issue of Georgia O'Keeffe's giant irises and peonies and the notion of "feminine imagery," speculation of dubious value today and even less justified in the pre-Freudian innocence of the nineteenth century.

If the subject of *The Grain Sifters* remains richly indeterminate, the sense of dominating energy of the central figure grasping the *crible* is unequivocal in its forcefulness. A similarly posed, back-view figure of a working woman from Velázquez's *Hilanderas*, a figure which may in fact have inspired Courbet, looks positively lackadaisical in comparison, and the central figure of Jules Breton's near contemporary *Cribleuses de Colza* of 1860 is a pretty, lifeless caryatid, merely holding the sieve as though it were a kind of attribute rather than really working with it.[46] Indeed, the only figures which suggest the kind of confident muscular expansiveness characteristic of Courbet's grain sifter are male ones, like Tintoretto's marvellously energetic back-to iron-worker from his *Forge of Vulcan.* This is not, of course, to suggest a specific influence, but merely to point out that the kind of pose chosen by Courbet here is rare in the ranks of representations of nineteenth-century women workers.

By the beginning of the twentieth century, the situation has changed. Even Courbet's monumental figure of the grain sifter seems frozen and self-reflexive in its energy compared with the wild vertical propulsiveness of the peasant-woman protagonist in Käthe Kollwitz's *Losbruch* of 1905, the central etching from her graphic cycle, the *Peasants' War.* As a visual manifestation or woman's energy, self-assertion, and power, it is to Millet's *Gleaners* that Kollwitz's image offers the most startling contrast. One might even think of Kollwitz's image as a kind of "anti-glaneuses," a counter-pastoral, with the dynamic, vertical thrust of its angular, female protagonist, who galvanizes the crowd behind her into action, serving to subvert the message of passive acquiescence to the natural order created by Millet's composition. One might say that what Millet scrupulously avoided by resorting to the peasant woman in his representation of the agricultural worker, and what Courbet kept cannily hidden, Kollwitz openly asserts through her: rage, energy, action. Kollwitz turned for historical as well as pictorial inspiration for her dominating figure of Black Anna, a leader of the sixteenth-century German peasant uprising, to Wilhelm Zimmermann's classical account, *Geschichte des großen deutschen Bauernkriegs* of 1891, which vividly described this powerful proletarian woman and, in addition, provided a popular woodcut illustration of her.[47] No doubt Delacroix's classic revolutionary image, *Liberty at the Barricades*, lingered in the back of Kollwitz's mind when she created *Losbruch:* indeed, a similar allegorical figure had been represented by her as the inciter of peasants to riot in a much earlier version of a similar theme, *Revolt*, of 1899. But the significant thing about Delacroix's powerful figure of Liberty, of course, is that she, like almost all such feminine embodiments of human value – Justice, Truth, Temperance – is an allegorical figure rather than a real human being, a perfect example, in fact, of what Simone de Beauvoir has called "woman-as-other."[48] In Delacroix's painting, it is the men behind the female figure who are concretely described and realistically differentiated. Black Anna, on the other hand, as Françoise Forster-Hahn has pointed out in her discussion of this series, is extremely concrete; it is the surging crowd of figures behind her that are, on the contrary, relatively anonymous: perhaps the dynamic generalization of individual forms is meant to convey a sense of the active unity of the aroused proletariat. Significantly, as Forster-Hahn points out, Kollwitz has foreshortened historical distance into the present by introducing into the foreground of the scene the back-view figure of a powerful woman of the people, thereby, this author feels, persuading the viewer to identify with the event as the artist herself does.[49]

For Kollwitz, a feminist and a socialist, who had been deeply influenced by August Bebel's pioneering document of feminism, *Die Frau und der Socialismus*,[50] specifically identified herself with Black Anna, and told her biographer that "she had portrayed herself in this woman. She wanted the signal to attack to come from her."[51] In *Losbruch*, for perhaps the first time in art history, a woman artist has successfully pierced through the structure of symbolic domination with conscious, politically informed awareness. Indeed, the whole seven-part cycle of the *Peasants' War*, although ostensibly, and actually, an account of the tragic sixteenth-century revolt of the German rural proletariat, is also a narrative of evolving feminine consciousness, perhaps, on the deepest level, an account of Kollwitz's own personal awakening to socialist feminism. The series progresses from the inert, helpless passivity of *Rape* to the ponderous thoughtfulness and incipient activism of *While Sharpening the Scythe*, to the explosive violence of catalytic feminine energy in *Losbruch*.

It is also significant that Kollwitz selected a narrative of outright social disorder for the representation of a powerful, directing, female figure. The *topos* of woman on top, to borrow the title of Natalie Zemon Davis's provocative study of sex-role reversal in pre-industrial Europe,[52] has always been, and remained in the nineteenth century, as a popular woodcut like *Les Réformes du ménage* testifies, a potent image of unthinkable disorder. Generally, during our period gestures of power and self-affirmation, especially of political activism, on the part of women were treated with special visual viciousness. Daumier, in 1848, the very year of the democratic revolution fought in the name of greater equality, in his *Voilà une femme qui, à l'heure solonelle …* from his *Divorceuses* series, treats the two feminists to the left as denatured hags, saggy, scrawny, uncorseted creatures, whose dissatisfied gracelessness is vividly contrasted with the unselfconscious charm of the little mother to the right who continues to care for her child heedless of the tumult of history.[53] The working-class women activists of the Commune, the so-called "pétroleuses," were mercilessly caricatured by the Government of Order, and depicted as frightening, sub-human, witch-like creatures, demons of destruction intent on literally destroying the very fabric of the social order by burning down buildings.[54] In the sixteenth century, Pieter Brueghel had used the figure of a powerful, active woman, Dulle Griet or Mad Meg, to signify contemporary spiritual and political disorder.[55] Indeed, it is possible that Kollwitz herself may have turned to this, one of the most potent images of the menace of the unleashed power of women, for her conception of Black Anna in the *Peasants' War* series, an image more or less contemporary with her subject itself: Mad Meg, who, with her ferocious band of female followers, serves as the very emblem of fiery destruction, of brutal oppression and disorder; to borrow Natalie Zemon Davis's words once more, a visual summary of the reversal of the proper power relations and the natural hierarchy of a well-ordered world. Brueghel's *Dulle Griet*, unloosed from its contemporary political significance, might well serve as the perfect illustration for Yeats's "mere anarchy is loosed upon the world." For Brueghel, as for the nineteenth-century imagination, the most potent natural signifier possible for folly and chaos was woman unleashed, self-determined, definitely on top: this was the only image sufficiently contrary to "normal" power relations, rich enough in pure negative significance, to indicate the destruction of value itself.

In creating her image of the powerful proletarian woman, Black Anna, then, Kollwitz has transvaluated the values of Mad Meg, so to speak, and made them into positive, if frightening and ultimately tragic visual signifiers. The dark, chthonic force of the peasant woman, those malevolent, sometimes supernatural powers associated with the unleashing of feminine popular energies and not totally foreign to those most menacing of all female figures – the witch – here assume a positive social and psychological meaning. The force of darkness, in the context of history, is transformed into the harbinger of light.

Courbet's notion of the powerful female agricultural worker is of course vastly different from that of Kollwitz: yet different though they may be as conceptual and pictorial conceptions, both the grain sifter and Black Anna share in certain characteristics: both in some way subvert the acceptable nineteenth-century imagery of the woman worker as conventionally come-hither, resigned, pious, or maternal; both imbue her, in vastly different ways and to different purposes, to be sure, with unaccustomed energy and physical expansiveness, and both insist on a context for the working woman which is historical rather than atemporal. Courbet's figure, of course, is far from conveying the feminist and socialist implications of Kollwitz's cycle. His political engagement, his profound sense of rebellious independence rarely ran to the overt expression of a precisely defined political position in his art. A figure like that of Black Anna springs from a very different kind of socially conscious impulse running through art history: a more romantic, dynamic, expressive current, often depending heavily on allegorical representation and dramatic narrative to convey its message. Courbet's strategies as a subverter of the status quo are radically different from those of a Goya, a Delacroix or a Kollwitz. He never created a sequel to or even an equivalent of Delacroix's *Liberty at the Barricades.* Indeed, if he had been asked to create an interpretation of the ideals of 1848 like "Equality at the Barricades" in celebration of the 1848 Revolution, he might well have answered, as he did when asked why he had never painted an angel, that he could never paint a figure of Equality because he had never seen one.[56] At the same time, his conception of woman, as a motif for art-making, was vastly different from what might be thought of as either revolutionary or feminist in any sense of the word. His portraits of women, specific ones, that is, are often sensitive, sometimes alluring, from time to time frankly coarse, like that of the so-called Mère Grégoire, but hardly innovative. His rather extensive repertory of sleeping women, clothed or dressed, like *The Sleeping Spinner*, suggest attitudes quite opposed to that of feminine activism or heroism: his female nudes like *Sleep* [36, p.58] or *The Bathers* [47, p.82] are, if sometimes overtly anti-academic, often mannered and artificed, and almost always overtly sensual in their poses as well as in the richly seductive materiality of their paint surfaces. It is the nudes, ironically, which, in the context of feminine nakedness available to the high art of his day, constitute the subversive impulse in Courbet's imagery of women, but it is an impulse which, in its overt sexual exhibitionism, its celebration of popular and semi-popular visual tastes in erotica, and its overt, unidealized presentation of women as objects of delectation for (presumably) male admirers, which makes them rather difficult for many observers of today to accept at all wholeheartedly, much less to accept as the daring essays into radical sensual visualization that they were at the time Courbet created them.

6 | In Detail: Courbet's *A Burial at Ornans*

Even today, Gustave Courbet's *A Burial at Ornans* [pl.2, pp.66–67] has the power to strike us with a kind of confrontational audacity. One hundred and thirty years after it was painted, the picture still reminds us that there was a time when art, politics, and a sense of class identity were inextricably mingled, when ideas such as democracy and freedom were seen to be inherent in the very structure of the work of art. Filing across the surface of the long, low canvas, Courbet's sturdy, black-clad farmers and their wives – the artist's own parents and sisters among them – stare stolidly ahead or raise crumpled handkerchiefs to their faces.

Gathered with them by the grave are several village dignitaries, a child or two, a pair of red-hatted beadles, the local priest, a kneeling gravedigger [pl.1, p.65], and an old veteran of the revolution, whose angular stance and brilliant turquoise calves mark the foreground of the picture stage [pl.3, pp.68–69]. To this day, these awkward, rough-hewn figures refuse to be assimilated to the other works of monumental ambition in the nineteenth-century galleries of the Louvre.

The *Burial* displays neither the suavely orchestrated pomp and glitter of David's ceremonial *Le Sacre* [50] (also a group portrait), nor the storm-tossed melodrama of Géricault's *Raft of the Medusa*, nor yet the jewel-like sensuality of Delacroix's *Death of Sardanapalus*. In this company, the *Burial* stands alone, isolated by its deliberate restraint and the air of defiantly graceless veracity that made Courbet notorious as the leader of the Realist movement in mid-nineteenth-century France.

Conventional critics and the conventional public reacted to the *Burial* with shock, even outrage. The response was the more violent because the work burst into public notice at the Salon of 1850–51, at a time when the humanitarian ideals of the 1848 Revolution had been replaced by a climate of political reaction and an increasingly authoritarian government. To many right-thinking Parisians of the time, Courbet's

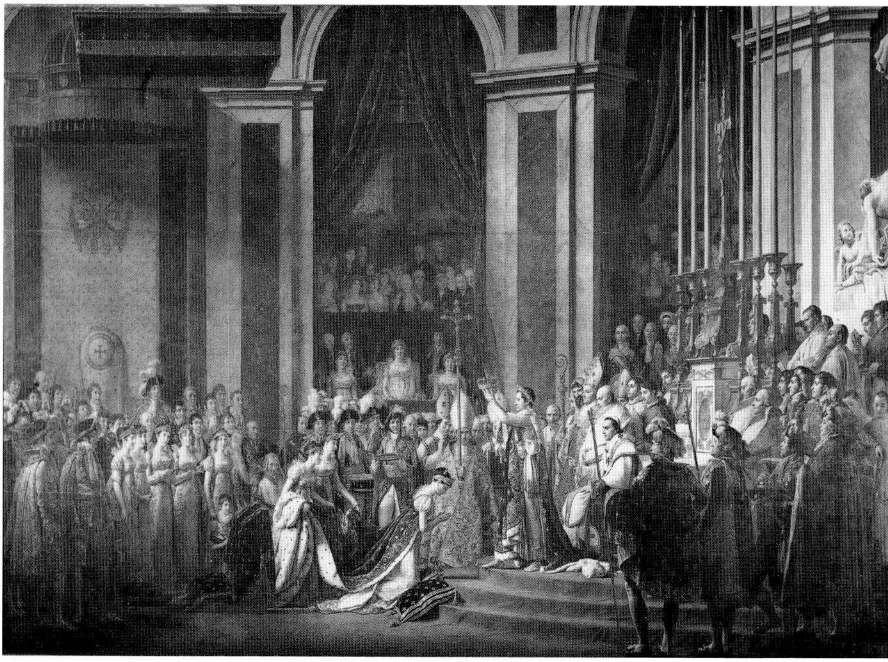

50 **Jacques-Louis David**, *Le Sacre*, 1807. Oil on canvas, 610 x 970 cm, 240⅛ x 381⅞ in.

painting, assertive in scale and subject, seemed a terrible reminder of their narrow escape from the threat of take-over by the working classes.

Such political animosity was almost automatically sublimated into aesthetic denigration by frightened salonniers. In the eyes of the conservative critic Louis de Geofroy, for example, the *Burial at Ornans* failed, not on account of its subject, but because of the way Courbet treated it: the compositional weaknesses of the painting, rather than the artist's decision to make an ambitious "tableau historique" out of a hometown news item, dismayed de Geofroy. He argued that, "If M. Courbet had deigned to elaborate his ideas to interrelate the various parts by playing down or concealing the unpleasant portions, by emphasizing the more pleasing motifs, he would have produced a good picture .... It is merely a question of first, not localizing the subject, and second, of emphasizing the interesting parts of such a scene." If these are family portraits, declared de Geofroy scornfully, they should be left in Ornans where they belong; those of us who are not from Ornans require something more. That "something more" for the critic was "the natural sentiment which accompanies such a scene," a sentiment he finds distressingly absent from Courbet's haphazard recording of local phenomena.

De Geofroy's demand for such "natural sentiment" would have been amply fulfilled by a small-scale, mediocre painting of the same subject by the now forgotten Augustin Roger, *A Village Burial* [7, p.23], which had appeared in the Salon of 1822. In

Roger's modest canvas, painted under the Bourbon Restoration, both cast and composition "know their place." The potential subversiveness of lower-class subject matter is thereby rendered not merely inoffensive but positively edifying. Courbet's cast of characters, on the contrary, are seen, quite correctly because of the artist's innovative pictorial strategies, not as charming peasants whose quaint customs might be recorded for the delectation of their urban betters, but as unsettlingly concrete representatives of the rural petty bourgeoisie. For de Geofroy, the major shortcoming of Courbet's realism resulted from the artist's apparent inability to go beyond the recording of crude reality: in the *Burial*, he had simply failed to produce a work of art.

If a conservative critic such as de Geofroy was quick to point out the connection between Courbet's regrettable lack of spiritual elevation and his formal weaknesses, it was for the very unorthodoxy of his pictorial structure that Courbet's progressive supporters praised him. His most articulate champion, the writer and critic Champfleury, declared that it was precisely through the composition and the arrangement of the groups in the *Burial* that Courbet broke with academic tradition. "Without knowing the admirable canvases of Velázquez," Champfleury asserted, "he finds himself totally in accord with that illustrious master, who placed his figures one next to the other and didn't worry about the laws posited by pedantic, second-rate minds." At the time he painted the *Burial*, Courbet was ignorant of the work of Velázquez. But he may nevertheless have drawn courage for both the boldness of his composition and its stark contrasts of black, white, and red from a thematically similar work by Zurbarán, another great seventeenth-century master, whose *Saint Bonaventure on his Bier*, then known as *Funeral of a Bishop*, was in the Soult Collection in Paris.

Whatever their sources, Courbet's democracy of vision and egalitarian composition were seen as the concomitants of a democratic outlook by conservatives and radicals alike. The relationship of the *Burial of Ornans* to the ideals of 1848 seemed to go deeper than any overt political message. And the connection of the painting with the advanced social thought of the mid-nineteenth century appeared to lie not merely in Courbet's decision to paint his fellow townspeople life-size, but also in the fact that by giving equal emphasis to all the elements of his composition, by breaking with traditional methods of constructing a painting, the *Burial* could be directly related in its simplicity and awkwardness to the art language of the people – that of the popular French woodcuts known as *images d'Epinal* [8, p.25].

In the view of many, truth and democracy were both judged to be functions of the same stalwart confrontation of actuality. Far from being trivial in the *Burial*, declared the Fourierist François Sabatier, Courbet "is truthful ... and this is democracy in art." It was Champfleury who first compared Courbet's style in the *Burial* to the naïveté of popular art, maintaining that this was one of its chief virtues. Courbet was the first major nineteenth-century artist to look deliberately

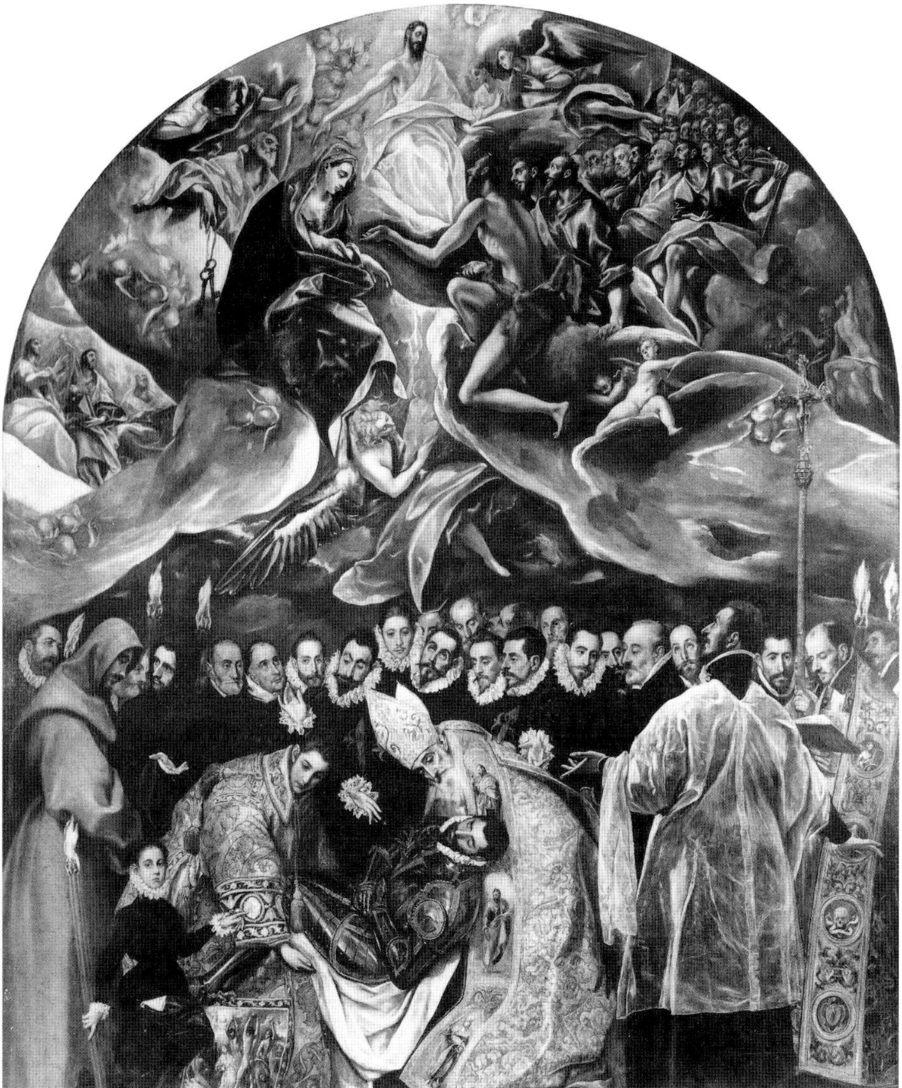

51 **El Greco**, *The Burial of Count Orgaz*, 1586. Oil on canvas, 480 x 360 cm, 189 x 141¾ in.

toward the "primitive" and, by creating a "historical painting" that reminded contemporary critics of such imagery, he made a statement that could be considered both politically and aesthetically radical.

Yet Courbet's painting may be considered innovative not simply because of the artist's conscious choices of style and subject. It was Courbet's friend, the anarchist philosopher (predecessor and later enemy of Karl Marx) P.-J. Proudhon, who observed of the *Burial:* "We have lost the religion of the dead; we no longer understand that sublime poetry with which Christianity, in harmony with itself, used to surround it." Courbet is not being consciously anti-religious or irreverent in this picture, as his denigrators seemed to believe. It is merely that he honestly sees the occasion as completely secular. The traditional Christian notion of death as the meeting place of heavenly and earthly realities and the funeral ceremony as the occasion of the ultimate journey of the soul – a notion perhaps most impressively made visible in El Greco's *Burial of Count Orgaz* of 1586 [51] – is foreign to Courbet's conception. For the nineteenth-century painter, the concreteness of the event here and now is the point of his subject. Courbet intended the *Burial* to fulfill his declared intention, set forth in the catalogue introduction to his 1855 Realist Exhibition, to "translate the customs, the ideas, and the appearances" of his time into his art.

Although Courbet's view of death may have been completely secular, it was by no means reductive. For Courbet, the death of a human being was more than a mere physical occurrence – the extreme Positivist position of his day – and the nature of its significance is implied in the *Burial* by a predominantly horizontal composition departing from the vertical relationships which had dominated traditional funerary art: it involves not the ascent of the soul to heaven, but the joining together of social bonds on earth. Courbet's reality consisted of his friends, family, and fellow townsmen aligned against the cliffs of their natural habitat. His painting is thus not an "irreligious" treatment of a religious theme, but an affirmation of entirely different values: those of the human community.

One might almost say that for Courbet the funeral served simply as a pretext for getting these fifty people together. Evidently the whole town of Ornans was eager to participate in Courbet's picture, and painting it took on the aspect of a community project. Courbet wrote to Champfleury: "Here the models are cheap; everyone wants to be in the *Burial*. I'll never be able to satisfy them all." Part of the two-dimensional, additive quality of the work may well be due to the fact that the *Burial* was created as a series of individual portraits, with Courbet working in a studio which was only sixteen inches longer than the canvas itself and about fourteen feet wide. While he was painting, he was never able to step far enough back to view the effect as a whole.

The *Burial* owes its power and originality to more significant factors than the difficulties attending its creation – or to mere empirical observation. It is part of Realist mythology that the artist produces his picture merely by looking at and recording what he sees. Yet if we examine what is obviously the first thought for the *Burial*, a charcoal drawing [6, p.21] that records the event (perhaps the funeral of Courbet's maternal grandfather) that the artist transformed into his painting, we are led to suspect some mediating image. The *Burial*, despite its apparent directness, is far more astutely composed than the drawing. In the drawing there is none of the sense of focus provided by the open grave, toward which figures converge from left and right; nor of the relieving asymmetry provided by the gravedigger's kneeling but assertive posture to left of center; nor the slight but telling sense of antiphonal statement and response from one side of the grave to the other provided by the gesture of the priest and that of the old republican to the right of the grave.

The most probable source of inspiration for Courbet's final composition was the tradition of the Dutch group portrait. Indeed, Courbet might have been inspired to paint the *Burial* by a Civic Guard portrait that he saw during the course of a trip to Holland in 1847: Bartholomeus van der Helst's *Company of Captain Bicker* [9, p.26]. The scale and format of van der Helst's work, and the poses of some of the figures (most notably those of the kneeling burgher and of the boy to far left), have clearly been adapted by Courbet, despite the fact that the *Burial* remains far less hierarchical in its composition than this seventeenth-century prototype.

Courbet was delighted with Holland and wrote home that a trip to the Low Countries was indispensable to an artist. Indeed, from his earliest visits to the Louvre, Courbet exhibited enthusiasm for Dutch art, an enthusiasm that lasted throughout his career. This interest was not merely a simple aesthetic preference. The taste for Dutch art, the decision to create an important work in the tradition of – and as a challenge to – the Dutch group portrait is tied to deeper social issues. Dutch art, from at least the time of the 1848 Revolution, was clearly associated with ideals of political liberty, rebellion against oppression, and republican government. Dutch art, as opposed to Italian, was considered the expression of a sturdy, independent, and anti-aristocratic people.

The greatest historian of Dutch art in the nineteenth century, Théophile Thoré, also one of Courbet's staunchest supporters, was a political radical who did most of his research on Dutch collections when in exile from imperial France. Thoré connected the originality and realism of seventeenth-century Dutch art with the freedom of religion and government enjoyed by the citizens of the Low Countries. In choosing to make a major statement in the form of the group portrait, then, Courbet was declaring his allegiance to the democratic traditions of Holland as well as proclaiming his loyalty to the traditions of his native Ornans. Indeed, as he himself put it in the *Realist Manifesto* of 1855, in the *Burial* he drew forth from tradition the "reasoned and independent consciousness" of his own individuality.

Almost by definition, the portrait fulfills the Realist requirement of "being of its times." In addition, though, the *group* portrait suggests the integration of the individual into some larger social order. It is the conformation of a certain class, a national or professional coterie, or a family, which is at issue, not the nuances of individual character. The group portrait, established as a Realist theme *par excellence* by Courbet in the *Burial at Ornans*, has remained a viable Realist motif ever since: in the pictorial manifestos of Henri Fantin-Latour; in Manet's vividly immediate yet highly artificed depictions of the *monde* and *demi-monde* of his time; in the sociable gatherings of the Impressionists; in Marie Laurencin's faux-naïf recordings of Cubist affiliations; right on to the present in the works of such artists as the painters Alex Katz and Al Leslie, and the photographer Neal Slavin.

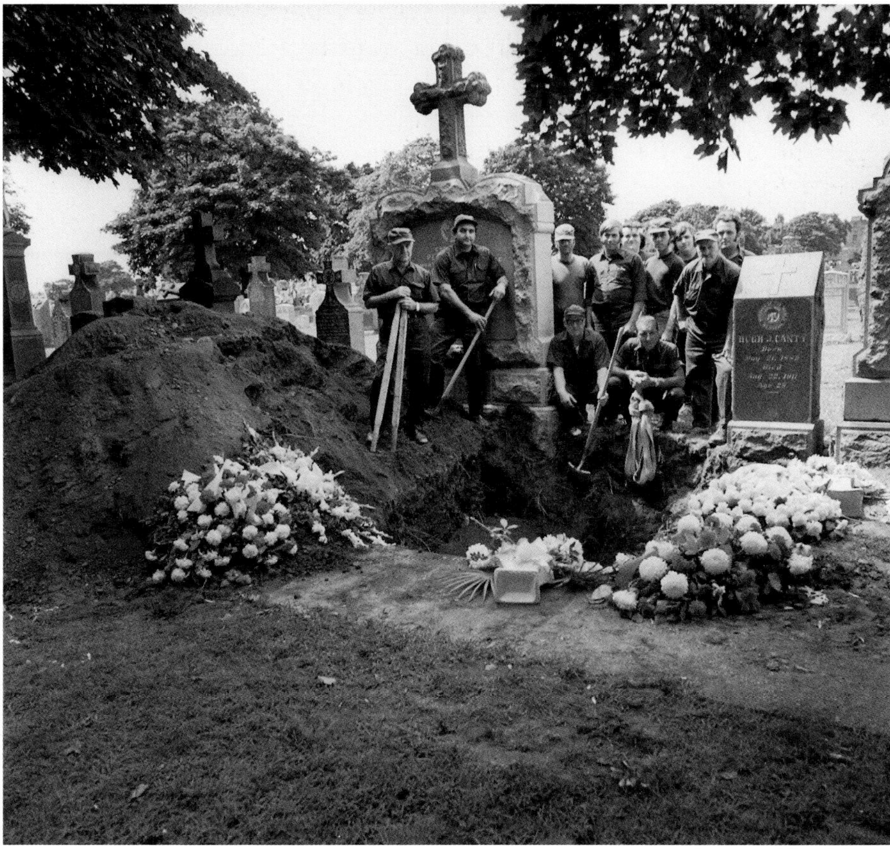

52 **Neal Slavin**, *Cemetery Workers and Greens Attendants Union ...*, 1973

Indeed, it is above all in the documentary mode of photography that the Realist group portrait flourishes today. Slavin, for example, in his *Cemetery Workers and Greens Attendants Union ...* of 1973 [52], like Courbet in his *Burial*, defines his subjects through the concrete details of their situation and setting. Like Courbet, the photographer has taken over and transformed elements from a popular art form – in this case, the local group shot – and mingled them with memories of classic photography, traditional art, and film. And like Courbet, the contemporary group portraitist infuses a time-honored Realist genre with new life. As a challenge to conventional notions of reality – and the visual structures through which they are mediated – the lessons of the *Burial at Ornans* are still valid in the world of our own experience.

7 | The De-Politicization of Gustave Courbet: Transformation and Rehabilitation under the Third Republic

Two quite different pursuits lead to the place from which to contemplate the late nineteenth-century "rehabilitation" of Gustave Courbet. The first is my ongoing investigation of Courbet within the framework of those issues of realism that were his concern. The second is a meditation on the questions feminism poses for art history and theory: the pair, of which one part is "Why have there been no great women artists?" and the other, its corollary, "Why *have* there been great male ones?" Why has this entity, the great artist, existed at all, in short? And more specifically, what configuration will the notion of the great artist have at given moments in history? How is this entity "the great artist" constructed? And to what purposes? What political needs, what psychological yearnings, what ideological functions, does such a notion serve? And more concretely, how was a former Communard, an exile, a still-controversial and prickly painter like Courbet transformed, during the decade between 1879 and 1889, into something approaching a cultural hero of the Third French Republic?

The steps in Courbet's actual rehabilitation are easy enough to follow and have been succinctly outlined in the current literature.[1] In 1877, a year before his death, Courbet was still in official disfavor, in exile in Switzerland, as a result of his participation in the Commune, and more to the point, his supposed responsibility for the destruction of the Vendôme Column. As late as November 26, 1877, a little more than a month before the artist's death, the court-ordered sale of his works for payment of the reconstruction of the column brought in, altogether, the derisory sum of 10,000 francs. Courbet died on New Year's Eve of 1877, on the uneasy brink of the Republic of the Opportunists, a year before MacMahon was replaced by Jules Grévy, a veteran of 1848, a year before the republic was actually controlled by the republicans.

In 1878, Courbet made a minor showing at the Exposition Universelle and a far larger one at the Retrospective Exhibition of Modern Masters at Durand-Ruël, where he was represented by thirty works. But it was not until 1881–82 that a more definite and official blow for the rehabilitation of the artist was struck with the brief ascension of Gambetta and the left wing of the Opportunist Republicans to power, and the creation of a Ministry of Art, with Antonin Proust, the boyhood friend of Manet, at its head. It was during this period that Courbet's family donated the *Burial at Ornans* [pl.2, pp.66–67] to the Louvre, and the state and the city of Paris bought five major works for a price of 150,000 francs, an impressive sum. It was during this period, too, that the critic Jules Castagnary, friend and supporter of the painter; Courbet's family; and the government got together to organize a major exhibition of his works at the Ecole des Beaux-Arts, an exhibition sanctified by the approving presence of the president of the republic himself.[2] By 1889 Courbet was quite literally enshrined within the great tradition of French art in a major republican celebration of that tradition: eleven of his works were featured in the great centennial exhibition of one hundred years of French art at the Paris World's Fair of 1889, an exhibition celebrating the hundredth anniversary of the Revolution.

These, then, are the basic facts of Courbet's promotion to the ranks of greatness: it is the how and the why of this promotion which is of more interest. Both the goals and the strategies of the reconstruction of Courbet need to be examined through several critical texts from this period, texts that both justified and at least to some degree prompted this new republican interpretation.

In the years from 1878 to 1889 there seem to have been three main tasks, all of them interrelated, facing Courbet's republican reconstructors. First, and perhaps most urgent, Courbet had to be definitively separated from his politics. Not, of course, from his wholesome and sympathetic interest in the peasant and the popular subject, which was – within certain limits of decorum – laudable, and even necessary to republican ideological strategy.[3] But more specifically he had to be detached from his all-too-well documented participation in the Commune – a terrible thorn in the side of the supporters of the Republic of the Opportunists – and from his equally notorious responsibility for the destruction of the Vendôme Column.

Secondly, Courbet's practice and his production had to be firmly attached to the realm of nature. In all the republican critics we will be concerned with, a dichotomy is established between the sociopolitical and the natural. Externalized, this dichotomy is envisioned as an opposition between his subject paintings of the 1850s (seen as bad or, at best, as limited) and his later landscapes, hunting scenes, nudes, and still lifes (seen as poetic, expansive, more universal). Internalized, it is posed as an opposition between the "natural" Courbet, the creature of pure intuition and "unerring instinct," and what one might be tempted to call the "corrupted" or "fallen" Courbet, the Courbet who misguidedly attempted to make choices or formulate theories, to participate – in short – in history.

And third, these critics, Castagnary especially, attempt to transform Courbet into a suitable great artist by inserting him into the ongoing, uninterrupted tradition of great art – great French art above all – in a ploy that is at once aesthetic and nationalistic, elevating and neutralizing. The Courbet of 1889 has been assimilated to the pantheon of national artists who shed glory on the republic. In so doing, Courbet is, like his predecessors, transformed into a kind of commodity – a French tourist attraction, as it were – and hero at once.

One hundred years after Courbet's birth, Théodore Duret, journalist, art critic, long-time republican, supporter of Manet and the Impressionists, could state with complete assurance: "Today, in 1918, Time has made its action felt. Courbet the political man has vanished from our attention; the passing judgments brought to bear on his works by his contemporaries are forgotten. The works themselves remain in all their power." But in the early days of the Third Republic, the case was less clear-cut. One could not eradicate the memory of the political Courbet quite so easily. In 1878, the year following Courbet's death, when the artist becomes the object of history, so to speak, rather than an agent still acting upon it, the situation was less assured; the political Courbet, Communard and fabled destroyer of the Vendôme Column, was still a living memory. Nor had the works themselves yet been recuperated, bought by the nation,

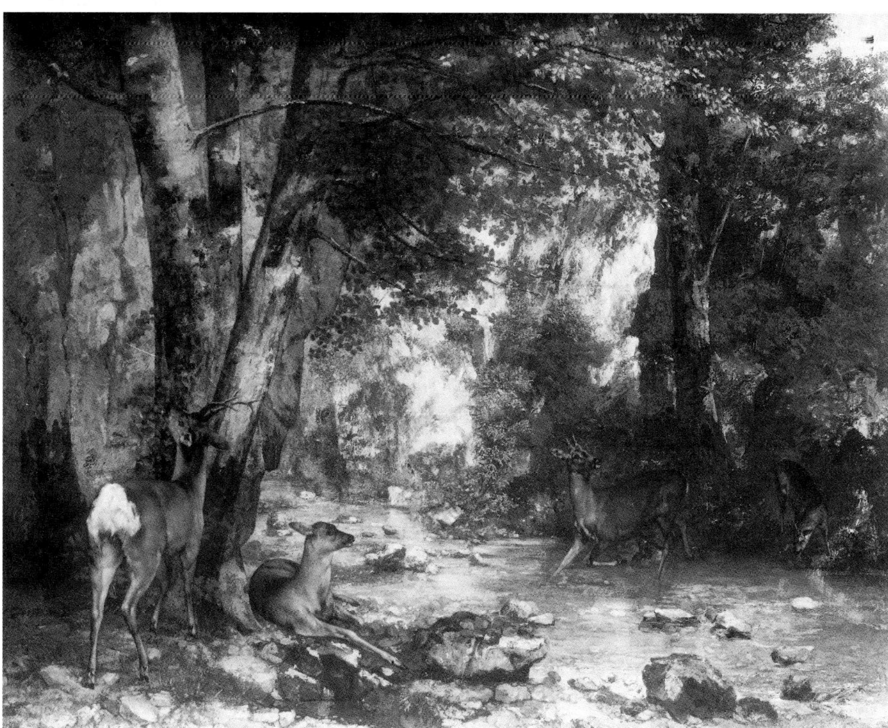

53 *Covert of Roe Deer,* 1866. Oil on canvas, 174 x 209 cm, 68½ x 82¼ in.

exhibited at the Ecole des Beaux-Arts. In 1878, the artist was, if no longer among the living, still problematic. His status as a Communard could not so easily be dismissed in the years preceding the General Amnesty of 1880, years in which the questions of whether Communards should be forgiven and to what degree were still much debated.

In 1878, three relatively serious studies of the recently deceased artist appeared, two in the form of books, by Camille Lemonnier and by the Comte d'Ideville, and one book-length, three-part article in the *Gazette des Beaux-Arts* by Paul Mantz. Mantz, one of the *Gazette*'s most active writers, had been a government administrator in a minor capacity under the Second Empire and was finally but briefly promoted to the post of director general of the Beaux-Arts in the early 1880s, under the Republic.[4]

The first two studies can be disposed of fairly easily; Mantz's work, more ambivalent and complex, deserves more detailed analysis. But what seems clear, first of all, about all three – ranging in tone as they do from the skeptically positive to the positively ecstatic – is that they are as anxious as Duret to detach their version of Courbet as effectively as possible from the taint of the political. D'Ideville's strategies are fairly simple-minded. He admits that Courbet's politics are indeed interesting, and goes so far as to devote a whole chapter to "Courbet homme politique," but ends up by completely discounting Courbet's political activities and ideas on the grounds of the artist's total incapacity in that realm. "If we have a deep admiration for Courbet the painter; if, despite its faults, we place the author of the *Covert of Roe Deer* [53] in the ranks of the greatest artists of our century, we must admit with no less sincerity that Courbet, as a philosopher, as a moralist, and as a politician, seems to have been a simple idiot .... Politics," d'Ideville declares, as though this were a self-evident proposition, "has nothing to do with art .... Even if he actually took down the [Vendôme] Column, which he denies, the friend of Proudhon has nevertheless painted – and it is both his glory and ours – the *Covert of Roe Deer*, the *Stags at Bay* ..., which will be the glory of our museums." In his clumsy way, d'Ideville has effectively, if unconsciously, set about the task of "professionalizing" the artist by declaring that his is a very specialized realm of competence; by the same token, his very proficiency as an artist is what renders him incompetent in any other areas of expertise – the political above all.

What is it that saved Courbet the painter from what d'Ideville terms these "pernicious influences," that is to say, complex or political ideas, and made him the marvellous interpreter of nature that he in fact was? Nothing else but Courbet's unique intuitive powers, or what d'Ideville terms "une intuition de paysan contemplateur." Courbet's intuition, like his political naïveté, becomes an article of faith of Third Republic Courbet hagiography, an essential feature of the "difficult but talented" artist. More than once, Camille Lemonnier reiterates this notion of the instinctive Courbet: "Courbet was an instinct more than a brain" and "He painted things as they are, with a dumb instinct which had something of genius in it." Paul Mantz, who from the start insists upon Courbet's faulty intellectual culture, declares that for him "many things remained in a state of instinctuality."

Mantz's entire formulation of Courbet is marked by a kind of irritated or regretful ambivalance. He begins what is after all an extended obituary notice not with the expected encomium, but with a put-down, a long, rambling account of the artist's exaggerated opinion of himself: "Courbet s'est follement aimé." By privileging the notion of Courbet's overweening pride, Mantz achieves two things. He distances himself and, by implication, his readers, from his subject; and he prepares the ground for the artist's eventual downfall: Courbet's hubris serves to justify his future punishment. Throughout, although Mantz expresses sympathy and admiration, he at the same time emphasizes formal flaws and missed opportunities. If in 1851 Courbet seemed to be the ideal opponent of the modish insipidness of the time, he aroused hopes that to a large measure remained unfulfilled, hopes that he would be an artist of poetry, of feeling, an artist who might have expressed the pathos of the life of the poor and disinherited, a kind of Octave Tassaert writ large, as Mantz put it, or, to borrow another of his phrases, "un Shakespeare de la rue Mouffetard."

But such, alas, was not to be. Courbet was not the long-awaited poet. It is around the words *poet* and *poetry* that Mantz's invention of Courbet begins to intensify. Mantz worries the notion of poetry like a dog with a bone. He is never quite sure where the artist stands in relation to poetry, or to put it another way, where he is going to make his version of Courbet stand in relation to it. The reconciliation of Courbet with poetry might at first seem like an impossible dream, Mantz admits, but, nevertheless, he maintains, in Courbet's best work of the later 1850s and 1860s, above all in his landscapes and seascapes, the impossible occurs: Mantz's Courbet becomes a poet in spite of himself. He literally falls under the spell of poetry, the seductress. "At the very moment when the artist proclaims himself the humble translator of external spectacles and objective realities, he invariably adds, often without realizing it, something that he takes from his own thought." This personal feeling, this legitimate exaggeration, is his concession involuntarily made to the ideal. "Courbet," Mantz concludes, "railed against poetry just when he submitted to her adorable despotism."

Courbet's practice, or at any rate a certain part of it, can be summed up to contravene his foolish theories, his fatal manifestos, his misguided participation in the Commune, which Mantz slides by so discreetly that we hardly realize what he is talking about, excusing himself all the while by saying that such "events" (as he calls them) are simply outside the framework of his habitual competence. Rather, it is only in contact with nature that this unconscious, seductive, but redeeming poetry finds its best expression in Courbet's work – and, one might add, that Courbet's political theories, his awkward notions of subject matter, and what Mantz thinks of as his errors in taste and construction are most notably absent. "What is best in the work of Courbet," Mantz concludes, waxing rather poetic himself, "are his landscapes, his green valleys of the Franche-Comté, his rocks carpeted with gray moss, his wooded interiors where hidden streams flow, and, above all, his blond banks of the

Mediterranean or the Atlantic, where, in the midst of fiery redness, the sun sinks slowly into the infinity of the sparkling sea."

These themes, sounded by the proto-republican writers of 1878, are taken up and developed with far greater range, depth, and sophistication by Jules Castagnary in his biography of Courbet, left unfinished at the time of the critic's untimely death in 1888.[5] Castagnary was a long-time republican, friend, and defender of Courbet in the disastrous aftermath of the Commune; and, for a brief period from 1887 until his death in May 1888, director of the Beaux-Arts under the ministry of Eugène Spuller. His fragmentary study of Courbet can only be understood in the context of the writer's other critical efforts at the time.

First of all, Castagnary's construction of Courbet must be interpreted in the light of his ongoing attempt, throughout the 1860s, to establish France as the preeminent artistic nation of the time on the basis of her achievement in landscape, which he held to be the most progressive form of painting. Second, and more materially, Castagnary's vision of Courbet in the later 1880s must be seen against the critic's engagement in the plans for the great exhibition of one hundred years of French art that he had conceived to celebrate the centennial of the French Revolution. Castagnary's Courbet, then, must be located in the context of the biographer's ongoing engagement with landscape as both French and progressive, but even more particularly, with the critic's attempt to create a continuous French – specifically a post-revolutionary republican French – tradition.

His account begins with a simple statement of origins in which the national and the natural aspects of his subject neatly coincide. "Gustave Courbet was born June 10, 1819 in Ornans, a little town of the Franche-Comté in the valley of the Loue. No other territory seems to have been as well prepared as this to be the cradle of a painter. The picturesque abounds there." Courbet, Castagnary maintains, comes from a region at once profoundly rooted in French traditional culture and unparalleled in its richness and variety of natural beauty.

For Castagnary, Courbet's realist masterpieces of the early 1850s were great achievements, expressions of contemporary life rooted in his Franc-Comtois heritage, devoid of any conscious or overt political overtones. Of Courbet's three major offerings to the 1851 Salon, the *Burial at Ornans*, *The Peasants of Flagey Returning from the Fair* [54], and *The Stonebreakers* [pl.7, p.71], Castagnary declares, "One might have said that these were a fragment of the Franche-Comté detached from that robust province and transported to Paris."

Yet it is clear that the critic's heart is with the later works, the landscapes above all. His Courbet, the hero of that French tradition he is in the process of constructing, must be something more than a mere regionalist; he must have ambitions on a national scale. To use Castagnary's own words, "The Franche-Comté is not all of France, popular customs are not all customs. Courbet, without abandoning his ideas in any way, felt the necessity of enlarging his frame of reference." What Castagnary

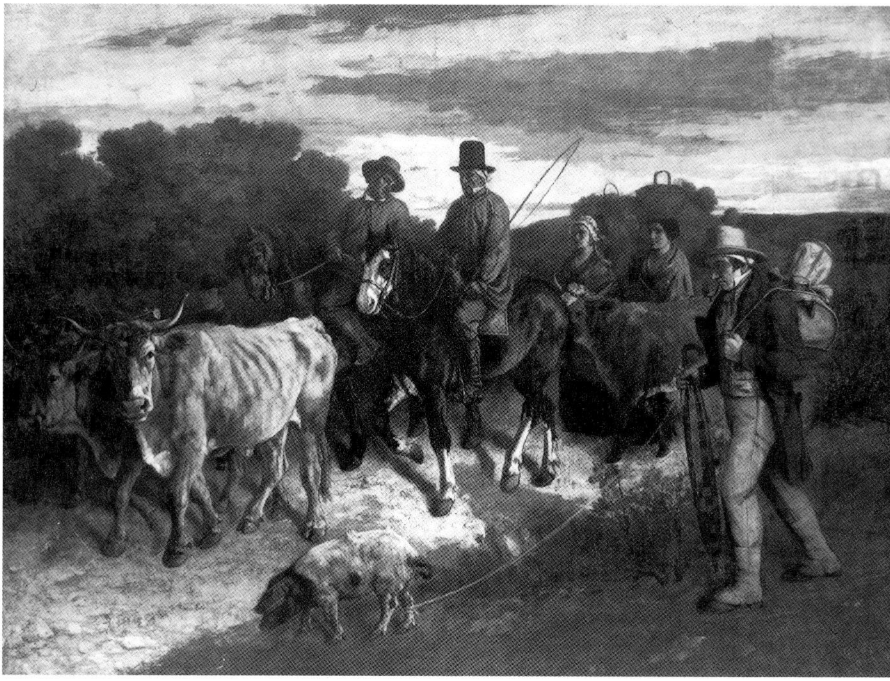

54 *The Peasants of Flagey Returning from the Fair*, 1850 (reworked 1855). Oil on canvas, 208.5 x 275 cm, 82⅛ x 108¼ in.

means by "enlargement" is Courbet's turning away from concrete subjects taken from contemporary life to a more diffuse, varied, and, although Castagnary never says it in so many words, a less politically provocative kind of subject. "Without exactly fleeing humanity, [Courbet] now considered to a greater extent the sky and the sea, leafage and snow, animals and flowers. He loved them with a particularly tender feeling." Courbet's abandonment of his earlier projects, the depiction of contemporary, popular subjects, Castagnary breathlessly mythologizes as a fantastic voyage of discovery into the mysteries of nature, a *symboliste* journey into an invigorating realm of the unknown:

> Avid to see and to penetrate the world open to his observation, he had in his quest the happy surprises of the ancient navigators: he discovered virgin territories where no one had yet set foot, aspects and forms of landscape of which one might say that they were unknown before his arrival. He climbed free heights where his lungs could expand; he plunged into mysterious caves; he was curious about unnamed places, unknown retreats. Each time he plunged thus into the deep bosom of Nature, he was like a man who has gone through a beehive and comes out of it covered with honey; he returned weighed down with perfume and poetry.

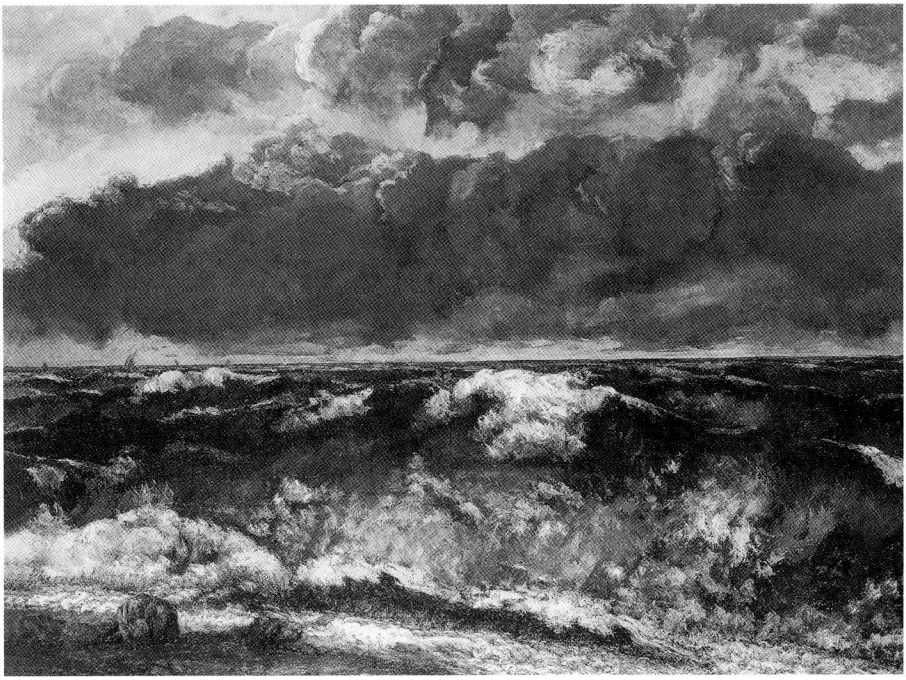

55 *The Wave*, 1870. Oil on canvas, 112 x 144 cm, 44⅛ x 56¾ in.

The penetration of the unknown and of nature, the transformation of nature into landscape – these are Courbet's triumphs [55], and poetry the prize of this mythic daring. *Poetry* – once more this word comes to the fore in the Third Republic's image of Courbet. If Mantz's Courbet, the Courbet of 1878, had been a painter plagued by weakness, who from time to time succumbed to the lure of poetry more or less in spite of himself, Castagnary's Courbet is a painter for whom poetic sensibility is a defining virtue. An exquisite sensibility, an incomparable technique, with these, "Courbet has made a new stream of poetry gush forth," declares the critic.

Yet even this is not enough to justify Courbet as a great painter, an artist hero of the Third Republic. To complete his project, Castagnary feels another step must be taken. Courbet must be made secure not merely within the feminine bosom of nature but within the more masculine precincts of tradition – French tradition above all. To secure tradition for Courbet and Courbet for tradition, however, Castagnary must temporarily abandon his Courbet the poetic landscape painter, and return to the earlier Courbet, the pictorial translator of the social realities of his time.

Having established firm historical precedents in the Dutch school of the seventeenth century, in the German Holbein, and the Spaniard Velázquez, all of whom, like Courbet, represented the society of their times with unmediated veracity, Castagnary turns to the tradition of France itself, above all, that established by the major artists of the preceding hundred years. In his penultimate paragraph he calls forth that grand procession of painters of living history in which his Courbet will now take a place. Castagnary calls the role with rhetorical questions: "Did not Louis David look for truth above all, when, seizing the events of his time, he sketched *The Oath of the Tennis Court* and captured on canvas the portrait of the murdered Marat?" "And Gros?" he continues, "Has there ever been anyone more taken with contemporary events, more in love with the human spectacle? The whole society of his time lives again in his painting. And Géricault?" Castagnary demands, "In what path was he going when death stopped him. Is not *The Raft of the Medusa* a simple *fait divers de journal* writ large, dramatized, and translated into painting by means of the most eloquent of compositions?" Courbet's art is authorized by precedents at once national and revolutionary, in the broadest sense of the term. By this process, innovation itself can be justified by precedent, daring assimilated to the best of tradition and transformed from contemporary scandal into cultural contribution.

I might say, parenthetically, that, of all the strategies employed to transform the ambiguous Courbet of the pre-republican period to Courbet the culture hero of 1889, the strongest and most enduring is the one based on the premise that there is in fact an ongoing and continuous stream of great art with which the artist can be fused. This is that same tradition that Harold Bloom has recourse to in his formulation of the great (male) writer, and the lack of which Virginia Woolf postulated as equally responsible for the difficulties faced by his female counterparts when, in *A Room of One's Own*, she declared, "But whatever effect discouragement and criticism had upon their writing ... that was unimportant compared with the other difficulty which faced them when they came to set their thoughts on paper – that is that they had no tradition behind them, or one so short and partial that it was of little help." Nor is the avant-garde by any means immune to the blandishments of tradition when it comes to asserting their claims to greatness. It was Guillaume Apollinaire who, in 1912, established the pedigree of Cubism as a valid art by declaring that "Courbet was the father of the new painters," as though this recourse to the tradition of French art, albeit a revolutionary tradition, in some way justified the new movement.

To return to Castagnary's account of Courbet, it is not so much that the critic, a good, leftish republican, eliminates Courbet's politics from his painting in his account of the artist, but that he neutralizes it. For Castagnary's Courbet was not being outrageous when he painted his *Stonebreakers* or his *Burial at Ornans*, he was simply following something called the dictates of the times: he could hardly have done otherwise. "Certainly," Castagnary asserts, "in 1848, at the time when Pierre Dupont rimed the miseries of the workers and when George Sand wrote *La Mare au diable*, there was nothing excessive in the fact that a painter, born of the people, republican by custom and education, took for the subject of his art the peasants and burghers of the milieu in which his childhood had unfolded. The humility of his subjects in no way militated against their aesthetic value; the important thing was to treat them with force and seriousness. In painting them on a natural scale, in giving them the force and character which had hitherto been reserved for gods and heroes, he created an artistic revolution." So much for Courbet the political painter. This is the Courbet of the survey of art history and of canned culture. With very few changes, Castagnary's paragraph could serve as the catalogue introduction for a present-day Courbet exhibition without attracting any particular notice. Castagnary's construction of Courbet is not so far from what one might term the contemporary "mainstream" view of Courbet.

But what of Courbet the political activist of recent memory, his undeniable participation in the Commune, his implication in the destruction of the Vendôme Column?[6] Castagnary first of all dulls the effect of Courbet the Communard by carefully embedding his brief account of the matter in a more general one of Courbet's patriotic activities during the defense of Paris that preceded it and the unjust severity of the punishment that followed. This technique resembles that of the child who disguises the taste of a particularly unappetizing morsel of food by embedding it in a heavy coating of mashed potatoes.

In the second place, Castagnary effectively detaches Courbet from his own political activity by constructing Courbet the Communard entirely in the passive voice. The Commune, by implication, was simply something that happened to poor, unwise Courbet. "Named member of the Commune in the complementary elections of April 16," Castagnary explains, "he did not have the wisdom to decline this mandate .... After the taking of Paris by the troops of Marshall MacMahon, he was arrested, led a prisoner to Versailles, and included in the general accusation which weighed on all the members of the Commune, accused more specifically of having toppled the Vendôme Column." With this latter issue, Castagnary breaks out of the passivity of historical apologia into contemporary indignation. "The Vendôme Column!" Castagnary explodes. "He was as foreign to the affair as you or I." And Castagnary has the documents to prove this. There follows an account of Courbet's trial, his imprisonment, the wild exaggeration of his fine, and his exile, followed by the assertion that concludes Castagnary's discussion of the political Courbet: "With his death, hatreds and rivalries are obliterated and justice, which was silent, rises to formulate the indisputable judgment." What Castagnary means, of course, is that Courbet the artist has been redeemed by history, while Courbet the Communard has conveniently been forgotten. The Commune, then, was simply something that happened to poor, naïve Courbet, his complicity in the destruction of the column simply part of a plot on the part of the closed-minded and the envious to discredit – and ultimately, to destroy – the artist.

In a way, this sounds like a credible account. It goes along with the Courbet we have become familiar with during the course of this text – a countryman, not too bright, a powerful observer and recorder of peasant customs, a poet deeply involved with nature and intuitively capable of transforming it into substantial art, gullible, enamoured with his own not too clear-headed ideas, quick to fall under the sway of political agitators – a marvellous, mindless artist who unwittingly got himself into trouble.

This sounds like the truth and seems to be supported by a certain amount of evidence. Or, at the very least, one might say that it is the consensus of Courbet's supporters in the first decade following the artist's death. Yet not quite. Before we accept this as a balanced view of Courbet, we should at least become aware that other views – positive views, that is – were possible. We should realize that another Courbet could be articulated in 1878, a very different one from any of those we have been considering: a Courbet for whom the experience of the Commune was central, a Courbet whose political and artistic practice were seen as inseparable – two sides of a single being, rather than opposing tendencies. This is the Courbet of Jules Vallès, novelist, journalist, and fellow Communard, who wrote about his Courbet a week after the artist's death, on January 6, 1878, under the name Jean de la Rue, when Vallès himself was still in exile in England.

In Vallès's account of Courbet, it is the Commune that provides the controlling imagery for Courbet's achievement. Far from trying to detach the artist from his political activism, he centers his Courbet within it. He begins his obituary notice solemnly, with the column itself: "The Column has lost its hostage; the one who had to pay the damages." Nor is the image of Courbet he creates that familiar one of the passive, bumbling political naïf, but rather, of a lucid participant. "Man of peace, thrust into battle, he looked for the blow he could strike without any arms," Vallès explains. "He who painted *The Spinner*, *The Stonebreakers*, the *Burial at Ornans* inevitably had to be – the day when he had to choose – on the side of labor, poverty, and paving stones." Unlike Castagnary, who spares no effort to exonerate Courbet in the affair of the destruction of the Vendôme Column, Vallès credits him with participation in the event. "Poor mad man," says Vallès ironically, "you don't attack bronze fetishes with impunity." But no, he goes on, "He wasn't so crazy; he knew perfectly well what would happen to him. The day that the Column was toppled, he was there, at the *Place*, with his twenty-sou cane, his four-franc straw hat, his ready-made overcoat .... 'It'll crush me as it falls, you'll see!' he said, turning to a group of friends."

If Vallès's Courbet, like Mantz's and Castagnary's, is a man of nature, it is a very different relationship of artist to nature that Vallès projects. If for Courbet's other biographers, Courbet the nature lover, the painter of landscapes, the countryman is constructed as the redemptive antithesis to Courbet the man of the left and of political scandal, for Vallès, nature is firmly united with the political. In Vallès's final peroration, the final paragraph of his obituary for a dead friend, nature itself is politicized, swept up into the élan of the vanished Commune:

> He crossed the great streams; he plunged into the ocean of the crowds; he heard the heart of a people beat like the thuds of a cannon; he ended up in the heart of nature, in the midst

> of trees, breathing the scents which had intoxicated him in his youth, beneath a sky unstained by the fumes of great massacres, but which tonight, perhaps, set ablaze by the setting sun, will spread itself out on the house of the dead man like a great red flag.

Finally, far from trying to aggrandize his Courbet by inserting him into a great tradition, Vallès explicitly cuts his artist off from it: his Courbet was a "deserter" who boldly rejected the barracks of established art, and was singled out for punishment because of that. "The pistol shots that are fired against tradition, even when the barrel of the pistol is a paint brush, disturb the tranquillity or the servility of those who lick their fingers over paintings, who lick their fingers over ministers," declares Vallès. This shooting against tradition irritates even the independent spirits, who, although they may be worthy in the face of people, are cowardly when it comes to theories. If Delacroix had been alive, would he have saved Courbet from execution, if Courbet had started to say, with his coarse laugh, speaking of the Louvre ceiling, or the frescoes of Saint-Sulpice, of *The Entry of the Crusaders into Constantinople*, "You actually knew them, then, you, Apollo, and Saint Thingamabob and Jesus Christ?" The bourgeois, Vallès concludes bitterly, are more pitiless than the soldiers. Not for Vallès the easy connection of Courbet with an existing tradition of great art. On the contrary, it is Courbet's difference, his irrevocable disjunction even from the most innovative achievements of the recent past that arouses Vallès's admiration and sympathy.

If I have cited Vallès's text last and at length, it is not because it is "right" and the others "wrong," but rather to indicate that like his the others are selections, constructions, based on an ultimately limitless material; that the "facts" in each case are chosen; that the vision of the artist embodied in each text, far from being a mere recounting or commonsense description is to a greater or lesser extent a work of creation, like a short story or a novel but with different intentions, strategies, and premises. Vallès's text, then, must not be taken as an antidote but rather as an alternative, the alternative of an outsider, a *réfractaire*, an alternative that, however, sets the basically constructed and ideological character of all the other accounts of his time into the sharpest possible relief.

At the present time, when the artist's biography is introduced more and more to explain the work of art, it is interesting – if not particularly original – to consider how the artist's biography, or rather the texts that set forth the artist, are no more privileged as empirical givens – as a species of raw data – than the art works themselves that such texts are called on to explain. Rather, they are complex constructions. Artists' biographies must be considered as artistic creations, mediating the various ideological and psychological positions of those who create them.

8 | Courbet, Oller, and a Sense of Place: The Regional, The Provincial, and the Picturesque in Nineteenth-Century Art

The slogan "il faut être de son temps" has often been cited as central to the conception of nineteenth-century Realism. "One must be of one's times" was the battle cry of Courbet and his followers: the admonition to reject the atemporal generalization of classical art or the anachronistic historicism of the Romantics and turn instead to the contemporary world in all its detailed concreteness for inspiration. Yet no less crucial to the Realist project, it would seem to me, was another admonition, sometimes related to, sometimes in contradiction with, the concern to be of one's times: "One must be of one's place" – that is to say, the injunction to deal with one's native country, region, or even, at its most extreme, one's own property (for this, essentially, is what John Constable did, spending his life painting his father's mills and the river Stour within a two-mile radius of the family lands) in order to grasp the singularity, the concrete veracity of reality as well as one's deepest and most authentic relation to it.

This injunction to be of one's place, in the case of both Gustave Courbet, the Frenchman from Ornans, and the Puerto Rican painter Francisco Oller (1833–1917), is even more central than the admonition to be of one's times. "Il faut être de son temps" seems somehow more germane to the up-to-date modernity of a basically urban vision like Manet's. To be of one's place implies an attachment to more lasting values, to a certain type of natural scene associated with rural life and folk customs. Indeed, one might say of Courbet that for no other painter outside of Constable did the well-loved and well-known physiognomy of his native countryside play such a seminal role in the creation of the work. A vivid sense of place is central to Courbet's achievement.

The American writer and critic Eudora Welty has claimed that creating a sense of place is one of the most effective ways that the writer has to maintain the ties of his work to reality. Place, says Welty, is where the writer has his roots: "Place is where he stands; in his experience out of which he writes it provides the base of reference, in his work the point of view .... Location pertains to feeling, feeling profoundly pertains to place."[1] Although she was writing about *Wuthering Heights* and *The Sound and the Fury* and thinking about the deep South from which she came, her words apply with equal appositeness to Courbet's *Oak of Flagey* [pl.13, pp.142–43] and to his Franche-Comté landscapes generally. They apply to a painter like Oller as well, as we shall see.

"Place" of course, referred in the nineteenth century, as today, to what was by definition the regional, the marginal, the peripheral. It was so defined by a dominant code in which the classical in the form of an imaginary Greco-Roman or biblical generalization functioned as the transgeographic – the *atopical*, so to speak. Or occasionally, provincial life might be presented in a suitably sweetened, idealized form as the "picturesque." But in general, one might say that a sense of place, in the form of provincialism or regionalism, was something the ambitious artist wished to discard rather than encourage in the mid-nineteenth century. Then, as now, power accrued from immersion in the so-called mainstream, in acquiescence to an imaginary ideal of the placeless.

How might a sense of place be constructed in the middle of the nineteenth century? The problem must be contextualized historically as well as geographically. A sense of place is obviously going to be construed differently in France in the nineteenth century in the context of Realism versus Academic-Classical and Romantic art than in Puerto Rico in the 1880s or 1890s – or today.

Courbet, in his monumental and ambitious *Burial at Ornans* [pl.2, pp.66–67], has insisted upon the ungeneralized, unidealized configuration of his own gnarled, unclassical, rocky countryside, the Franche-Comté, as a basic ingredient in his construction of a sense of place – harsh, unmodulated, insistently horizontal – and in the same way, insisted on a direct, unprettified representation of his fellow citizens of Ornans, which was interpreted as caricature, or in some cases, like that of the red noses of the beadles, as sacrilege by many viewers and most critics at the Salon of 1850–51.

But in addition, Courbet felt the need of a new kind of contentious visual language with which to state his opposition to the dominant code of representation of his time; he found it in popular imagery, the crude simplified woodcuts of so-called *imagerie d'Epinal*. Popular imagery offered two different but related variables to Courbet's construction of a sense of place: first, a mode of composition which, in its simplicity, directness, reduction, and naïveté, could signify "Le Peuple" and the cultural values associated with the 1848 Revolution, which had stressed both the popular and, to some degree, the regional and the folkloric. Secondly, in the context of 1848, an art related to popular imagery, in its apparently willful stiffness and gracelessness, on the enormous and "arrogant" scale of the *Burial*, could be read as provocative, oppositional, and even revolutionary. The sense of place conveyed by Courbet's painting understood in these terms was decidedly subversive of the dominant culture.

It is interesting to look at Francisco Oller's work from the vantage point of a sense of place and its pictorial construction. It is clear that, like Courbet in the *Burial* or his *Funeral Preparations* (a work, now overpainted, which underlies his much altered painting, *Toilette de la mariée*, now in the collection of Smith College) Oller too wished, in his major work, *El Velorio* (*The Wake*) of 1893 [56], to convey a sense of *both* his native region and, perhaps less consciously and with more difficulty, a sense of *himself as a Puerto Rican artist* – not just someone who comes to Puerto Rico to paint local color. In the same way, Courbet had insisted on conveying a sense of being an Ornanais, not just a tourist visiting Ornans.

In contrast to the Scottish painter John – known as "Spanish" – Phillip's treatment of a similar theme from Spanish popular culture, *La Gloria*, of 1864, where figures are idealized and smoothed out, the bereft mother assimilated to sentimental English notions of maternal grief; and where the colorful crowd is united in a smooth, theatrical dance – that is to say, where composition is unified and harmonized by conventional, sentimental narrative strategies and an idealized figure style – Oller, insisting on an insider's critical discourse rather than a tourist's patronizing and glamorizing one, creates a strikingly different image. Indeed, Oller, in *The Wake*, while intending to body forth an "orgy of brutish appetites under the guise of gross superstition" (his own statement), succeeds in creating an image which is much more interesting than a mere condemnation would be.[2] "Location pertains to feeling, feeling profoundly pertains to place," said Eudora Welty. It is precisely amid these "brutish appetites," these "gross superstitions" that Oller the Puerto Rican has his roots. Yet at the same time, as a member of the cultivated Puerto

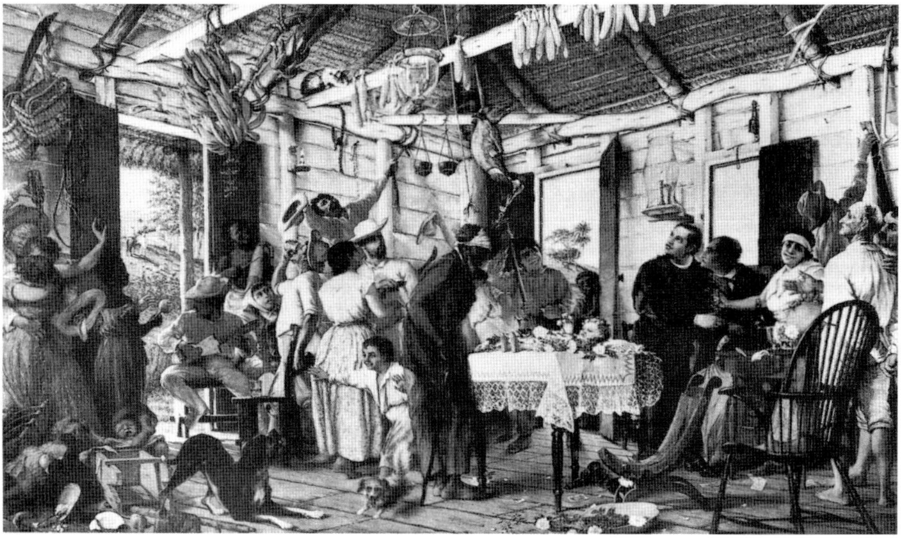

56 **Francisco Oller,** *El Velorio* (*The Wake*), 1893. Oil on canvas, 258.6 x 458.9 cm, 101¾ x 180¾ in.

Rican middle class, the tree itself (to continue the analogy) had grown and flourished far away, in France, in Spain, and within cosmopolitan vanguard and academic circles in both countries. *The Wake*, it seems to me, represents an attempt to reconcile tree and roots, as it were, under the guise of social or, more precisely, moral criticism.

It is clear that Oller has a profound attachment to the folkloric details, the accurate descriptive configuration of Puerto Rican popular and rural customs of the times. And of course, he relished the still-life aspects of the scene: the plantains; the baskets hanging from the rafters; the structure of the house itself; the lace of the table cover: all have been depicted with loving, one might almost say with a deliberately obsessive specificity. Indeed, there is a certain sense of willed naïveté, of deliberate exaggeration of awkward gestures, a separation of individual elements into independent statements which may, on the one hand, harken back to the broad comedic mode established by Courbet in *The Return from the Meeting* of 1863, a painting also highly critical of the clergy, a work Oller may in fact have seen in France at a time when he was probably in contact with Courbet and his circle. But on the other hand, although this is mere speculation on my part, it would seem to me that Oller may have turned to some form of local popular art for inspiration. Crude broadsides? Cheap, mass-produced lithographs? Journalistic caricature? I don't know which or what, but still the impact of popular art, probably some form of Hispanic popular art, makes itself felt in the anti-academic, generally anti-High Art, anti-mainstream characteristics of *The Wake*.

In addition, Oller's major work establishes its oppositional character by refusing to be a "pretty" picture or an ingratiating or a unified one. Or rather, it relegates loveliness, along with a more sophisticated Impressionist style to the place it belongs: out the door, in the form of two deliberately contrasting landscape vignettes. The very ease and tranquillity of these vignettes offer a striking contrast to the crowding, awkwardness, and popular energy, even grotesquery, of the main interior space. It is not merely the rich mixture of physiognomic and racial types, or the recording of folk customs and rituals, which of course had had a vigorous tradition in Spanish even more than in French nineteenth-century painting, or even the incorporation of authentic Puerto Rican objects and elements, not to speak of the localism of the theme of the *baquiné* which establishes *The Wake* as an expression of national identity. Rather, it is its conscious and unconscious refusal to conform to contemporary standards of either the academic *or* the vanguard center – i.e., Paris or Spain of the 1890s – which makes it a difficult painting and at the same time, because of its very combination of awkwardness and ambition, confers upon it a genuine sense of place mediated through its author's conflicted but authentic sense of his Puerto Rican identity.

A sense of place can be closely allied to a sense of class, and therefore suggested by means of the human figures rather than literally described in a landscape or interior. Neither Oller nor Courbet relied simply on local color to communicate a sense of local experience in this case, which can be represented by Oller's drawing *Laundress* or Courbet's painting *Grain Sifters* [pl.5. p.70]. Rather, a certain kind of forceful drawing style, a marked deviation from conventions of benign, idealized generalization, a striking departure from the reigning notion of the charming or the acquiescent female worker separates both Courbet's and Oller's versions of the theme from the more regularized and prettified and universalized versions of a Breton or a Bastien-Lepage. Interestingly enough, it is a nearly contemporary drawing by the Dutchman van Gogh, *Peasant Woman Putting Corn in Sheaves* of 1884, that comes nearest to Oller's *Laundress* in some ways. Like Oller, van Gogh communicates a genuine sense of a specific type of peasant and of the backbreaking difficulty of routine manual labor through the deliberate anti-classicism of the pose and a boldly emphatic exaggeration of the awkwardness, crudeness, even, of the contour.

When we turn to Oller's portraits, such as *Colonel Contreras* (1880) or the poet *José Gautier Benítez* (1885), we confront a different problem and a different solution. Here, after all, we have the artist confronting men of his own class, his own type: outstanding figures, not typical ones; heroes and cultural leaders, not peasants. How can one reconcile the demands of a sense of place, conceived of as a sort of aesthetic-egalitarian imperative, with those of the signification of heroism, by definition an elitist notion? Oller chooses to emphasize the idea of the specificity of the heroic in *Colonel Contreras* by placing this figure in a landscape, which is clearly meant to serve as a background for the military prowess of the hero, who maintains a comfortable if dominating position within his native habitat, rather like Courbet in his rocky setting in the *Self-Portrait with a Black Dog*.

In the case of the quite beautiful and moving representation of the poet, José Gautier Benítez, the situation is more complicated. Despite the fact that Benítez was a strong nationalist as well as a Romantic poet, and converted "the geography and physical beauty of Puerto Rico into symbols of the growing national consciousness of the creole population;" a poet who "became one of the island's most popular writers" for singing "the praises of the beauty of the countryside,"[3] it is the romantic rather than the national aspect of Benítez's achievement that Oller has chosen to stress in this painting, which was done as a memorial after the poet's death, in 1880, as Courbet had painted his friend the philosopher P.-J. Proudhon after the latter's death in 1865. But whereas Courbet had chosen to emphasize the everydayness of Proudhon's setting, placing the anarchist in his backyard with his children, having him wear a workman's *blouse* and posing him looking up from scattered books, as though interrupted in the middle of work, Oller chooses not to dwell on the details of the authentic Puerto Rican landscape, but rather on the more cosmopolitan, romantic notion of the pathetic fallacy: nature transformed into an analogue of human emotions. The prominent gray clouds in the sky convey a sense of melancholy, in conjunction with the low horizon and the thistle with its yellow flowers; and the leafless branches of the bushes behind the poet undoubtedly symbolize "the grief of Nature at the loss of her bard."[4]

In this poignant painting, then, we are confronted by a genuine dilemma faced, now as then, by the provincial or so-called provincial artist vis-à-vis a sense of place: that is, the need to adhere to the codes of the mainstream versus the desire to create a sense of national and personal identity through the language of art. This was, and still is, a source of conflict. After all, what other ways are there of communicating with a large, confirmatory audience and feeling that one has succeeded in terms of high quality, of genuine excellence in a craft one has struggled to perfect over many years, except in terms of the standards of the mainstream? The alternative to so-called universality (i.e., adherence to the criteria established by the centers of power) then as now was marginality or lack of "quality." Then as now, universality was understood to be identical with high quality, and both were felt to be identified with the center, the art world. In Oller's terms, the appropriate setting for a hero of Puerto Rican culture, suitable for asserting his genius, was one that played down the sense of specific place in favor of the aura of universal meaning.

For nineteenth-century artists like Courbet and Oller, who were painting during what might be called, to borrow a phrase from John Berger, "the moment of landscape," this genre was most important of all in establishing a sense of place. For Courbet, for example, *The Oak of Flagey*, which he subtitled "Chêne de Vercingétorix, Camp de César près d'Alésia" when he showed it at his private exhibition in 1867, was an image rich in implications: personal, in that the oak could be read as a kind of self-image of the artist, rooted in his native soil of Flagey, near Ornans; political, in the association of the tree with Vercingetorix, the Gallic chieftain who had died for the cause of his people's national struggle against Julius Caesar at the Battle of Alesia, and whom Courbet could identify with the French left's struggle against the modern Caesar, Napoleon III; historical, in that the oak had been associated both with the Tree of Liberty of the French Revolution and with popular notions of national self-determination (i.e., the Great Oak of Guernica). In short, without being directly symbolic, the painting of the oak – like landscape in general – could convey a range of implications, rooted in local meanings and concretized in the historic oak of Flagey.

Like Courbet's oak, one might imagine that Oller's *Palms* conveyed a range of implications, personal and political, as well as national. (This was, of course, before the adaptation of the palm as the logo of the statehood party in the twentieth century.) It is hard to believe, certainly, that the *Landscape with Royal Palms* [57] could be "just another motif" for Oller on his return to Puerto Rico from France in about 1897. The dominating uprightness of the central palm, isolated from its smaller, more wavering neighbors; the overgrown pathway; and the crumbling fence give the image overtones that go beyond the merely picturesque or the aesthetically satisfying. Indeed, one might well be tempted to subtitle it, following Courbet's lead, "The Great Palm of Borínquen: Tree of Puerto Rican National Identity." For, like the oak for Courbet, the palm must have had for Oller an emblematic as well as a merely pictorial significance.

But the styles of these paintings, the means used to convey the sense of place, are very different. In Oller's *Palms*, the open brushwork, the high-keyed color, the attempt to embed light and atmosphere in the very fabric of the image point to his recent trip to France and his contact with Pissarro. His style is a signifier not of Puerto Rican identity but of what, for Oller, was the latest stylistic fashion in France. For some observers of the time, the specifically Puerto Rican implications of the work – its very sense of place, in fact – might have been felt to be attenuated, even contradicted, by the aesthetic vanguardism of its style. This can only be viewed as ironic, for Pissarro and Guillemet thirty years earlier had overtly associated their Impressionist style with the politics of revolutionary anarchism, as the letters from these artists to Oller reveal.[5] But in the context of Puerto Rican art at the end of the nineteenth century, such a stylistic language seems more to proclaim the artist's affiliation with international Modernism than with the concrete, national character of the motif it is employed to depict.

Oller himself may have been aware of such contradictions in his work of the 1890s. Whatever the reasons, he reverts to a more sober, less conspicuously "aesthetic" style in the landscapes of the turn of the century, those specifically dedicated to capturing a vanishing Puerto Rican past, representations of the obsolete sugar factories, a motif both objectively historical, personally nostalgic, and, of course, profoundly national at the same time – a time, it must be said, of great national turbulence during which the comforting emblems of a simpler, vanished way of life and the apparently unchanging verities of nature might seem particularly appealing.

Ultimately, however, Oller most successfully, if paradoxically, establishes a sense of place mediated by an original visual language in the form of still life. I say "paradoxically" because still life is often considered, to be the most neutral, inherently "pure" genre of all, a kind of abstraction before the fact, in which the artist is concerned only with formal relationships and nothing more. We, from Europe and North America, tend to think of apples and oranges as "neutral," "natural" still-life components, as though they were universals, and as though still lifes composed with them had no particular national identity. Oller, to a degree, shared this view. In *Guavas*, a still life heavily based on both Fantin-Latour and Cézanne, he simply substituted a tropical fruit, the guava, for a northern one and let this substitution stand for geographical difference. The same might be said of his *Mangóes* of 1901–3, which is even more strongly, I believe, based on a specific prototype, Cézanne's *Apples and Basket* (in the Bartlett Collection, Art Institute of Chicago), and which, despite the tropical subject, looks distinctively mainstream French, its Puerto

Rican products deliberately and coolly neutralized, an effect that is even more apparent if one compares this painting with the deliberately exoticized, primitivized still lifes of Gauguin. It is Gauguin the Frenchman, not Oller the Puerto Rican, who emphasizes the primitiveness of his still lifes by the way each object is clearly and "crudely" distinguished from the next, or set off by deliberate, angular outline, or presented on an up-tilted table to imply a mysterious, irrational primitive ritual or offering.

Obviously, then, it is not the subject matter *per se*, apples or guavas, that establishes a sense of place in still life. Indeed, Courbet, painting in prison after the fall of the Commune, in his still lifes with apples reminds us that there is nothing necessarily abstract or universal about apples. These dimpled, bumpy, juicy objects are not mere counters in a game of formal relationships but emblems of deep, personal yearning, of the lost pleasures of home and freedom. They can be experienced as concrete, sensuously differentiated tokens of place – at once desired and absent.

There is a group of Oller's still lifes that evokes a quality of profound rootedness in Puerto Rican reality. Certainly the subjects are the fruits of his native country and recognizably distinctive as "exotic"; certainly the impact of contemporary French still-life painting by Cézanne and Fantin-Latour is discernable. But equally present, as an important variable in a Latin American sense of place, is the impact of the Spanish Bodegón tradition, stretching back to the seventeenth century, with its moral seriousness and austerity offering a counter to French formalism and neutrality of the object. And this sense of moral weightiness, a solidity and heaviness at once

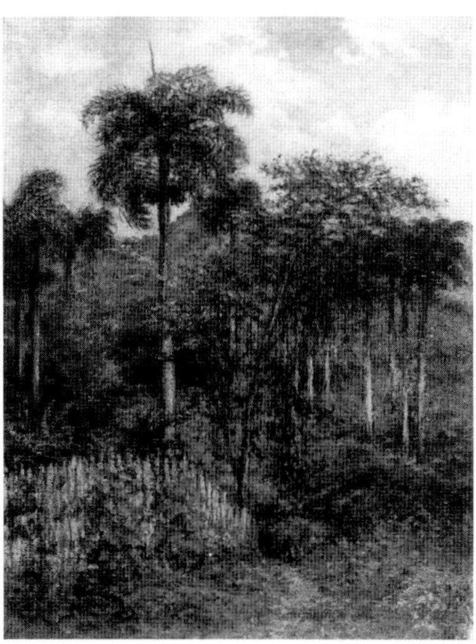

57 **Francisco Oller**, *Landscape with Royal Palms*, *c.*1897. Oil on canvas, 46.7 x 34.9 cm, 18⅜ x 13¾ in.

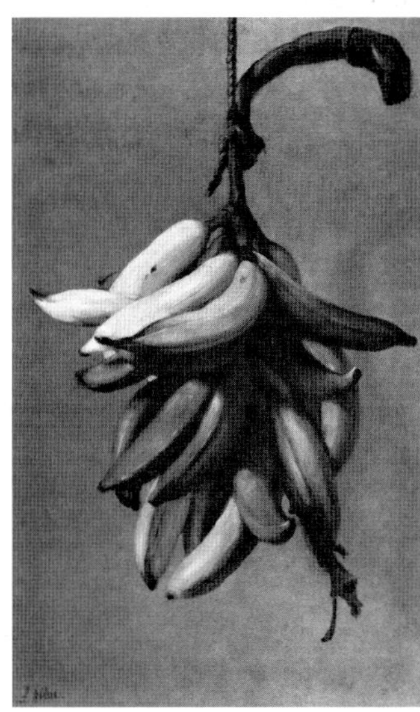

58 **Francisco Oller**, *Ripe Plantains*, 1892–93. Oil on canvas, 83 x 51.5 cm, 32⅝ x 20¼ in.

material and spiritual, achieved through pictorial concentration and the willed divestment of all extraneous distraction, marks Oller's still-life masterpiece of 1892–93, the *Ripe Plantains* [58]. Here the artist has managed to "monumentalize this simple fruit of the earth, which was the main staple of the Carribbean diet"[6] so that this Puerto Rican version of our daily bread assumes an unpretentious but almost sacramental solemnity. Here indeed, with minimal means and no apparent conflict, Oller has managed to project a sense of place, and of his own identity as an artist at the same time.

This discussion of Courbet, Oller, and a sense of place in nineteenth-century art has, I hope, raised more questions than it has answered: questions that are still central to the so-called provincial or marginal artist today. First of all, what do we mean by provincial and who decides who *is* provincial? Why was Cézanne's painting at Aix or Monet's at Etretat "mainstream," or central, whereas Oller's painting in Puerto Rico was not? Or, to put it another way, why was Cézanne's painting the Montagne Sainte-Victoire in Aix-en-Provence not considered regionalist? Or what if Pissarro had gone back to Saint Thomas to become the "national" painter of this Caribbean island, as Oller did for Puerto Rico? Clearly, the variables are not merely aesthetic ones, but relate to far broader issues of power and domination.

And what is the difference between what is thought of, generally in belittling terms, as provincialism, and what has come to be known as "regionalism," a positive expression of local difference? And further, what is the function of the picturesque in the nineteenth century? Does it function as a way in which the dominant culture may confirm its judgments of outsiders? Can one's equals ever be viewed as "picturesque"? Above all, one must confront the ongoing conflict, for the so-called provincial, often third-world, artist among the demands of the local culture, the expression of national identity, and the frequently internalized demands for high quality, in which quality is inevitably equated with the standards of the world center.

Yet at the same time, one must not underestimate the importance, expecially in the nineteenth and earlier twentieth century, but today as well, of modernity and modernization as liberating, expansionist concepts, which opened doors, knocked down walls, expanded the cramped, often conventional roles inflicted on people by traditional village culture. Both nineteenth- and twentieth-century fiction offers us many visions of the talented or the unusual individual oppressed by or languishing in restrictive, stultifying provincial settings, from *Madame Bovary* to the *Three Sisters*. The center, then – Paris above all for the nineteenth-century artist – should be thought of not just in terms of oppression or domination, but as the source of liberation and stimulation as well. In this conflict, so central to the meaning and direction of art, and indeed, of all cultural creation today, Francisco Oller stands as an exemplary figure, one whose importance extends far beyond the island which nourished him with that all-important sense of place.

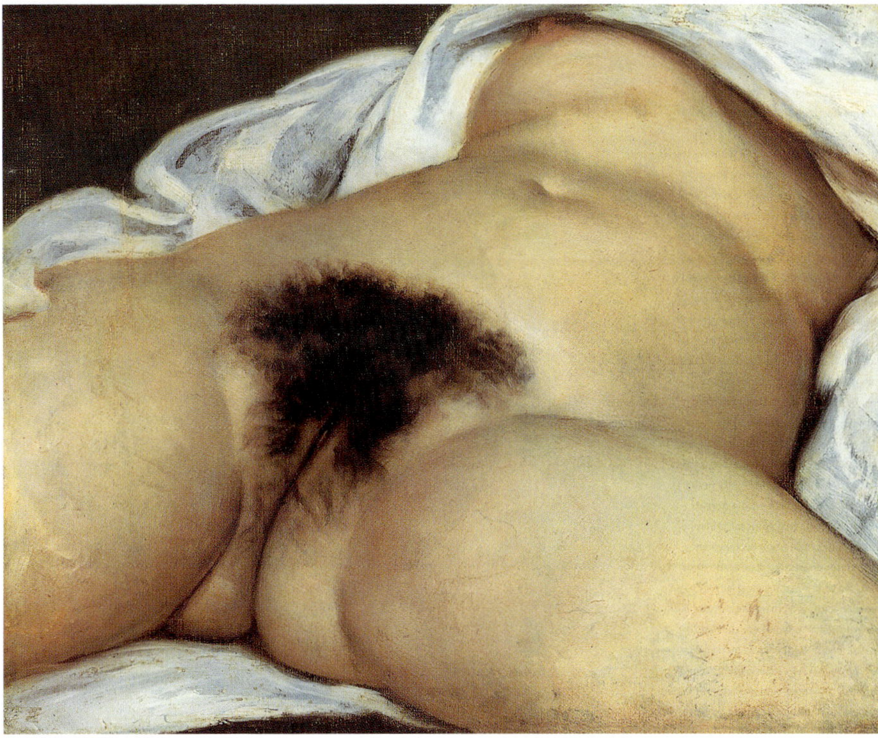

PLATE 10 *The Origin of the World*, 1866.
Oil on canvas, 46 x 55 cm, 18⅛ x 21⅝ in.

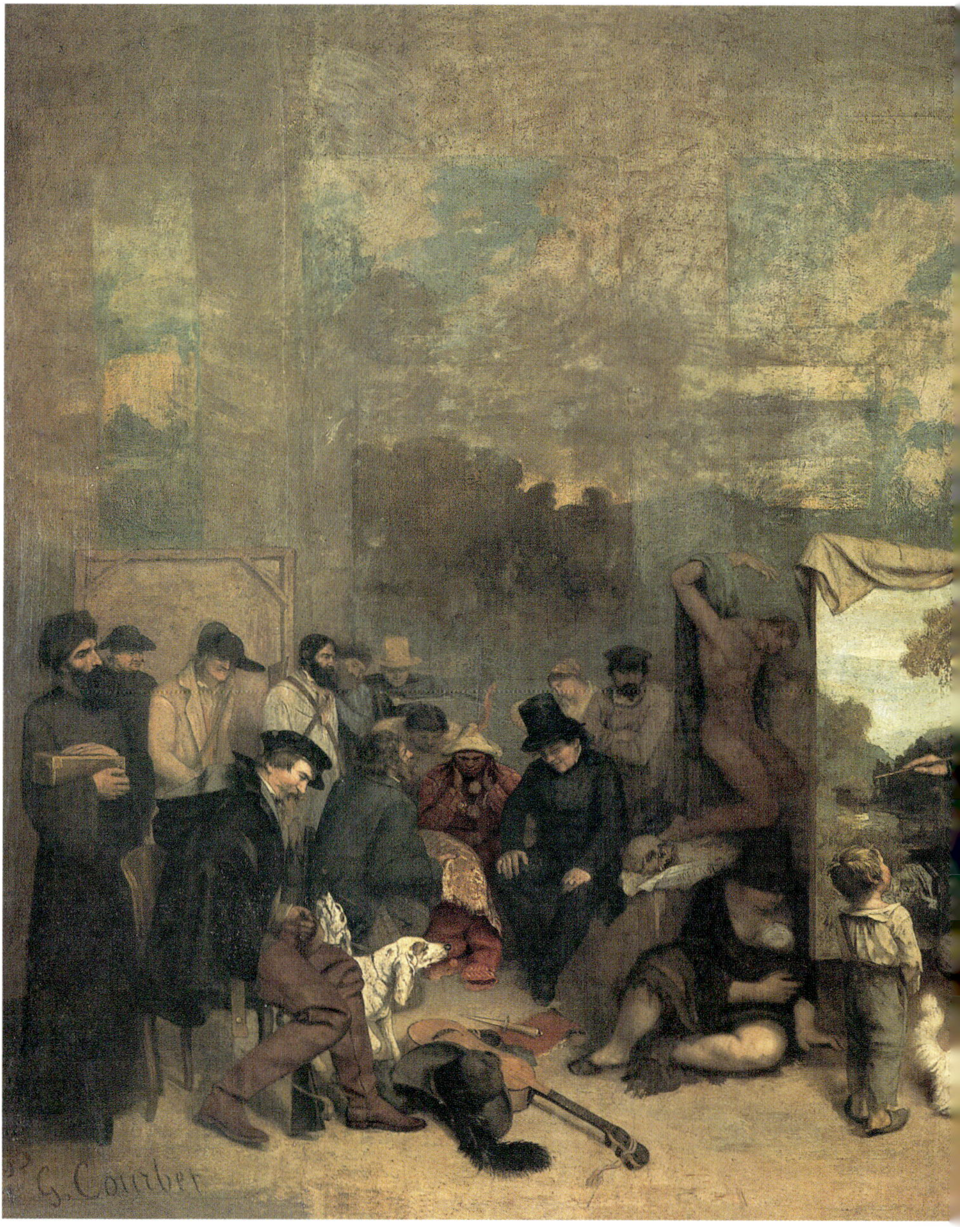

PLATES 11 AND 12 (detail, overleaf)
The Painter's Studio: A Real Allegory Summing Up Seven Years of My Artistic and Moral Life, 1855.
Oil on canvas, 359 x 598 cm, 142¼ x 235½ in.

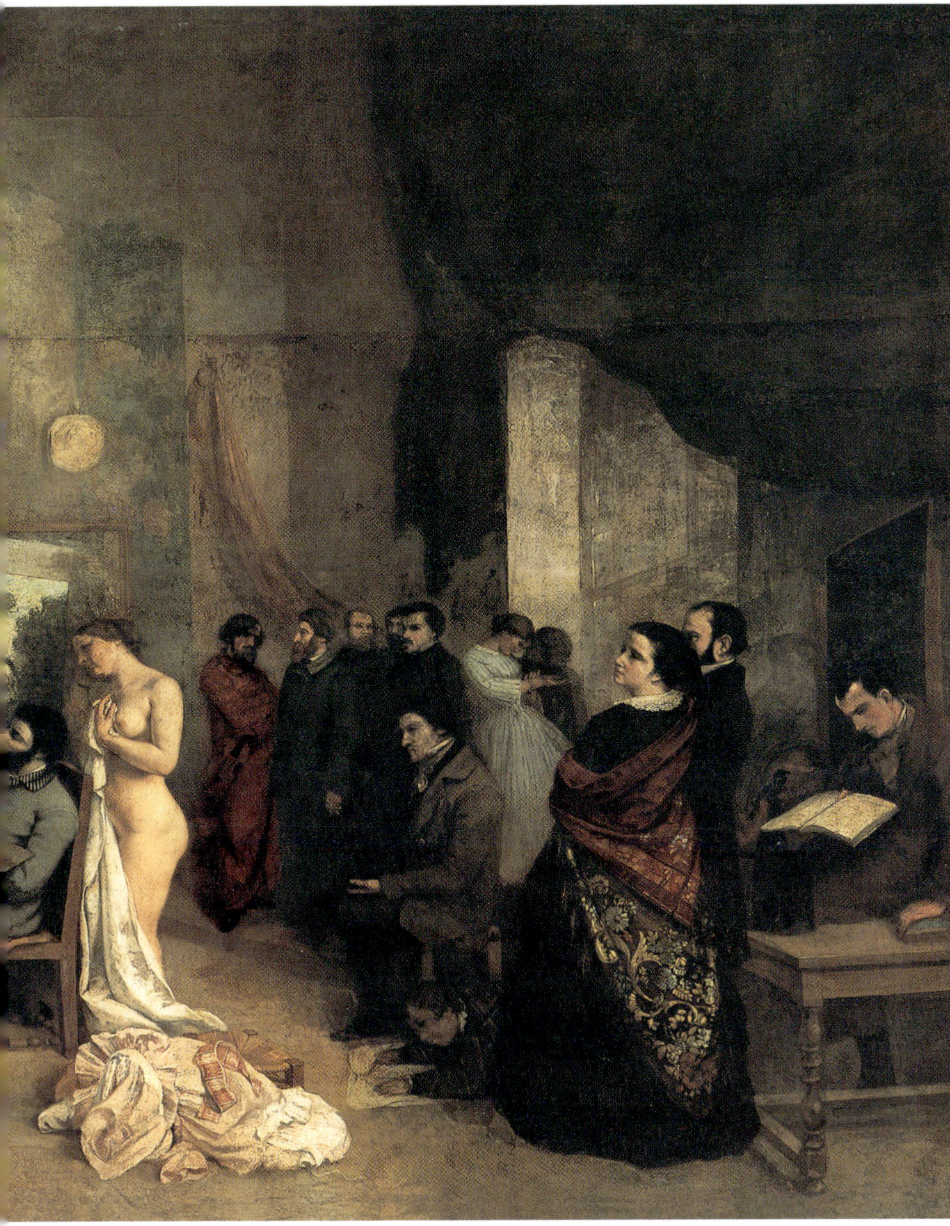

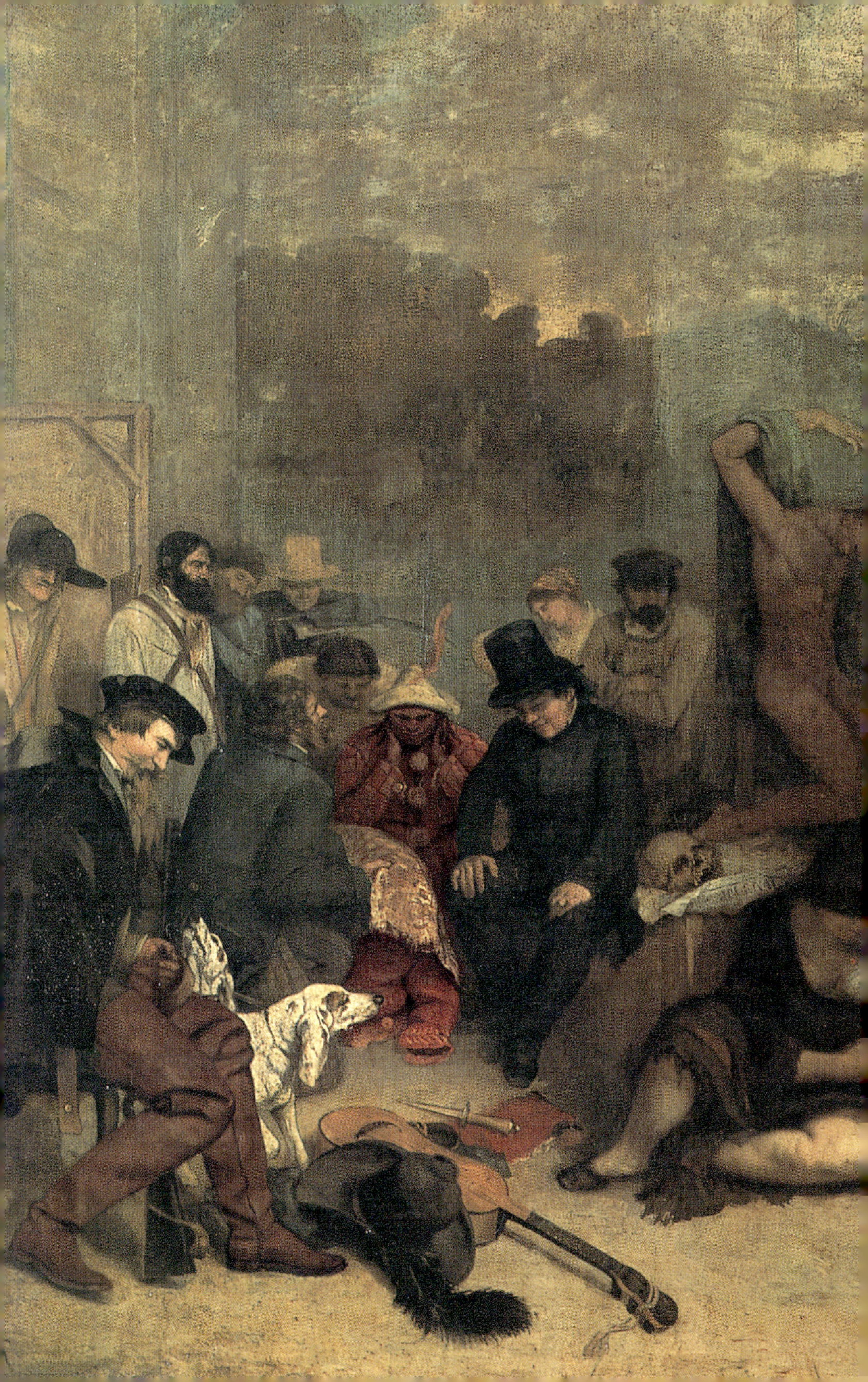

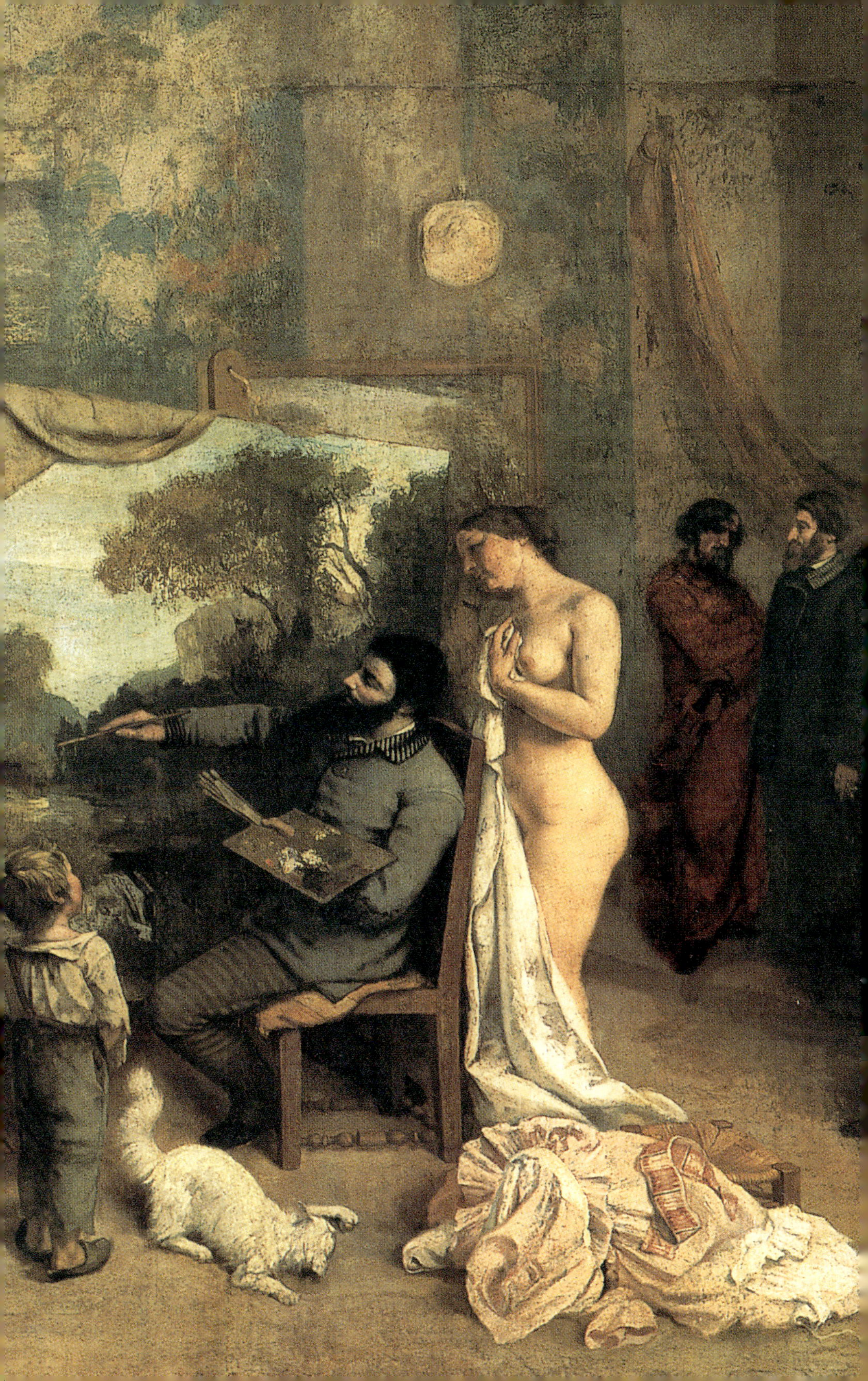

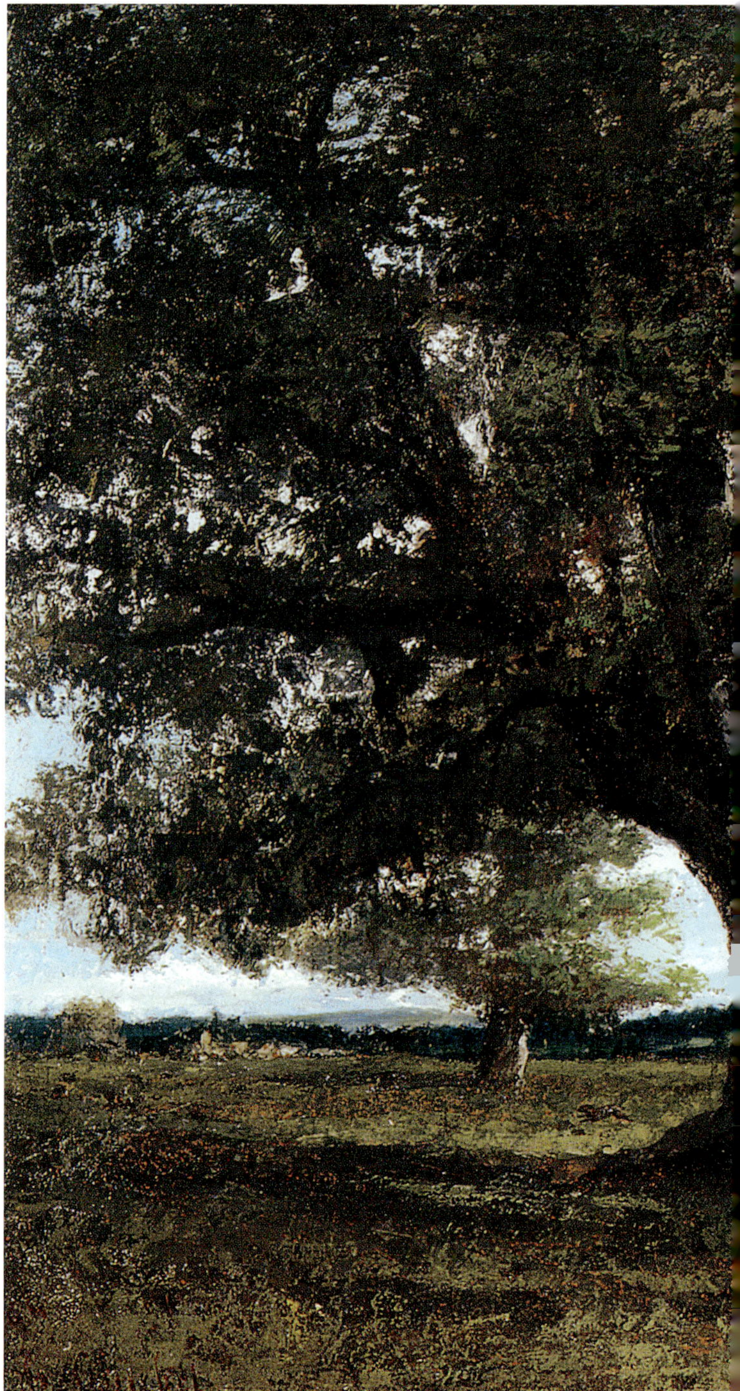

PLATES 13 AND 14
(detail, overleaf)
The Oak of Flagey, 1864.
Oil on canvas,
79 x 110 cm,
35 x 43⅜ in.

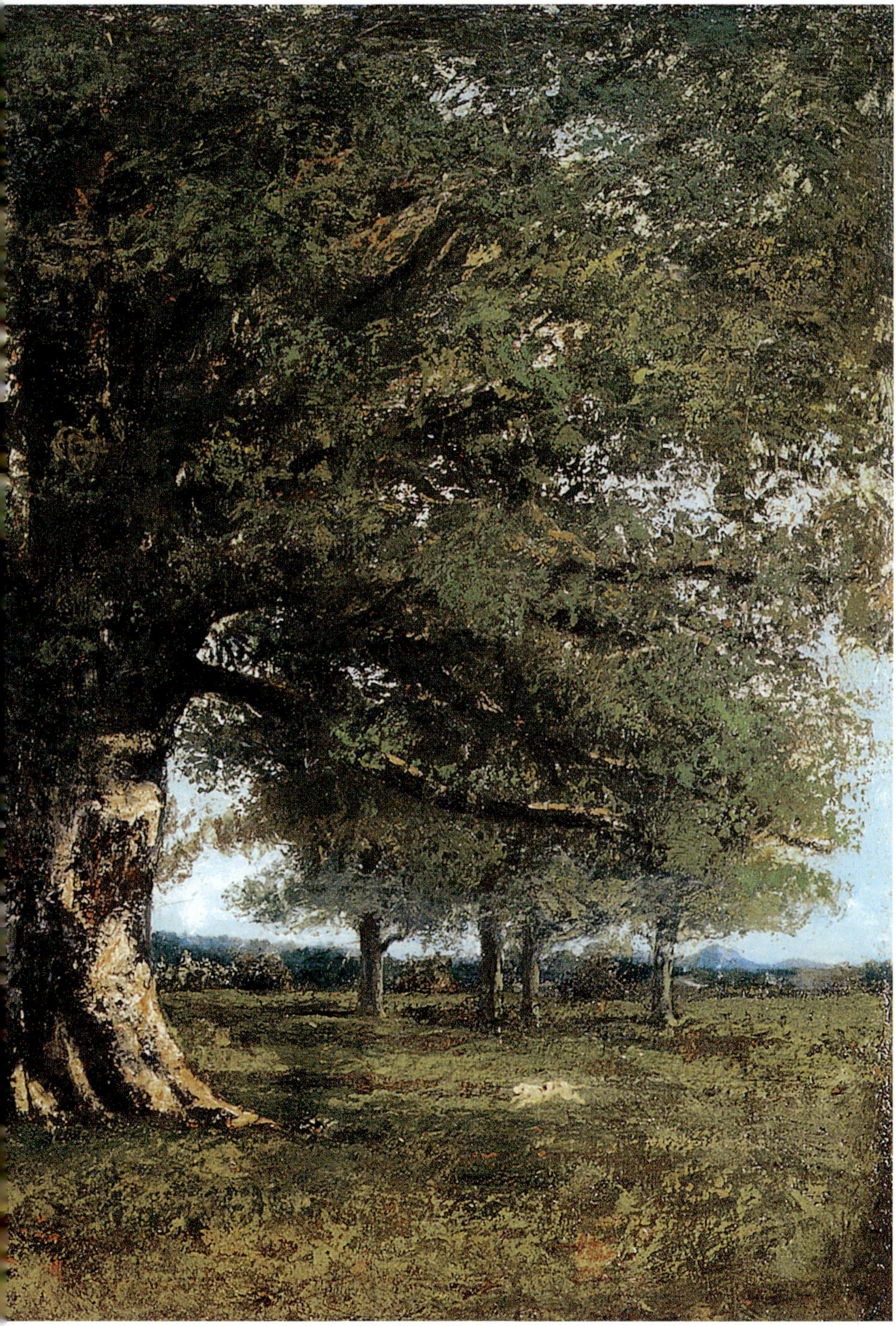

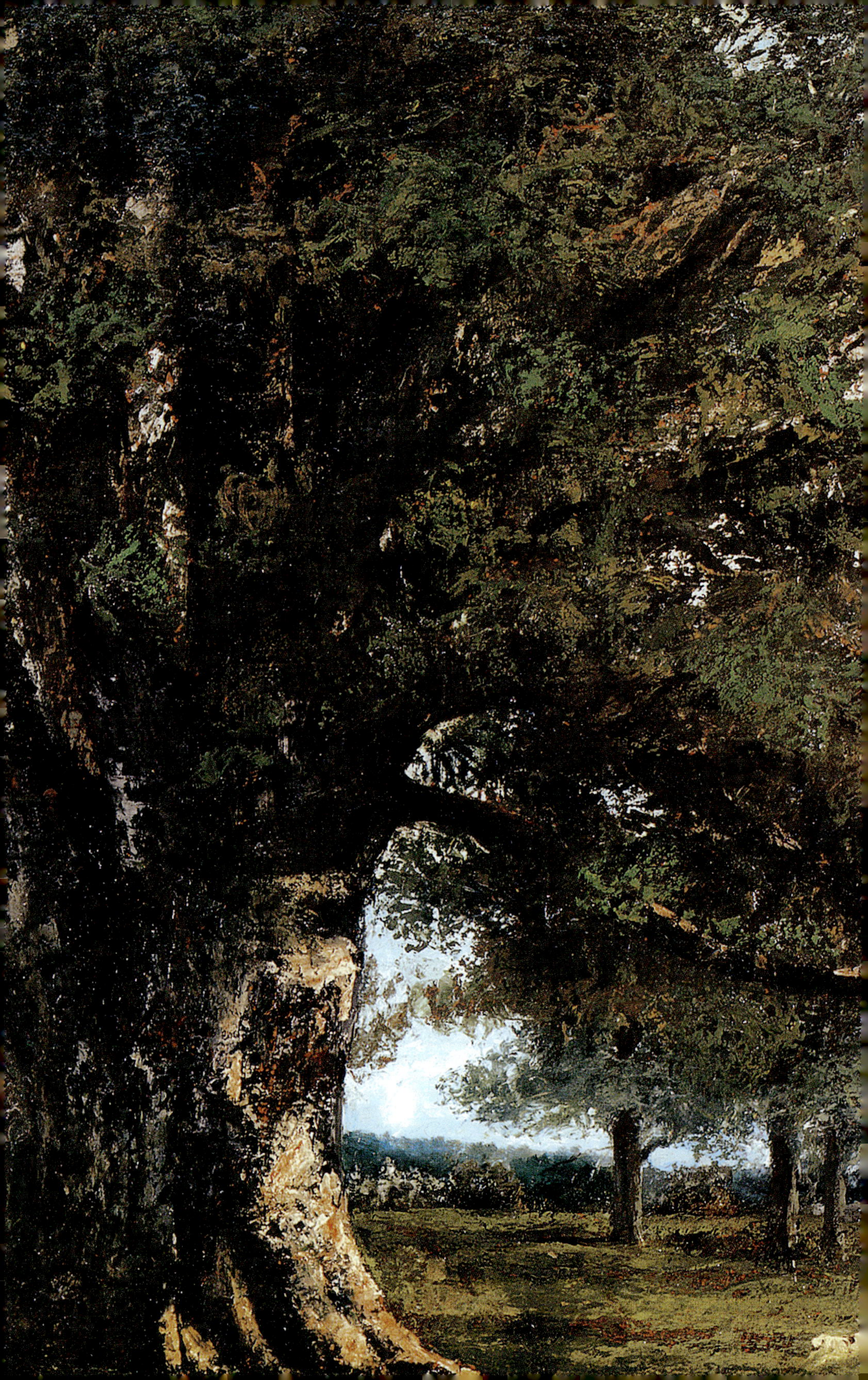

9 Courbet's *L'Origine du monde*: The Origin without an Original

Nothing could be more Freudian than the scenario I am about to rehearse in this narrative, for it concerns the endlessly repetitive quest for a lost original, an original which is itself, in both the literal and the figurative senses of the word, an origin. I am referring to Courbet's painting, *The Origin of the World* [pl.10, p.137], a work which is known to us only as a series of repeated descriptions or reproductions – an *Origin*, then, without an original [59]. But I shall also be discussing notions of origination and originality as they inform the discipline of art history itself: the founding notion that through the logic of research – i.e., the repetitive act of searching over and over again – one can finally penetrate to the ultimate meaning of a work of art. In the case of Courbet's *Origin*, this ultimate-meaning-to-be-penetrated might be considered the "reality" of woman herself, the truth of the ultimate Other. The subject represented in *The Origin* is the female sex organ – the cunt – forbidden site of specularity and ultimate object of male desire; repressed or displaced in the classical scene of castration anxiety, it has also been constructed as the very source of artistic creation itself.

The first part of my scenario has to do with a failure: the failure to locate the original of Courbet's *Origin of the World* for a forthcoming exhibition of the artist's work. I had gone about my art-historical business in the usual way: tracing the work back to its origin in the Courbet literature, and then, working forward, attempting to discover its present location – to no avail. Not only was the original *Origin* impossible to find, but the clues to its location seemed to be perversely, almost deliberately, misleading, fraught with errors in fact. Nor did the errors seem to me to be entirely fortuitous. Rumors that *The Origin*, now veiled behind a canvas by André Masson, was actually in the collection of Sylvie Bataille Lacan – former wife of both Georges Bataille and Jacques Lacan – seemed almost too good to be true, even when they were

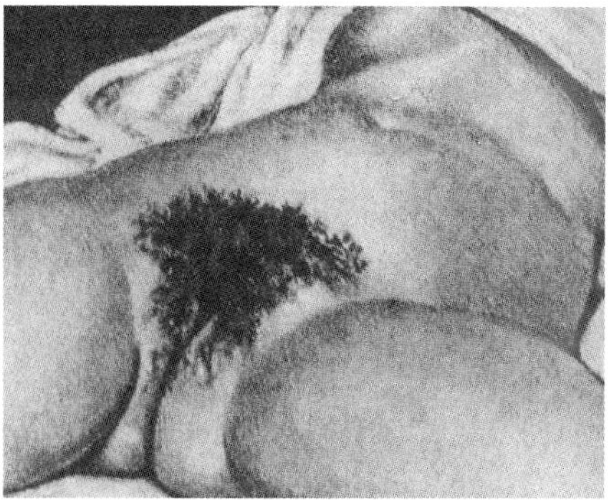

59 *The Origin of the World*, as reproduced in Robert Fernier, *La Vie et l'œuvre de Gustave Courbet*, 1977–78

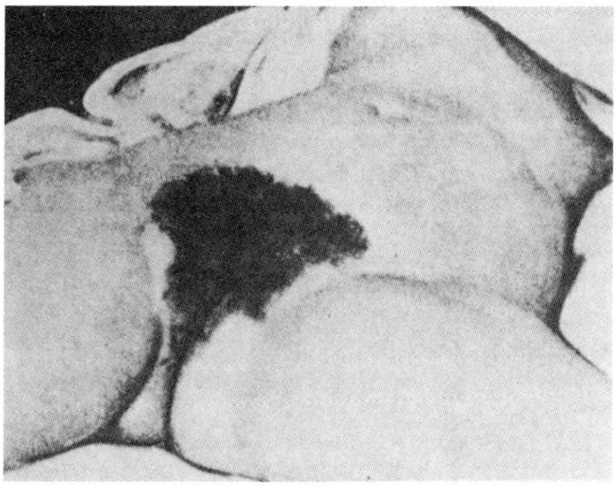

60 *The Origin of the World*, as reproduced in Neil Hertz, *Medusa's Head*, 1983

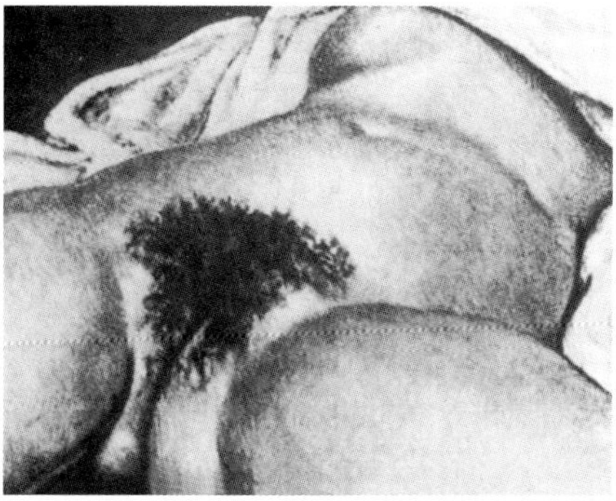

61 *The Origin of the World*, as reproduced in Peter Webb, *The Erotic Arts*, 1975

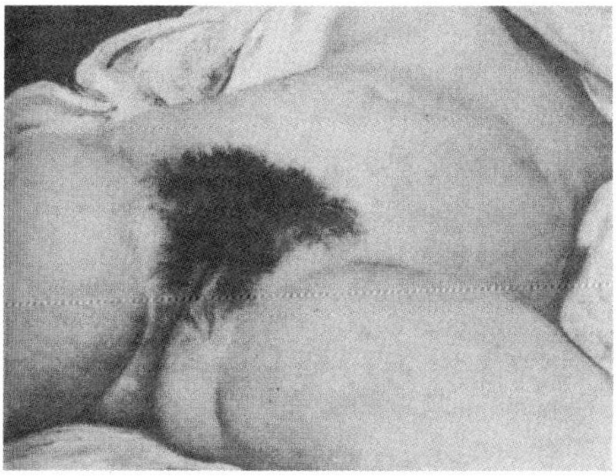

62 *The Origin of the World*, as reproduced in Gerald Zwang, *La Sexe de la femme*, 1967

confirmed by a French expert who claimed to have seen the *The Origin* in Mme. Lacan's apartment. This hot lead, sending my colleague and myself to a sure address in the sixth arrondissement, left us standing frustrated in the lobby. On a subsequent trip another French expert, the head of the Societé des amis de Gustave Courbet, assured us that the work was not in France at all, but in the United States, in a collection on the West Coast the name of which he had forgotten – perhaps the Norton Simon Collection, perhaps not. My heart leaped when I discovered a photograph of the work [60] accompanying Neil Hertz's provocative article, "Medusa's Head: Male Hysteria under Political Pressure,"[1] credited to the Boston Museum of Fine Arts – certainly the most unlikely possible location, one would imagine, for a work that might be thought of as prototypically "banned in Boston"! A call to the curator of the Boston Museum confirmed my doubts. After helpfully going through all the files of the museum, including those of visiting exhibitions, he assured me that there was no record of *The Origin* in Boston. A call to Neil Hertz revealed that the attribution to the Boston Museum had been a printer's error – an error more recently repeated by Denis Hollier in *his* provocative article, "How to Not Take Pleasure in Talking about Sex":[2] perhaps Boston is the literary critic's preferred mislocation of *The Origin*? Hertz told me that he had really meant to credit the *Budapest* – not the *Boston* – Museum of Fine Arts. Yet the hope that *The Origin* might be in Budapest was dashed by further research. Peter Webb, in his discussion of Courbet's work in his 1975 publication, *The Erotic Arts* [61], states that this painting, which had been reproduced in hand-tinted full color in Gerald Zwang's *Le Sexe de la femme* [62][3] – a limited edition, luxe, pseudoscientific, soft-porn production – with the provenance "Museum of Fine Arts, Budapest, formerly collection of Professor Hatvany," was not in fact in the Budapest Museum any more than it had been in the Boston one. Says Webb, "In a communication to the author dated 4 February, 1972, the Director of the Museum of Fine Arts at Budapest (Dr. Klara Garas) wrote, 'Courbet's painting has never been in our museum; it was in a private collection in Budapest and disappeared during the war.'" Webb continues, "During a visit to Budapest in October 1972, the author learned that the painting had been stolen by the Germans during the war and had then been appropriated by the Russians. Professor Hatvany had bought it back and later taken it to Switzerland. Wayland Young, in *Eros Denied*,[4] reports a rumor that the painting was sold in America in 1958." At this point, Webb simply throws up his hands in despair: "This painting has rarely been seen or even heard of, and judgment of its quality is difficult from the blurred photograph that remains." He concludes rather lamely, "This painting was last heard of in Budapest in 1945"[5] – which leaves us more or less where we began, although, to be sure, Robert Fernier, in his catalogue raisonné of Courbet's work, asserts, without further substantiation, that *The Origin* returned to Paris after the war, where it was sold to an unspecified "amateur" in 1955.[6]

More secure, in terms of the art-historical quest for the original *Origin*, is the reference to the Hatvany Collection. In his 1948 publication, *Courbet et son temps*, Charles Léger, one of the major Courbet scholars of the earlier twentieth century, states that the work was bought in about 1910 by the Baron Francis Hatvany of Budapest.[7] Baron Hatvany had seen the painting at the Bernheim-Jeune Gallery in a double-locked frame, hidden by a panel representing, Léger asserts, not a "church in the snow" as Edmond de Goncourt had described it in his diary in 1889, but rather a "castle in the snow." Even the supplementary details relating to *The Origin*, it must be reemphasized, tend to be frought with error. One might almost say that no statement can be made about it – including my own – that does not contain some deviation from empirical factuality, much less from "truth" in the larger sense. Léger continues, "M. de Hatvany, with whom I was formerly in correspondence, for he owned *The Wrestlers* of Courbet [a work now in the Budapest Museum, 66, p.156], naturally spoke to me about this *Origin of the World*, acquired at Bernheim-Jeune, with the frame, while the little panel hiding the canvas, the *Castle in the Snow*, became the property of Baron Herzog, of Budapest."[8]

Working ever backward in our search for the original *Origin*, we come upon a sighting in June 1889, recorded in the pages of Edmond de Goncourt's *Journal.* Goncourt writes that a picture dealer had shown him a painting of a woman's *bas-ventre* which made him want to make "honorable amends to Courbet." That belly, declared Goncourt, "was as beautiful as the flesh of a Correggio."[9] Also dating from the 1880s, May 27, 1881, to be precise, is Ludovic Halévy's account of Gambetta's spirited recollection of the work, which the latter had encountered, many years earlier, in the company of Courbet, at the home of its owner, the notorious art collector and Turkish ambassador to St. Petersburg, Khalil Bey.[10] Here is Gambetta's rather scrappy reminiscence as recorded by Halévy in his memoirs: "*L'Origine du monde.* A nude woman, without feet and without a head. After dinner, there we were, looking ... admiring .... We finally ran out of enthusiastic comments .... This lasted for ten minutes. Courbet never had enough of it."[11] Still earlier, we have the notorious "hysterical" description of the work by Maxime du Camp in his four-volume denunciation of the Paris Commune, *Les Convulsions de Paris*, written ten years after the fact:

> To please a Moslem who paid for his whims in gold, and who, for a time, enjoyed a certain notoriety in Paris because of his prodigalities, Courbet ... painted a portrait of a woman which is difficult to describe. In the dressing room of this foreign personage one sees a small picture hidden under a green veil. When one draws aside the veil one remains stupefied to perceive a woman, life-size, seen from the front, moved and convulsed, remarkably executed, reproduced *con amore*, as the Italians say, providing the last word in realism. But, by some inconceivable forgetfulness, the artist, who copied his model from nature, had neglected to represent the feet, the legs, the thighs, the stomach, the hips, the chest, the hands, the arms, the shoulders, the neck, and the head.[12]

The search, then, ends, fruitlessly, in the dressing room of an Oriental *bon vivant*, or rather in a textual allusion to Khalil Bey, who commissioned the work from Courbet in 1866. Ultimately we find the origin of *The Origin* in the desire of its possessor, the exotic collector of erotica, Khalil Bey, but it is still an origin without an original: we have come no further in our search for the lost painting itself. In this almost parodic – because failed – rehearsal of a familiar art-historical scenario, which has turned into a kind of allegory of the scholar's enterprise itself, I wish to emphasize the repetitiveness at stake here, within the context of a discussion focused on originality and repetition. Each new find simply repeats, as though original, a new set of false clues. Each so-called discovery simply mimes the "truth" it supplants without bringing the quest any nearer to completion. One might go further and say that art-historical practice is itself premised on the notion of originality as repetition, an endless rehearsal of the facts which never gets us any closer to the supposed "truth" of the object in question.

Yet the presumed origin of *The Origin* in masculine desire leads to still another scenario of origination, that of the origin of art itself. In an article entitled "The Origins of Art," Desmond Collins and John Onians attempted to "trace back" historically the origin of art to the engraving of crude but recognizable vulvas on the walls of caves in Southern France during the Aurignacian Period, about 33,000 to 28,000 BC.[13] According to this scenario, masculine desire literally led lusting but frustrated Aurignacian males to represent in stone the desired, absent object – the female sex organ – and thereby to create the very first artwork. In the light of this assumption, all other artworks ought to be considered simulacra of this originating male act, and representation must itself be considered a mere simulacrum of that desired original. What a perfect example such art-historical scholarship offers of the assumption that "everything has to begin somewhere," referred to by Rosalind Krauss in her introduction [see *October*, vol. 37, Summer 1986]! What a perfect disregard of the "always already" is demonstrated by such an enterprise!

It is equally clear that Courbet shared in this myth of the originating force of the artist's desire. To construct still another scenario implicated in the quest for *The Origin* without an original, one must turn to *The Painter's Studio*, a work in which Courbet clearly and literally turns his back on the social and political contextualization which had marked his earlier achievements – *The Stonebreakers* [pl.7, p.71] or *A Burial at Ornans* [pl.2, pp.66–67]. The central portion of *The Studio* [pl.12, pp.140–41] constitutes Courbet's most complex and profound meditation on art as an originating act and the position of the artist in relation to that act of origination.

In *The Studio* Courbet positions himself at the very heart of what must be read as the oedipal triangle, classic site of origins, a configuration constituted by the female model – the mother – the little boy spectator – the son – and the dominating figure of the painter – the father. In a single, powerfully determined image, Courbet has locked into place patriarchal authority and pictorial originality as the inseparable foundations of Western art: great or ambitious art, needless to say.[14] Turning away from the nude model and her forbidden sexuality, the patriarch-painter is absorbed in his act of progeneration, the supremely originating thrust of brush to canvas. And what he is represented as creating in the painting-within-a-painting is not an image of the nude model, who functions unthreateningly as a kind of motherly muse behind his back, but rather a landscape. The reading of landscape as a manifestation of the psychoanalytic process of displacement in Courbet's œuvre becomes even clearer if we consider a work like *The Source of the Loue* – itself the representation of an origin, or source – whose morphological relationship to *The Origin of the World* has often been asserted in the Courbet literature [63]. Nor is it any accident, to continue this Freudian scenario, that, at the crucial heart of a crucial painting, Courbet-as-patriarch is represented as inscribing sheer matter – the actual pigment on the palette – as the origin of his creation. Not only is the pigment emphasized by its denseness, thickness, and brightness; not only is it unequivocally centralized; but also, by calling

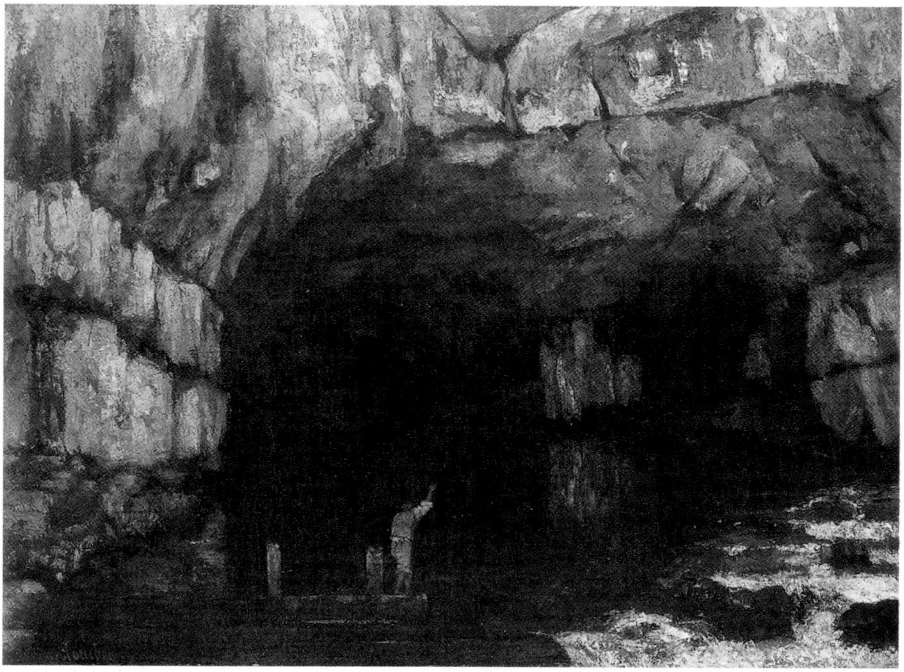

63 *The Source of the River Loue*, 1864. Oil on canvas, 98.4 x 130.4 cm, 38¾ x 51⅜ in.

attention to the shape of the canvas-within-the-canvas, as well as the shape of the *actual* support of the painting, the rectangular palette which supports that pigment focuses our attention on the manipulation of matter, the application of paint to canvas, as the originating act of the artist. It is this that makes his work authoritatively original. Here, the strict Freudian, or the reductivist one, might say that the patriarch/originator becomes identical with the child who plays with his feces.

Which leads us to the final scenario: that of the quest for originality in Courbet's *Origin*. In the absence of the painted materiality of the original, that incontrovertible evidence of the father-generator's presence constituted by Courbet's unique mode of applying his *matière* to the canvas; in the absence, in short, of all the identifying signs of the artist's imperious originality in the available images of the work, there is really no satisfactory way of differentiating Courbet's painting from a thousand ordinary beaver shots available at your local newstand. In its blurry, reproduced repetitions, most of which seem to have been printed on bread, *The Origin* is literally indistinguishable from standard, mass-produced pornography – indeed, it is identical with it [64].

Critics have, understandably, attempted to read the signs of originality back into these inadequate reproductions of Courbet's *Origin of the World:* it is a practice in which almost all of us who work with reproductions must inevitably engage. Here is Neil Hertz, in an otherwise exemplary article, having a try at establishing the authoritative originality of *The Origin:*

> The darkness of the paint combines with the pull of erotic fascination to draw the eye of that central patch, but this centripetal movement is impeded, if not entirely checked, by the substantiality of the figure's thighs and torso, by details like the almost-uncovered breast ... and by what I take to be (judging from black-and-white reproductions) Courbet's characteristic care in representing the surfaces of his model's body – the care, at once painterly and mimetic, that can be observed in his rendering of the rocks surrounding the cave of the Loue. *The Origin of the World* ... explores a powerfully invested set of differences – the difference between paint and flesh, between a male artist and his female model, between sexual desire and the will to representation.[15]

Surely, the last two sets of differences fail to distinguish Courbet's *Origin* from any other representation of the female nude, in whole or in part; and in the absence of the original, the first set of differences is unsubstantiated by the visual evidence. This passage simply indicates the degree to which eyes have been strained and discourse put under pressure in the vain attempt to find traces of the patriarchal caca, the spore of genius, in an unprepossessing black-and-white, infinitely repeatable, reproduction.

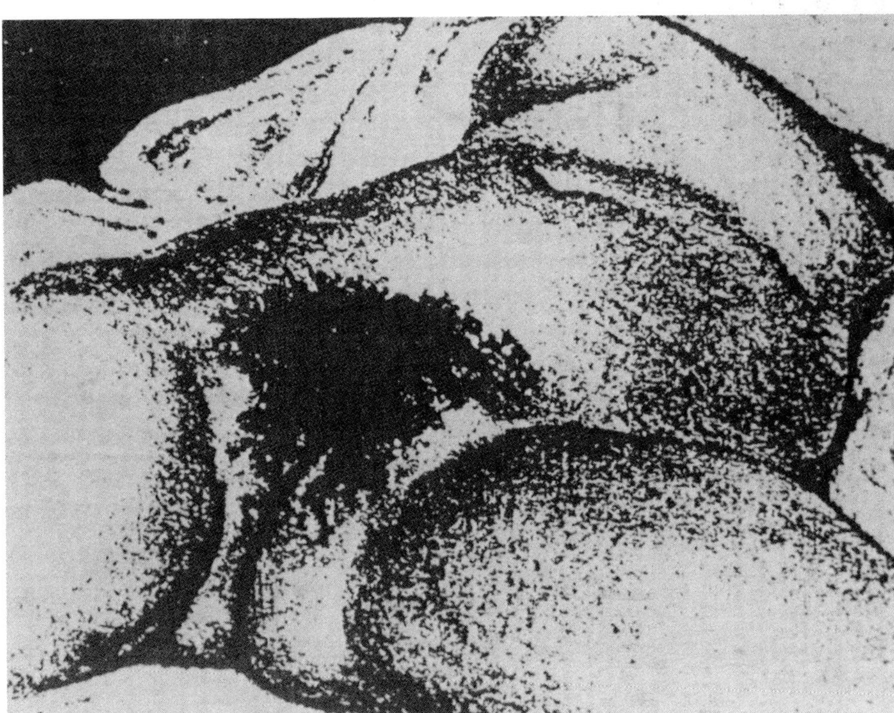

64 *The Origin of the World*, as reproduced in Werner Hofmann, *Courbet und Deutschland*, 1978

But it is this infinite repeatability, ironically enough, which characterizes the very *subject* of Courbet's *Origin:* a metonymy, which, in Lacanian terms, poses the question of lack and desire. Desire itself, according to Lacan, is a metonymy, for metonymy expresses itself as "eternally stretching forth towards desire for something else."[16] Courbet's *Origin of the World*, then, finally re-enacts the infinite repetitiveness of desire, the impossible quest for the lost original. Or, to return to our original Freudian scenario, one might say that in the case of Courbet's *Origin of the World*, as in that of the founding myth of Oedipus, the search for lost origins leads ultimately to blindness.

10 Courbet's Real Allegory: Rereading *The Painter's Studio*

Je fais penser les pierres.
Gustave Courbet

Allegories are, in the realm of thoughts, what ruins are in the realm of things.
Walter Benjamin

One can effectively undo authority only from the position of authority, in a way that exposes the illusions of that position without renouncing it, *so as to permeate the position itself with the connotations of its illusoriness, so as to show that* everyone, *including the "subject presumed to know," is castrated.*
Jane Gallop

Beginning from the beginning: Wrestling with the meaning

"It's pretty mysterious. Good luck to anyone who can make it out! (*Devinera qui pourra!*)," Courbet wrote to a friend about the big picture he was working on for the Paris Exposition Universelle in 1855.[1] The painting in question is entitled *The Painter's Studio: A Real Allegory Summing Up Seven Years of My Artistic and Moral Life* [pl.11, pp.138–39]. It represents, in a format reminiscent of the tripartite divisions of the traditional triptych, an oddly assorted group of people in an artist's studio, assembled around the central focus of the figure of Courbet, who is shown working on a landscape, in the company of a nude model, a ragged little boy, and a sumptuous white cat. To the left are those whom Courbet described in a crucial letter to Champfleury, his friend and supporter, as "the world of commonplace life"; to the right is a less anonymous group, including such recognizable figures as Champfleury himself, the poet Baudelaire, and the philosopher P.-J. Proudhon, a group that Courbet refers to in the letter as "his friends, fellow workers, and art lovers."[2] People have been struggling to figure out the meaning of the painting ever since Courbet issued his challenge. The title is almost as enigmatic as the painting it glosses, but it does provide an invaluable key to the interpretative strategy most suitable for unlocking the iconographic code of *The Painter's Studio*: in it, the painting is specified as an allegory.

According to Littré's *Dictionnaire*, the highest authority on French definitions, the term *allégorie* means: "Saying something other than one appears to say. A kind of continuous metaphor, a species of discourse presenting a literal sense but intended, by way of comparison, to convey another sense which is not expressed."[3] "In the simplest terms," says Angus Fletcher in the introduction to his magisterial study, *Allegory: The Theory of a Symbolic Mode*, "allegory says one thing and means another."[4]

Even without the title, however, the visual evidence alone might lead us to suspect that Courbet was working in the allegorical mode in *The Painter's Studio*. The confluence of this oddly assorted group – which includes a rabbinical looking figure, a clown, a beggar woman, an elegantly dressed couple, a ragged child, a famous poet, a naked model, and, in the center, the artist himself, natty in a bottle-green jacket and horizontally striped trousers – cannot be accounted for in terms of any sort of internal logic: clearly, this crew is not meant to represent a group of actual visitors to the painter's studio, such as is the case in a nearly contemporary work, no doubt known to Courbet, by the Montpellier painter Glaize [62]. Only allegory, it would seem, could account for the strangely muted, isolated, fragmentary, and, indeed, alienated, effect produced by Courbet's painting. *The Painter's Studio* seems bathed in a palpable atmosphere of melancholy, the melancholy of lost presence. Unlike the normal narrative painting of the time, and in contradistinction to the rules of

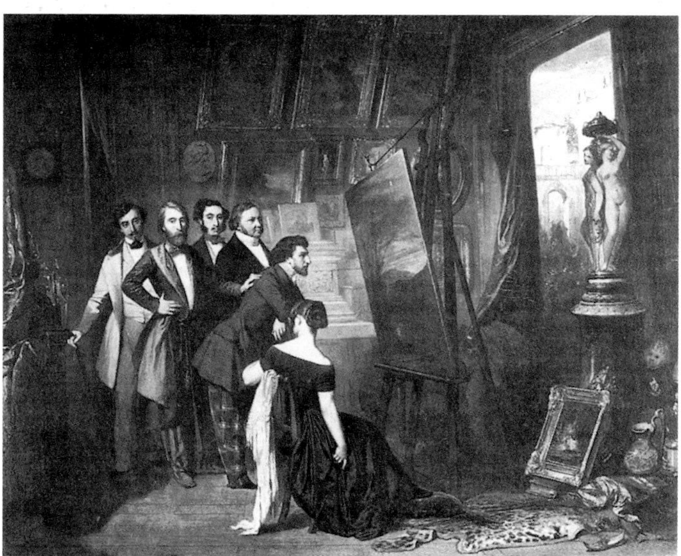

65 **Auguste Barthélemy Glaize**, *The Interior of the Cabinet of Alfred Bruyas*, 1848. Oil on canvas, 60 x 49 cm, 23⅝ x 19⅜ in.

academic composition generally, *The Painter's Studio* offers the viewer no meaningful interaction among the figures, no story-producing give-and-take of gesture or attention. Poses are, with rare exceptions, apparently unmotivated: each figure seems frozen into place the way children "freeze" into odd or haphazard postures in the game of "Statues"; no figure is made to seem aware of or to pay attention to any other. It is precisely this strange, dead, frozen quality marking the composition of *The Painter's Studio* that tells us that the key to its significance lies somewhere outside the perimeters of the painting itself; that there is information to which we, the viewers, are not immediately privy controlling the system of meaning here. Faced with the striking absence of "natural" relationships within the framework of the pictorial given in an allegorical painting like *The Painter's Studio*, the viewer is forced to conceive of its significance as problematic.

Courbet, the artist, plays a dual role in relation to the allegorical meaning of *The Painter's Studio*: he is figured within it as one of its personifications – indeed, as its leading character – but at the same time, he has also chosen to play a role outside it in relation to its meaning. That is to say, in his customary provocative way, he provided his friends, and the present-day viewer, with some confusing hints about his general intentions in *The Painter's Studio*, as well as a deceptively generous amount of data about the surface identities of the individual figures within it. At the same time, in the same document, a long letter to his friend and supporter Champfleury (like Courbet himself, a character in this charade), the artist deliberately withholds information about the arcane, hidden meaning of the allegory, although he constantly drops broad hints about its existence, teasing the reader-viewer like a naughty child with a tantalizing secret. "I have explained all this very badly, the wrong way round," he concludes lamely after his unrevealing enumeration of almost every item in the picture to Champfleury, "I ought to have begun with Baudelaire, but it would take too long to start again. Make it out as best you can. People will have their work cut out to judge the picture – they must do their best."[5]

Although many of Courbet's contemporaries rejected the artist's attempt to suggest that his work hid profound meaning as characteristic pretentiousness and obscurantism,[6] more recent art historians have certainly taken Courbet at his word. Responding to his challenge, they have attempted to subdue the recalcitrant hidden meaning of *The Painter's Studio* like wrestlers – Courbet's own painting by that name provides a suitable painted equivalent of the situation [66] – in hand-to-hand combat. Ever since the painting first appeared in the Louvre, in 1920, they have been attempting to decipher the meaning of Courbet's allegory, both as a general program and in terms of the individual elements within it. Such attempts have included the objective documentary approach of Huyghe; the imaginative, wide-ranging interpretation of Werner Hofmann; the more empirical analyses of the late Benedict Nicolson, and of Alan Bowness; my own reading of the work as a Fourierist allegory; and James Rubin's interpretation of it as a Proudhonian one.[7] All of these

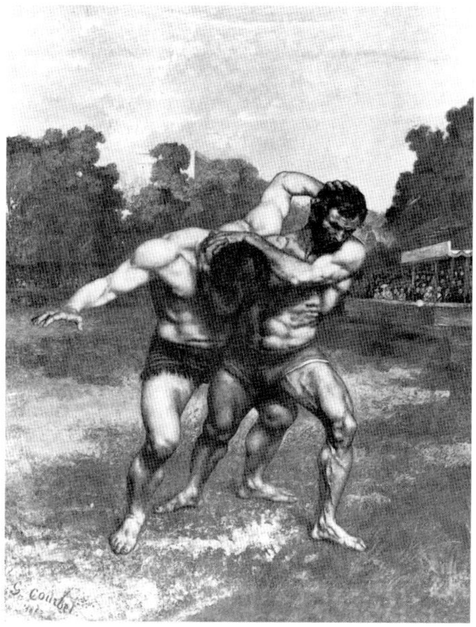

66 *The Wrestlers*, 1852–53. Oil on canvas, 252 x 198 cm, 99¼ x 78 in.

interpretations, however, were based on a more or less literal acceptance of the identity of the figures in the left-hand group, the "world of commonplace life," as Courbet had described them in the crucial letter to Champfleury: the Jew was a figure he had seen once in England; the curé was simply a curé, the huntsman a huntsman, the old-clothes man just that. Their allegorical function, it was believed, was simply to represent different aspects of the social order, to create an anonymous opposition to the world of "shareholders," constituted by the concrete portraits of Courbet's friends on the right.[8]

Then in 1977, on the occasion of the great exhibition celebrating the centenary of Courbet's death, Hélène Toussaint of the Louvre made an interpretative breakthrough. Starting from a hint given by Courbet himself within the letter to Champfleury about the identity of the "weather-beaten old man" next to the curé,[9] she discovered that most of the figures on the left-hand side of the painting had specific if well-hidden identities. Far from constituting mere general references to the poor and downtrodden masses, each one referred to a specific, generally contemporary public figure.[10] The adjective *real* describing the allegory in Courbet's title could now be understood not merely as a paradoxical allusion to the putative realism of the artist's style, but rather as a reference to the work's status as a commentary on real-life political events and positions. Its "real" meaning rescued from obscurity, *The Painter's Studio* could now be read once again – as it originally must have been, if only by a relatively small group of initiates – as a kind of political cartoon writ large.[11] The "weather-beaten old man" was now revealed to be a portrait of Lazare Carnot, once a member of the Convention, who had had a checkered career under subsequent governments;[12] the Jew was apparently a disguised representation of the contemporary financier and statesman Achille Fould, a warm supporter of Emperor Napoleon III who had been Minister of Finance from 1849 to 1852. The "curé" was actually the reactionary Catholic journalist Louis Veuillot; the figure identified in the letter to Champfleury as an "undertaker's mute" was in fact the editor Emile de Girardin, who had initiated popular journalism in France in the 1830s.[13] The "old-clothes man" (*marchand d'habits-galons*) could be identified with Louis-Napoleon's close associate, Persigny, who was nicknamed the "hawker" of the *Idées napoléoniennes*, a tract written by the emperor; and the huntsman behind him to the left regarded as the representative of the Italian Risorgimento in the form of Garibaldi.[14] The man in the cap, in Toussaint's reading, would be Kossuth, representing insurgent Hungary, a figure not, in fact, mentioned by Courbet in the important letter to Champfleury but inserted later; the man with the scythe is now to be read as a portrait of Kościuszko, standing for the Polish freedom movement; and the laborer with folded arms next to him a portrait of Bakunin, representing Russian socialism.[15]

Most startling of all, given Courbet's supposed animosity to the Second Empire and all that it stood for, as well as the fact that direct representation of the imperial person in cartoons or caricatures was forbidden by the régime, was Toussaint's convincing identification of the booted and mustachioed figure with the hunting dogs who dominates the left foreground as a covert representation of Emperor Napoleon III himself.[16]

Having made these crucial discoveries about the hidden, and manifestly contradictory, agenda of *The Painter's Studio*, Toussaint was understandably reluctant to draw any sweeping conclusions from them. Instead, she ended her decoding of Courbet's real allegory with a series of questions about the implications of this oddly assorted assemblage on the left-hand side of Courbet's painting. "Was Courbet," she asks, "being pessimistic or cynical when he assembled the 'betrayers of the Republic' on the left-hand side of his picture, as if to show that the best way of achieving dictatorial power is to use democracy as a stalking horse? Is his work a testament of hope or disillusionment, an Inferno or a Paradiso, a farce or a tragedy? Is its message one of total forgiveness or total skepticism?"[17]

Shortly thereafter, a young German scholar, Klaus Herding, responding to the challenge of Courbet's allegorical conundrum, now rendered even more complicated by the presumed political identity of the figures on the left, wrested a complex and convincing solution to the meaning of *The Painter's Studio* from Toussaint's discoveries. In addition, Herding provided convincing answers to the more general questions of interpretation raised by *The Painter's Studio*. In an article entitled "The Studio of the Painter: Meeting Point of the World and Site of Reconciliation,"[18] Herding responded to Courbet's challenging "*devinera qui pourra*!" with an interpretation of *The Painter's Studio* that was at once analytically incisive and synthetically inclusive. Basing his reading of Courbet's real allegory on the long but still viable tradition of the *adhortatio ad principem*, or exhortation to the ruler, Herding interpreted the painting as a complex pictorial lesson designed for the instruction and edification of Emperor Napoleon III. Herding correctly and convincingly reads, and makes sense of, Courbet's hidden intentions in this work: to teach the emperor, on the propitious occasion of the great Exposition Universelle of 1855, a lesson of rulership. In Herding's view, Courbet in *The Painter's Studio* set out to construct a vast didactic panorama of reconciliation, of peaceful coexistence and harmony among opposing factions, classes, and nations – to create an allegorical "balance of power" in short – organized around the redemptive and productive centering of the artist who is himself in harmony with the source and origin of all social and personal reconciliation: unspoiled nature, represented by a landscape of Courbet's native Franche-Comté on the easel before him.[19] Herding has accounted for every aspect of the painting's iconography and has satisfactorily contextualized it within the historical and discursive framework constituted by the Exposition Universelle, with all its attendant hopes and ambitions. One might say that from the standpoint of art history, indeed from that of a social history of art, Herding, in his closely reasoned and masterfully inclusive argument, has finally solved the riddle of *The Painter's Studio*. The search for meaning is apparently exhausted: there is nothing left to discover. We have come to the end of interpretation.

Beginning with the end: From work to text, or the allegorical fumble

Having written this, I immediately feel a twinge of annoyance; indeed, a surge of rebellion. I have been put in a position of intellectual distress. It would seem that the more I know about *The Painter's Studio*, the less access I have to collaborating in the production of its meaning. There would seem to be nothing more to say about Courbet's painting, no room for doubt: the interpretation is finished, the airtight case is closed; I, and by implication, every other viewer, have been shut out of the house of meaning. The only way I can get back in, it would seem, is by bowing down to authority, and I don't bow easily; in fact, I don't usually bow at all. What I would like to do is force the doors, or, shades of Delacroix, storm the barricades! Partly, this feeling has to do with the role of authorial authority in allegory, an authority that calls forth a similar authoritativeness, not to say authoritarianism, in its interpreters. Allegory, to borrow the words of Angus Fletcher in his discussion of the literary variety, "necessarily exerts a high degree of control over the way any reader must approach any given work. The author's whole technique 'tries to indicate how a commentary on him should proceed.' … Since allegorical works present an aesthetic surface which implies an authoritative, thematic, 'correct' reading, and which attempts to eliminate other possible readings, they deliberately restrict the freedom of the reader." Allegory, continues Fletcher, "does not accept doubt; its enigmas show instead an obsessive battling with doubt …. [The reader] is not allowed to take up any attitude he chooses but is told by the author's devices of intentional control just how he shall interpret what is before him."[20] My distress may also be related to the way that the devices of allegory seem to accord so effortlessly with the hermeneutic practices of art history itself, in which the production of meaning is all too often foreclosed by restricting its operations to the field of iconography, and within it, to unequivocal interpretations. Art history in this sense may be understood as an allegory of allegory: a rebus-like translation of elements in the pictorial "program" into verbal equivalents, with an edifying synthesis at the end. Meaning is understood to be finite, the interpretation of meaning restricted for the most part, as in allegory, to deciphering the intentions of the author. I seem to be faced with an open-and-shut case, the end of interpretation rather than the beginning; the suppression of doubt and ambiguity rather than an opening up to them; the death of meaning in the painting rather than its vivification.

This sort of interpretation, based on the assumed authority of the One Who Knows, while necessary from the vantage point of art history, tends not merely to close off the possibility of interpretation rather than opening it, but even more dubiously, to militate against coming to terms with the myriad concrete meanings produced by the painting itself, independent of any intentions of the artist and at times in opposition to his intentions. Although Courbet may indeed have meant to create a grand vision of harmony, *The Painter's Studio* in its existence as a system of signs producing meanings is anything but harmonious. This is so for several reasons. First of all, because allegory can be looked at from a very different viewpoint from that of authoritative closure and constriction of meaning; rather, it may be understood as a mode that operates in a theater of disjunction and disengagement. The presence of allegory signals to us the very opposite of that system of organic unity presupposed by the vision of harmony Herding has convincingly demonstrated to be present in *The Painter's Studio.*

Courbet as an artist came to maturity at a time when political revolution and, later, the failure of political revolution destabilized all socially produced meanings, calling such meanings, including the meaning of art, into question. Like most of the interesting painters of the mid-nineteenth century, working in the uncertain space between the older Academy-Salon system and the still nascent one of free enterprise production for an uncertain public and an equally uncertain private market mediated by dealers, Courbet realized that he had to choose a way of painting: he could not merely inherit one. It was unclear where painting was going; what relation it had to tradition; what constituted a new or modern direction for art. What indeed was "tradition" in the 1840s or 1850s? Could it be understood as anything but fragments, ruins, fleeting and partial visions?

Allegory, as Walter Benjamin suggested in his great study of German Tragic Drama,[21] bears a natural affinity to disintegrative moments of history: times that are not merely disorganized, but, so to speak, "dis-organicized"; when the ideological

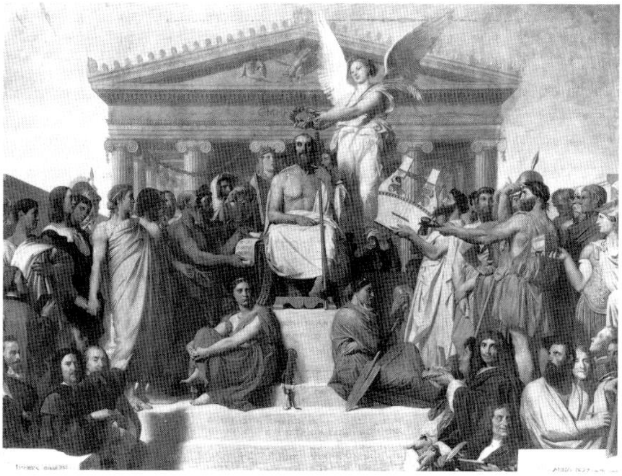

67 **Jean-Auguste-Dominique Ingres**, *The Apotheosis of Homer*, 1827. Oil on canvas, 306 x 515.6 cm, 152 x 203 in.

assumptions holding things together and the power structures engaging with such unity begin to fall apart – when the center no longer holds. "Allegory," says Fredric Jameson in his penetrating analysis of Benjamin's study, "is precisely the dominant mode of expression of a world in which things have been for whatever reason utterly sundered from meanings, from spirit, from genuine human existence."[22] Central to Benjamin's understanding of allegory, in his *Trauerspiel* study, is its wresting apart of the unity of signifier and signified, what is often, in the case of metaphor, and by extension, in the case of allegory, referred to as the "vehicle" and the "tenor" of the figure;[23] its insistence upon the material density and independence of the signifier, and the dead, mutilated insubstantiality of the signified. Allegories like Courbet's, in attempting acts of visible reunification, inevitably show their hand: "The more things and meanings disengage, the more obvious become the material operations of the allegories that fumble to reunite them," declares Terry Eagleton in his discussion of Benjamin's *Trauerspiel*.[24] "Fumble" is certainly the operative word here since no allegory ever succeeds in its attempted reunification. Indeed, there is a certain dark, even tragic pessimism implicit in the way allegory re-enacts the dilemmas of disconnectedness, dilemmas that perhaps, in the last analysis, are not merely moral and epistemological, but ontological. Given what Jameson, in the analysis of Benjamin's *Trauerspiel* cited above, terms the "historical impossibility in the modern world for genuine reconciliation to endure in time," allegory becomes "the privileged mode of our own life in time, a clumsy deciphering of meaning from moment to moment, the painful attempt to restore a continuity to heterogeneous, disconnected instants."[25]

Of course, to return to the nineteenth century and to painting, there is allegory and allegory. Ingres, in his allegory of the position of art and the artist, *The Apotheosis of Homer* [67], constructs a figural equivalent of the most rigid authority, firmly positioning each figure within the hierarchy of creative achievement on either side of Homer, the blind father figure of all art, who holds sway in the exact center of the composition. The figure of the artist here rules over his belated cohorts with the hieratic authority of an archaic Zeus. In *The Apotheosis of Homer*, history is transformed by the allegorical impulse into an enabling myth of origins under the aegis of the classical, ordered by static symmetry into a permanent emblem of the pedigree and permanence of power. Aesthetic control in Ingres's work is overtly equated with a politics of domination. An almost desperate smoothness of surface, a near compulsive perfection of finish here anxiously attempts to secure a conviction of the perfect unity between things and meanings. Yet it is interesting to see to what extent Ingres has failed to convince us of the absolute authority of his expression of artistic totalitarianism; how, exactly because Ingres works so hard at the *retour à l'ordre*, we are made more than ever aware of the arduousness of the effort at the expense of the assumed "naturalness" of the order he tries to instate. No more than in Courbet's far more destabilizing and imperfect allegorical image does the relation between form and meaning seem natural in Ingres's work, much less convincing. This of course has something to do with the history of the nineteenth century, not just the history of its art. To repeat Eagleton's phrase: "The more things and meanings disengage, the more obvious become the material operations of the allegories that fumble to reunite them." In the case of the allegorical mode operating in *The Painter's Studio*, its "material operations" are made all the more evident by Courbet's realist language, which calls our attention unrelentingly to the disjunctions between the things represented and their latent meanings, surely the very opposite of a "harmonious" relationship. But it is precisely in that "fumble" – that uncolonized territory between ball and hand, as it were – in the gaps between things and meanings, that is to say in the failure, spatially, to restore unity to fragments or, temporally, to impose continuity on disconnected instants, that the really interesting meanings of Courbet's allegory are produced: what one might be justified in calling the "real allegory" of *The Painter's Sudio.*

What is interesting to me, as a reader who has been shut out of the house of meaning, is how Courbet's allegory fails, how it cannot create a complete and finished system of meaning. It is, after all, both figuratively and literally incomplete and unfinished – therefore, in Baudelairean terms, open to the infinite interpretative field of the imagination. This encourages me – and all those who insist on enjoying art as a text rather than merely consuming it as a work, to borrow Roland Barthes's terms – to collaborate in the production of meaning in Courbet's allegory.[26] For Courbet's real allegory is, in an important sense, also an allegory of the unfinished, of the impossibility of ever finishing in the sense of imposing a single, coherent meaning on a work of art.

Because it is literally unfinished, it is more than ever possible to consider *The Painter's Studio* as a field of uncertainty, in which vague and more substantial incidents rise, assert themselves for a while, and then fade away on the vast projective screen of the canvas. The slippery flow of unfixed meaning, the interminable production of significance has a material source in the painting's incompleteness. Undoing the phallic illusions of the author as well as the authority of the central image of the artist, an image that speaks to our own phallic illusions of plenitude, the unfinished condition of the painting counters the apparent closure of Courbet's *tableau vivant* by creating other meanings, totally apart from authorial intentions and often working against them.

The unfinishedness of *The Painter's Studio* is a major element enabling me to read it against the grain. In the most literal way possible, *The Painter's Studio* speaks itself as an unharmonious fumble: it is, after all, unfinished, incomplete: can one really speak of an incomplete harmony, an unfinished unity? The fact that *The Painter's Studio* is unfinished is rarely discussed in terms of the meaning of the work.[27] Generally, it is simply mentioned as a contingency with little or no effect, simply an empirical accident in the history of the painting's creation. Courbet, it seems, caught jaundice and, despite working day and night, was unable to bring it to completion in time for the deadline for the submission of works to the jury of the Exposition Universelle.[28] Yet of course, even speaking on the level of biography and personal intention, Courbet could have finished it after the fact if he had wanted to or been able to. For whatever reasons, it is an unfinished painting and our reading of it must be based on it as unfinished or, rather, as partly sketchy, with elements barely adumbrated, and partly richly painted, quite highly wrought: I maintain that this equivocal and disharmonious condition of the work must enter into our reading of it as much as its iconography, for it produces meanings as much as, though in a different way from, the iconography. *The Painter's Studio* would be a very different work, would mean something very different if it were completed, finished as highly as an allegorical painting like Ingres's *Apotheosis of Homer*. Indeed, one might say that the air of "mystery" by which the work is so frequently characterized is produced just as much by its unfinishedness as by its "hidden" iconographical implications, and that the mystery produced by this sketchiness, or figural un-clarity and openness, continues even after and in opposition to the clarification provided by the authoritative readings of the hidden message of the piece provided by Toussaint and Herding. As such, *The Painter's Studio* constitutes an allegory of unfinishedness.

So far, I have been using "unfinished" and "incomplete" as though they were the same thing. Indeed, they are almost synonymous in English, although not in French. Baudelaire, in fact, in his famous discussion of the subject, made a good deal of the difference between a work that is completed (*fait*) and a work that is finished (*fini*). "In general," maintains Baudelaire, "what is *complete* is not *finished*, and ... a thing that is highly *finished* need not be *complete* at all."[29] Courbet's *Painter's Studio*, however, is one of the few major paintings to be both incomplete, that is to say, left unfinished by the artist, and at the same time, not highly finished in many of the parts that the painter did bring to completion. Ironically, the painting is least highly "finished," is most overtly unmanipulated pigment, just where one might say it is most "complete" – in that part of the image of the artist where he may be said to demonstrate the originary roots of art: in the demonstrable lumps of highly visible paint on his palette.

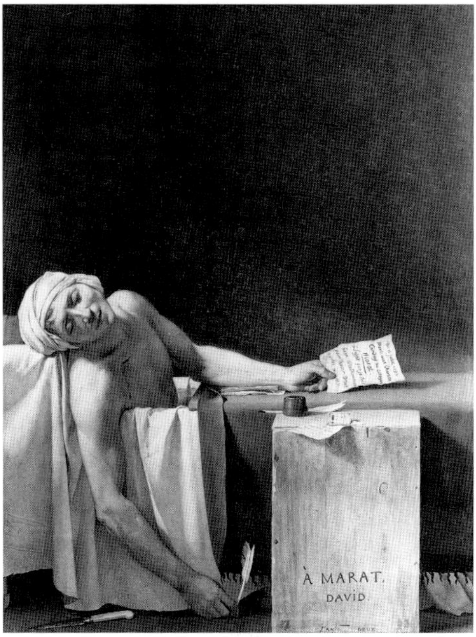

68 **Jacques-Louis David**, *Death of Marat*, 1793. Oil on canvas, 165 x 128.3 cm, 65 x 50½ in.

Now there is a historical precedent for this contrast between the sketchy, with its overtones of evocation, of openness to imaginative possibility, and the finished, which implies perfection, closure, and deliberateness, and painters have long used this contrast to produce meanings.[30] There is one order of meaning in quite classical painting where a certain vagueness or sketchiness, an obliteration of clarity and specificity, has a primary function: that is, in producing significations of temporal distance or of universality. In David's *Death of Marat* [68], for instance, the vaguely adumbrated background removes the dead figure, with all its specificity of circumstance, from the immediate present and sets it in the vast, unclarified spaces of History and Universal Truth. This speckled, luminous surface works on us like some angelic choir singing the hero Marat's praise in the background, moving us both backward in time to ennobling historical precedent and forward to a Utopian future. Closer to Courbet's time, Thomas Couture, in his *Romans of the Decadence* [5, p.20], used the relative sketchiness of the depths of his painting to suggest a kind of pictorial pluperfect, the past within the past: a time, in fact, when the Romans had been upright and self-denying, the very opposite of decadent. In Courbet's *Painter's Studio*, the contrast between the parts of the painting that are merely adumbrated as opposed to those brought to completion also work to create temporal distance: his own past, explicitly cited in the title by the phrase "seven years of my artistic life" and constituted by the paintings hanging on the back wall, is hardly more than a ghostly presence, through whose transparent skeleton the texture of the canvas makes its appearance. Although in the letter to Champfleury, Courbet mentioned specific titles – *The Return from the Fair* [54, p.122] and *The Bathers* [47, p.82] – of works to be depicted on the back wall, they are hardly recognizable as individual works. Rather, there is a constant shifting taking place between our awareness of these "canvases" defining the back wall of the studio in the painting as painted images, and the intrusive presence of the actual canvas that serves as a support to the painting itself.

This perceptual oscillation between represented surface and literal one serves further to undermine the reading of *The Painter's Studio* as a finished product and to render it open to interpretation as process, a process of paint coming into being as

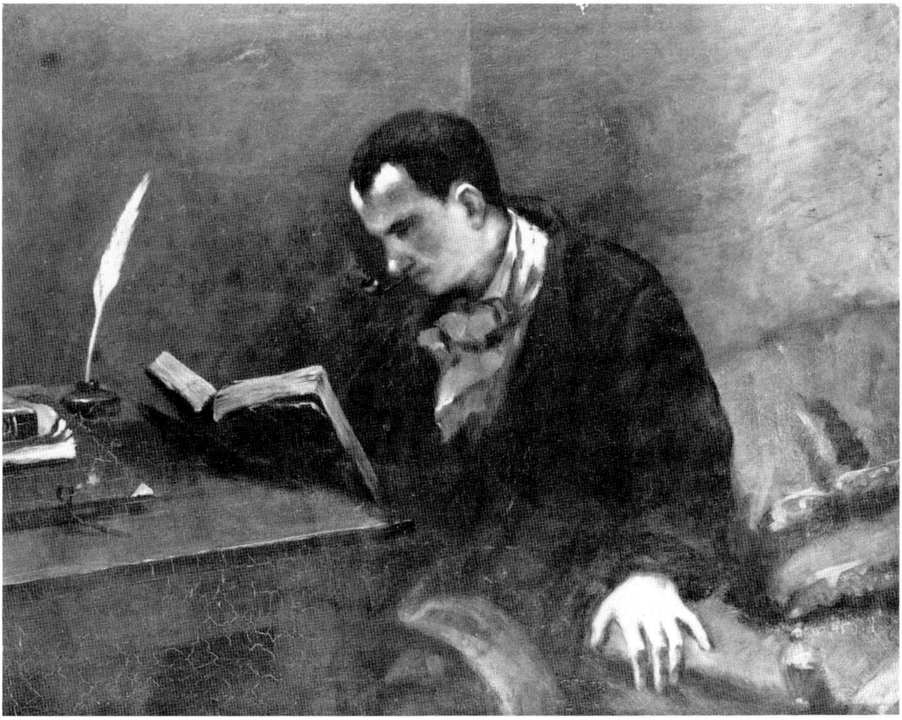

69 *Portrait of Baudelaire*, *c.*1848–49. Oil on canvas, 54 x 65.5 cm, 21¼ x 25¾ in.

form on canvas. Similarly, the contrast between the completeness and plenitude of the central section and the relative thinness and insubstantial vagueness of many portions of the lateral areas, as well as the light and dark contrast between them, tends to de-emphasize the social and political community "in the wings," as it were, in favor of the dominating group of the individual artist, his work, and his model, along with his two wealthy patrons. Inconsistencies of scale add to the sense of floating vagueness complicating the spatial relations of *The Painter's Studio:* figures in the rear of the painting, like the worker's wife, are so small in scale that they seem illogically distant; the position of the lovers on the right is undefined and indefinable; the back wall of the studio provides a spatially uncertain, as well as an almost transparent, boundary for the composition. The fact that Courbet based most of his images of his friends and associates – Champfleury, Bruyas, Buchon, Baudelaire – on pre-existing portraits he had made of them [69], rather than having them come and pose for him in the studio, adds to my sense of the painting as a collage of temporally fragmented and materially unintegrated parts, in this case, parts obtained by a re-appropriation of his own previous work.

As I look at the unfinished *Painter's Studio* with a full awareness that it is unfinished, that it is, in essence, a construction of fragments more or less successfully but by no means finally or definitively sutured together, hence, eminently deconstructable, and/or reconstructable, separate motifs begin to detach or combine themselves, insisting on their fragmentary presence, refusing to reintegrate themselves within the totalizing authority of the composition as a whole. One motif in particular floats up from the brownish, undersea depths of the painting, commanding my gaze. What thrusts itself most insistently on my attention is the motif on the left – which can be read as a miniature allegory in itself – constituted by the descending trio of the *croque-mort*; the skull on the newspaper; and the black-clad Irishwoman, whom Courbet claimed he had seen "in a London street wearing nothing but a black straw hat, a torn green veil and a ragged black shawl, and carrying a naked baby under her arm."[31]

If an allegory is, as Benjamin has stated, in some sense a ruin, then the impoverished Irishwoman, emerging from the *non finito* of Courbet's composition, is the very epitome of allegory; at the same time, in the context of Courbet's iconography, she can be read as a figure more concretely signifying the unfinished. As Herding has pointed out, in his reading of *The Painter's Studio* as an *adhortatio ad principem*, this exhortation "implies mourning, warning and hope: a silent mourning is articulated with the mother dressed in rags, sitting near the feet of the Emperor; she proves drastically that his promise to eliminate poverty had by no means been fulfilled – after all Louis-Napoleon had written a book in 1844 bearing the title *De l'Extinction du paupérisme*."[32] The ruinous Irishwoman, then, stands for unfinished business, an incompleteness in the realm of the political as well as that of the pictorial, a fumble in the unifying modality of allegory itself – an *aporia* in the realm of Utopian possibility.

Herding contrasts the beggar woman with the figure of the emperor, as a signifier of unfinished political business, but there are other important oppositions established by the figure. There are, first of all, intertextual readings within the history of art itself that endow this melancholy mourning figure, a figure of lack *par excellence*, with new significances: the historically delimited meaning embodied in Louis-Napoleon's failure to "extinguish" poverty is only the tip of the iceberg. I propose to read the Irishwoman as a modern figure of Melancholy. As such, within the context of a feminist hermeneutics,[33] she points directly back to the great mother figure of Melancholy herself, Dürer's

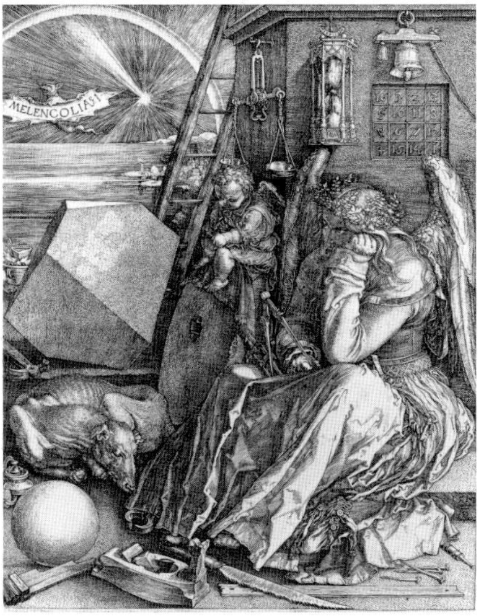

70 **Albrecht Dürer**, *Melancolia I*, 1514. Engraving, 24.3 x 18.7 cm, 9½ x 7⅜ in.

Melancolia I [70], which, in a certain sense, can also be figured as the mother of allegory as it has been interpreted for our times.

At the heart of Walter Benjamin's study of allegory lurks *Melancolia I*, that massive emblem of saturnine genius disenabled, unproductive, in mourning for what one might think of as both a lost transcendence and a damaged immanence: the loss of meaningfulness itself. Indeed, a whole section of Benjamin's study of the *Trauerspiel* is devoted to the subject of melancholy, of which Dürer's *Melancolia I* is the founding image and a constantly reinvoked object of contemplation. Benjamin associates melancholy with many other emblems. The prophetic wisdom of the melancholic is especially associated with the netherworld: "For the melancholic," he says, "the inspirations of mother earth dawn from the night of contemplation."[34] Norman Bryson elaborates on Benjamin's meditation on this figure by declaring:

> In Dürer's *Melancolia I*, the world ceases to be plenitude and becomes first allegory, existing piece by piece to transmit its emblematic meanings; but then once the allegory has been grasped and the content of signification has been released, the world is emptied, drained, sorrowful. Its signification has gone, the world persists but it has now lost something that can never be replaced or retrieved – its meaningfulness. After their excited discharge of meaning, its objects are *spent*, and the game of melancholy follows on the gaze of allegory. Dürer is clearly the classical source of statement of the connection between meaning and sadness.[35]

The "connection between meaning and sadness" is clearly at stake in any serious interpretation of Courbet's figure of the beggar woman as she relates to the overwhelming precedent of Dürer's *Melancolia I*. If, in addition, like Dürer's *Melancolia*, the beggar woman is indeed an allegorical figure, which she surely is, then her meaning is subject to almost endless interpretation. In other words, she cannot be reduced to standing merely for poverty or the condition of Ireland or any other single "tenor." Both her meaning and her sadness are too large for this. If, says Benjamin, allegory "'enslaves objects in the eccentric embrace of meaning,' that meaning is irreducibly multiple."[36]

I am in this instance insisting upon another aspect of allegory, one almost diametrically opposed to the one I posited above when I complained so bitterly about the authoritarian control the allegorist, Courbet in this case, maintained over the reader-viewer, and the authoritarian reductivism of the resulting "translation" of the painted text. But allegory offers the reader very different possibilities, as Eagleton points out, citing Walter Benjamin to make his point. The nature of these possibilities is important enough to reproduce the passage at length. Says Eagleton:

> The very arbitrariness of the relations between signifier and signified in allegorical thought encourages "the exploitation of ever remoter characteristics of the representative

objects as symbols." In an astounding circulation of signifiers, "any person, any object, any relationship can mean absolutely anything else." The immanent meaning that ebbs from the object under the transfixing gaze of melancholy leaves it a pure signifier, a rune or fragment retrieved from the clutches of an univocal sense and surrendered unconditionally into the allegorist's power. If it has become in one sense embalmed, it has also been liberated into polyvalence: it is in this that for Benjamin the profoundly dialectical nature of allegory lies. Allegorical discourse has the doubleness of the death's head: "total expressionlessness – the black of the eye-socket – coupled to the most unbridled expression – the grinning rows of teeth."[37]

I, in my role of interpreter of *The Painter's Studio*, also have a certain doubleness, vis-à-vis the meaning of the allegory. If I am its prisoner in one sense, I am also its creator in another. "All commentary is allegorical interpretation, an attaching of ideas to the structure of poetic imagery," declares Northrop Frye, speaking of its literary variety.[38] If, as I believe, all interpretation is in some sense allegory, then in rereading Courbet's *Painter's Studio*, I am in turn really allegorizing the "real allegory." I am not, however, free to read this figure in any way I choose. Just how I allegorize the beggar woman depends on who I am and where and when I am doing the interpretation: interpretation occurs concretely, in specific historical circumstances, and, since the figure is a woman and I am a woman quite consciously reading *as* a woman, gender is a crucial issue here as well.

Beginning with the end: Reading as a woman

For me, reading as a woman but nevertheless reading from a certain position of knowledge and hence privilege, in the United States in the twentieth century, the Irish beggar woman constitutes not just a dark note of negativity within the bright Utopian promise of the allegory of *The Painter's Studio* as a whole but, rather, a negation of the entire promise. The poor woman – dark, indrawn, passive, source of melancholy within the painting as well as reference to it outside its boundaries – constitutes both a memorial to melancholy past and the repressed that returns, turning against both the triumphant harmony of Courbet's allegory and the sermon of art's triumph that dominates its center. The Irish beggar woman is thus the really realist vehicle of the allegory, interrupting the flow of its intentional meaning. In her, the would-be allegorical connection between thing and meaning is really fumbled.

Because of the material specificity of Courbet's language, we are made aware, in the most substantial and moving way possible, of allegory's other potential: to emphasize the signifier at the expense of the signified. Embodying in a single figure the convergence of gender and class oppressions, a figure of lack *par excellence*, the Irishwoman for me becomes the central figure, the annihilation-cancellation of Courbet's project, not merely a warning about its difficulty. Figuring all that is unassimilable and inexplicable – female, poor, mother, passive, unproductive but reproductive – she denies and negates all the male-dominated productive energy of the central portion, and thus functions as the interrupter and overturner of the whole sententious message of progress, peace, and reconciliation of the allegory as a whole. In my rereading of Courbet's *Painter's Studio*, the Irishwoman as a figure refuses to stay in her place and be a mere vehicle of another more general meaning, whether that meaning be Poor Ireland or the Problem of Pauperism, an incidental warning signal on the high road to historic reconciliation. In her dumb passivity, her stubborn immobility, she swells to the dimensions of an insurmountable, dark stumbling block on that highway to constructive progress. Uneasily positioned within the composition, pressing up almost against, yet somewhat behind the edge of the canvas that establishes a barrier between the defeated world of the anonymous downtrodden and the triumphant one of the artist, her unstable spatial position reinforces the spatial ambiguity of the composition as a whole, at the same time that it threatens the apparent stability of the central group. Visible only by the fitful glow cast by the pallid skeletons of Courbet's own past work on the wall behind her, radiating an ineluctable darkness that is also the substance of her body, the Irishwoman resists the light of productive reason and constructive representation, that luminous and seductive aura surrounding the artist and his minions.

Take her legs, for instance: bare, flabby, pale, unhealthy, yet not without a certain unexpected, pearly sexual allure, the left one folded back in on itself, exposing its vulnerable fleshiness to the gaze of the viewer yet suggestively leading to more exciting, darker passages, passages doubly forbidden because this is the figure of a mother as well as an object of charity. This pose of exposure in a woman, this revealing of naked legs is, in the codes of nineteenth-century decorum, a signifier of degradation, an abandonment of self-respect. The implication of self-abasement is reiterated by the place where she sits, directly on the ground, so that the bare legs also figure in a secular and untranscendent updating of the Madonna of Humility, a topos that we all have inscribed with our own uneasiness and guilt, having seen it often enough in the flesh, the flesh of those pale, varicosed, naked, unhealthy, sometimes filthy, often scabbed and scarred female legs, on the sidewalks of our own cities, in my case, New York, precisely as Courbet, it is said, saw them on the streets of London in his own time.

But the legs of the Irishwoman signify powerfully within the text of the painting itself, as the antithesis of another pair: that of Courbet himself. For a long time, I have been if not obsessed, at least fascinated by Courbet's legs – shapely, perky, aggressively thrust both forward toward the spectator and back into the pictorial space – but mostly by the green-striped trousers the artist has chosen to wear in the painting.[39] This fascination was intensified when I discovered, from what source I no longer remember, that Picasso too was fascinated by those green-striped legs, fascinated enough, so the story goes, although it may be apocryphal, to have trousers of his own made up just like them, at great expense, with the unusual horizontal, rather than vertical stripes. Perhaps Picasso associated such stripes with a notion of criminality – horizontally striped clothing conventionally defines the convict in the United States, and Courbet himself was not just an artistic rebel but condemned by the court as a bona fide lawbreaker after the Commune – so that the stripes may have connoted that transgressiveness so closely allied with the avant-garde project itself; in assuming the trousers (rather than donning the more conventional mantle) of Courbet, Picasso was symbolically assuming his role as the leader of artistic and social rebellion as well as literally stepping into the pants of an overtly phallic master painter. This difference, then, between the legs of lack and the legs of mastery and possession, establishes the gender terms underpinning the meanings generated by the painting as a whole.

There are still other infratextual readings possible for the figure of the Irish beggar woman in *The Painter's Studio*, other figures that construct its meaning. If, as a woman, I can read any other figure in *The Painter's Studio* in relation to the Irishwoman, it is inevitably Baudelaire to whom I must turn: Baudelaire, another dark negator of Utopian promises, the Baudelaire who later sardonically dismissed Courbet with the phrase "Courbet sauvant le monde,"[40] and who, like the beggar woman in the painting, is marked with the dark sign of melancholy. This crucial connection-opposition between Baudelaire and the poor woman is carried out on the formal level, too: the woman all emergent but muffled roundness, created by an out-pressing, fore-shortened fullness of form; Baudelaire curiously flattened, planar, outlined, a surface phenomenon, as sunken in his reading as she is extrusive in her embodied misery; together they constitute a paired vehicle connoting privatized absorption versus public demonstration.[41]

There is a sense, too, in that the woman may be read as a Baudelairean type, one more *exemplum* of that flotsam of the modern city that it is the project of *flâneur* to glimpse in the course of his peregrinations. If she is not old enough to figure as one of the little old ladies of the "Petites Vieilles," she is surely a prefiguration of one of those "singular, decrepit and charming beings" who take refuge in the "sinuous folds of old capital cities," and whose mysterious eyes harbor "mysterious charms / For him whom austere Misfortune nursed at her bosom."[42] Through the poet's eyes, or rather, his diction, we can see/read Courbet's beggar woman not merely as a conventional type, but as a figure as resonant with ambivalent values as Baudelaire's metaphoric nurse – "austere Misfortune" – nurturant yet denying in a single trope, she who nourished the poet at her breast. Especially potent in light of Courbet's triumphant self-assertiveness as the painter-creator in the center of *The Painter's Studio* is Baudelaire's self-denying projection of himself as the artist in the figure of "he whom austere Misfortune nursed." If we think of the Irishwoman as in some sense identical with Baudelaire's Misfortune, then the artist (the one nursed at her breast) is reduced from masterful protagonist to almost nothing, a mere nursling beggar, whose frail and dependent existence is pitifully signified by the little white blob of the baby's cap, almost invisible in the dark folds of the Irishwoman's shawl, a white blob that refers at once to the fragile, moonlike tondo suspended on the wall slightly to the right above the central group, and, at the same time, to the ominous, shadowy skull on the newspaper to the left and behind the mother and child. Precarious life, inevitable death: What could constitute a more devastating response to the intended lesson of Courbet's allegory about the authoritative position of the artist than this alternative allegorization of the figure of the beggar woman and her almost invisible child?

Part Two

Ending with the beginning: The centrality of gender

Although Courbet's allegory may indeed have been designed to teach a lesson of peace, harmony, and reconciliation to the emperor, there is another lesson inscribed, unconsciously, no doubt, at the very heart of Courbet's "Allégorie réelle": that is the all-important lesson about the gender rules governing the production of art – great art, needless to say. As such, it constitutes a lesson about the origin of art itself in male desire.[1] Although it is hidden to eyes blinded by the Oedipal construction of all meaning in patriarchy, there is nothing ambiguous about this lesson. No amount of analysis of Courbet's formal innovations[2] can obfuscate the message constituted by this central group, a group in which the major players literally replicate the Oedipal triangle. It is crystal clear in this, Courbet's construction representing representation:[3] the artist-father, Courbet, his Assyrian profile tilted at a confident angle, brush in hand, is unequivocally male, unambiguously active. The model-mother, to his right, and upon whom he turns his back, is equally unambiguously female, and passive. The pupil-son, follower or representative of the next generation who looks up at the artist's work, presumably with awe and admiration, like his alter ego, the little boy artist sprawled out sketching on the floor to the right, is as unambiguously male as the artist himself, or as any of the youthful ephebes in Harold Bloom's study of the uninterruptedly male, if anxiety-ridden, chain of poetic creativity.[4] The implications are, to me reading it as a woman, that if the next generation looks at Courbet's work and is stirred with fires at once imitative and competitive, so did Courbet look at Rembrandt, Rembrandt at Raphael, Raphael at Rome, and so forth. That is how it is, how it has always been, how it is always going to be. If the artist leans from his space into ours, breaking down the barriers between fictive and actual presence, it is almost as though to reinforce this message: "as it is in representation, so it is in the real world." This too is part of the "real" in the real allegory. The only touch of ambiguity comes in the multiple roles assigned the female model, who may be read as either wife, mother,[5] mistress, or inspiring muse: but this is relatively inconsequential, since the sign "woman" is infinitely malleable in the representation of representation and can stand for any or all these positions in its anonymous objecthood.[6]

Courbet, then, allegorized as the artist in the heart of *The Painter's Studio*, is definitively gendered, and this gendering is underlined by the position of his opposite – his would-be object included in the image: the female model. Here gender is overtly and blatantly positioned as opposition – and domination. One might say that Courbet goes so far as to cross out woman in the Lacanian sense by substituting "nature" for her as the signifier of his creation on the canvas-within-the-canvas, a strategy of deletion he resorts to, incidentally, quite literally in the case of the *Portrait of P.-J. Proudhon in 1853* later on, where he literally "erases" the adult female member of the family, Mme. Proudhon, from his composition, leaving only her work basket behind as a synecdoche of her absence-presence [1, p.14]. This easy replacement of the woman's body by landscape – an incarnation of the nature/woman dyad *par excellence* – bears a precise relation to the almost infinite mutability of the feminine itself under patriarchy. "Femininity," says Klaus Theweleit in his provocative study of gender relations, *Male Fantasies*, "has retained a special malleability under patriarchy, for women have never been able to be identified directly with dominant historical processes ... because they have never been the direct agents of those processes; in some way or other, they have always remained objects and raw materials, *pieces of nature* [my emphasis] awaiting socialization. This has enabled men to see and use them collectively as part of the earth's *inorganic body* – the terrain of men's own productions."[7] This seems to be exactly the point at issue in Courbet's real allegory: women and nature are interchangeable as objects of (male) artistic desire – and manipulation.

To reinforce this (totally unintentional) message, Courbet has underlined this powerful strategy of displacement by introducing a surrogate male beholder right into his picture in the figure of the little boy gazing, in the position of the spectator, at the picture.[8] Woman nevertheless has a role, and a crucial if not an active one, in the image of origins Courbet has inscribed in the generative center of his real allegory: she stands as the passive Other to the artist's active subjecthood, and, at the same time, she forms an apex of the Oedipal triangle inscribed by painter, model, and observing child. Here, at the generative center of the real allegory, Courbet, separating the mother figure from that of the child, functions unequivocally as father, enforcing patriarchal law, in this case, the law of visual representation. If Courbet feels free, like many male artists, to "merge corporeally" with some of the female objects of his representation, as Michael Fried asserts in his catalogue essay,[9] he certainly does not wish to "feminize" himself represented in the act of painting, where, on the level of vulgar Freudian symbolism, he depicts himself as fully and unequivocally phallic, actively giving form to inert matter with his probing, dominating brush.

All the productive ambiguities proper to or characteristic of the murky wings of the altarpiece dedicated to the dominant position of male artistic genius are banished in the central portion, what Fried has aptly seen as the place where Courbet is "representing representation." It is perfectly clear who is meant to be represented with the phallus here. Thus, although Courbet may occasionally exercise the time-honored privilege of entering the bodies of women in his painting,[10] he rarely allows the opposite to happen – that is to say, he rarely lets women enter *his* represented body: allows himself to be "feminized," as it were. Courbet may well have represented himself as the passive, wounded lover in *The Wounded Man*[11] [pl.9, p.72], positioning himself as castrated (that is, vulnerable, womanish) in order to emphasize the extremity of the suffering caused by the female companion who nestled close to him in the original version of the painting, but whom he subsequently erased.[12] Reading as a woman, I might see the erasure of the woman as more significant than the suffering of the man, and the implication that being positioned as a woman functions as the unquestioned signifier for the one who suffers, the one who is abandoned, the helpless (wounded or castrated) victim, as more significant than either. Courbet constructs a position of femininity as a potent signifier for his defeated masculinity here – literally his "unmanning"; if this is an "openness" to the "feminine" side of his nature, it's a pretty negative formulation. "Womanishness" has always stood for a high degree of masculine failure, for the specific failure of masculinity; it is never a sought-after position in the representational schemata of heterosexual males.

Michael Fried, in his essay "Courbet's 'Femininity'", makes a strong case for Courbet's openness to femininity, his ability, as it were, to enter into the bodies of his female subjects. Now to say that Courbet enters into the bodies of the women in his paintings is hardly to say anything new about the male representation of women, or of Courbet specifically. Men have always had the privilege of "entering," identifying or empathizing with, the female bodies they depict. One could certainly say this of Delacroix and the murdered women his surrogate-self watches so coolly in *Sardanapalus*. "Je suis la plaie et le couteau!" ("I am the wound and the knife") declared Baudelaire in "L'Héautontimorouménos" – another way of saying "I am the vagina, I am the penis"; more literally, for Courbet, the visual artist, "I am the female flesh, I am the male brush or palette knife." Male artists have had that dual privilege for a long time; women's bodies have always served as allegorized objects of desire, of hatred, of elevation, of abasement – of everything, in short. That is the point: woman's body has never "counted" in itself, only with what the male artist could fill it with, and that, it seems, has always been himself and his desires. To assert that Courbet has "entered" the bodies of his women – the nude bodies, above all – is hardly the same as postulating a protofeminist Courbet. After all, entering and/or taking over women's bodies have always been the privilege of the male artist, a privilege reinforced in the nineteenth century by the specific historical conditions associated with capitalism. Above all, it is a totally asymmetrical privilege; no such entry is provided for women artists. Courbet's apparent identification with the bodies of the women he represents would, in this reading, be simply more of the same thing, transgression as usual.[13]

The gender rules inscribed in the center of *The Painter's Studio* – the artist is male and active, his model is female and passive – are, in my reading, manifestly in place in the construction of the erotic in Courbet's œuvre as a whole. If, as Fried contends, Courbet came close to "thematizing the activity of painting as simultaneously man's and woman's work" in *The Sleeping Spinner*,[14] it is hardly "the *activity* of painting" that is at stake here: the female figure, if it indeed thematizes painting, is notably asleep at the switch. If painting is woman's, as well as man's, work, the female figure is overtly *not* engaged in it; painting as woman's work is characterized by disenablement, not activity, and the female figure, asleep at the job, whether spinning or, allegorically, painting, is thereby made available as the seductive object of the male gaze.

If, as Fried sees it, the powerful central figure of *The Grain Sifters* [pl.5, p.70] owes some of its unassimilability to current conventions for the representation of female labor, to Courbet's projecting of his own body image into the *cribleuse* in question,[15] doesn't its unusual, unsettlingly "masculine" configuration – embodied in the powerful musculature of the working arms, above all – owe something to a more conventional source for deviant imagery of women at the time? I refer to what might be called the imagery of perverse desire – an underground source nevertheless readily available and pointing to certain kinds of aberrant erotic preferences in men of Courbet's time. The strong woman plays a discreet but omnipresent role in the nineteenth-century iconography of fetishism. Such a preference, for example, is embodied in the unusual photographic collection of the Englishman Arthur Munby, who had heavily muscled, young working-class women, often wearing masculine clothing, photographed for his private pleasure.[16] Muscular arms were particularly admired [71]. The muscular arms of the female figure in *The Grain Sifters* might suggest the identification of the artist with the representation; I might also, reading as a woman, suggest that the artist, like Munby, finds something vital, sexy, desirable, in women's muscular arms. A body like that of Courbet's *cribleuse* offers something both resistant and ultimately yielding to the male

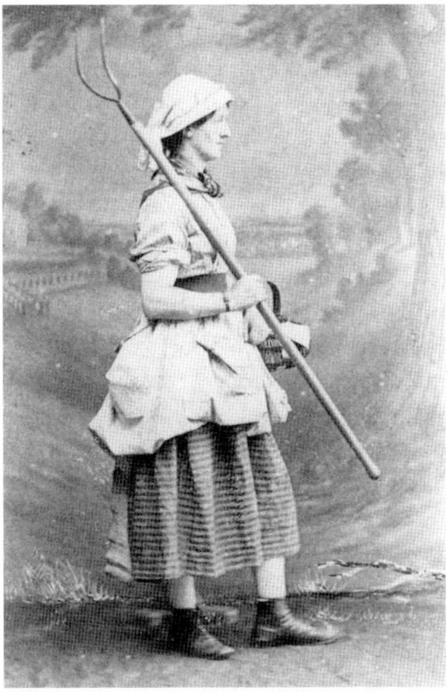

71 **H. Howle**, *Hannah in Traditional Shropshire Peasant Dress.* Studio photograph with rustic backdrop, 1872

gaze, and this something has to do with the fetishization of the signifiers of class in nineteenth-century representation. Upper-class women, ladies, never have such arms; working-class ones frequently do. It is these vigorous, firmly grasping arms combined with the smallness of the waist, the inviting, rich swelling of the skirt, and the piquancy of the little feet that constitute the desirability of the whole image, as well as its ambiguity; the erotic persuasiveness of the composition as a whole is enhanced by the way the vigor of the central imagery is opposed by the more familiar languor of the female figure to the left.

Languor, sleep, resting are more characteristic modes of representation for female figures in the nineteenth century, for Courbet above all: and in Courbet's case, as well as for other artists, like Carolus-Duran [72] and the Catalan Realist Ramon Martí Alsina [73], for occasional male ones as well.[17] There is a tendency to assimilate all sleeping figures within a single signifying position within this pictorial discourse. But surely here is where gender-as-difference is most consequential: precisely where it is most unapparent, where the manifest content seems most similar, indeed, identical. Although sleep is a topos representing both men and women, it is figured differently for each. Of all the figures represented sleeping, only the female ones are represented nude: male ones are always represented clothed. Courbet's only nude male figures, *The Wrestlers* [66, p.156], are only partly so and vigorously active. The vulnerable flesh of the sleeping male figure in Courbet's work, or that of his followers, is veiled flesh, protected from the prying and possessive gaze – of women as well as of other men; male vulnerability is posited as momentary and conditional in a general state of potency. The meanings produced by this difference – sleeping women often nude, sometimes clothed versus sleeping men never nude, always clothed – must therefore be different. Gender makes a potent difference precisely within topical similarity or near identity: it is precisely within the same topos that the gender differential reveals itself most vividly. The sleeping male, with rare exceptions, does not suggest sexual availability to the male heterosexual gaze. Rather, it suggests a sort of poetic or imaginative availability open to the male viewer through identification with the sleeping male figure, embodiment of *le repos du guerrier*, as it were. The process of identification for the female viewer of the female sleeping figure, nude or clothed, however, is quite different: such an identification is inevitably either masochistic or narcissistic and connotes sexual availability, especially in the case of the nude, but even in the case of the clothed female sleeper, as in *The Sleeping Spinner*. The sleeping or dozing female nude is the preeminent topos, open to and designed for the pleasure of the desiring male gaze. There is thus no symmetry between sleeping male and sleeping female. The naked woman can inscribe only passive available flesh. In the form of muse or model, mistress or mother, asleep or awake, the nude female can inspire, perhaps reproduce, but cannot produce or create – that is the crucial distinction.

Paradoxically, however, it is in the representation of clothed female figures, in *The Young Ladies of the Banks of the Seine* [74], of 1857, that Courbet most vividly inscribes

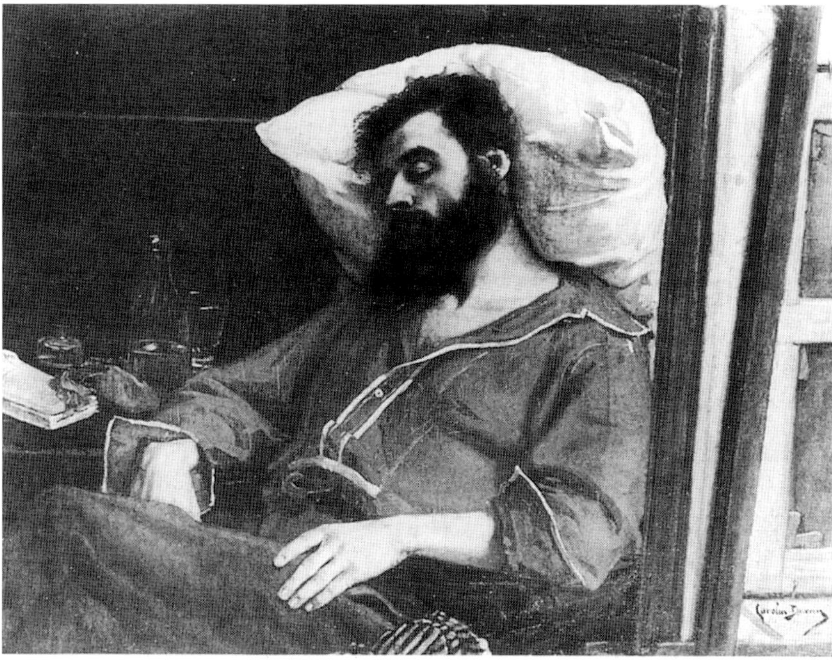

72 **Emile-Auguste Carolus-Duran**, *The Convalescent*, *c.*1860. Oil on canvas, 99 x 126 cm, 39 x 49½ in.

73 **Ramon Martí Alsina**, *The Siesta*, *c.*1884. Oil on canvas, 53 x 56 cm, 20⅞ x 22 in.

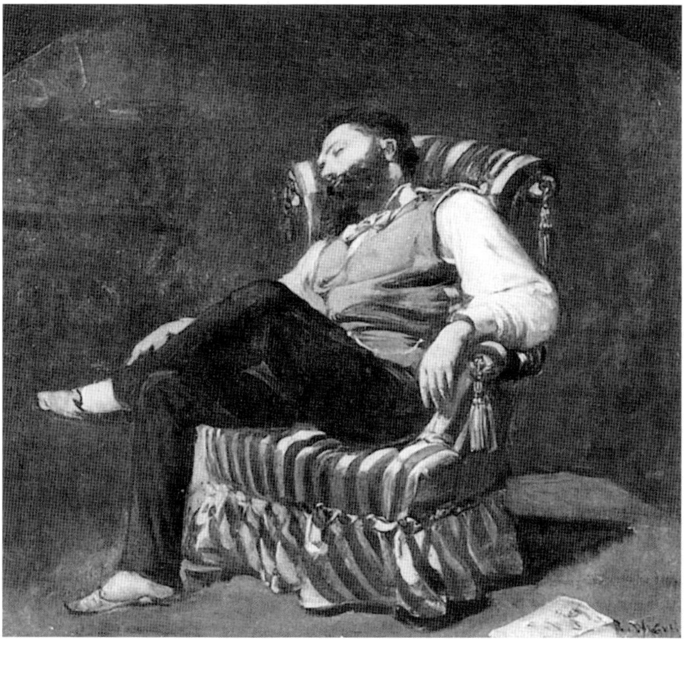

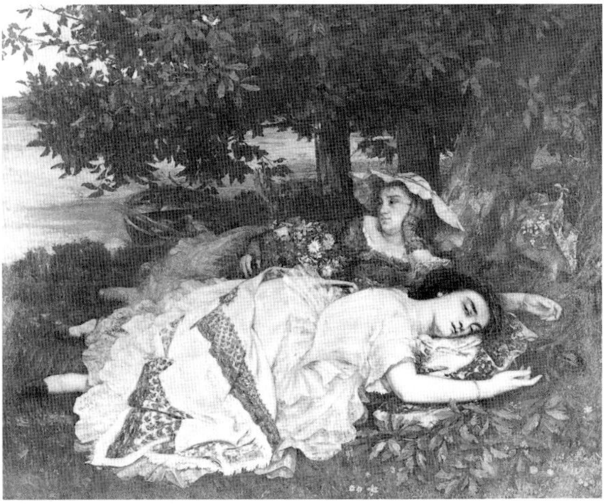

74 *The Young Ladies of the Banks of the Seine*, 1857. Oil on canvas, 174 x 200 cm, 68½ x 78¾ in.

the discourse of female sexual availability on the topic of sleep. To be more precise, the foreground "demoiselle" is not, in fact, either fully asleep or fully "clothed," or certainly would not be considered fully clothed to the nineteenth-century viewer; rather, she is what might be thought of as lounging or resting and "half-clothed," committing the solecism of wearing her corset-cover and petticoat in public, a sure sign of impropriety. She is in an intermediary, and all the more scandalous state, between being properly clothed and, for the purposes of painting, permissibly nude.[18]

The whiteness of lingerie, the very signifier of erotic availability in nineteenth-century sexual fantasy, could also serve in pictorial discourse, in its very purity (the material analogue it offers is to the blank page) as an ideal symbolic field on which to inscribe acts of desecration. *The Young Ladies of the Banks of the Seine*, in its potent concatenation of whiteness, supineness, sleep, and sexual scandal, offers a striking visual analogue to a passage describing the degradation of prostitutes from Flora Tristan's *Promenades dans Londres*, first published in France in 1840. In this passage from her heartrending chapter on prostitution in London, Tristan describes in some detail the way English upper-class males make their prostitute-companions drunk and then, when the poor women are lying senseless on the floor, amuse themselves by pouring drinks on their unconscious bodies. "I have seen," declares Tristan, "satin dresses whose colour could no longer be ascertained; they were merely a confusion of filth. Countless fantastic shapes were traced in wine, brandy, beer, tea, coffee, cream and so forth – debauchery's mottled record. Alas! the human creature can sink no lower!'[19] The analogy with painting conjured up by Tristan's image of "debauchery's mottled record" is striking. But more striking still is the passage in which she describes the fall and desecration of a prostitute dressed in *white*,

> an extraordinarily beautiful Irish woman ... She arrived toward two in the morning, dressed with an elegant simplicity which only served to heighten her beauty. She was wearing a gown

75 **William Holman Hunt**, *The Awakening Conscience*, 1852. Oil on canvas, 76.2 x 55.9 cm, 30 x 22 in.

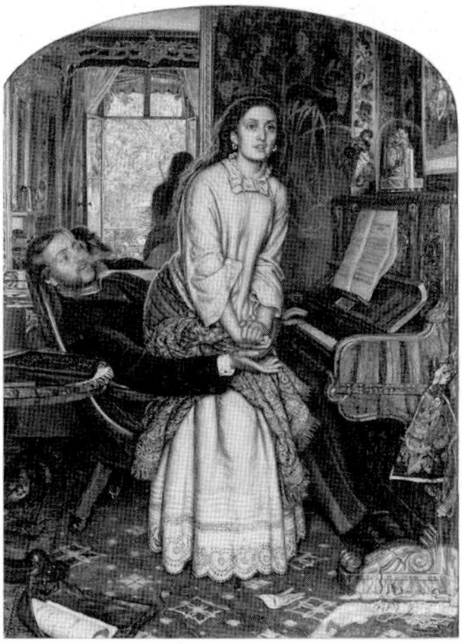

of white satin, half-length gloves revealing her pretty arms; a pair of charming little pink slippers set off her dainty feet, and a kind of diadem crowned her head. Three hours later, that same woman was lying on the floor *dead drunk*! Her gown was revolting. Everyone was tossing glasses of wine, of liqueur, etc., over her handsome shoulders and on her magnificent bosom. The waiters would trample her under foot as if she were a bundle of rubbish. Oh, if I had not witnessed such an infamous profanation of a human being, I would not have believed it possible.[20]

Courbet's representation of the white-clad fallen woman in the foreground of the *Demoiselles* does not go to quite the same lengths of moral allegorization as Tristan's, but it lends itself quite nicely to a pejorative reading within the codes defining nineteenth-century female decorum. Is it a mere coincidence that the gorgeously painted cashmere shawl in the foreground re-echoes the position and function – veiling yet calling attention to the sexual part of the body – of the similar shawl draped about the hips of the heroine of Holman Hunt's *Awakening Conscience* [75], the quintessential Victorian morality painting on the theme of the fallen woman?[21]

The misogynistic and moralistic P.-J. Proudhon, who figures prominently among the group of friends and supporters in *The Painter's Studio*, author of the major antifeminist text of the period, *La Pornocratie ou les femmes dans les temps modernes*,[22] found ample material for allegorical interpretation in the *Demoiselles*. He deals with the painting at length in his study of Courbet, *Du Principe de l'art et de sa destination sociale*.[23] For him, as for so many other male allegorists, ranging from Emile Zola to Otto Dix, the sexual ("fallen" or "vicious") woman functions as the prime allegorical vehicle of social corruption. Behind Proudhon's paranoid diatribe against the moral scandal represented by this painting, one must imagine another, very different representation of the feminine: the good, of course, married, woman, plainly and soberly dressed, sitting with her spindle or standing, her children about her, at the stove; a woman completely controlled, mindless, sexless, privatized, powerless. It is hard to say what enrages Proudhon most: the fact that the women in Courbet's painting are represented as publicly available to the male gaze, that is to say, to the pleasure of *others*; or that they are represented as experiencing pleasure *themselves*, in some way independently, outside patriarchal control and authority, pressing their bodies lazily and voluptuously against the bosom of the earth. Proudhon immediately attempts to distance himself from the immediate sexual scandal of the *Demoiselles* by allegorizing it in terms of contemporary social failure: what Courbet really would have entitled the painting, if it had not seemed seditious at the time, was "Two fashionable young women under the Second Empire." The implications of this title are, in Proudhon's reading, manifold, and ultimately political. They have to do with the moral corruption of the regime of Napoleon III, a corruption centered in the venality of women: their unwillingness to marry and have children; their tendency, as embodied in the foreground demoiselle, to be at once "somewhat virile," and at the same time to "swim in erotic revery";[24] their unslakable thirst for luxury at its most refined. But what Proudhon hates most of all about the female types he sees embodied in *The Young Ladies of the Banks of the Seine* is their grotesque attempt to be fully human, that is to say, the preemption of the male prerogatives of creativity: "They cultivate what is called the ideal; they are young, beautiful, adorable; they know how to write, to paint, to sing, to declaim; they are real artists." Obviously, for Proudhon's allegorical imagination, such presumption on the part of women can only reap punishment, and it can only be, in visual terms, represented by the ugly: "But pride, adultery, divorce and suicide, replacing love affairs, hover about them and accompany them; they bear these in their dowry; it is why, in the end, they seem horrible."[25]

Although all of Courbet's paintings of eroticized women, like the *Demoiselles*, are open to allegorical interpretation based on gender difference, some of them would appear to be more resistant to the traditional, moralistic variety practiced by P.-J. Proudhon. Often, Courbet, like many of his contemporaries and followers, seems to have turned to the theme of sleep or "resting" – *La Blonde endormie* or *Femme couchée: Le Repos* – simply as a pretext for painting the nude female model. Often, and increasingly as the century progresses, even that pretext becomes unnecessary, and we are faced by what in English is designated by the *Reclining Nude* or simply *Nude* (female understood) *tout court*.

Detaching the female nude from its relatively constrained position within traditional iconography in the nineteenth century, positioning it – and, significantly, not the male nude – outside of narrative (or within the thinnest possible narrative pretexts as "Sleeping Model," "Odalisque," or "Bather") as an object at once of desire and of formal innovation may be read as a courageous step in the progressive evolution – or revolutionary progress – of modernism. Women's naked bodies have played a major role in modern artists enterprise of "making forays into and taking up positions on the frontiers of consciousness," their attempts to "advance further in the dialectic of outrage." This is Susan Sontag and she is in fact talking about pornography,[26] not about the high-art nude, but what she says has not a little resonance in the case of Courbet – and later, that of Manet, of Gauguin, of Picasso, of Matisse, and of the German Expressionists. The female nude as such is the contested site of vanguard versus conservative practices in the nineteenth century. The question is: How different are these presumably adversarial practices from each other, and, if different, how significant are these differences, and even more germane to the point at issue, in whose reading are these differences between the vanguard and the conservative nude stipulated as significantly different?

Reading as a woman, I might well come out with a different answer to these questions than if I were reading as a man.[27] Following Susan Suleiman's complex analysis of the centrality of the concept of transgressiveness in the strategies of modernism,[28] I would suggest that in the case of Courbet's more excessively eroticized nudes – his *Sleep* [36, p.58], for instance, or his *White Stockings* (Barnes Collection), his *Woman in the Waves* [93, p.204], and certainly, his part-image, *The Origin of the World* [pl.10, p.137] – we are invited by a certain modernist discourse, or, perhaps, more accurately, a postmodernist one, to read the transgressive content of the work as a metaphor for the transgressive formal practices involved. Transposing Suleiman's analysis from the realm of fiction to that of art, one might say that what we see here is the transfer or slippage of the notion of transgression from the realm of experience (whose equivalent, in painting, is representation) to the realm of figuration (or form), with a corresponding shift in the roles and importance accorded to the signifier and the signified. The signified becomes the vehicle of the metaphor, whose tenor is the signifier. The sexually scandalous iconography of Courbet's *Sleep* – two naked lesbians locked together in a sexually explicit pose – is there to signify Courbet's formally scandalous pictorial practice: his tender, miraculously modulated, sensual handling of paint, the pulsating suggestiveness of the lush curves of breasts and thighs, the daring play of pearly blond flesh tones against deeper, rose-flushed brunette surfaces, the delicate threading of blue veins into an almost imperceptible weave of pinks and umbers connoting skin, the caress of the artist's supple brush or palette knife on the receptive surface of the canvas.[29]

Yet is this an adequate analysis for a painting like Courbet's, where "effects of the real" may in fact constitute the dominant formal practice, where brushwork, intentionally, tends to vanish into palpable flesh, palette-knife work into illusory breast or thigh, and where, as much as in any *Playboy* centerfold, arousal is the issue – arousal with a certain aesthetic bonus? Reading as a woman who happens to be an art historian, I cannot entirely accept the first reading; reading as an art historian who happens to be a woman, I cannot wholly accept the second. Yet I must arrive at a position that maintains that simply to bracket the content and function of the work in a case like *Sleep*, or in any of Courbet's nudes, is to be blind to what they are doing, how they affect us specifically as women who view images. Surely I cannot simply take over viewing positions offered me by men – either the creator of the picture or his spokesmen – nor can I easily identify with the women in the picture as object of the gaze, which necessarily involves a degree of masochism on my part;[30] nor can I easily invent some other, alternative, position. Once more, I find myself at once invited into, but shut out of, the house of meaning, uneasily hovering on the brink of, moving into, withdrawing from the potentialities of the painting: the familiar shifty, feminine subject-position.[31] Ultimately, though, such work would seem designed to put me – the viewer who is a woman – in her place. This place is, as usual, problematic, and it might best be formulated as a question: Am I going to be one of the boys (that is, am I going to "enjoy it" as erotic stimulation, as artistic daring, as vanguard transgression) or one of the girls (am I going to acquiesce to [male] authoritative interpretations, am I going to reject it as "oppressive," am I just going to give up my status as viewer and lie down and identify with the bodies in the picture)? Or to end this discussion with still another question: Why must transgression – social and artistic alike – always be enacted (by men) on the naked bodies of women?

The obvious answer to this question lies in what I have read as the Oedipal center of *The Painter's Studio*. To answer it, I have to end with a still larger question, a question posed, in a different context, by Susan Suleiman: "Is there a model of *textuality* possible that would not necessarily play out, in discourse, the eternal Oedipal drama of transgression and the Law – a drama which always ultimately ends up maintaining the latter?"[32] Reading as a woman, I see Courbet's vision of Utopia less as an ideal vision of the future, or even as unfinished business, than as business as usual; certainly, it does not seem transgressive in any deeply serious sense. It has become clear to me that it is only in gender difference that a real allegory of the transgressive might be constructed.

I can, with difficulty, imagine another scenario, a real allegory of transgression. Since it is a scenario that denies Oedipus, invokes gender reversal, it can only be read as a kind of – threatening – joke, a joke in bad taste. It will, of course, be written off as mere frivolity by serious critics and a desecration by serious art historians. I will now stop reading as a woman and write as one.

Rosa Bonheur now sits in the central position of *The Painter's Studio*. Courbet, nude, or rather partly draped, stands modestly behind her. She is wearing a striped skirt (we can leave her Courbet's jacket; with a few alterations, it will do), and vigorously painting, with her loaded brush – a bull. A ragged little girl watches her intently. Suddenly, Champfleury can't stand it any longer. He rises from his seat in the wings and approaches the center. "But she's not even a *great* artist," he protests; "Why are there no great women artists?" The little girl turns around; we see that she is, in fact, the young Mary Cassatt (or Berthe Morisot or Georgia O'Keeffe or Hannah Höch – any number of possibilities are available). Now, the anonymous women in the picture, led by the Irishwoman, begin to converge on the center of the stage; the men gradually sink into the shadows, where they take off their clothes, and, equally important, lose their names: they are no longer Champfleury or Bruyas or Max Buchon, they are just naked male bodies.[33] Little by little, they take up their positions in a series of *tableaux vivants*: one of them holds a parrot over his head, offering his substantial nudity to the audience; two others are locked in a passionate, muscular embrace on a piece of blue drapery; another displays his buttocks to us in front of a waterfall backdrop; still another exposes his luminous but hairy flesh, recumbent, on white sheets before a landscape. Two of the women try to urge the naked Proudhon, misogynist author of *La Pornocratie ou les femmes dans les temps modernes*,[34] to join them in a picnic on the grass, but he resists; perhaps it is still too early; they leave him alone. Now all the women are gathered together in the center of the painting; the "rich patroness" lends her shawl to the nude model. They all have names: they are Marie, Angèle, Claire. They introduce themselves to each other and engage in animated conversation; they have a lot of catching up to do. They turn to look at the naked men in their ridiculous poses and suddenly they all burst into laughter, great gales of body shaking, uncontrollable laughter; they laugh and they laugh and they simply cannot stop .... As they laugh, as though a result of their laughter, the solidity of the painted matter begins to sparkle, melts, flows, diffuses "in an architecture of pure color, the sudden brightness in turn opening up color itself – a last control of vision, beyond its own density, toward dazzling light."[35]

End of the scenario; but we have obviously left realism far behind for a kind of surrealism, although this is an allegory of the transgressive the Surrealists never quite got around to. This is the unreal allegory, and perhaps the never real one as well:[36] an allegory of what can never be as long as we live in the land where Oedipus rules. The absurdity of my paraphrase of Courbet's real allegory could only be paralleled by rephrasing Freud's famous question "What does a woman want?" as "What do *men* want?" It is absurd because what *men* want is what want *is*; men's want defines desire itself.

Ending with the ending: The politics of place, the place of hope

If Courbet's *Studio* can in no sense be read as subverting the laws of gender – the ultimate subversion – it was nevertheless successful in fulfilling its author's intention to shake up some of the social and political assumptions of its time. Such a transgressive strategy might, from a certain point of view, even appear appropriate to the occasion for which it was painted: the Exposition Universelle of 1855. Courbet, following a time-honored tradition of carnival-sanctioned infraction of the rules, does resort to a trope of role reversal in *The Painter's Studio*: that popular imagery of "the world upside down," the destabilizing of the accustomed social hierarchy countenanced by carnival, in which all normal relations of domination and subservience are reversed.

In the carnival atmosphere created by the Paris World's Fair, Courbet, it would seem, felt free – indeed, called upon – to reverse the "normal" order of the world: now it is the monarch who must listen and learn, the artist who is on top, who grants the benefit of his example to the ruler. In this reversal of customary roles, his allegory and mine of gender reversal, no matter how different in every other aspect, share a common ancestry in popular tradition, for the laws controlling gender were exactly those most outrageously violated by the carnivalesque suspension of the normal mode of life, when men could dress as women and women, as Natalie Davis has demonstrated, could, during the Utopian days of carnival, however briefly, find themselves "on top."[37]

There are other ways, too, in which Courbet, in *The Painter's Studio*, contravenes accepted practices: those, for example, governing the codes controlling high art. There is a sense, as I indicated at the beginning of this essay, in which *The Painter's Studio* must be read as a political cartoon writ large: an allegory of the venality, or at least the futility of present political conduct and hope for a more positive political future.[38] In hiding politically subversive meanings under the cloak of allegory, *The Painter's Studio* looks back to a time-honored tradition connecting this rhetorical mode with political subterfuge. "Allegory," says Angus Fletcher, "presumably thrives on political censorship."[39] Certainly, Courbet's choice of an allegorical form for his painting owes a great deal to specific political conditions, most notably official censorship, at the beginning of the Second Empire. But the *kind* of allegory he chose, an allegory related to the "low" form of the political cartoon rather than the "high" one of, say, classical mythology or antique epic points to another kind of politics at work in his painting: a cultural politics involving that shifting and provocative relationship between high art and the materials of low or mass culture which has been posited as one of the defining characteristics of modernism in the recent literature.[40] In Courbet's work at the post-revolutionary Salon of 1850–51, in paintings like the *Burial at Ornans* [pl.2, pp.66–67], as T. J. Clark and Thomas Crow have pointed out in different contexts, the innovations that pointed ahead to fully fledged modernism "were carried forward in the name of another public, excluded outsiders, whose own emergent or residual signifying practices these pictures managed to address."[41] By 1855, such "excluded outsiders" had to be addressed more circumspectly than they had been five years earlier, if indeed they, or they primarily, were the intended public for *The Painter's Studio.*

Indeed, the political implications of the work are impossible to grasp without a consideration of the public for which it was intended; and this notion of a public is in turn impossible to understand without a knowledge of the place and circumstances for which Courbet designed *The Painter's Studio.* It was executed for a specific historical situation: the Exposition Universelle in Paris, inaugurated by Napoleon III on May 1, 1855, an exhibition to which the emperor had devoted a great deal of detailed attention over a considerable period of time.[42]

Within the context of the Exposition Universelle, an exhibition designed to enable France to display her technological prowess and cultural achievement to the world in competition, primarily, with its arch rival, England, certain of the figures in Courbet's painting assume new importance. The "old-clothes merchant," for instance, positioned in the center of the left-hand group of figures, displaying his wares to exotic personifications of Turkey and China (– a figure whose centrality to the allegorical message Courbet indicated in his letter to Champfleury by declaring of him: "he presides over all this … displaying his frippery to all these people, each of whom expresses great interest in his own way"[43] –) can now be read as a crucial, and deflationary, figuration of that hawking of commodities that was the ultimate point of the Exposition Universelle itself. If the Irish beggar woman may be said to call into question the emperor's economic policies on one level, then the ludicrous rag-and-bone seller may be said to question it on another. This debased and parodic representative of the world of commerce – selling that which is devoid of value – provides an effective opposition to the image of the artist, engaged in producing that which *is* of value. Courbet, by representing himself in his own painting surrounded by his past and present pictorial production, has created an allegory of his beneficent role as a producer of valuable cultural goods. The real allegory then, in the context of the Exposition Universelle of 1855, may be read as Courbet's production of himself as a counter-commodity – a free and self-determined man producing objects of genuine value – for a new and relatively unfamiliar public. That this public might include prosperous and enlightened purchasers is indicated by the pair of wealthy patrons prominent in the right foreground of the painting as well as the inclusion of Courbet's own patron, Alfred Bruyas, among the group of friends and supporters. *The Painter's Studio*, then, in the context of the year in which it was created, 1855, and the place for which it was intended, the French section of the painting exhibition of the Exposition Universelle, may be conceived of as a kind of miniature "universal exhibition" in its own right, in which the artist displays his wares to an interested public in much the same way as Napoleon III displayed his nation's commodities to would-be buyers and investors.

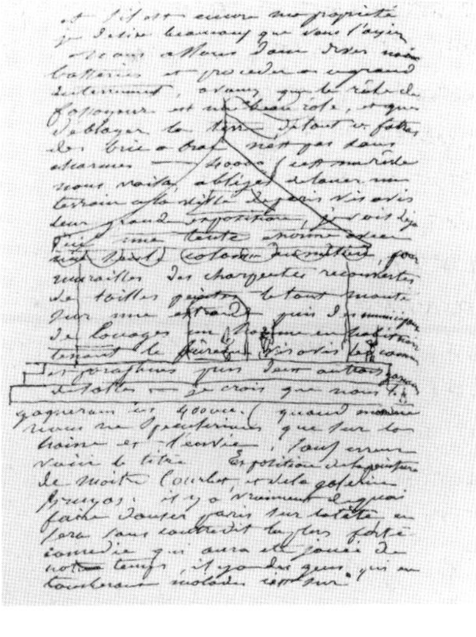

76 *The Pavillon du réalisme*, letter from Gustave Courbet to Alfred Bruyas, 1854

The public to be addressed was a vast, international, and socially heterogeneous one, and Courbet's sense of competition was keen. He intended his new painting to function as the keystone of an extended group of his works, fourteen in all. But his relationship to the government-sponsored exhibition, and especially to the powerful superintendent of the fine arts, Count Nieuwerkerke, was a stormy and ambivalent one,[44] leading ultimately to the rejection of *The Painter's Studio* from the official exhibition and Courbet's implementation, with the financial and moral encouragement of his patron, Alfred Bruyas, of his own private exhibition featuring *The Painter's Studio*, in the so-called Pavillon du réalisme on the Avénue Montaigne [76], an exhibition that competed with the official one in which he also showed a group of eleven paintings. "Whether inside or outside the official exhibition," as Herding points out, "Courbet wanted to participate and to maintain at the same time his independence from the organizers."[45]

The position of *The Painter's Studio* was thus at once marginal – Courbet's private exhibition was, so to speak, "marginalized" in relation to the official one – yet central in that it dominated the space, proclaiming Courbet's independence of government demands and stipulations. The real allegory, then, constituted within the context of Napoleon III's Exposition Universelle, declared Courbet's centrality within the terrain of the marginal, a position that vanguard artists ever since have avidly sought after and established as their own. Thus, if the political allegory embodied within the painting was hidden, the allegory of cultural politics enacted by the placing of the painting in a specific site at a concrete moment of history was far more overt. Courbet had indeed maintained his independence, but at a price. This "price" – with its inevitable appeal to a "special" or in some sense "marginal" public – the price of uncertainty, of non-centrality in relation to the still-powerful government art establishment, and finally, of being in opposition to that establishment – would eventually, transvalued, define the position of modernist art in Paris and indeed, the world.[46]

The cultural politics involved in the physical placement of *The Painter's Studio* and its relation to the public – or publics – play major roles in the evolution of the critical discourse surrounding it. After the exhibition in the Pavillon du réalisme, *The Painter's Studio* languished for more than half a century in near oblivion, until it was rescued by public subscription for the Louvre in 1920.[47] It became, as a result of this transaction, at once, a part of the French cultural heritage, inserted into the "great tradition" of national art production, and at the same time, as part of the same operation, a work more or less completely divested of political implication. As a "great work," hallowed by its position of honor in the galleries of the Louvre, its meaning was now secured by the elevated language of the aesthetic, not the mundane discourse of politics; its references to contemporary issues, though hinted at from time to time, were, to all intents and purposes, as lost to the comprehension of a public blinded by the ideology of art-historical interpretation as its gender lessons are today made invisible to a public blinded by the ideology of patriarchy.[48]

If the place where a work is shown bears a crucial relationship to its meaning, then the new location of *The Painter's Studio* in the Musée d'Orsay rather than the Louvre would seem to demand new readings. Whereas in the Louvre, *The Painter's Studio* –

far more than the ever-inassimilable *Burial at Ornans* – seemed to announce the end of a great tradition, now, in the Orsay, a museum devoted to the work of the second half of the nineteenth century, it seems to point ahead, if by no means unequivocally, to the modernist future.[49] I say "not unequivocally" because there are ways in which, set against the postmodern stoniness of Gae Aulenti's new walls, in the company of Manet's *Olympia* (if not that of Bouguereau or Bastien-Lepage) and beneath the galleries full of Cézanne, van Gogh, and Gauguin, *The Painter's Studio* looks, if not precisely "traditional," at least touchingly old fashioned in some respects. Certainly, its iconography owes something to nostalgia for that sweeping and totalistic yet compulsively detailed Utopian vision characteristic of Fourier and his disciples.[50] Yet if in the context of its new placement in the Musée d'Orsay, Courbet's *Painter's Studio* looks Utopian, it does so not merely by preaching a pictorial lesson of reconciliation, by resorting to eccentric iconography, or even by transforming old traditions of popular resistance into new iconographic form. Rather, seen in the context of later nineteenth-century art and, thus, through imaginative projection, in the context of modernism and the vanguard of the future, it is not Courbet's iconography that seems to point ahead as a "principle of hope," to borrow the Marxist philosopher Ernst Bloch's eloquent phrase, but rather his pictorial practice in *The Painter's Studio.* In relation to the work of the Impressionists and Cézanne, the choice of landscape, considered by progressive critics of the time as the perfect democratic genre, as the motif on Courbet's easel becomes the vehicle of a progressive and liberating tenor within the allegorizing totality of the painting. The pure pigment on the palette and the insistence on the surface and substance of the painting as elements of its meaning point even further ahead to the rejection of representation itself in the modernist practices of the twentieth century. The collage-like dissonances of the composition and its fragmentation as well as its appropriation of ready-made imagery and its rejection of finish and completeness point to still other vanguard strategies of the future. *The Painter's Studio*, read in this way, is Utopian in that it allegorizes the future of art and its – mostly unfulfilled – hopes of instrumentality in the production of revolutionary change. For Utopia is clearly not so much a place – how could it be? – or even an ideal, but, rather, once more to borrow the words of Ernst Bloch, who spent so much of his life considering it: "the methodological organ of newness."[51]

CODA: It may be of interest for the reader to note that this two-part essay allegorizes in textual form the pictorial structure of *The Painter's Studio.* At the "heart" or "vital center" of the essay (the second half of the first essay and the first of the second), I take over Courbet's role of "creator" and assume my femininity (as he has his masculinity) in the construction of a discourse of gender from the raw material offered by the visual artifact. In the "wings" (the first half of the first part and the last part of the second), I assume the "normal" voice and position of the art historian – a sort of neutro- or neutered-masculine one and give a more empirical – and entirely ungendered – account of the painting and its context.

11 Courbet and his Territory: How Landscape Means

In this essay, I will examine the specific sites and strategies used by Gustave Courbet in his landscape paintings. In doing so, I will confront the many ways in which landscape may be said to create meaning, despite its lack of narrative or story line. To do this, I will examine Courbet's landscapes in detail, as well as the landscape production of his contemporaries, his predecessors and later landscape painters and photographers, in order to explore the particularity of Courbet's landscape practice.

In order to contextualize Courbet's landscapes, I will start by examining three trees: Courbet's *Oak of Flagey* [pl.13, pp.142–43]; Cézanne's *Great Pine and Red Earth* [77], and the contemporary photographer Robert Adams' *Sitka Spruce, Cape Blanco State Park, Curry County, Oregon* [78]. All three of these images represent specific trees in specific places. The trees have names, and at the time they were created one could find these trees *in situ*. Yet only Robert Adams' – the photographer's – tree

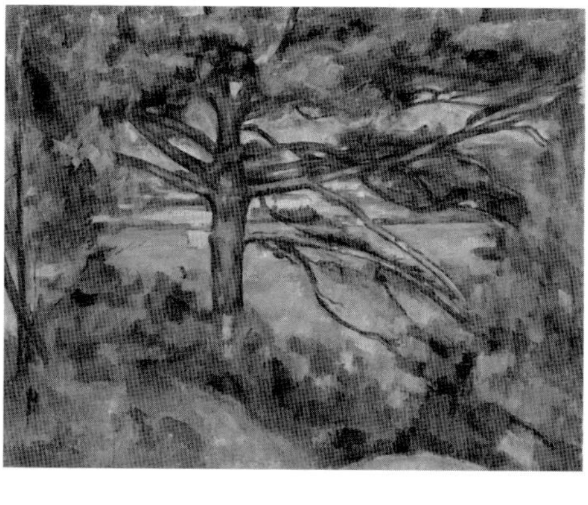

77 **Paul Cézanne**, *Great Pine and Red Earth*, c.1895. Oil on canvas, 72 x 91 cm, 28⅜ x 35⅞ in.

is what one might call indexical – that is to say, one might point to the exact tree in the world that produced the image and is identical with it. The two paintings are representations, created out of paint.

The power of all three of these tree images is greatly enhanced by the intelligence of the crop. We tend to associate this strategy of cutting off the image at its borders with photography specifically, but clearly, painters used it too. Having said this, I want to make it clear that I am not interested in similarity as much as I am absorbed by difference. That is to say, I have no interest at all in so-called influence, either of painting on photography, photography on painting, or earlier painting on later painting. I find "influence chasing" more important to scholars playing art-history-as-usual than in actually illuminating what is going on within particular images or the work of particular artists. Specifying difference is another thing altogether, a maneuver that lets us get closer and closer to the object in question and its meanings.

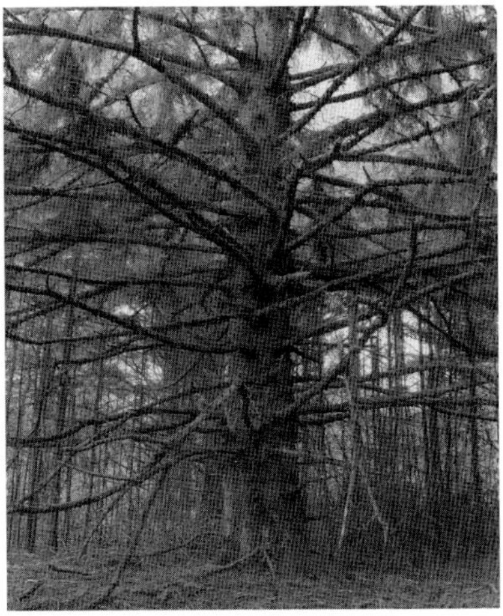

78 **Robert Adams**, *Sitka Spruce, Cape Blanco State Park, Curry County, Oregon*, 1999–2003. Gelatin-silver print, 32.4 x 26 cm, 12¾ x 10¼ in.

Courbet's *Oak of Flagey* is a remarkable portrait of a remarkable tree. Titled "Chêne de Vercingétorix, Camp de César près d'Alesia, Franche-Comté" and dated 1864 when it was first shown at Courbet's private exhibition in the Pavillon de l'Alma in 1867, it is not quite like any other tree-painting of its time, a time when many of the most interesting artists were turning to landscape motifs.[1] In no other tree-painting of the nineteenth century does the indomitable quality of the oak, its sense of firm rootedness in the earth, its expansive upward and outward branching, receive such forceful treatment. A sense of absolute yet natural authority is created by the way the shape of the tree is made to coincide with the rectangle of the canvas – the crop is perfectly calculated. Yet there is no feeling of either accommodation to the demands of the format or gratuitous imposition on the facts of experience. The coincidence of frame and foliage merely increases our sense of the oak's imperious quiddity.

Courbet has placed the tree firmly in the center of the canvas, but he has not forced a rigid symmetry on his composition: there is a good deal of textural and directional variety within the trunk, the roots, and the dense web of leafage that crowns them. Thick, salmon-colored impasto is built up in energetic yet controlled flicks of the palette knife to form the right side of the trunk [pl.14, p.144]; to define and emphasize the sinewy shape of the roots; and to create a general sense of vigor that reinforces the sheer material solidity of the massive trunk, a solidity thinned out with shadow on the left. Different kinds of energy and shaping are visible in the brush and palette-knife work, and even within the all-over texture of the foliage there are variegated intrusions of light and air, the paint and the intensity of treatment thinning out most conspicuously to the right, where the great oak's branches coincide with and overlap the four subordinate trees in the background. Indeed, the composition itself is a synthesis of the absolute and the relative, on a variety of levels: the smaller tree to the left and the four smaller ones to the right submit to but are not entirely subdued by the dominating close-up presence of the oak in the foreground. They lean slightly inward, like the columns of the Parthenon, as though drawn toward the oak by magnetic force; but their presence softens what might otherwise be an effect of hieratic centralization. The great oak would have been a much more absolute, and a more banal, invention without their presence. They add the mundane authority of experienced reality to the image and also help to break up the strong contrast between vertical and horizontal – foreground close-up and background long view – which Courbet tended to avoid in his best work. The rich scumbles and palette-knife work of the tree trunk, its massiveness literally reinforced by the thickness of the impasto highlights to the right, and of the leafage, are echoed in softer form, to create equivalences of grass and moss at its base, then thinned out but not totally abandoned in the gentler slopes of the hills at the horizon.

If organic endurance and material longevity combine in the leitmotif of the painting – an arboreal triumph over time – then these qualities – solid, dense, unshakable – are intensified by the volatility of the only two representatives of the animal world in the painting: the white dog pursuing the brown hare, one on each side of the tree, running leftward. Tiny harbingers of instantaneity, they emphasize the oak's endurance by suggesting its opposite, the ephemeral existence of living beings. Yet of course the oak is living too. But the time scale is different, presented as an opposition by the artist.

Cézanne makes the same statement about contrasting temporalities in *Mont Sainte-Victoire, Seen from Bellevue* of 1882–85 [79], where the foreground tree plays

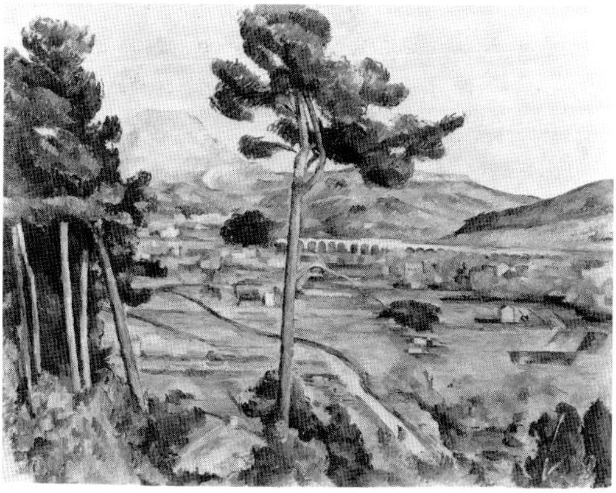

79 **Paul Cézanne**, *Mont Sainte-Victoire, Seen from Bellevue*, 1882–85. Oil on canvas, 65.4 x 81.6 cm, 25¾ x 32⅛ in.

against the emergent viaduct to the right. Here, temporality is asserted by the emergence of form from hypothetical formlessness as the arches of the viaduct entering on the right pick up shape – clarity and substance – just the way a train picks up speed, as they drive toward the soaring tree at the heart of the picture. This element of temporality versus permanence is something Courbet shares with Cézanne in *The Oak of Flagey*, however different the means used to suggest it.

Of course, Courbet, like Cézanne, was painting a landscape, not making a philosophical statement. Nevertheless, the assertiveness of his image, and his choice of title for it, suggest some intention beyond the mere record of a landscape motif. Or rather, one might say that for Courbet, as for many other artists of his time, there was nothing "mere" about a landscape subject: it meant something to choose to paint landscape. The great oak, for Courbet, was an image rich in multiple evocations: personal, political, historical, and artistic: in short, it had meaning for him.

In Cézanne's *Great Pine and Red Earth*, the pine, created with a palette of rich, almost iridescent blues, violets, and greens, sweeps across the surface of the canvas, anchoring the boundaries of its energy and the edges of its burgeoning foliage firmly at the borders of the picture plane. Every touch of Cézanne's brush demonstrates both his mastery and his ability to make use of the spontaneous rightness of his visual judgment. See, for example, in this canvas, how the apparently haphazardly placed white rectangle to the left of the tree trunk complements the multiplicity of its intertwined horizontal branches to its right; or the way this crucial white flat rectangle echoes the volumetric rectangular forms of the houses scattered in the background. The meaning of a specific paint-shape is contextual in Cézanne's late landscapes. It can, on the one hand, signify difference – a white rectangle may function as highlight; as a cluster of pine needles under daylight; as a farmhouse in a distant field – or it can act as a forceful agent of pictorial unity, tying together the disparate elements of the landscape composition.

Robert Adams' *Sitka Spruce, Cape Blanco State Park*, the most recent of the tree images, published in Adams' volume *Turning Back* in 2005, is the only one in black and white and the only photograph of the trio. It, like the paintings, depends on a sagacious crop for part of its power – indeed, as I mentioned above, we associate the crop with photographic practice rather than painting. Yet unlike the tree paintings, it depends on value alone – black, white, and all the values in between, for its pictorial construction. Of course, value is itself one of the three elements of color, the others being hue and intensity. Courbet depends much more heavily than Cézanne on variations of value for his effects, working his tree up from a dark underpainting to the pale impasto of the highlights. Yet we perceive black, white, and gray as much more than lack in Adams' photograph. According to the late Louis Marin, who turns to the seventeenth-century theorists Charles-Alphonse Dufresnoy and Roger de Piles for support, both black and white are colors, "or rather, *meta*colors, if we dare to use such an expression."[2] I, for one, have no desire to see the Sitka spruce in full

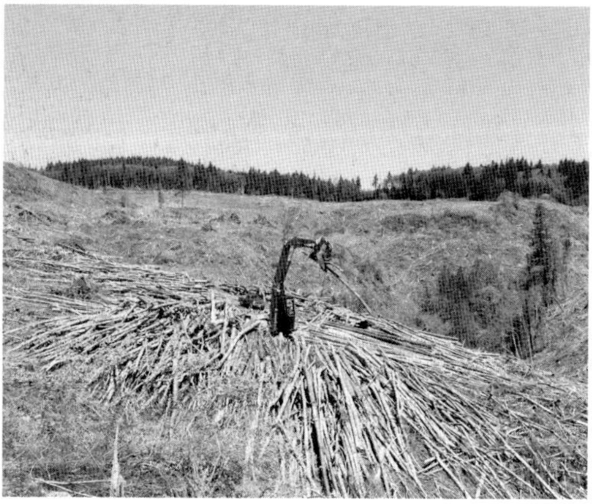

80 **Robert Adams**, *Stacking the de-limbed trunks of an immature "harvest", Columbia County, Oregon*, 1999–2002. Gelatin-silver print, 22.9 x 26.7 cm, 9 x 10½ in.

technicolor. It is lack of color that gives the dense, close-packed skeletal structure of the trunk and branches, set off by feathery gray areas of misty needles, its black-and-white austerity. The spruce has a foreboding presence that it would not have had in color. The looming tree in black and white stands for something, reaches out to the viewer in a way that color would destroy. Delicate and powerful at once, it communicates both its strength, its endurance, and, in the context of contemporary ecology – its vulnerability.

Adams' *Sitka Spruce* assumes its full – or fuller – meaning only in the context of a series of works recording the destruction of the Oregon forests, images such as *Stacking the de-limbed trunks of an immature "harvest"* [80] or *Clatsop County*. Together, the series constitutes a powerful and moving ecological indictment, countering the iconography of endurance produced by both Courbet's and, to a lesser extent, Cézanne's trees in the nineteenth century.[3] No, asserts Adams' contemporary series, the image of a great tree may signify power, but in reality, nothing is more vulnerable. In minutes or days, what took centuries to grow can be destroyed, eliminated from the earth by faceless profiteers who mow down whole landscapes with their machinery. The fallen, murdered trees conjure up memories of corpses strewn over the battlefield, like Mathew Brady's Civil War set pieces of fallen soldiers, or, at the farthest extreme, but certainly not unthinkable, the horrifying postwar pictures of the corpses at Auschwitz, piled up, to reverse the metaphor, like so much dead wood in front of the barbed wire. These, then, are pictures of trees replete with meaning, the great powerful standing spruce only a prelude and a foil to a longer narrative of total devastation.

In the case of Courbet's Oak, the title "The Oak at Falgey, known as the Oak of Vercingetorix, Caesar's Camp near Alesia, Franche-Comté" gives us several clues, both about Courbet's attachment to his native turf, his Franc-Comtois territory and, more specifically, the painting's position as evidence in a heated historiographic battle, a subject I will consider in more depth below. Many of Courbet's landscapes bear the names of local sites – *The Grotto of the Loue* [87, p.198], *The Source of the Lison*, *The*

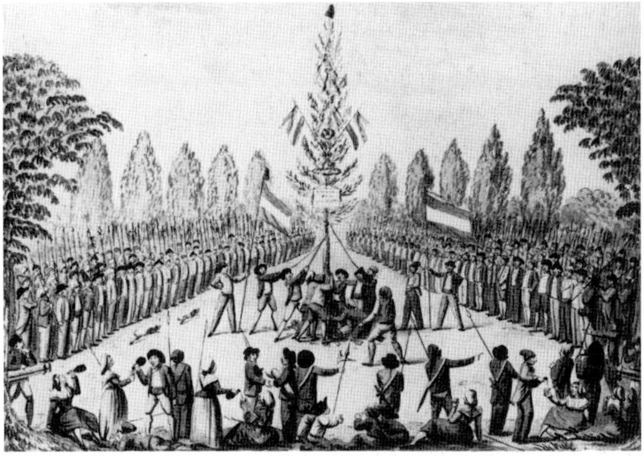

81 **Etienne Béricourt,**
The Planting of a Liberty Tree,
*c.*1791. Gouache

Puits Noir, The Gour de Conche – and many of them are "tourist spots" which had previously been commemorated in the elegant lithographs of the *Voyages pittoresques* edited by Baron Taylor,[4] and later immortalized as ubiquitous picture postcards.

The oak tree itself had had a long history of significance in European religious and secular practice. It had played a major role in the religious rituals of the Druids in pre-Roman Britain. Sir James Frazer devoted a whole chapter to the "Worship of the Oak" in *The Golden Bough* (1890), and the very name of Druid, he said, is believed to mean nothing more than "Oak Man." They built their altars beneath the chosen oak, marked out by the growth of mistletoe upon it.[5]

More germane to the significance of Courbet's painting, the oak had also played an important role in the imagery of secular history in ancient Europe, commemorating the civic rights and political self-determination of a region or province. The best known of these is the famous oak of Guernica, venerated as the emblem of the independent government of the Basque people, where the Diet of Vizcaya met to administer the laws of the nation. The national anthem of the Basque nation was, and is, in fact "Guernikako Arbola." It was the existence of this tree that made Guernica the "holy town" of the Basques, compounding the outrage of the Fascist bombing of the city commemorated in Picasso's *Guernica,* for the oak was the embodiment of the freedom and independence of the province. The original oak of Guernica is now dead and a replacement that grew in front of the City Hall died in 2004; it was replaced by still another oak grown from the old tree's acorns. The original oak's gnarled trunk is preserved and venerated as a secular relic. This is but one of many such secular icons of civic independence that flourished throughout Europe during the Middle Ages and the early modern period. The French Revolution sharpened that image with the many popular representations of the planting of the Tree of Liberty [81]. The Liberty Tree was usually a poplar rather than an oak, based on the false etymology relating the French word for "people" (*peuple*) with the tree: the "peuplier."

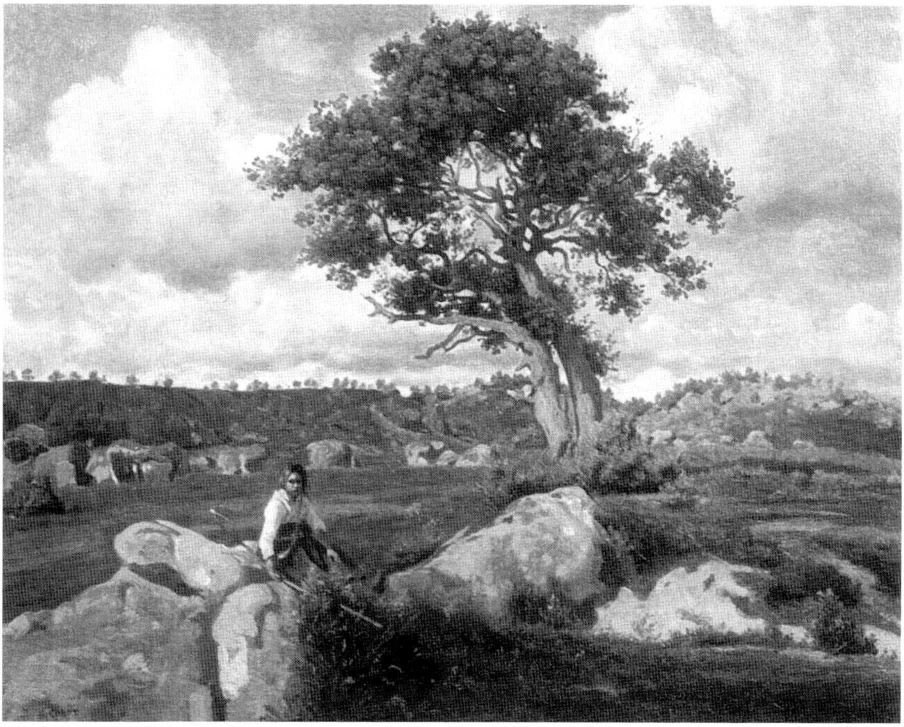

82 **Jean-Baptiste-Camille Corot**, *Le Rageur*, 1830–34. Oil on canvas, 50.8 x 61 cm, 20 x 24 in.

A simple sense of regional pride was expressed quite frequently in famous tree images, often images of oaks, in the period of Courbet's painting: Corot's *Le Rageur* of 1830–34 commemorated a great oak of the Forest of Fontainebleau [82], and a less celebrated artist, Charles Bavoux, who came from Courbet's own region, living in Besançon, showed his *Oak of my Village* in the Salon of 1867, the very year that Courbet exhibited his *Oak of Flagey.*

Yet the regional tree, often the oak, was not merely celebrated in painting. Popular journals ran illustrated articles, dedicated to the promotion of well-known local trees. In 1850, the *Magasin pittoresque* published an illustration of the *Giant Oak of Montravail*, as part of a series of publications of noteworthy trees of the various regions of France [23, p.39]. In 1862, the popular journal *L'Illustration* published an ambitious article "Quelques arbres célèbres," which, after mentioning such world famous specimens as the Bo tree of Ceylon, the "venerable patriarch of vegetation;" the Oak of William the Conqueror in Windsor Forest, and the Parliament Oak in Clipstone Forest, went on to show its readers a variety of less widely publicized regional trees illustrious for age, size or association, trees such as the Chêne d'Allouville, near Yvetot, an oak so enormous that it contained a chapel in its gnarled trunk.

Practitioners of the relatively new medium of photography were keen to record nature in all its forms, and trees in particular. Gustave Le Gray was known for his photographs of the Forest of Fontainebleau in the late 1840s and 1850s [83], Henry le Secq for his work in the Forest of Montmirail.[6] For these early photographers, trees, like architecture – and unlike people or animals – had the advantage of immobility. In their concreteness, and their implicit if not always explicit recording of specific locality – the photographer, after all, had to be there, on that spot, in order to capture the image – such tree-pictures both depended on and at the same time called into question, with a new kind of unchallengeable veracity, that profound sense of authentic localization so central to the Realist enterprise in painting.

Courbet's *Oak*, however, evokes something more than either its realist veracity or its regional affiliation. The subtitle of the painting when it was shown in 1867 asserted that it was not merely the Oak of Flagey but also, that it is "known as the Oak of Vercingetorix, Caesar's camp near Alesia, Franche-Comté." As such, the painting was to be understood as a counter in one of those heated archeological disputes of the nineteenth century that involved far more than the dispassionate methodology of science. On the contrary, this dispute, the so-called Battle of Alesia, involved a strong element of regional patriotism as well as a heavy dose of encoded political rancor. The "Battle of Alesia" referred to an argument about the precise location of the historic plateau that had served as the ground for Julius Caesar's decisive defeat of the Gallic chieftain Vercingetorix in the Battle of Alesia in 52 BC. By the late 1850s, the choice of sites had narrowed down to Alaise near Flagey, where Courbet's family owned property, or the Mont Auxois near Alise-Sainte-Reine in the Côte d'Or. On the side of Alaise in the Franche-Comté were ranged a large cast of local *erudits*, most prominent among them Jules Etienne Joseph Quicherat; professor at the Ecole des Chartes and one of the founding fathers of French archeology. Quicherat published two combatative papers, "L'Alesia de César rendue à la Franche-Comté" (1857) and "Conclusion pour Alaise dans la Question d'Alesia" (1858), attempting to establish, with a good deal

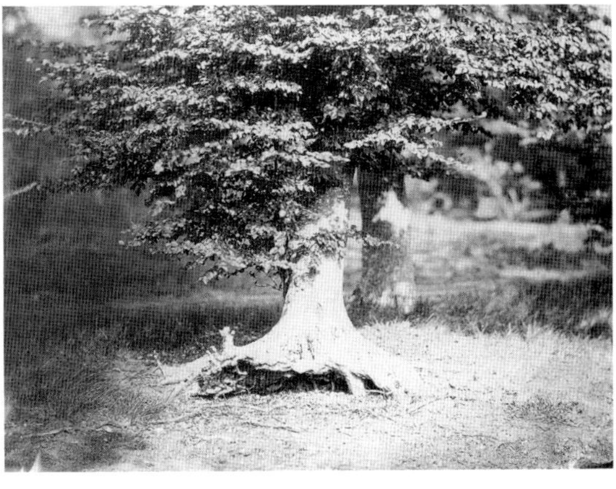

83 **Gustave Le Gray**, *Beech Tree, Fontainebleu*, *c.*1855–57. Albumen print from collodion-on-glass negative, 31.9 x 41.3 cm, 12¾ x 16¼ in.

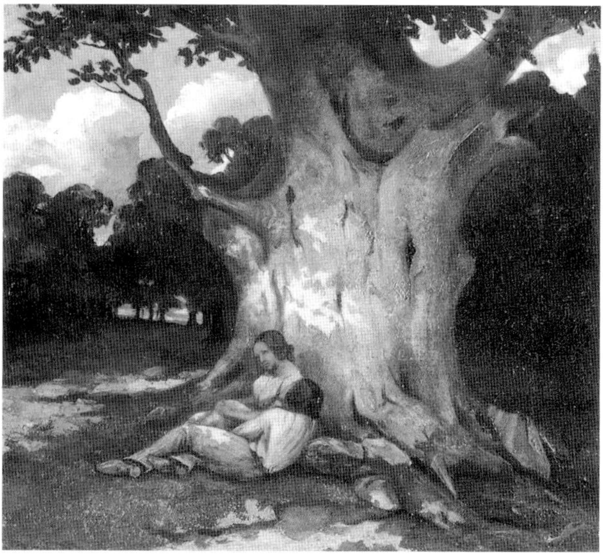

84 *The Large Oak*, 1843–44. Oil on canvas, 29 x 32 cm, 11½ x 12⅝ in.

of etymological sophistication, but many archeological errors, the claims of Alaise as the site of the Gauls' defeat and concluding in no uncertain terms: "Alaise est l'antique Alesia."[7] The victory of Courbet's Alaise was shortlived, however, and the ultimate blow to the Franc-Comtois claims was dealt by none other than the Emperor Napoleon III himself. In May 1866, the Emperor published the second volume of his *Histoire de Jules César*, parts of which had already appeared in the press, in which he fully substantiated the authenticity of the site in the Côte d'Or with overwhelming archeological evidence and documentation, basing his conclusions on the evidence supplied by state-sponsored digs executed around the Mont Auxois from 1862 to 1865.[8]

These discoveries had already been broadly disseminated to the general public as well as to specialists, in journals such as the *Moniteur universelle*, in 1863, and, by 1865, even more public, official and visible sanction had been given to the imperial claims of Alise-Sainte-Reine as the authentic site of the historic battle in the form of a gigantic statue of Vercingetorix, commissioned especially for the plateau d'Alise-Sainte-Reine, which made a conspicuous appearance in the Salon. Dubbed "the monument of the boiler-makers" ("le monument des chaudronniers") by disrespectful art students, the work, created by the now forgotten Aime Millet, was castigated by Courbet's friend and supporter Théophile Thoré, who declared of it: "The truth is that the large and patriotic figure of the defender of Gaul against the Roman Empire has not been poetically felt by M. Millet. This long tube of copper signifies nothing at all. Perhaps the art of our epoch understands Caesar better than Vercingetorix." This last remark was of course a veiled attack on Napoleon III and his "caesarism" by a left-wing critic of the regime. Napoleon III did, in fact, strongly identify his aims, his achievements, and his very persona with those of his Roman predecessor. In his account of the Roman conquest of Gaul, the Emperor's sympathies were clearly on the side of Caesar and against the Gauls and their lack of a strong central authority, their clinging to the kind of democratic regionalism that was precisely what Courbet was celebrating in his *Oak of Flagey*. Courbet's painting then, has a hidden political agenda, understandable only if we are aware of the specific relationship of this realistic depiction of a local oak tree to larger and more general political issues of the day in France. In terms of genres, we can compare Millet's state-sponsored academic monstrosity – everything Courbet hated – to his own conception of the Vercingetorix theme: a landscape motif rather than a heroic monument, positing the authority of nature, to borrow Klaus Herding's term, against the trumpery of ill-conceived artifice. In short, it was rich in provocative meaning, political and otherwise.

However, I wish to conclude this investigation of the meanings invested in Courbet's *Oak* with more than a purely political reading. The oak tree motif also serves as a profound revelation of the self at different stages of the artist's *personal* history. A dominating oak had appeared several times in Courbet's œuvre, in contexts of deep personal meaning, before reaching its apotheosis in *The Oak of Flagey*. The tree had played a leading role in *The Large Oak* of 1843–44 [84], in which a male figure, presumably the artist, and a female one, presumably the Lise whose name is carved on the trunk, recline at the base of the mighty trunk. In *The Portrait of the Artist*, called *The Wounded Man*, begun in 1844 and altered to its present state, and highly melodramatic subject, perhaps ten years later, the artist lies expiring in seductive close-up at the foot of the very oak that had sheltered him and his lover in the earlier *Large Oak*. In the original version of this canvas Courbet had depicted himself with his arm about a young woman whom he later painted out and, as a rejected lover, substituted

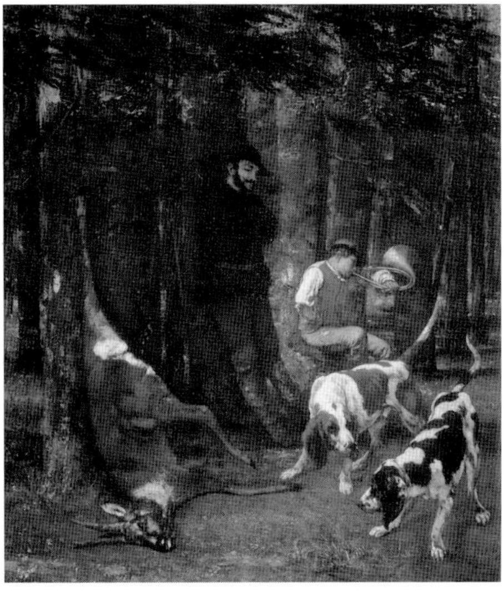

85 *The Quarry*, 1857. Oil on canvas, 210 x 183.5 cm, 82¾ x 72¼ in.

his literally bleeding heart for the image of his faithless sweetheart [pl.9, p.72]. In *The Quarry*, a work of 1857 [85], Courbet had represented himself as a triumphant hunter, contemplatively leaning against a tree trunk, in a self-image that almost seems to illustrate his highly romantic thoughts about the implications of the hunter's role in society. "The hunter," he said, "is a man of independent character who has a free spirit, or at least the feeling of liberty. He is a wounded soul, a heart that goes to stimulate its languor in the vagueness and melancholy of the woods."

In his most elaborate self-portrait, *The Painter's Studio* of 1855 [pl.11, pp.138–39], Courbet had indentified his mission with the painting of nature, depicting himself working on a landscape of his native territory at the center of his ambitious, multifigured canvas. In *The Oak of Flagey*, almost ten years later, he has created a kind of self-portrait, too, a portrait of the artist as an oak tree, rooted firmly in the ground, energetic and powerful, outreaching and expansive in his generous creation. Nature and artist, landscape and art have assumed a single identity here. Still later, pathetically, nature and the artist separate, after the ordeal and the persecution of Courbet following the fall of the Commune. Then, when he paints himself in prison, it is a tree – not a powerful oak, but a wispy, uncertain little tree, poised wistfully between the bars of his cell in the courtyard of Sainte-Pélagie – that offers an alternative to, rather than identity with, the figure of the incarcerated artist [48, p.85]. As a small epitome of nature, of light, of growth, a token of lost liberty – of everything, in short, that prison, personal and political defeat, and humiliation are not – the little tree offers a poignant contrast to the artist in his dark reclusion.

In many of Courbet's other landscapes, the meanings are less complex or multilayered, depending more on formal choices than historic references. To begin with, the implications of close-up vision in Courbet's construction of the natural motif must be considered. Courbet is at his best doing close-ups – another term, like "the crop" borrowed from photography – of landscape motifs. Indeed, the close-up seems to me to be an essential component of what might be called his Realist vision in general.

In a work such as *The Young Ladies of the Village* of 1852 [pl. 4, p.70] Courbet brings the whole landscape vista close to. He cannot let go of the defining detail of individual elements, even when they interfere with the effects of spatial recession demanded by conventional linear and aerial perspective. The *Young Ladies* was pilloried for its incompetent handling of perspective and diminution of scale by critics when it appeared in the 1853 Salon: the cows seemed like dogs, too small for their place in the perspective scheme: the cliffs in the background were represented with the same amount of surface detail as the terrain in the foreground.[9] Some of Courbet's best landscapes, such as his various versions of *The Grotto of the Loue* [63, p.150, and 87], embody this sense of literal nearsightedness, a feeling of intimate acquaintance, dependent on the landscape motif being close to rather than distant from the artist, and by extension, close to the spectator as well.

When Courbet backs up, he tends to lose focus and formal integrity, as he does in the recently rediscovered *The Gust of Wind* [86], a meaningless, ambitiously large-scale hodgepodge of disparate landscape motifs that falls apart in the center rather than leading into depth, and has an unpleasant, blurry, badly painted foreground. This is Courbet showing all his stuff in a single big canvas, probably at the demand of a single patron, and straying, as he sometimes does in the later work, out of his area of competence as a landscape painter. In short, this is a meaningless painting, a kind of made-to-order pastiche of tasty motifs and slipshod brushwork.[10]

Having mentioned the word "patron," I would like to interject an important scholarly disagreement about the meaning and status of Courbet's landscapes. This battle of interpretations is constituted by two important articles about Courbet's landscapes: Anne Wagner's "Courbet's Landscapes and Their Market," which appeared in *Art History* in 1981, and Klaus Herding's "Equality and Authority in Courbet's Landscape Painting," originally published in German in 1977 and republished in his book *Courbet: To Venture Independence* in 1991.[11] I am oversimplifying Wagner's complex and sophisticated argument when I maintain that her article asserts that Courbet sold out in his later landscapes, and that he tailored his compositions quite explicitly to fit the desires of his patrons, those urban businessmen who were his major source of income. To fulfill these desires, the artist relied on the seductive generalizations of *effet* to produce works devoid of the harsh and hard-won pictorial specificity of his earlier figural painting: these landscapes were, in the terms we have been considering, more or less devoid of meaning. For Wagner, many of

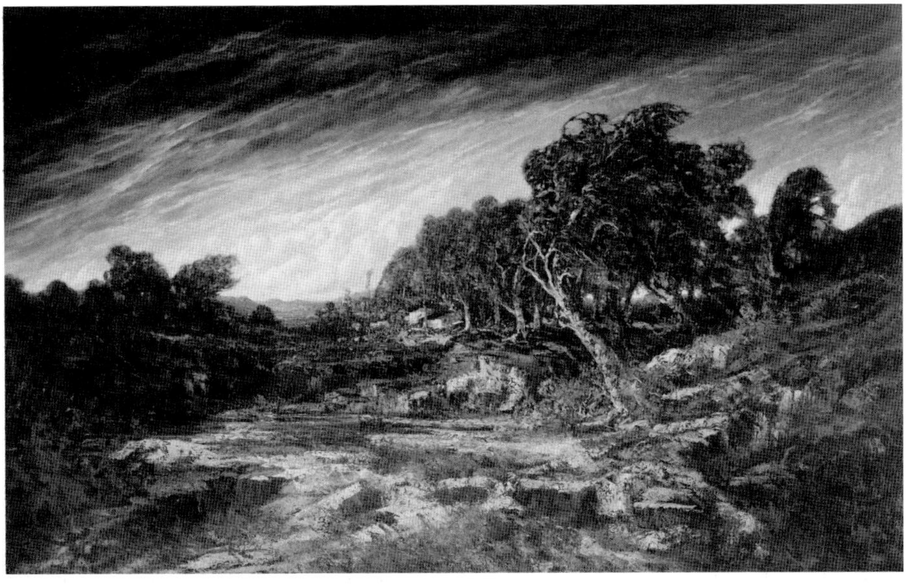

86 *The Gust of Wind*, c.1865. Oil on canvas, 143.5 x 228.5 cm, 56½ x 90 in.

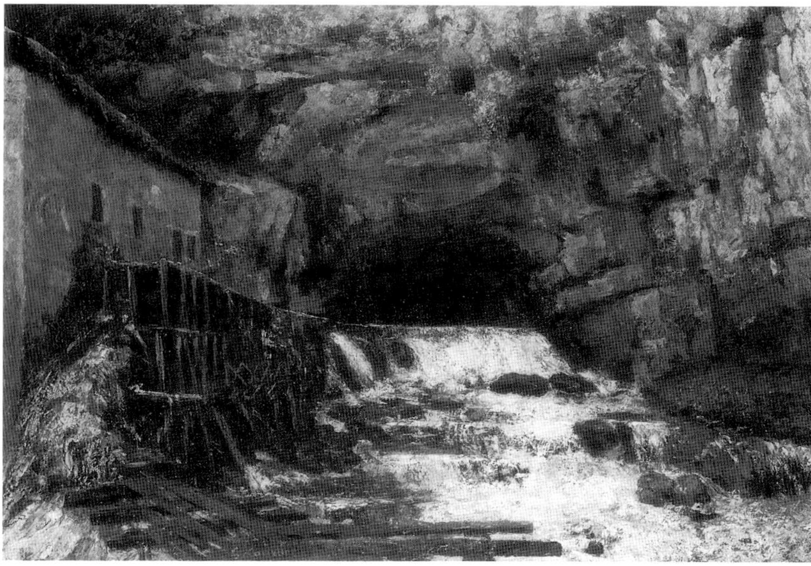

87 *Grotto of the Loue*, 1864. Oil on canvas, 99.7 x 142.2 cm, 39¼ x 56 in.

Courbet's later landscapes are to be considered as mere counters in the creation of exchange value, shoddy goods in the marketplace.

Klaus Herding, on the other hand, feels that Courbet turned to landscape as a covert political stratagem during the Second Empire, a period when overt political meanings were unacceptable in a work of art. He thinks the landscapes were assertions both of artistic independence and anti-establishment commentary. To borrow Wagner's neat summary of Herding's position on the landscapes: "His thesis works from the claim that after 1857 these pictures were the core of Courbet's production, not just in numbers, but in the meanings they contain. For Herding they are, like the figure paintings, vehicles for a social critique. He suggests that Courbet's choice of particular landscape motifs conveys an implicit challenge to governmental power as located in the person of Napoleon III. Moreover, the argument runs, Courbet's hierarchical, equal treatment of compositional elements over the whole surface of the canvas results in a uniform planarity which permits the transference of certain abstract ideas, like equality or solitude, to the canvas. Their form allows the pictures to stand as embodiments of such ideas and their message, he asserts, is consistent with Courbet's increasing adherence after 1857 to a politics of anarchy."[12]

Of course, both these readings may be true to some degree. Producing work in accordance with a patron's wishes does not necessarily result in bad or "meaningless" art any more than painting from pure inspiration means good art. Bach wrote almost all his greatest music for patrons, while many second-rate Sunday painters certainly "venture independence," to borrow the title of Herding's book on Courbet, and paint from their own hearts desire and individual inspiration with less than happy results.

Nor do I believe that one can generalize about all of Courbet's landscapes during the Second Empire and after; there are great variations in the quality of his production. I think there are significant variables visible in the landscapes of the 1860s and 1870s, variables that affect both Courbet's approach to his territory and the production of meaning in his work. To understand these variations in quality and approach, we need to scrutinize what I have called his close-up vision in greater detail.

The various versions of *Source of the Loue* are paradigms of this close-up vision, problematizing the issues of both territoriality and meaning [63, p.150]. They are near-sighted visions of one of Courbet country's major tourist attractions: the source, or head, of the Loue river. I was surprised when I visited Ornans to find that the landscape element in question is a vertical one, the cliff rising high above the grotto itself. As Courbet zeroes in on the source, it becomes a compact, anti-recessional motif; at its purest, in the Metropolitan Museum version [87], an intense close-up view, a horizontal squarish composition that pulls stratified rocks, rickety wooden structure and foam up to the surface of the canvas for the viewer's delectation: Courbet pays careful attention to two kinds of foaming stream – less purely white where it is reduced to a relatively weak trickle on left, richly stippled and variegated at the main waterfall. There is a meaningful contrast between nature and culture intimated by the smoother brushwork and regularized form used for the structure of the brown wooden shack to the left as opposed to the variegated palette-knife work – incrusted and smeared greens, pinks, yellows – in the rocky strata to the right. Courbet's vision is naturally geological, so to speak, in works like these, as Petra Chu revealed in an important article on Courbet and contemporary geological research several years ago.[13]

Yet there is deep recession in all the *Sources*, a veritable black hole at the heart of the image, pulling us into dark, mysterious depths as adamantly as the richly painted foaming waterfall pulls us forward. It is the presence of this dark hole at the center of the composition that suggests that along with territorialism, attachment to local sites of the Franche-Comté, and a desire to make them the motifs of his art, there are other issues of meaning inscribed in this landscape series.

Certainly, the "meaning" is far less intentional and political in the various versions of the source of the Loue than it was in *The Oak of Flagey*, but it is certainly present, even if it is evocations and analogies rather than intentionalities. First of all, there is the historical association of such natural

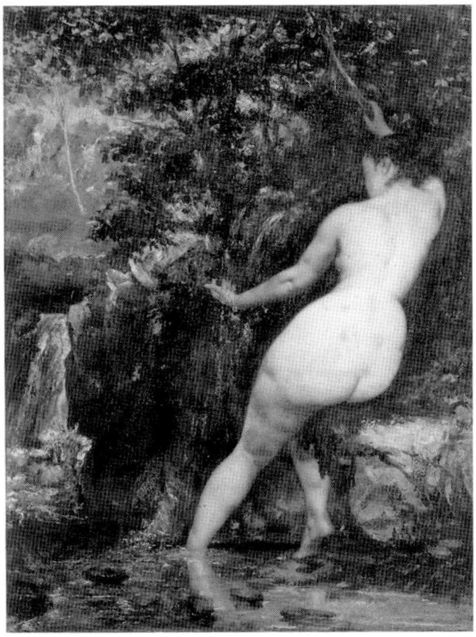

88 *The Source*, 1868. Oil on canvas, 129 x 97 cm, 50¾ x 38⅛ in.

sites with the female body, preferably the nude female body. Courbet not only was aware of such associations but painted several works drawing on that associative tradition. Such a work is *The Source* [88] of 1868, an updated version of the classical "Nymph of the Spring" topos, a nymph whose wasp-waisted form and generous buttocks conform more to the fashion dictates and corsets of the mid-nineteenth century, not to speak of Courbet's personal taste, than to the ideals of classical antiquity or the Italian Renaissance .

Of course, there are the analogies to be drawn between grotto and female sex, between that deep dark metacolor at the heart of the Source paintings and Courbet's commissioned pornographic rendering of the so-called *bas ventre* of a naked model in the notorious *Origin of the World* [pl.10, p.137], painted at roughly the same time as the landscapes. Is this a meaningful connection that Courbet intentionally constructed or something we, post-Freudians, hot on the trail of the fetish wherever it may lead us, have attached to the image? (I might add that in the strictly Freudian sense, *The Origin of the World* is the farthest possible remove from a fetishistic image.) There is, of course, a tradition of analogizing landscape and female bodies. Then there is the fact that Jacques Lacan, post-Freudian supreme, owned this painting and seems to have commissioned his surrealist friend André Masson to create a landscape version of it as a kind of cover .... Did Courbet himself think of this analogy between cunt and cave? Did he paint the source of the Loue over and over again because he was secretly painting the sex of a woman? This is not very likely. *The Origin* was not his spontaneous creation. It was commissioned, by Kahlil Bey, the Turkish ambassador to the Court of St. Petersburg, bon vivant and avid collector of erotic art, for whom Courbet created his pair of Lesbian nudes, *Sleep* [36, p.58], and who also owned that masterpiece of tightly packed female flesh, Ingres's *Turkish Bath*.[14] Yet the analogies between the

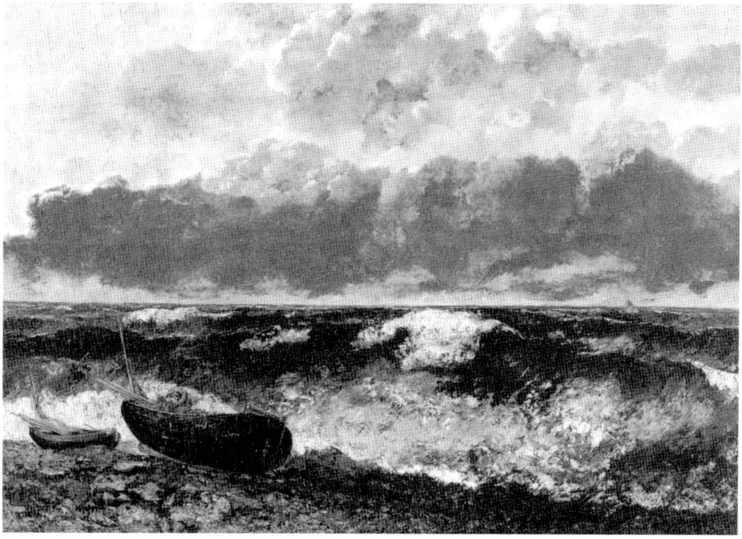

89 *The Wave*, 1870. Oil on canvas, 117 x 160 cm, 46 x 63 in.

landscape motif and the female sex certainly exist, and once we have seen them, they do not disappear but color our vision of the natural theme forever: in short, these analogies become part of its meaning. Certainly, they must have colored the vision of Marcel Duchamp, who seems to have made reference to both Courbet's landscape and his *Origin* in his notorious *Etant donnés* of 1946–56.[15]

In contrast to the many canvases devoted to the valley of the Loue and its environs, Courbet's sea paintings of the 1860s and 1870s – what he called his "paysages de mer" – are obviously not attached to his native territory. Rather, these sea motifs are the common property of the artists who settled on the Normandy coast during this period, or for part of the year at least, in such popular spots as touristic Trouville and picturesque Etretat. The group included Boudin and Monet, as well as Courbet and many lesser-known figures such as Eugène Le Poittevin, from whom Courbet rented a beach house.[16] Courbet painted in both places: Trouville in 1865 and Etretat in 1869, when he created many versions of the wave motif, none of them done out of doors, incidentally.[17] Guy de Maupassant, who also frequented the Normandy coast, has left a description of a visit to Courbet *in situ*, in his rented house on the beach.

> In a great bare room, a fat, dirty, greasy man was spreading patches of white paint onto a big bare canvas with a kitchen-knife. From time to time, he went and pressed his face against the windowpane to look at the storm. The sea came up so close that it seemed to beat right against the house, which was smothered in foam and noise. The dirty water rattled like hail against the window and streamed down the walls. On the mantelpiece was a bottle of cider and a half-empty glass. Every now and then Courbet would drink a mouthful and then go back to his painting. It was called *The Wave* and it made a good deal of stir in its time.[18] [89]

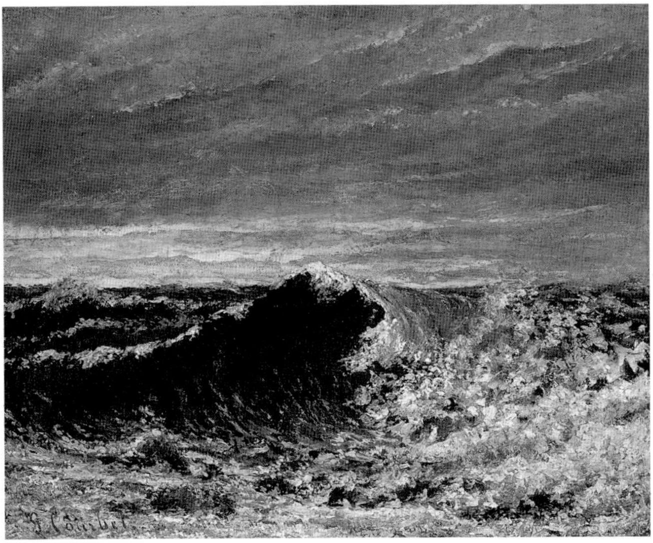

90 *The Wave*, c.1871.
Oil on canvas,
46 x 55 cm, 18⅛ x 21⅝ in.

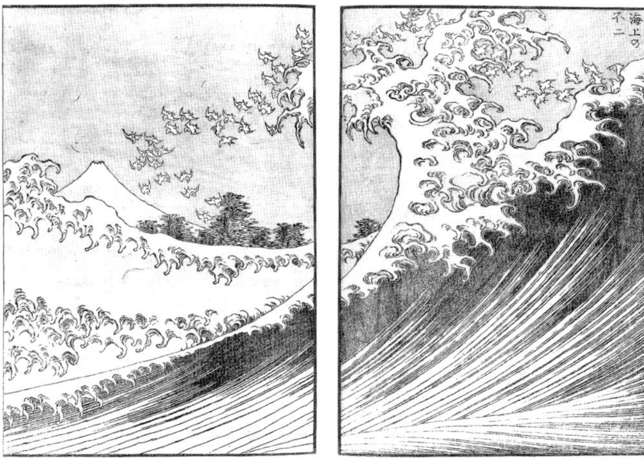

91 **Katsushika Hokusai,** *Fuji at Sea.* Woodcut, *One Hundred Views of Mount Fuji*, vol. 2, 1835

In another, later version, this one in the National Gallery of Scotland – the wave is a thick, dense, congealed, indeed, frozen, image [90]. Its force lies at its center, its ephemerality at the margins, where brilliant streaks, blots, blobs, and splashes of white paint re-enact the dynamics of the wave's muscular up thrust from the turbulent sea-surface. One thinks back to Aby Warburg's ascription of the vitality of antique and renaissance nudes to the movement and agitation of their transparent drapery, fluttering veils at the margins of the placid nude figures they both covered and revealed.

Storms at sea, shipwrecks, and maritime disasters were staples of traditional marine painting – think of Turner, Géricault or Delacroix, or Claude-Joseph Vernet, who specialized in imagery of marine disaster – but the single wave, unaccompanied by a storm-tossed boat or other elements of narrative implication, was a relatively new topic in Courbet's time. It was not a motif without precedent, however, for the Japanese printmaker Katsushika Hokusai had popularized the theme of the great wave with his woodblock print, *Fuji at Sea*, published in his *One Hundred Views of Mount Fuji* in the 1830s [91]. Courbet, moving as he did in the circle of Monet and Manet in Paris and on the Norman coast as well, must certainly have been familiar with Japanese prints of this sort, and it is unthinkable that he did not have Hokusai's prototype in mind when he went to do his own version from nature. However, I do not believe it is a question of influence or even of Harold Bloom's "anxiety of influence" here, in this, the most stylized of Courbet's wave paintings, although the latter may have entered into the relationship between the Courbet *Wave* and the Hokusai woodblock. Neither of them, of course, bears much relationship to the look of a real wave, indexically correct in the photographed version by Gustave Le Gray [92]. I took Courbet's image to the beach on stormy days both in Long Island and on the Normandy coast, and I am quite sure that there is no wave that looks exactly like it, or the Hokusai, of course. Real waves look more like the photograph – they come in curling

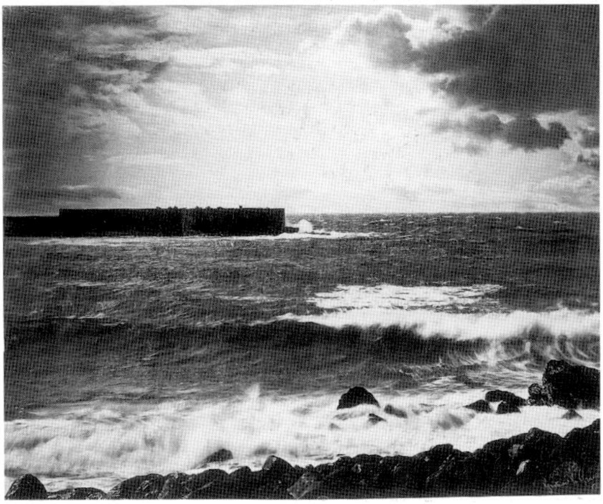

92 **Gustave Le Gray,** *The Great Wave, Sète,* 1857. Albumen print from two collodion-on-glass negatives, 35.7 x 41.9 cm, 14 x 16½ in.

rows.[19] But Courbet's wave is more forceful, scarier, in short, more "wavelike" – akin to the wave fixed in our imagination – than any actually viewed wave. It is not real, but better as a wave, rather in the way that the traditional flying gallop – depicting the rushing horse with front and back legs extended like a bird in flight – looked more like a horse's racing gait than any tame photo of the actual way a horse's legs are deployed when it gallops. Courbet may have looked at the Japanese woodblock, admired it, and then said to himself, "But I can do you one better, Hokusai. I can make a powerful, muscular, realist wave direct from nature, a giant three-dimensional wave in spritzy impasto that will knock your fairytale decorative version clear off its rice paper." Yet Courbet, like Hokusai, sticks to the surface, although building up layers of thickness on it with paint, a practice foreign to the literal flatness of the woodblock medium.

So what does the wave mean? Or rather, what do the various waves mean, for there are quite a few different versions of the subject [55, p.123]. Klaus Herding offers the most consistent and substantial interpretation of their meaning. The wave pictures, he asserts, are particularly important because they represent "the culmination ... of the artist's complex relationship to nature, especially as regards the factors of equality and authority [....] The lack of distance common to all of Courbet's wave paintings again confronts the viewer with nature as a threat [...] their masses of water and clouds affect the viewer like a surprise attack." "In the wave paintings," Herding continues, "he qualifies both the notion of human subjugation to a natural order that brings everything to its own level, and the ideology of human domination and omnipotence. His attack is directed equally at the belief in nature as a quasi-mythological redeeming force and its total utilization – both of which were publicly propagated under Napoleon III." But neither of these concerns was wholly negative. The waves also "attempt, through exact observation of nature, to collect experience which could be fed back as imagery into society, in conformance with Courbet's

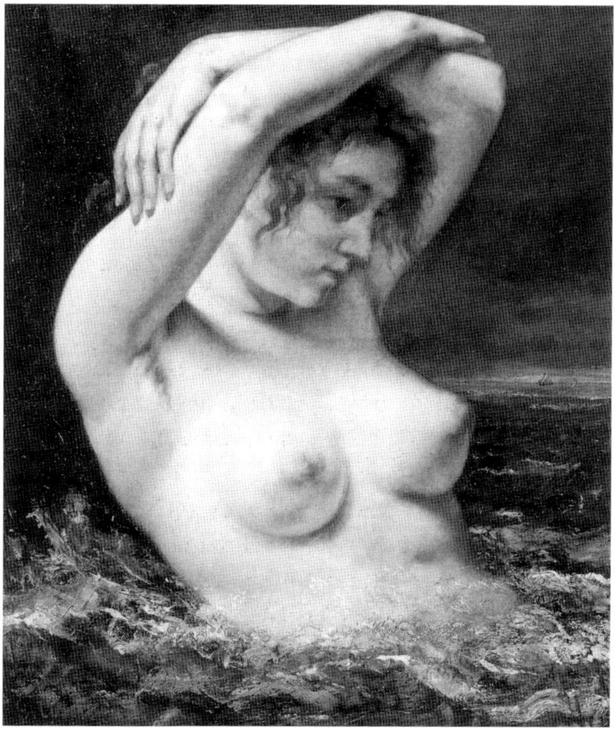

93 *The Woman in the Waves*, 1868. Oil on canvas, 65 x 54 cm, 25⅝ x 21¼ in.

desire to work through art for individual freedom and finally for democracy."[20] This seems to me, despite its complexity and conviction, quite a tall order for Courbet's wave paintings, a reading that, although brilliant and politically hopeful, lies more in the realm of speculation and wishful thinking than empirical evidence and visual analysis. Certainly, Courbet was far from rejecting the "belief in nature as a quasi-mythological redeeming force," albeit on his own terms, as he powerfully demonstrates in his modernized version of the Venus Anadyomene theme, with a lusty, busty nineteenth-century country girl taking a dip in the sea substituting for the time-honored Venus in the waves motif of traditional painting: one of the most robustly sensual, sexually provocative images in his repertory [93].

Courbet, in short, whether in his own territory or an adopted one like the Normandy coast, often reverts to what we might call the "primordial form" of the natural object, whether it be tree, wave or grotto, an image, however naturalistic in some respects, which is at the same time true to the felt reality of the motif in question. Although waves break, characteristically, in horizontal rows, the foam appearing when the wave folds over, the single, vertical wave conveys a greater sense of power, of natural agency, even of "masculinity" than the experienced wave. The horizontal row of waves curling over and breaking suggests against the grain and, despite the noisy splash and the activated palette-knife work, a mood of peace, harmony, and rest.

Horizontality is a restful direction, according to Seurat and his theoretical guide, Charles Henry, who constructed a convenient code of directional meaning in composition.[21] Courbet, in his wave paintings looks toward individuation and verticality as his compositional basis, to increase the sense of ominous power in the motif, just as he emphasizes the verticality and at the same time the spreading horizontality of his oak – power and protective peace combined in a meaningful dialectic of compositional rhetoric, based on, but not subordinated to, objective observation of nature.

Much has been made recently, especially by feminist art historians, of the hitherto neglected sense of touch in painting, an art that obviously privileges the sense of sight. In a recent Cézanne symposium, in fact, the audience was regaled with several learned and theoretically sophisticated discourses directed toward greatly enlarged, eminently tactile daubs, streaks, smears and gobbets of paint – all in the interest of intensifying our awareness of touch as a determining factor in the creative process. But what about the sense of taste? No one, as far as I know, even in thrall to the trendiest abjection, has admitted that some paintings make us salivate, want to eat them, gobble them up or least lick their tempting surfaces – Courbet's among them. I am not talking about iconography – fruit or bread on a table – but on material quiddity, the gooey or crusty painterly substance. Look at all that delicious whipped cream, icing, hot fudge, Swiss cheese and so on.[22] Courbet's materialism knew no sensuous bounds it would seem; in much of his best work, it is overflowing the sedate categories separating real-life enjoyment from esthetic delectation, mundane sensuality from refined synesthesia. Isn't this germane to the meaning of Courbet's landscapes?[23]

At this point, it is worth asking if there are no limits separating the exploration of meaning in painting from wild speculation and personal flights of fancy. One can well imagine Courbet returning to earth and objecting. "Hey, pal, are you nuts?" or words to that effect. "You think I can't tell a cunt from a cliff? Or a cliff from a cheese? You want to eat my paintings? You should join the circle of my poor friend Vincent who ate his paints in a fit of madness, not me, I know what my paintings are and what they mean or don't mean. Don't bother me with your self-indulgent nonsense." That is what Courbet might say if he returned to us.

Well, sorry, my friend Courbet. Painters do not own the meaning of their works any more than they own the sites they paint. They may not even be conscious of some of the meanings their paintings have produced over time. Once that painting is out in the world, its meaning is up for grabs; anyone may interpret it. That does not mean all interpretations are equal of course. A reading of Courbet's painting may be more or less well supported by empirical evidence, art-historical experience of painterly strategies or hermeneutic brilliance. In other words, neither Courbet, nor anyone else, is obliged to accept my interpretations but I am certainly entitled to make them and my readers to judge them.

I am going to end this essay with an image referencing the very institution at which I gave the lecture on which it is based: the J. Paul Getty Museum and Art Center in Los

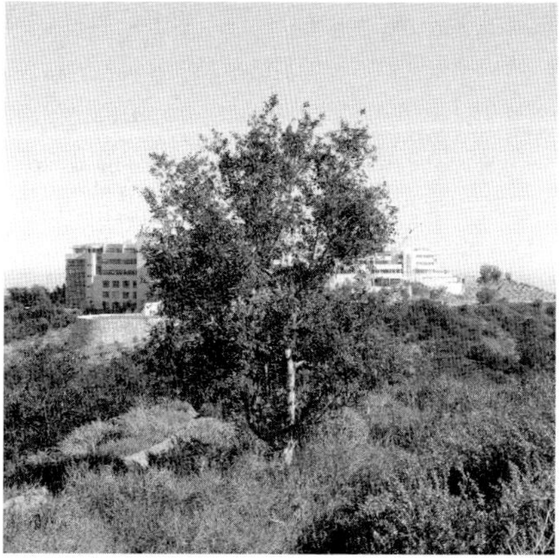

94 **Joe Deal**, *August 1997, Looking South.* Photograph of the Getty Center from the *Topos Portfolio*, 1984–97

Angeles [94]. This photograph of a nondescript tree standing before a building in the process of construction is part of a photographic essay by Joe Deal, recording the creation of the Getty and its larger social and cultural implications.[24] Nature and Culture are the critical elements here, and, as with Courbet's *Oak of Flagey*, the implications are surely political in the final instance. The tree in Joe Deal's essay, like Courbet's oak, asserts its authority, but, as in the case of Robert Adams' *Sitka Spruce*, for how long? Nature, in the visual arts, is itself a product of culture, a carefully "posed" view, manipulated by the artist, photographer and viewer to best advantage, for a purpose. The production of meaning, then, as announced in the title of this essay, is an inescapable part of the visual object. A sense of place, on the contrary, gets harder and harder to find, to settle on as more and more of the world gets transformed into a giant airport or parking lot or Hyatt Regency – places totally devoid of any sense of place whatever, as geography is rendered literally "atopical," hence, unreal.

The American writer Eudora Welty once claimed that creating a sense of place is one of the most effective ways that the writer of fiction has to maintain the ties of his work to reality. Place, says Welty, is where the writer has his roots: "Place is where he stands; in his experience out of which he writes it provides the base of reference, in his work the point of view .... Location pertains to feeling, feeling profoundly pertains to place."[25] Although she was writing about *Wuthering Heights* and *The Sound and the Fury*, her words apply equally to Courbet's *Oak of Flagey* or his *Source of the Loue*. I hope that through an examination of Courbet's landscapes and their meanings, I have illuminated the complex relationships tying Courbet's work, at its best, with reality, in the broadest, and the narrowest, senses of the term.

Notes

Introduction

1 Charles Baudelaire, "Salon of 1846," *The Mirror of Art*, ed. Jonathan Mayne (London, 1955).

2 The political interpretation has stood up over the test of time; the Masonic interpretation has fared less well.

3 Clearly a reference to *The Oak of Flagey*, until recently in the Pennsylvania Academy of the Fine Arts in Philadelphia. The painting was then in the collection of Henry C. Gibson in Philadelphia. Cited by Cecilia Beaux in her autobiography, *Background with Figures* (Boston, 1930), p. 38.

4 The dissertation was published by Garland Publishing, New York and London, in 1976, as part of their Outstanding Dissertations in the Fine Arts series. The original title of the dissertation, which was accepted for the doctorate in 1963, was "The Development and Nature of Realism in the Work of Gustave Courbet."

5 The article references George Sand's long section in *La Mare au diable* devoted to "La Noce de Campagne," the country wedding, in which the marriage customs incorporate references to violence and death. See Marie-Hélène Huet, "Ritual Violence: Courbet and George Sand," *New Literary History*, 26:4 (1995), pp. 833–55.

6 Elizabeth Bronfen, *Over Her Dead Body: Death, Femininity and the Aesthetic* (Manchester, 1992), pp. 259–60.

7 *Realismus als Widerspruch: Die Wirklichket in Courbets Malerei*, ed. Klaus Herding (Frankfurt, 1978), pp. 249–62 and 316–18.

8 "Paris Commune Photos at a New York Gallery: An Interview with Linda Nochlin," Jon Wiener, *Radical History Review*, 32 (1985), 59–74.

9 Manchester University Press, 1995.

10 It was published in *October*, 37 (Summer 1986), pp. 76–86. I am grateful to Rosalind Krauss, editor of *October* and longtime friend, for her generous and highly intelligent assistance in preparing the article for publication.

11 See for example, the admirably complete, even replete, publication by Thierry Savatier, *L'Origine du monde: Histoire d'un tableau de Gustave Courbet* (Paris, 2006), which offers the most thorough account of the painting's complicated provenance and a history of reception. Bernard Teyssèdre, in his lively *le roman de l'Origine*, offers a thoughtful and eminently readable account of and commentary on the painting. Also see Michèle Haddad, in *Khalil-Bey, un homme, une collection* (Paris, 2000), who denies the pornographic aspect of the *Origin* and implies that the impetus of the painting is the syphilis contracted by its commissioner, Khalil Bey; also A. Bessières, who, in *Courbet, Narcise ou Dionysos* (Paris, 1994) questions the painting's title and suggests it functions as a metaphor for Courbet the child of nature, or Dominique Massonaud, who, in *Courbet Scandale. Mythes de la rupture et Modernité* (Paris, 2003), puts forth a socio-political significance for the work, reading the female sex organ as a site for artistic creativity. Jean-Jacques Fernier, in his exh. cat., *Les Yeux les plus secrets* (Ornans, 1991) relates the *Origin*'s imagery to the Surrealist concept of eroticism linked irrevocably to death. There are many, many more publications and theories. I am grateful to Nicole Myers for assembling this material.

12 Valérie Bajou, *Courbet* (Paris, 2003), p. 344. The erotic photographs in question are by Belloq, and they were stereoscopic, enhancing their realism. For reproductions of the stereoscopic photographs in question, for whom the model is Augustine Legaton, see Dominique de Font-Réaulx, "Les Bouches d'Ombre" in Sylvie Aubernas, et al., *L'Art du nu au XIX siècle: le photographe et son modèle* (Paris, 1997), fig. 127, p. 119.

13 For an account of the important relationship, personal and intellectual, between Proudhon and Courbet, see James H. Rubin, *Courbet* (London, 1997).

14 Linda Nochlin, *Bathers, Bodies, Beauty: The Visceral Eye* (Cambridge, Mass., 2006), p.48.

15 More faithful to the spirit, if not the letter, of Courbet's *Origin* is Austrian artist Valie Export's performance piece, *Genital Panic* of 1969 in which she marched around and sat fully clothed except for the entire crotch of her jeans, which was cut out, revealing her naked sex to the world.

16 Smart Ass Press, Los Angeles, 2005.

17 When Balthus's first New York show opened at the Pierre Matisse Gallery in 1938 (J. T. Soby, *Balthus: Catalogue of the Exhibition at the Pierre Matisse Gallery*, New York, March 21–April 13, 1938), both James Thrall Soby and Alfred Frankfurter included Balthus's statement: "Je fais du Surréalisme à la Courbet" in their catalogue entries. The citation reveals that Balthus was engaged both with the Freudian Unconscious (which he denied) and Courbet's realism and painterly facture. I am grateful to my student Nate Donahue for this reference.

18 P.-J. Proudhon, *Du Principe de l'art et de sa destination sociale*.

Chapter 1

"Innovation and Tradition in Courbet's *A Burial at Ornans*." First published in *Essays in Honor of Walter Friedlaender, Marsyas*, suppl. 2 (Institute of Fine Arts, New York University, 1965), pp. 119–126.

1 Courbet contributed nine works to this Salon, which opened on December 30, 1850. The *Burial*, which was listed as no. 661 in the Salon catalogue, was erroneously entitled "Un enterrement à Ornus." See *Explication des ouvrages de peinture, sculpture, architecture, gravure et lithographie des artistes vivants, exposés au Palais National le 30 décembre 1850* (Paris, 1850), p. 73.

2 For a collection of outraged critical opinion about Courbet's work in this Salon, see Georges Riat, *Gustave Courbet, peintre* (Paris, 1906), pp. 86–88.

3 This was the term Courbet himself used for the *Burial at Ornans*. See Meyer Schapiro, Review of *French Painting between the Past and the Present* by Joseph C. Sloane, *Art Bulletin*, 26 (1954), p. 164.

4 Courbet began the *Burial* in 1849 and completed it in 1850.

5 Thoré praised the painting for its social significance in his *Salon* of 1847, although he admitted that Couture lacked the genius to be a great artist and did not claim that he represented a new movement in art. See Francine Lifton Klagsbrun, "Thomas Couture and the *Romans of the Decadence*" (M.A. thesis, New York University, 1958), pp. 23–24. Proudhon wrote in 1847 that Couture's painting was the "seul tableau vraiment remarquable" at the Salon of that year and pointed out its political implications. *Carnets de P.-J. Proudhon*, ed. Pierre Haubtmann, Suzanne Henneguy, and Jeanne Fauré-Fremiet (Paris, 1961), 2, p. 63.

6 Klagsbrun, op. cit., p. 22.

7 *July 28, 1830: Liberty Guiding the People*, now in the Louvre.

8 See Klaus Berger, "Courbet in his Century," *Gazette des Beaux-Arts*, 24 (1943), pp. 22–24, for a similar view of this aspect of the artist's style.

9 Louis de Geofroy, "Le Salon de 1850," *Revue des Deux Mondes*, 9 (1851), pp. 929–30. English translation: "The *Burial at Ornus* is indeed the most important work, the history painting of Mr. Courbet. If Mr. Courbet had bothered to elaborate his thought, to adjust the various parts by cutting out or dissimulating those that are distasteful to the benefit of the interesting motifs that a scene like this could include, he might have produced a good painting. The subject is suitable enough: it is not necessary to go very far in order to produce a moving work; in our opinion, the burial of a peasant is no less touching than the funeral processi on of Phocion. But he should first of all not have localized the subject, and secondly he should have emphasized the interesting portions of such a scene .... If they are family portraits, leave them at Ornus. To us, who are not from Ornus, we need something more to attract us. What he should have aroused in the spectator is the natural sentiment which accompanies such a scene."

10 E. Bénézit. *Dictionnaire critique et documentaire des peintres, sculpteurs, dessinateurs et graveurs* (Paris, 1952), 7, p. 316. The painting was reproduced by Bellay in J. Vatout and P. Quenot, *Galerie lithographiée de son Altesse Royale Monseigneur le Duc d'Orléans* (Paris, n.d.), 2, n.p., and might have been known to Courbet.

11 De Geofroy, op. cit., pp. 937 and 939.

12 Ibid., p. 930.

13 Ibid.

14 Champfleury [Jules-François-Félix Husson], *Grandes Figures d'hier et d'aujourd'hui* (Paris, 1861), p. 251.

15 Ibid., p. 235.
16 The *Burial at Ornans* measures 315 cm × 668 cm.
17 Sabatier-Ungher is identical with François Sabatier, one of the leading disciples of Fourier of the period, who conducted an important left-wing salon in his home near Lunel, La Tour-de Farges, close to Montpellier. Sabatier was almost the only critic capable of appreciating Courbet's merits on both the aesthetic and the social levels in 1850–51, aside from Champfleury. He was a friend of Courbet's patron, Alfred Bruyas, and it was no doubt through the latter that the artist was invited to Sabatier's home during the summer of 1854 which he spent with Bruyas in Montpellier. (The information about Sabatier was communicated to me in personal conversation with M. Jean Claparède, curator of the Musée Fabre at Montpellier, during the winter of 1963.)
18 F. Sabatier-Ungher, *Salon de 1851* (Paris, 1851), pp. 62–63.
19 Champfleury, op. cit., p. 244.
20 De Geofroy, op. cit., p. 928.
21 This analogy was originally suggested by Meyer Schapiro in his important study of the artist, "Courbet and Popular Imagery," *Journal of the Warburg and Courtauld Institutes*, 4 (1941), pp. 165ff.
22 This image can be dated some time prior to 1837. See Jean Mistler, François Blaudez and André Jacquemin, *Epinal et l'imagerie populaire* (Paris, 1961), p. 184.
23 Robert J. Goldwater has, of course, pointed out the complexity of the implications of the term "primitive" in relation to European art of the 19th and 20th centuries, and the mixture of aesthetic, social and psychological factors which brought about the appreciation of primitive art in *Primitivism in Modern Painting* (New York and London, 1938).
24 This term was applied to the Le Nains by Champfleury in his *Essai sur la vie et l'œuvre des Lenain, peintres laonnois* (Laon, 1850), p. 48.
25 *Stanley Meltzoff*, "The Revival of the Le Nains," *Art Bulletin*, 24 (1942), p. 265 and *passim*.
26 *Les Peintres de la réalité sous Louis XIII*: *Les Frères Le Nain* (Paris, 1862), p.16.
27 Sabatier-Ungher, op. cit., pp. 36 and 62.
28 The painting is now in the Louvre under its correct title: *Saint Bonaventure on his Bier*.
29 Robert Fernier, "En marge de *L'Enterrement d'Ornans*," Société des Amis de Gustave Courbet, *Bulletin*, 10 (1951), pp. 8–10.
30 H. van der Tuin, *Lex Vieux Peintres des Pays-Bas et la critique artistique en France de la première moitié du* XIXe *siècle* (Paris, 1948), pp. 125–26.
31 Undated letter cited in Champfleury's *Souvenirs et portraits de jeunesse* (Paris, 1872), pp. 174–75.
32 Ibid., p. 175.
33 Cited in Théodore Duret, *Courbet* (Paris, 1918), p. 32.
34 See, for example, the criticisms of the *Burial* cited by Champfleury in *Grandes Figures*, op. cit., pp. 232–33 and Riat, op. cit., p. 86.
35 P.-J. Proudhon, *Du Principe de l'art et de sa destination sociale* (Paris, 1865), p. 210.
36 Haavard Rostrup, *Trois tableaux de Courbet*, Collections of the Ny Carlsberg Glypothek, 1 (Copenhagen, 1931), p. 118.
37 Meyer Schapiro, Review of *French Painting between the Past and the Present* by Joseph C. Sloane, *Art Bulletin*, 26 (1954), p. 164.
38 *L'Avenir de la science*: *Pensées de 1848* (extraits), ed. Bernard Lalande (Paris, 1954), p. 48. The work was written in 1849 but not published until 1890.

Chapter 2

"Gustave Courbet's *Meeting*: A Portrait of the Artist as a Wandering Jew." First published in the *Art Bulletin*, 49:3 (September 1967), pp. 209–22.

1 See, for example, Louis de Geofroy's criticism of the *Burial at Ornans* for its "indifferent reproduction" of whatever happened to come before Courbet's eyes, in the critic's "Le Salon de 1850," *Revue des Deux Mondes*, 9 (1851), p. 930. Courbet's friend Champfleury praised the painting for precisely the same qualities in his article on Courbet published in *Grandes Figures d'hier et d'aujourd'hui* (Paris, 1861), p. 251. Courbet is even supposed to have painted a bundle of faggots from a distance without knowledge of their identity: "I didn't need to know it," he said; "I painted what I saw without realizing what it was." Cited by Francis Wey, "Mémoires inédits," *Courbet raconté par lui-même et par ses amis*, ed. P. Courthion, 2 vols (Geneva, 1948, 1950), 1, pp. 90f.
2 For the relation of the *After Dinner at Ornans* to Louis Le Nain's *Repas de Famille* of 1642, see Stanley Meltzoff, "The Revival of the Le Nains," *Art Bulletin*, 24 (1942), p. 264 and figs 4 and 5. The connection of the *Burial at Ornans* with popular imagery has been dealt with extensively by Meyer Schapiro in "Courbet and Popular Imagery," *Journal of the Warburg and Courtauld Institutes*, 4 (1941), pp. 166f and pl. 39, probably the most significant of all studies of Courbet and his milieu. Further sources for the *Burial* are convincingly demonstrated by Robert Fernier, "En marge de *L'Enterrement d'Ornans*," Société des Amis de Gustave Courbet, *Bulletin*, 10 (1951), pp. 8–10, are discussed in Chapter 1 of the present volume and will be briefly reconsidered once more on pp. 32–33. The dependence of Courbet's *Wrestlers* upon Guido Reni's *Heracles and Acheleous* in the Louvre, suggested by Cesare Gnudi and Gian Carlo Cavalli in *Guido Reni* (Florence, 1955), p. 71, which was mentioned by the author in her Ph.D. dissertation ("The Development and Nature of Realism in the Work of Gustave Courbet," New York University, 1963, p. 187), is further discussed by Robert L. Alexander in "Courbet and Assyrian Sculpture," *Art Bulletin*, 47 (1965), p. 451. The sources of *The Painter's Studio* have been most extensively considered by René Huyghe, Germain Bazin, and Hélène Jean Adhémar in *Courbet: L'atelier du peintre: Allégorie réelle, 1855, Monographies des peintures du Musée du Louvre*, 3 (Paris, 1944), pp. 14–18, and in Werner Hofmann's *The Earthly Paradise: Art in the Nineteenth Century*, trans. Brian Battershaw (New York, 1961), p. 19
3 Alexander provides a notable exception, but his contention ("Courbet and Assyrian Sculpture," p. 448) that *The Meeting* is based on a motif from Assyrian relief sculpture is far from convincing. Robert L. Herbert ("Millet Revisited – II," *Burlington Magazine*, 104, 1962, p. 378 and figs 16 and 17) has justly pointed out the "patently artificial construction" of *The Meeting* in contrast with two Millet drawings after the work but of course does not go into the problem of the genesis of Courbet's painting in the context of his discussion of Millet's more plausibly lifelike reinterpretations of it.
4 *Transformations* (New York, 1956), pp. 47–48.
5 Klaus Berger, "Courbet in his Century," *Gazette des Beaux-Arts*, 24 (1943), p. 24.
6 Ibid., pp. 24 and 28. An anonymous reviewer of Gerstle Mack's *Gustave Courbet* ("The Challenge of Courbet," *Times Literary Supplement*, 51, June 27, 1952, p. 414), refers to "the curiously low angle of vision and the 'snapshot' effect" of *The Meeting*, which he feels "anticipate Degas by 20 years." This same reviewer considers *The Meeting* "one of the most significant pictures of the whole nineteenth century."
7 See, for example, Edmond About's discussion of Courbet's self-flattery and the disposition of the shadows in the work: "Neither the master nor the valet cast their shadows on the ground; there is only a shadow for M. Courbet: he alone can stop the rays of the sun" ("Voyage à travers l'Exposition des Beaux-Arts, 1855," in Courthion, op.cit., 1, p. 120).
8 The work in question, with the title "Le Juif-errant d'après une image de fabrication parisienne," was to serve as the frontispiece of both the 1869 and 1886 editions of Champfleury's book, but was doubtless known both to Champfleury and to Courbet long before that time; see below, p. 39. Whether or not Courbet simply reversed the composition of the example in question in order to emphasize his own person, or whether he actually based *The Meeting* on a slightly different variant of the same *image*, where the composition itself is reversed, can, of course, not be stated with certainty. Champfleury himself mentions several variants of this particular version in a long list of examples of Wandering Jew *images*, appended to his essay, "Le Juif-errant," *Histoire de l'imagerie populaire* (Paris, 1869), pp. 95–105. It is, therefore, not inconceivable that Courbet actually based *The Meeting* on a version in which the figure of the Jew appeared on the right-hand side, as he himself does in the painting.

The only specific 19th-century reference to the relationship between *The Meeting* and the Wandering Jew theme, possibly a fortuitous one, is a two-verse parody of the traditional *complainte* by one G. Randon, which appeared in the 1867 *Journal amusant* beneath a caricature of the painting:

Deux bourgeois de la ville,
Deux notables d'Ornans,
D'une façon civile
L'abordent cheminant.

—N'êtes-vous point cet homme
De qui l'on parle tant?
—Oui, c'est moi, mes enfants,
Qui suis Courbet le grand.

Cited in Charles Léger, *Courbet selon les caricatures et les images* (Paris, 1920), p. 68.

9 Max [Maximilien] Buchon, *Recueil de dissertations sur le réalisme* (Neuchâtel, 1856), cited in Charles Léger, "Courbet, ses amis et ses élèves," *Mércure de France*, 201 (1928), p. 14. Some contemporary observers even went so far as to make Courbet out as a semi-illiterate, in order to stress the instinctual component of his creativity: "As for reading, he did not overindulge in it," states Castagnary. "By not reading, he remained closer to instinct. The idea escaped him; he grasped the world through form and color" ("Manuscrit inédit," in Courthion, op. cit., 1, p. 156). Gros-Kost repeats the same idea in almost identical words in his *Souvenirs intimes* (Paris, 1830); see Courthion, op. cit., 2, p. 287.

10 Recounted by his close friend Francis Wey, "Mémoires inédits," in Courthion, op. cit., 2, p. 194.

11 "Le Titien, Léonard de Vinci sont des filous. Si l'un de ces deux-là revenait au monde et passait à mon atelier, je prendrais un couteau!" Cited by Théophile Silvestre, *Les Artistes français* (1861), in Courthion, op. cit., 1, p. 52.

12 See Théophile Silvestre, *Les Artistes français* (1861), in Courthion, op. cit., 1, pp. 50f.

13 Letter from Holland, 1847, in Courthion, op. cit., 2, p. 74.

14 Cited by Silvestre, *Les Artistes français*, in Courthion, op. cit., 1, p. 52.

15 "Jamais Vélasquez, Rembrandt, ni moi nous n'avons mieux fait." Cited by Castagnary, "Manuscrit inédit," in Courthion, op. cit., 1, p. 148.

16 See Courbet's letter to Castagnary from Interlaken, November 20, 1869, in Courthion, op. cit., 2, p. 116. An editor's note informs us that the letter was found among Castagnary's unpublished papers with the date 1869 added by the latter. Courbet's copy of Hals's *Malle Babbe*, signed and dated 1869, after the Munich painting, is in the Kunsthalle, Hamburg; his copy of Rembrandt's *Self-Portrait*, after the famous Munich work, signed and dated 1869 and with the inscription "Copie, Musée de Munich," is now in the Louvre. No copy after a Velázquez portrait is, to my knowledge, still in existence, although Gerstle Mack (*Gustave Courbet*, New York, 1951, p. 232), mentions a copy after "a portrait of Murillo by Velázquez" without further elucidation. See the catalogue, *Exposition Gustave Courbet*, Musée des Beaux-Arts de Besançon, Aug. 23–Oct. 10, 1952, cat. nos 42 and 43 for information about the Rembrandt and Hals copies.

17 Both Champfleury and Louis de Geofroy make the analogy between the *Burial at Ornans* and popular imagery. See Champfleury, *Grandes Figures*, op. cit., p. 244, and De Geofroy, op. cit., p. 928. Also see Schapiro, op. cit., p. 164.

18 See ibid., pp. 171–188, *passim*, for a detailed account of this phenomenon.

19 Buchon, *Recueil*, cited in Léger, "Courbet, ses amis et ses elèves," op. cit., p. 14.

20 *Carnets de P.-J. Proudhon*, ed. Pierre Haubtmann, Suzanne Henneguy, and Jeanne Fauré-Fremiet (Paris, 1960–61), 1, p. 349.

21 *Histoire de l'imagerie populaire*. See above, p. 30 and note 8 and below, pp. 39–40, for additional information about this important work.

22 Ibid., p. xxxiii.

23 Schapiro, op. cit., pp. 190f, suggests this interpretation. Since the sources of the *Burial at Ornans* have already been thoroughly investigated (see above, note 2), the discussion of this work and relevant illustrative material will be restricted to a minimum.

24 Robert Fernier ("En marge de *L'Enterrement d'Ornans*") establishes the relationship between Courbet's painting and the Dutch work, which he erroneously calls the *Banquet du Capitaine Bicker*, confusing it with another large group portrait by van der Helst, painted in 1648 and now also in the Rijksmuseum in Amsterdam, in which the figures are seated around a table.

25 H. van der Tuin, *Les Vieux Peintres des Pays-Bas et la critique artistique en France de la première moitié du XIXe siècle* (Paris, 1948), pp. 125f.

26 Zurbarán's so-called *Funeral of a Bishop*, then in the Soult Collection in Paris, may have provided a source of inspiration for the *Burial*. The painting is now in the Louvre under its correct title, *Saint Bonaventure on his Bier*. See Martin S. Soria, *The Paintings of Zurbarán* (London, 1953), cat. no. 27 and pl. 11.

27 See for example, François Sabatier-Ungher, *Salon de 1851* (Paris, 1851), pp. 36 and 62. For the popularity of Zurbarán in the period, see Paul Guinard's introduction to the catalogue, *Trésors de la peinture espagnole: Eglises et musées de France*, Palais du Louvre, Musée des Arts Décoratifs, Paris, Jan.–Apr., 1963, p. 23.

28 Schapiro, op. cit., p. 167 and pl. 39.

29 Georges Riat, *Gustave Courbet, peintre* (Paris, 1906), p. 100.

30 Proudhon used these words to recommend subject matter appropriate for treatment by the artist of the present in *Du Principe de l'art et de sa destination sociale* (Paris, 1865), a work devoted mainly to a study of Courbet, with whom the author had discussed his ideas on art.

31 J.-P. Séguin, "Antoine Chassaignon, imprimeur, libraire et canardier parisien (1810–1854)," *Arts et traditions populaies*, 3 (1955), pp. 18f, discusses the theme of fires in Parisian *canards*.

32 *Magasin pittoresque*, 10 (1842), p. 281.

33 *L'Illustration*, 13 (July 21, 1849), p. 336.

34 "Le Sapeur-Pompier," *L'Illustration*, 1 (July 29, 1843), pp. 339–41, illustration on p. 340.

35 Pierre Dupont, *Chants et chansons* (Paris, 1855), 3, p. 110. The illustration facing p. 110, by Andrieux, also reveals some similarities with elements in Courbet's painting, or perhaps points to a common prototype. Dupont's poem had first been published in 1851, and it is certainly possible that Courbet was familiar with it before he began work on his *Firemen*.

36 These two figures would seem to be an earlier counterpart of the well-dressed couple – the so-called *amateurs mondains* – in the right foreground of Courbet's *Painter's Studio* of 1855.

37 The *Toilette de la mariée* is generally dated *c.* 1865, although no valid reason has ever been given to substantiate such a late date. More recently, Douglas Cooper has suggested a far more reasonable date of about 1858 for this work, on the basis of its close thematic relation to Courbet's works of the 1850s and its formal relationship to *The Painter's Studio* of 1855; see "Reflections on the Venice Biennale," *Burlington Magazine*, 96 (1954), p. 322.

38 [Etienne Achille] Réveil, *Musée de peinture et de sculpture, ou, Recueil des principaux tableaux, statues et bas-reliefs* ..., 17 vols (London-Paris, 1829–34). This collection, easily available to artists, as Paul Guinard has pointed out (Louis Réau, "Velázquez et la peinture française du XIXe siècle," in *Velázquez, son temps, son influence*, Paris, 1963, p. 106), contains an engraving of the *Maids of Honor*, entitled "Vélasquez Faisant le portrait d'une Infante," 14, p. 971, and one of the *Spinners* entitled "Fabrique de tapisseries," 14, p. 987.

39 On the relation between Millet's *Portrait of Antoinette Hébert* and Velázquez's *Infanta Margarita* in the Louvre, see Guinard in Réau, ibid., p. 107, This portrait by Velázquez had been published in the *Magasin pittoresque*, 9 (1841), p. 177.

40 André Chastel in Réau, ibid., p. 109.

41 *Characteristics of French Art* (London, 1932), p. 111.

42 Cited in "'La Mariée' en Voyage: Smith's Courbet Abroad," *Smith College Museum of Art Bulletin*, 35–36 (1954–55), p. 17.

43 Alexander, op. cit., p. 447.

44 Shapiro, op. cit., p. 190.

45 Courbet himself hints at the derivation of this work from that of the English artist, when, in a description of his *Stag* in a letter of April 19 and 20, 1861, to Francis Wey, from Ornans (in Courthion, op. cit., 2, p. 92), he states: "The expression of his head ought to please the English; it recalls the feeling of Landseer's animals." The inspiring engraving had appeared in the *Magasin pittoresque*, 19 (1851), p. 385.

46 William M. Kane has suggested this source for Courbet's figure in "Courbet's 'Chasseur' of 1866–67," *Yale University Art Gallery Bulletin*, 25 (1960), pp. 32–34, and has illustrated both Courbet's painting, now in the Musée des Beaux-Arts, Besançon, and its prototype, in figs 2 and 3 of the same article.

47 "A Landscape by Gustave Courbet," *Museum Notes*, Museum of Art, Rhode Island School of Design, 4:5 (May, 1946), pp. 2f.

48 See the catalogue, *Gustave Courbet, 1819–1877*, Philadelphia Museum of Art; Museum of Fine Arts, Boston, 1959–60, cat. no. 44.

49 *Magasin pittoresque*, 18 (1850), p. 220.
50 Courbet characterized his aim in this manner in the so-called Realist Manifesto, the preface to the catalogue of his Realist Exhibition of 1855. It is published in Courthion, op. cit., 2, pp. 60f.
51 Letter from Courbet to Alfred Bruyas, dated May, 1854 by Pierre Borel (Pierre Borel (ed.), *Lettres de Gustave Courbet à Alfred Bruyas*, Geneva, 1951, p. 28).
52 Letter from Courbet to Alfred Bruyas of May, 1854 (ibid., p. 22). Courbet and Bruyas had met in the spring of 1853, at a time when Bruyas had first seen Courbet's paintings in the Salon of that year, and had purchased *The Bathers*, *The Sleeping Spinner*, and the earlier *Man with the Pipe*.
53 See below, pp. 40–41, for a discussion of this work and its lithograph sequel.
54 See above, note 8.
55 Champfleury, *Histoire*, op. cit., p. xliv.
56 For this estimation of Champfleury's work, see George K. Anderson, *The Legend of the Wandering Jew* (Providence, 1965), p. 401. Anderson's study provides the most complete repository of literary material on the Wandering Jew available.
57 Champfleury, *Histoire*, op. cit., pp. 2f.
58 Jean-Louis Bory characterizes Süe's novel in this manner in *Eugène Süe: Le roi du roman populaire* (Paris, 1962), p. 298, *Le Juif errant* was published serially in the *Constitutionnel* from June 25, 1844, until July 12, 1845. What is striking about the work, as far as the figure of the Wandering Jew himself is concerned, is, as Anderson points out, "that Süe casts Ahasuerus as a champion of the working man – the humble shoemaker of Jerusalem has become a spokesman for labor, and his protest against the fate of the laboring man is the protest of all workers against their oppressors" (*The Legend of the Wandering Jew*, op. cit., p. 239).
59 Champfleury, *Histoire*, op. cit., p. 45.
60 Ibid., p. 43. Béranger's enormously popular song was first published in 1831. For "Le Juif errant," see P.-J. de Béranger, *Oeuvres complètes* (Paris, 1834), 3, pp. 278–82.
61 Champfleury, *Histoire*, op. cit., p. 45.
62 Pierre Dupont, the self-taught son of artisans, was the author of such popular ballads as "The Song of the Workers," "The Daughter of the People," and "The Song of the Firemen"; see above, p. 34. His *Légende du juif errant* was published in a sumptuous folio edition, illustrated with wood engravings by the then unknown Gustave Doré, in 1856 by Michel Lévy Frères, Paris.
63 Schapiro ("Courbet and Popular Imagery") discusses this work and its implications in great detail, pp. 167f, and suggests its relation to the Wandering Jew of popular prints as well as to the pilgrim St. Jacques of religious broadsides.
64 Alexander's suggestion ("Courbet and Assyrian Sculpture," p. 448) that Journet's pose in the lithograph (and in the now-destroyed painted portrait upon which it was based) was derived from that of Sargon in Assyrian relief sculpture, with the figure turned "ninety degrees to show Journet stepping toward the viewer," seems farfetched in light of the much closer prototype provided by the Wandering Jew *image*.
65 See fig. 11 and p. 30 above. The fact that the figure of Journet in Courbet's lithograph faces to the left, whereas the figure of the Jew in the popular image, reproduced as the frontispiece to Champfleury's book, faces right, gives added support to this hypothesis, since the composition would have been reversed in the printing of the lithograph.
66 Stanza 5 of the *complainte*, to be sung to the "Air de Joseph," surrounding the broadside of *L'Apôtre Jean Journet, partant pour la conquête de l'harmonie universelle*, printed in 1850 by Vion, 27 rue St.-Jacques, Paris. The author of the *complainte* is unknown.
67 Benedict Nicolson, "Courbet's 'L'Aumône d'un Mendiant'," *Burlington Magazine*, 104 (1962) p. 74.
68 Ibid.
69 Ibid., pp. 73f and 74, n. 1.
70 For the drawing, fol. 33r, in Louvre Carnet RF 9105, see Louis Aragon, *L'Exemple de Courbet* (Paris, 1952), pl. 87, p. 183. For Courbet's description of the Irishwoman in *The Painter's Studio*, see his long letter to Champfleury of January, 1855, in Huyghe, et al., op. cit., p. 23.
71 Champfleury, *Histoire*, op. cit., pp. 76f and 102.
72 Ibid., p. 77.
73 Nicolson, op. cit., pp. 73f.
74 Cited by Maurice Z. Shroder, *Icarus: The Image of the Artist in French Romanticism* (Cambridge, Mass., 1961), pp. 103 and 263f, n. 22. Baudelaire was to extend the image of the artist as a wanderer to its ultimate point in his poem "Le Voyage" (1859), in which the Wandering Jew figures as a simile for man fleeing Time:

… Il est, hélas! des coureurs sans répit,
Comme le Juif errant et comme les apôtres,
A qui rien ne suffit, ni wagon ni vaisseau,
Pour fuir ce rétiaire infame …

(Charles Baudelaire, *Oeuvres complètes*, ed. Y.-G. Le Dantec and Claude Pichois, Paris, 1961, p. 126). For the image of the great man as a wanderer in the 19th century, see Werner Hofmann, *The Earthly Paradise*, op. cit., pp. 238f.
75 Cited in François Fosca (pseud.), *Edmond et Jules de Goncourt* (Paris, 1941), pp. 30f.
76 Gustave Flaubert, Letter dated July 13, 1847, from St.-Malo to Ernest Chevalier, *Correspondance* (Paris, 1922), 1, 230.
77 Pierre Dupont, "Le voyageur à Pied," *Chants et chansons*, p. 25.
78 Published in Courthion, op. cit., 2, p. 78.
79 See above, p. 40 and fig. 24.
80 Baudelaire, op. cit., p. 637.
81 Borel, op. cit., p. 68.
82 See Saint-Simon's "Dialogue entre l'artiste, le savant et l'industriel," of 1825, cited by H. J. Hunt, *Le Socialisme et le romantisme en France: Etude de la presse socialiste de 1830 à 1848* (Oxford, 1935), p. 18.
83 Emile Barrault, *L'Appel aux artistes* (Paris, 1830), cited in H. J, Hunt, ibid., p. 34.
84 Victor Hugo, "La fonction du poète" (1839), 11, pp. 81–90, in *Oeuvres choisies*, ed. P. Moreau and J. Boudout (Paris, 1950), 1, p. 850.
85 Courbet did, in fact, express his solidarity with Hugo in a letter to the poet of November 28, 1864, written while the latter was in exile in Guernsey. In this letter, Courbet refers to Hugo's *Châtiments* with enthusiasm and adds that he joins with him in the salvation of "democratic art in France": "We are strong enough, despite the renegades, despite present-day France and its insane herds; we will save the art, the intelligence, and the honesty of our country" (Courthion, op.cit., 2, pp. 100f.).
86 Still less should this figure be considered a mere space filler, as has been suggested by Alexander, op. cit., p. 448.
87 See the account of Courbet by Théophile Silvestre, *Les Artistes français*, 1861, in Courthion, op.cit., 1, p. 30, and that by Dr. Paul Collin in Courthion, op.cit., 2, p. 258, as well as Schapiro, op. cit., p. 170, for details of Courbet's often self-conscious popularism.
88 Cited by Castagnary, "Manuscript inédit," in Courthion, op. cit., 1, p. 150.
89 Draft of a letter to Maurice Richard, Minister of Fine Arts, Paris, June, 1870; see Courthion, op. cit., 2, p. 121.
90 Letter to Francis Wey, 1850, in Courthion, op. cit., 2, p. 78.
91 "Voyage à travers l'Exposition des Beaux-Arts, 1855," in Courthion, op. cit., 1, p. 120.
92 Ibid., 119f.
93 Berger, op. cit., p. 24.
94 Champfleury, *Histoire*, op. cit., pp. 91f.
95 Lines from the *complainte* accompanying a popular image of the Wandering Jew from Pont-à-Mousson (Meurthe), *chez* Haguenthal, in the Musée des Arts et Traditions Populaires, Paris.
96 Letter from Courbet to Alfred Bruyas, probably of December, 1854 (Borel, op.cit., p. 75). The anonymous author of the review of Gerstle Mack's *Gustave Courbet* ("The Challenge of Courbet," *Times Literary Supplement*, 51, June 27, 1952, p. 414) suggests that this letter may have been written as late as January, 1855.
97 Both of these, head and shoulder portraits, are in the Musée Fabre at Montpellier. The more important of the two, in which Bruyas faces to the right, leaning his head in his hand, against the background of a lace antimacassar, the portrait that obviously provides the basis for Bruyas's likeness in *The Meeting* (see below, p. 51), is reproduced in color by Guy Dumur, "La Galerie Bruyas," *L'Oeil*, 60 (December 1959), p. 86. In the other portrait of 1854, Bruyas turns to the left in pure profile and wears a green cravat.
98 This portrait, in which the subject is represented in three-quarter length, was also in the Galerie Bruyas and is now in the Musée Fabre in Montpellier. Bruyas commissioned some thirty-five portraits of himself during his lifetime.
99 Courbet, Letter of November, 1854, from Paris, to Alfred Bruyas (Borel, op.cit., p. 47).
100 See Courbet's letters to Bruyas of November, 1854 (ibid., p. 52) and of about April, 1855 (ibid., p. 80), and Guy Dumur, op. cit., p. 92.

101 See Georges Wildenstein, *Ingres* (London, 1954), p. 183, cat. nos 118 and 119; p. 220, cat. no. 267; p. 185, figs 64, 65, and 66. The original version, signed and dated 1818, is lost.
102 Joseph Nicolas Robert-Fleury, *Charles-Quint ramassant le pinceau du Titien*, exhibited in the Salon of 1843, reproduced in the *Magasin pittoresque*, 11 (1843), p. 165.
103 Chateaubriand, Letter dated Feb. 5, 1823, in *Correspondence*, 4, p. 91, cited by Shroder, op. cit., p. 46.
104 Alfred de Vigny, Text dated 1848, in *Oeuvres*, 2, p. 1264, cited by Shroder, op. cit., p. 46.
105 Published by Eugen Weber (ed.), *Paths to the Present: Aspects of European Thought from Romanticism to Existentialism* (New York, 1960), p. 123. Weber, who dates the Beethoven letter August 15, 1813, instead of August 15, 1812, which is the more usual dating, mentions that the authenticity of the document is in doubt. I am grateful to Prof. H. W. Janson for having brought the Beethoven letter and its relevance to Courbet's painting to my attention.
106 Courbet, Letter to Alfred Bruyas of December, 1854, in Courthion, op. cit., 2, p. 81, The Comte de Nieuwerkerke was at the time Director General of the Imperial Museums and Commissioner of the Fine Arts of the Imperial Household.
107 The *Wounded Man*, refused by the Salon of 1844 and probably retouched in 1854, now in the Louvre.
108 *The Wounded Man* seems clearly related to Delacroix's *St. Sebastian Aided by the Holy Women* of 1836, in the Eglise de Nantua; for a reproduction of this work, see Louis Hourticq, *Delacroix: L'oeuvre du maître* (Paris, 1930), p. 61.
109 *The Lovers in the Country*, signed and dated 1844, Musée des Beaux-Arts, Lyons. It is no doubt to this self-portrait that Courbet refers, when, in a letter to Alfred Bruyas of May 1854 (Borel, op. cit., p. 20), he mentions "the portrait of a man in the ideal and the absolute love [*sic*] of the manner of Goethe, George Sand, etc." There exists another version of the *Lovers in the Country* in the Petit Palais, published in Courthion, op. cit., 1, facing p. 49, where it is dated 1845.
110 *Self-Portrait: The Man with a Pipe*, Musée Fabre, Montpellier, probably painted in 1846 and refused for the Salon of 1847. It is probably to this work that Courbet refers when he speaks of "the portrait of a fanatic, an ascetic, of a man disillusioned by the idiocies that served for his education" in the letter of May, 1854, to Bruyas (Borel, op. cit., p. 19). While the *Smoker* in the Louvre may not actually be by Brouwer, in Courbet's time it was certainly considered a self-portrait by this artist; see Ludwig Goldscheider, *Five Hundred Self-Portraits* (Vienna and London, 1937), pp. 41f and pl. 89.
111 Exhibited in the Salon of 1849 under the title, *Portrait of the Painter, a Study from the Venetians*. I am inclined to agree with Georges Riat (*Gustave Courbet, peintre*, Paris, 1906, p. 66) who dates the work *c.* 1845.
112 Letter from Courbet to Bruyas, May, 1854 (Borel, op. cit., p. 20).
113 Harry Levin, *The Gates of Horn* (New York, 1966), p. 70.
114 Meyer Schapiro has observed the same phenomenon in Courbet's style (op. cit., p. 184).
115 Information communicated to the author by M. Jean Claparède, curator of the Musée Fabre, Montpellier, in 1963. I am extremely grateful to M. Claparède for his generous assistance in providing me with information about *The Meeting* and Courbet's stay in Montpellier.
116 The *Ponds at Palavas* was executed during the course of Courbet's 1857 sojourn in Montpellier, but is remarkably similar in tonality and composition to the background of *The Meeting*. No specific sketch for the background of the latter is still in existence, to my knowledge, but since Courbet often executed such preliminary studies on cigar boxes, he may well have considered them unworthy of preservation.
117 See above, p. 47 and note 97 for the portrait of Bruyas in question. The prototype for Courbet's own portrait in *The Meeting*, the *Self-Portrait, in the Striped Collar*, was later to serve as the model for the artist's likeness in *The Painter's Studio* of 1855. Interestingly enough, in this small self-portrait, Courbet has represented himself wearing Bruyas's green jacket with the distinctive striped collar, the very jacket that his patron wears in *The Meeting*.
118 See Berger, op. cit., p. 24.
119 Berger (ibid., pp. 22–30) has given the most convincing account of the formal component of Courbet's realism.
120 Statement by Courbet that appeared in the *Précurseur d'Anvers*, August 22, 1861, cited by Georges Riat, *Gustave Courbet, peintre*, in Courthion, op. cit., 1, pp. 160f.
121 Paul André Lemoisne, *Degas et son œuvre* (Paris, 1946–49), 2, no. 368, The painting, formerly in the Gerstenberg Collection in Berlin, is now believed to be destroyed. A good reproduction is to be found in Jean Sutherland Boggs, *Portraits by Degas* (Berkeley and Los Angeles, 1962), pl. 88.
122 Michel Eyquem de Montaigne, *Les Essais de Michel de Montaigne*, ed. Pierre Villey (Paris, 1922–23), 3, p. 27.
123 For a reproduction of this work, in the Louvre, see William C. Seitz, *Claude Monet* (New York, 1960), p. 97.

Chapter 3

"Gustave Courbet's *Toilette de la mariée*." First published in the *Art Quarterly*, 34:1 (1971), pp. 31–54.

1 Guy Eglington, "An Unpublished Courbet," *International Studio*, 79 (September 1924), pp. 447–53. For further bibliographical references, see the exhibition catalogues *Gustave Courbet, 1819–1877* (Philadelphia and Boston, 1959–60), no. 50; and *19th and 20th Century Paintings from the Collection of the Smith College Museum of Art* (1970), no. 14.
2 A notable exception is provided by Jean Seznec's invaluable investigation of the iconography of the *Toilette* and his convincing relation of it to the "*scénario nuptial*" of the French provinces, in an article which originally appeared in the French student's journal of the University of Oxford (*La Chouette aveugle*, 5, 28 février, 1955) and was reprinted in "*La Mariée* en Voyage; Smith's Courbet Abroad," *Smith College Museum of Art Bulletin*, 35–36 (1954–55), pp. 15–17, and in the Société des Amis de Gustave Courbet, *Bulletin*, 16 (1955), pp. 7–9.
3 Eglington, op. cit., p. 453.
4 Douglas Cooper, "Courbet in Philadelphia and Boston," *Burlington Magazine*, 102 (1960), p. 245. Cooper admits that the dating is problematic but on the basis of style is inclined to place the *Toilette* in the period 1858–60.
5 J.-M. Garnier, *Histoire de l'imagerie populaire et des cartes à jouer* (Chartres, 1869); C. Nisard, *Histoire des livres populaires ou de la littérature du colportage depuis le quinzième siècle jusqu'à l'établissement de la commission d'examen des livres du colportage* (30 novembre 1852), (Paris, 1854); M. Buchon, *Noëls et chants populaires de la Franche-Comté* (Salins, 1863); Champfleury [Jules François Félix Husson], *Histoire de l'imagerie populaire* (Paris, 1869).
6 Charles Beauquier, *Chansons populaires recueillies en Franche-Comté* (Paris, 1894), p. 14.
7 George Sand's manuscript was published by M. Parent, *Bulletin de la Faculté des Lettres de Strasbourg* (May–June 1954), cited in Stephen Ullmann, *Style in the French Novel* (Oxford, 1964), p. 81.
8 See L. Nochlin, "Gustave Courbet's *Meeting*: A Portrait of the Artist as a Wandering Jew," *Art Bulletin*, 49:3 (1967), p. 210 (Chapter 2, pp. 31–32, in the present volume) for expressions of this attitude.
9 For a detailed, insightful investigation of the implications of rural imagery in the 19th century, see Robert L. Herbert, "City vs. Country: The Rural Image in French Painting from Millet to Gauguin," *Artforum* (February 1970), pp. 44–55.
10 George Sand, *La Mare au diable* (Paris, 1926; first published 1846), pp. 161–217. One might well contrast this picture of the wholesome, orderly, time-consecrated ceremonies of the rural peasant weddings with the chaos, vulgarity, and emptiness of the urban proletarian marriage celebration of Gervaise Coupeau described by Zola in *L'Assommoir* thirty years later.
11 Edmond and Jules de Goncourt, *Manette Salomon* (Paris, n.d.; originally published 1865), pp. 353–55. The work represented an elegant mass at Saint-Germain-des-Prés, with a large crowd present, and, as a *repoussoir* for all this splendor, a group of proletarian onlookers, including a ragged old woman, a working-class mother with her baby, and a young workman in a blue cotton shirt with a loaf of bread.
12 Emile Zola, *L'Oeuvre*, in *Les Rougon-Macquart: Histoire Naturelle et sociale d'une famille sous le Second Empire*, Pléiade edn (Paris, 1966), 4, pp. 86–87. *L'Oeuvre* originally appeared in 1885–86.
13 Ibid., pp. 288–89.
14 Seznec, op. cit., p. 16.
15 The work, in fact, appeared under the title *Toilette de la mariée* in the catalogue of Courbet's studio sale at the Galerie Georges Petit, July 9, 1919, where it was listed as no. 1.

16 Wilkie's *Bride at her Toilet* is now in the National Gallery of Scotland, Edinburgh. It was exhibited at the 1838 Royal Academy. The work was painted for a Herr Arthaber of Vienna and remained in his collection until 1868. Whether or not Courbet was familiar with it through engravings is conjectural. Certainly he was acquainted with, and seems to have admired, the work of other English artists, such as Hogarth, Northcote, and Landseer.

17 Eglington, op. cit., p. 453. For detailed studies of the continuation or revival of 18th-century art in that of the 19th century see: Seymour O. Simches, *Le Romantisme et le goût esthétique du XVIIIe siècle* (Paris, 1964); and Carol Duncan, *The Rococo Revival in Nineteenth-Century Painting* (unpublished Ph.D. dissertation, Columbia University, 1969). I am grateful to Dr. Duncan for her generosity in bringing to my attention obscure works relating to Courbet's painting and lending me photographs from her personal collection.

18 The painting, originally created in 1791 for Boydell's Shakespeare Gallery, was engraved by James Heath and published by T. Thoré-Bürger in his *Histoire des peintres de toutes les écoles*: *Ecole Anglaise* (Paris, 1863). There was a highly successful variant of Northcote's work by the German painter Ferdinand Hildebrant, dated 1836, repeated in three identical versions and perhaps known to Courbet, either through direct contact or through publication in the French edition of Raczynski's *Geschichte der neueren deutschen Kunst* (Berlin, 1836). I am grateful to Thomas Pelzel for the information about Hildebrant.

19 Such Lesbian themes were not uncommon in the semi-pornographic art of the times: see, for example, the pastel *Two Female Nudes*, by Delacroix's friend Jules Robert Auguste, where there is a similar contrast between light- and dark-skinned nudes (published in F. Trapp, *The Attainment of Delacroix*, Baltimore, 1970, fig. 45). Courbet himself had done an earlier version of the theme in 1863, *Venus and Psyche (The Awakening)*, Berlin, ex-Gerstenberg Collection, also partially inspired by Northcote's work. Indeed, he created the later *Sleep* in 1866 as a substitute for *Venus and Psyche* to fulfill the demands of Khalil Bey, when the earlier work was no longer available to this exigent collector.

20 The *Toilette* was thoroughly examined by means of ultra-violet, infra-red and x-ray by the Research Laboratory of the Museum of Fine Arts, Boston, in 1960. The complete results of this investigation were generously made available to me by Charles Chetham, Director of the Smith College Museum of Art. This x-ray photograph reveals not only that the bride was originally painted nude, but that the head was originally at a slightly different angle and the hair closer to the head; the left arm of the attendant on the left originally held the mirror; the bride's left arm was originally across her waist: *Report of the Research Laboratory*, Museum of Fine Arts, Boston, p. 3.

21 For reproductions of these, and others like them, see Malcolm C. Salaman, *French Colour-Prints of the XVIII Century* (Philadelphia and London, 1913), pl. XL, XLI, XLII, XLIII.

22 The *Bather Sleeping by a Brook* was painted in 1845. There is an almost identical version of the work in the collection of Oskar Reinhart, Winterthur, Switzerland.

23 The question of contemporary dress and local color, as opposed to the timeless universality of the nude, was of course a major issue of the so-called "*bataille réaliste*": see, for example, Champfleury's reference to "the serious representation of present-day personalities, the derbies, the black dress coats, the polished shoes or the peasant's *sabots*" in his letter to George Sand of 1855 (L. Nochlin, *Realism and Tradition in Art: 1848–1900*, New York, 1966, p. 40).

24 This tract, pieced together from an unfinished manuscript and additional "Notes et Pensées" by Proudhon's executors, was intended as a reply to attacks on Proudhon's anti-feminist views by Juliette La Messine and Jenny d'Héricourt. The anti-feminism of Proudhon is equally virulent, though more rationally expressed, in the anarchist's earlier works, *Les Contradictions économiques* and *La Justice dans la révolution et dans l'église*: see the excellent introduction to *La Pornocratie* by Jules L. Puech, *Oeuvres complètes de P.-J. Proudhon*, ed. C. Bouglé and H. Moysset (Paris, 1939), pp. 303–24, and the work itself, pp. 325–469.

25 The critique is part of a chapter entitled "De la prostitution dans l'art – sévérité de l'école critique 'Venus et Psyché'": see P.-J. Proudhon, *Du Principe de l'art et de sa destination sociale*, in *Oeuvres complètes*, op. cit., pp. 202–10.

26 In addition, this minor but interesting artist from Courbet's native Franche-Comté had created a pair of lithographs on the theme of the *lever*: *Le Lever à la ville* and *Le Lever au village*. I am grateful to Dr. Carol Duncan for having brought these works to my attention.

27 Diderot, *Salons*, ed. Jean Seznec and Jean Adhémar (Oxford, 1963), 3, pp. 197–99. A. Pigler (*Barokthemen*, Budapest and Berlin, 1956, 2, p. 512) traces the theme of the *coucher de la mariée* back to the Aldobrandini wedding and illustrates the early 17th-century Italian *Sposa Novella* by G. Manozzi, where the bridegroom is already in bed and reaches out his arms to the reluctant bride, who is surrounded by attendants. The earliest French version of the theme is apparently an engraving by Abraham Bosse, from his *Country Marriage* series of 1633.

28 Courbet, of course, had had recourse to the inspiration of popular imagery both in his *Burial at Ornans* and *The Meeting*: see Meyer Schapiro, "Courbet and Popular Imagery," *Journal of the Warburg and Courtauld Institutes*, 4 (1941), pp. 164–91; and L. Nochlin, "Gustave Courbet's *Meeting*," op. cit., *passim*. Seznec, op. cit., p. 16, mentions an *image d'Epinal* of the *Mariée de campagne* which had as a pendant *La Mariée de la ville*, but I have not been able to locate these prints.

29 Seznec, op. cit., p. 16.

30 Seznec, op. cit., p. 17; and E. Gros-Kost, *Gustave Courbet: Souvenirs intimes* (Paris, 1880), pp. 20ff.

31 While both Seznec and Gros-Kost seem to feel that Courbet was telling one of his (fairly common) tall stories about providing a sequel to the *Toilette* in the form of *The Wake*, Charles Léger (*Courbet*, Paris, 1929, p. 28) affirmed that such wakes were still customary in the Franche-Comté of his own day, and there seems to be no real reason to suspect that Courbet was not sincere in his intention to paint one.

32 *Catalogue de tableaux ... de Gustave Courbet ...*, Hôtel Drouot, 28 June, 1882. *La Toilette de la morte* is numbered no. XL on a supplementary list of works that were not put up for sale: Léger, op, cit., p. 218.

33 Published by Emma Boehm-Oller, "Francisco Oller: Puerto Rican Impressionist," *Americas*, 19 (September 1967), pp. 24–25. The Scottish painter John ("Spanish") Phillip represented a similar subject in a Spanish setting in 1860–64; entitled *La Gloria*, the work is now in the National Gallery of Scotland: see *National Gallery of Scotland: Catalogue of Paintings and Sculpture* (Edinburgh, 1957), no. 836.

34 It is difficult to say whether or not Courbet was familiar with either Bruegel's *Peasant Wedding Dance* or his *Peasant Wedding Feast* in Vienna. Certainly Bruegel's works were known in France since 1809, at least, when the French carried off the Vienna Bruegels to Paris and included them in a great exhibition of European art: see Fritz Grossmann, *Bruegel: The Paintings* (London, 1955), p. 30.

35 *The Penny Wedding*, first called "The Scotch Wedding," was painted for the Prince Regent in 1818. While totally different from Courbet's *Toilette* in attitude and conception, it nevertheless shares Courbet's concern with the folk customs of the artist's native region, in this case the custom whereby the guests defrayed the cost of the wedding. For a reproduction see Mrs. Charles Heaton, *The Great Works of Sir David Wilkie* (London, 1868), n.p. For bibliography see the exhibition catalogue *Royal Academy of Arts Bicentenary Exhibition, 1768–1968* (London, 1968–69), no. 198.

36 The painting is also known as "Grandmother's Bridal Crown." Tidemand, dubbed by Richard Muther the "Léopold Robert of the North," specialized in genre scenes of his compatriots, especially their holiday customs. Björnson evidently wrote one of his tales, *The Bridal March*, as a text to Tidemand's *Dressing the Bride* (probably a different work, of 1870, in the Art Museum in Göteborg): see Richard Muther, *The History of Modern Painting*, rev. edn (London and New York, 1907), 2, pp. 165–66.

37 Seznec, op. cit., p. 16.

38 The two songs illustrated with wood engravings after Courbet were "Les Scieurs de Long" and "Le Piocheur de Terre": see *Les Chansons populaires des provinces de France*. Notice par Champfleury, accompagnées de piano par J.-B. Weckerlin (Paris, 1860), pp. 133 and 181.

39 Seznec, op. cit., p. 16.

40 Charles Beauquier, *Chansons populaires recueillies en Franche-Comté* (Paris, 1894), p. 302.

41 Lafargue was the son-in-law of Karl Marx. His study, "Les Chansons et les cérémonies populaires du mariage," was published under the *nom de plume* "Fergus" in *La Nouvelle Revue* (1886), and later included in Paul Lafargue, *Critiques*

littéraires (Paris, 1936), pp. 1–33; the section dealing with the bride's farewell is on pp. 4–13. Julien Tiersot, in his *Histoire de la chanson populaire en France* (Paris, 1889), also stresses the universality of this song and cites a particularly apt example (p. 210):

Adieux châteaux brillants,
La liberté des filles;
Adieu la liberté
Il n'en faut plus parler.

42 Pierre Dupont, "Adieux de la mariée," *Chants et chansons* (Paris, 1855), 3, pp. 61–62.
43 Champfleury and Weckerlin (eds), *Les Chanson populaires*, op. cit., p. 108.
44 Henri Davenson (ed.), "Chanson de la mariée," *Introduction à la chanson populaire française: Le Livre des chansons*, 2nd edn (Paris, 1946), pp. 488–90.
45 Rouart, Larolle, et cie., (eds), "La Mariée," *Les Chansons de France*, 5ème année (Paris, 1911), p. 19.
46 Seznec, op. cit., p. 16; Léger, op. cit., p. 81.
47 Tiersot, op. cit., p. 203.
48 "Chanson des Mariés," in Beauquier, op. cit., p. 301.
49 For the complete song, "Le Chant des Livrées," see Davenson, op. cit., pp. 491–93.
50 The absence, or inconspicuousness, of the groom is often a feature of traditional wedding iconography: see W. S. Gibson, "Some Notes on Pieter Bruegel the Elder's *Peasant Wedding Feast*," *Art Quarterly*, 28 (1965), pp. 197–98.
51 Roger Fry, *Characteristics of French Art* (London, 1932), p. 111.
52 An engraving after Velázquez's work, so entitled, appeared in Réveil's *Musée de peinture et de sculpture* ... (London–Paris, 1829–34), 14, p. 987.
53 This interpretation of Courbet's style was convincingly set forth by Klaus Berger, "Courbet in his Century," *Gazette des Beaux-Arts*, 24 (1943), pp. 19–40.
54 Other examples of "a morsel of vision expanded into a larger picture" presented by MacDonald include the 1846 *Self-Portrait* in Besançon; *L'Après-dînée à Ornans*, of 1849, Palais des Beaux-Arts, Lille; the *Portrait of Alphonse Promayet*, of 1851, in the Metropolitan Museum of Art; the *Peasants of Flagey* on loan to the Petit Palais; *La Mère Grégoire* in Chicago; and *Les Trois Baigneuses* in the Petit Palais: Bruce K. MacDonald, "*The Quarry* by Gustave Courbet," *Boston Museum of Fine Arts Bulletin*, 69 (1969), no. 16, pp. 67–68 and *passim*. As MacDonald points out, the seams in the very large paintings by Courbet "probably simply reflect Courbet's need for larger canvases than those available to him." There would appear to be a seam of this latter type in the *Toilette*.
55 I have made a detailed analysis of *The Young Ladies of the Village* and critical reactions to it, with particular emphasis on Courbet's stylistic tendency to push "the subject, including the much-criticized cattle, up to the surface of the canvas;" his increase of "the plastic richness, density of detail and variety of paint surface throughout the entire work" in order to achieve "a sense of the near-view, hence a realism of direct, visual experience;" and concluding: "If the unity of effect thereby achieved is an additive one, based on the primary reality of concrete, separate material entities rather than a synthetic grasp of a consistent visual totality, this is no more the result of mere negligence or incapacity than is the unity achieved by Cézanne in his views of Mont Sainte-Victoire, where the artist has adopted almost precisely the opposite procedure." See Linda Nochlin, "The Development and Nature of Realism in the Work of Gustave Courbet: A Study of the Style and its Social and Artistic Background," Ph.D. dissertation, New York University, 1963, pp. 178–85.
56 For example, Alfred Vance Churchill claims that "all Courbet lovers will be glad ... that the picture is unfinished .... This work offers us a purer Courbet – a purer expression of his instinct – than we should otherwise have known": see "La Toilette de la Mariée by Gustave Courbet (1819–1877)," *Smith College Museum of Art Bulletin*, 10 (April 1929), p. 9.
57 M. Fried makes the claim that Couture took measures "to counteract or moderate the undeniable and, given his ambitions, inescapable theatricality of the painting as a whole" and continues: "Couture's dramaturgy in the *Romans* consisted ... in the minimizing of the theatricality of *particular* actions and expressions, and the rationalizing – and hopefully the neutralizing – of the theatrical as a *general* condition of action and expression as such": see "Thomas Couture and the Theatricalization of Action in 19th-Century French Painting," *Artforum* (June 1970), p. 44.
58 For a more detailed analysis of innovations in figure-space relations and the consequent radical shift of concomitant expressive and dramatic values in Courbet's major paintings of the 1950s, see L. Nochlin, "Innovation and Tradition in Courbet's *Burial at Ornans*," *Essays in Honor of Walter Friedlaender* (New York, 1965), pp. 119–26 (Chapter 1 in the present volume).
59 Eugène Delacroix, *Journal*, ed. André Joubin, rev. edn (Paris, 1950), 2, p. 18 (April 15, 1853).
60 John Richardson, *Edouard Manet: Paintings and Drawings* (New York, 1958), pp. 13–14. This criticism was convincingly countered by Alan Bowness, "A Note on Manet's 'Compositional Difficulties'," *Burlington Magazine*, 103 (1961), pp. 276–77. Alain de Leiris has also discussed Manet's additive compositions in "Manet – Sur la Plage de Boulogne," *Gazette des Beaux-Arts*, 57 (1961), pp. 53–62.

Chapter 4

"Courbet, the Commune, and the Visual Arts." First published in German in Klaus Herding (ed.), *Realismus als Widerspruch: Die Wirklichkeit in Courbets Malerei* (Frankfurt am Main, 1978).

1 For the most recent information on this painting, including reasons for later dating, see *Gustave Courbet, 1819–1877*, Grand Palais, Paris, 1977–78, cat. no. 128 (hereafter *Courbet, 1977*). For a suggestive account of prison imagery in 19th-century literature relevant to this painting, see V. Brombert, *La Prison romantique: Essai sur l'imaginaire* (Paris, 1975).
2 Seven post-Commune drawings by Courbet are reproduced by L. Aragon, *L'Exemple de Courbet* (Paris, 1952) (figs 95, 96, 97, 98, 99, 101, 102). The originals are in Louvre Carnet RF 29235. Two of these, Aragon nos 95 and 96 (f°4 and f°5) are not, in my opinion, from Courbet's hand. These drawings, especially Aragon no. 99 (f° 8), an execution in which the last standing victim is a woman in a Phrygian cap, are far more emotionally expressive in their treatment of Commune themes than is the prison self-portrait.
3 *Autoportrait à la pipe*, recently discovered by Georges Martin du Nord, charcoal on paper, 77 x 64. 5 cm.
4 Courbet evidently shaved off his beard when in hiding, to throw his pursuers off the track. (Clipping from *Le Petit Moniteur Universelle*, 11 June, 1871, "Capture and Trial of Courbet" in Paris, BN Estampes, *Papiers Courbet*, Boîte 4. Hereafter *PC*). For weight loss and white hair, see *Courbet, 1977*, cat. no. 128.
5 P. Courthion (ed.), *Courbet raconté par lui-même et par ses amis* (Geneva, 1950), 2, p. 124.
6 Courthion, op. cit., p. 140.
7 The literature on Courbet and the Column is vast and can only be summarily indicated here. For a view hostile to Courbet, see A. Darcel, "Les Musées, les arts, et les artistes pendant la Commune," *Gazette des Beaux-Arts*, 5 (February 1872), pp. 145–50; for a total exculpation of Courbet: J.-A. Castagnary, *Gustave Courbet et la colonne Vendôme. Plaidoyer pour un ami mort* (Paris, 1883). For a fairly objective, and well-documented account: R. Walter, "Un dossier délicat: Courbet et la colonne Vendôme," *Gazette des Beaux-Arts*, 81 (March 1973), pp. 178–84.
8 Published by Darcel, op. cit., pp. 147–48.
9 H. Lefebvre, *La Proclamation de la Commune, 26 mars 1871* (Paris, 1965), p. 394. For consideration of this dilemma, see L. Nochlin, "Museums and Radicals: A History of Emergencies," in *Museums in Crisis*, ed. B. O'Doherty (New York, 1972), pp. 7–41.
10 Réimpression du *Journal officiel de la Commune*, ed. V. Bunel (Paris, n.d.), 15 avril, p. 273 (hereafter *Journal*).
11 "... Nommé improprement art industriel." Ibid.
12 *Journal*, p. 27.
13 Ibid.
14 At the same time that it supressed the old Schools, the Committee proposed the creation of Communal Schools of Professional Art, possibly to be housed in empty military barracks. *Journal*, 10 May, 1871. p. 523.
15 *Journal*, 4 May, p. 459. The communiqué is mistakenly dated April 1 in the newspaper, but obviously the vote must have taken place on May 1.
16 See n. 7 above and discussion in *Courbet, 1977*, p 47. According to Castagnary, Félix Pyat claimed responsibility for the ultimate decision to topple the column in a letter the former member of the Commune's Executive Committee

wrote to the London *Times* on June 24, 1874. See Castagnary's *A Plea for a Dead Friend (1882)*, ed. and trans. A. Cannon and F. A. Trapp, in *Revolution & Reaction : The Paris Commune, 1871*, ed. J. Hicks and R. Tucker ([Amherst], 1973), pp. 136–37 (hereafter *Hicks and Tucker*).

17 *Courbet, 1977*, p. 47.

18 For illustrations see J. Bruhat, J. Dautry, and E. Tersen, *La Commune de 1871*, 2nd edn (Paris, 1970), pp. 265 and 266 (hereafter *Bruhat*).

19 Now in the Chambre Syndicale Typographique Parisienne. See C. Feld and F. Hincker, *Paris au front d'insurgé: La Commune en images* (Paris, 1971), p. 309 for the Varlin painting (hereafter *Feld and Hincker*). There is also a sketch or second version of this work, published by Feld and Hincker. The *Rue de Paris* is in the collection of the Louvre, gift of M. F. Luce, 1946.

20 Repr. *Bruhat*, p. 267.

21 Repr. ibid., p. 282.

22 Repr. *Feld and Hincker*, pp. 4–5. The painting, a lively "impressionist" work of a commemorative ceremony at Père Lachaise, was painted in 1883. See I. S. Grabar and I.S. Zil'bershtein, *Repin* (Moscow, 1948–49) 1, pp. 464–66, reprs. pp. 461 and 462.

23 A. de Leiris, *The Drawings of Edward Manet* (Berkeley and Los Angeles), 1969, cat. no. 342 and fig. 287 for *La Barricade*, a wash-drawing in the Budapest Museum of Fine Arts. For the lithograph of this subject, see J. C. Harris, *Edouard Manet: Graphic Works: A Definitive Catalogue Raisonné*, cat. no. 71, fig. 144. For the lithograph *Civil War*, ibid., cat. no. 72, fig. 146. J. Kaplow, "The Paris Commune and the Artists" (in *Hicks and Tucker*, pp. 162–63), describes a Manet painting, *Execution of the Communards*, now in the Folkwang Museum at Essen. As far as I know, this painting has not been mentioned in the Manet literature.

24 A. Boyd Houghton, *The Paris Mob – A Barricade in Paris* appeared in the *Graphic*, April 8, 1871, p. 313. His *Paris Under the Commune – Womens' Club...* appeared in the June 3, 1871 *Graphic*, p. 520.

25 Lefebvre, op. cit., p. 130.

26 Ibid. Of course the memory of Delacroix's *Liberty* lingered on.

27 See E. Thomas, *Les Pétroleuses* (Paris, 1963).

28 Repr. *Bruhat*, p. 260. For the same subject from the *Penny Illustrated News*, ibid., p. 192.

29 Repr. *Bruhat*, p. 180.

30 Repr. *Feld and Hincker*, pp. 308–9. The painting is in Geneva, the Modern Art Foundation.

31 Repr. E. Thomas, *Louise Michel ou la Velléda de l'anarchie* (Paris, 1971), "Documents" after p. 454.

32 Repr. ibid.

33 Repr. S. Lambert, *The Franco-Prussian War and the Commune in Caricature, 1870–71* (London, 1971), no. 137.

34 Paris, BN Estampes.

35 Lambert, op. cit., no. 125. The cartoon is there described as an example of the "vicious anti-clericalism ... common to all communards" although it is clearly anti-feminism that is the major issue here. The "orateuse" holds a copy of the divorce law.

36 Ibid., no. 127.

37 Gautrad, "1870–71: Les Photographes et la Commune," *Photo-Ciné Revue* (February 1972), p. 53.

38 Ibid., p. 56, and see numerous albums, Paris, BN Estampes.

39 Paris, BN Estampes (Album), E. Appert, *Crimes de la Commune*, 1871. Also see R. A. Sobieszek, "Composite Imagery and the Origins of Photomontage. Part 1: The Naturalistic Strain," *Artforum* (September 1978), p. 62.

40 Gautrand, op. cit., p. 53. Repr. *Bruhat*, p. 285.

41 Gautrand, op. cit., pp. 60–63, rediscovered Braquehais and discusses him extensively. See also Paris, BN Estampes (Album), B. Braquehais, *Paris pendant la Commune*, 1871, nos 14–25 for Place Vendôme series.

42 L. Nochlin, *Impressionism and Post-Impressionism, 1874–1904: Sources and Documents* (Englewood Cliffs, NJ, 1966), p.125 for English translation. The statement is an excerpt from an unpublished MS in the Signac archives of *c.* 1902.

Chapter 5

"The *Cribleuses de blé*: Courbet, Millet, Breton, Kollwitz, and the Image of the Working Woman." First published in *Malerie und Theorie, Das Courbet-Colloquium 1979* (Stadeslschen Kunstinstitut, Frankfurt am Main, 1980), pp. 49–73.

1 For the most recent, and complete, discussion of and references to the literature on Courbet's *Cribleuses*, see the catalogue *Gustave Courbet, 1819–1877*, Grand Palais, Paris, 1977 (hereafter *Courbet*, 1977). Also see Werner Hofmann's briefer discussion of the work in *Courbet und Deutschland* (Hamburger Kunsthalle, 1978), pp. 600–1. For Millet's *Glaneuses*, see the catalogue *Jean-Francois Millet (1814–1875)*, Grand Palais, Paris, 1975–76, no. 65. Also see "Le dossier des Glaneuses" in the same catalogue, pp. 143–49 and the catalogue *Jean-François Millet*, Hayward Gallery, London, 1976, pp. 81–116. Both of these catalogues owe much of their information to Robert Herbert, who also was a major contributor to the smaller catalogue, *Millet's "Gleaners,"* The Minneapolis Art Institute, 1978. For a more sociological examination of Millet and his work, see Jean-Claude Chamboredon, "Peintures des rapports sociaux et invention de l'eternel paysan: les deux manières de Jean-François Millet," *Actes de la recherche et sciences socials*, 17–18 (November 1977), pp. 6–28.

2 For a discussion of the complex issue of women's work in the context of the early period of industrialization, see Louise A. Tilly and Joan W. Scott, *Women, Work and Family* (New York, 1978).

3 For an excellent study of Daumier's anti-feminist caricatures, see Caecilia Rentmeister, "Daumier und das häßliche Geschlecht" in the catalogue *Daumier und die ungelösten Probleme der burgerlichen Gesellschaft*, Schloß Charlottenburg, Berlin, 1974, pp. 57–79. Also see Françoise Parturier's unfortunately titled *Lib Women* (Paris, 1974). Rentmeister discusses the *topos* of the baby who falls into the bathtub on p. 64 and illustrates the works in question. Daumier was, of course, perfectly capable of producing a monumental, allegorical representation of a woman nurturing her young to stand for the Republic in 1848. (See below, n. 56.) It was real women as activists or as independent forces apart from their maternal function that he, like most "right-thinking" men of his time, held anathema.

4 Jules Simon, *L'Ouvrière* (Paris, 1861). Not all authorities agreed with Simon, however. See Tilly and Scott, op. cit., pp. 1 and 2 for other opinions.

5 See such paintings as Max Liebermann's *Women Working in a Canned Food Factory*, 1879, Museum für Bildende Künste, Leipzig; A. Zorn's *The Large Brewery*, 1890, Kunstmuseum, Göteborg, or Edouard Rosset-Granger, *The Sugar Crushing Machine*, 1891, whereabouts unknown. These are reproduced in Edward Lucie-Smith and Celestine Dars, *Work and Struggle: The Painter as Witness*, 1870–1914 (New York and London, 1977), figs 27, 29, and 30.

6 Robert L. Herbert, "City vs. Country: the Rural Image in French painting from Millet to Gauguin", *Artforum*, 8 (February 1970), pp. 44–55.

7 See no. VI–61 in the catalogue *The Second Empire 1852–1870: Art in France under Napoleon III*, Philadelphia Museum of Art, 1978, for a discussion of Glaize's painting and contemporary reactions to it.

8 Eunice Lipton, "The Violence of Ideological Distortion: The Imagery of Laundress in 19th Century French Culture," *Heresies*, 6: *On Women and Violence* (Summer 1978), pp. 77–81, 85.

9 Legros: *Ex-voto* was originally intended as a funeral and then repainted. See Monique Geiger, "Alphonse Legros, L'ex-voto. Etude radiographique," *Bulletin du Laboratoire du Musée du Louvre* (1971), pp. 18–23. Also, see *Alphonse Legros: Peintre et graveur, 1837–1911*, Musée des Beaux-Arts, Dijon, 1957, no. 2.

10 Perhaps nowhere is the connection between raw sexuality and the daily life of the *paysanne* more forcefully asserted than in the beginning of Zola's novel *La Terre* of 1887, in which the adolescent farm-girl, Françoise, nonchalantly inserts a bull's penis into the waiting cow with her hand. (See Emile Zola, *La Terre* in Les Rougon-Macquart, IV, Paris, Bibliothèque de la Pléiade, 1966, pp. 374–75).

11 See Marius Vachon, *Jules Breton* (Paris, 1899), pp. 100, 125, 127–28.

12 I am grateful for this information to Madelaine Fidell Beaufort who permitted me to see her unpublished article "Jules Breton, Some American Appreciations."

13 The most extensive and provocative study of the erotic allure of the working-class woman, in England, rather than France, is provided by Derek Hudson's *Munby: Man of Two Worlds:*

The Life and Times of Arthur J. Munby, 1828–1910 (London, 1972). The subject of the book, Arthur J. Munby, gentleman, civil servant and minor literary figure, was obsessed with the muscular charms of the working woman, whom he interviewed and photographed in male attire. Eventually, he married, secretly, his servant Hannah. His biographer characterized his attitude as "benign perversity" (p. 77), but, in exaggerated form, it epitomizes the erotic stimulus provided upper-class men by lower-class characteristics. Christopher Isherwood makes the same point, from a homosexual viewpoint, about the allure of working-class boys to upper-class Englishmen in *Christopher and his Kind, 1929–1939* (New York, 1976), *passim.*

14 Marilyn Kluger, *The Joy of Spinning* (New York, 1971), p. 107.

15 For a reproduction, see Walter S. Gibson, "Some Flemish Popular Prints from Hieronymus Cock and his Contemporaries," *Art Bulletin*, 60 (December 1978), fig. 1, p. 673.

16 See for example Steven van Duyven's *Eingeschlafene Spitzen-Klöpplerin*, s and d, 1677, in W. Bernt, *Die Niederländischen Maler des 17. Jahrhunderts* (Munich, 1962), 4, no. 77. The theme continued in 18th-century France. See for example, the photograph of a sleeping spinner, not unlike Courbet's in its pose, attributed to Françoise Duparc (1726–78) in the files of the Witt Photographic Survey, London (A. S. Harris, L. Nochlin, *Women Artists: 1550–1950*, Los Angeles, 1976, p. 172). I am grateful to Professor Harris for calling this work to my attention. In addition, Michael Fried published a related but not exactly similar figure, after Greuze, *La Tricoteuse endormie* from the Salon of 1759, engr. by Jardinier as *Eighteenth-Century Studies*, 9 (1975–76), pp. 139–77. For studies of the moral implications of the sleeping servant-girl, particularly Jan Vermeer's *Girl Asleep* in the Metropolitan Museum, New York, see Seymour Slive "'en Dronke Slapende Meyd aen een Tafel' by Jan Vermeer," *Festschrift Ulrich Middeldorf* (Berlin, 1968), pp. 452–59, and Madlyn M. Kahr, "Vermeer's Girl Asleep: A Moral Emblem," *Metropolitan Museum Journal*, 6 (1972), pp. 115–32. For an analysis of the theme of the spinner in Dutch 17th-century art, see *Tot Lering en Vermaak*, Rijksmuseum, Amsterdam, 1976, pp. 40–43 and 48–49.

17 Kahr, *Metropolitan Museum Journal*, op. cit., pp. 126–27.

18 Slive, *Festschrift*, op. cit., p. 454 and Kahr, *Metropolitan Museum Journal*, op. cit., pp. 115–16.

19 Werner Hofmann, "Über die 'Schlafende Spinnerin'," in *Realismus als Widerspruch: Die Wirklichkeit in Courbets Malerei*, ed. K. Herding (Frankfurt, 1978), pp. 212–22 and "Courbets Wirklichkeiten" in *Courbet und Deutschland*, Hamburger Kunsthalle, 1973, pp. 605–8. Aaron Sheon's is an unpublished article, "Courbet, Grandville, Dreams and the Unconscious." The reference to Nodier's novel occurs on pp. 10–11. Professor Sheon also discusses a related drawing, Millet's *Sleeping Girl*, of *c.* 1846, very similar to Courbet's *Sleeping Spinner* in its pose and composition, a work that has now disappeared, to which Robert L. Herbert had called his attention. I, too, was struck by the similarity to Courbet's *Spinner* when Professor Herbert showed it recently at a conference in Frankfurt.

20 P.-J. Proudhon, *Du Principe de l'art et de sa destination sociale*, in *Oeuvres completes de P.-J. Proudhon*, ed. C. Bouglé and H. Moysset (Paris, 1939), p. 173.

21 See G. and J. Lacambre, *Champfleury: Le réalisme* (Paris, 1973), p. 190.

22 Vidal's work had appeared as no. 5046 in the Paris Salon catalogue of 1850, under the title *Le Fil rompu*. I am grateful to Professor Beatrice Farwell for calling the work to my attention. Other representations of spinners, knitters, and related fiber-workers had appeared in the Salons immediately preceding that of 1853, in which Courbet's *Fileuse endormie* figured as no. 301. These included, in the Salon of 1850, François Bonvin's *La Tricoteuse* (no. 295); Mlle. Marie-Laure Forestier's *La Tricoteuse* (no. 1089); François Montfallet's *Une Fileuse* (no. 2239) as well as his *Le Sommeil* (no. 2238), a suggestive combination; and in the Salon of 1852, Léon-Joseph Billotte's *Une Brodeuse* (no. 116) and Louis-Alexandre Maroller's *Fileuse du Béarn.*

23 A most interesting (possible) offshoot of Courbet's *Sleeping Spinner*, although in some ways more relatable to Millet in mood and style, is the even more overtly eroticized and far sweeter *The Spinning Wheel*, signed and dated 1859 by the English painter John Philipp, now in the Burrell Collection in Glasgow. Philipp's sleeping spinner has a frankly open, light-revealed *décolletage* and "fortituously" clutches her heart with her right hand, as she smiles in dreaming.

24 The most complete historical examination of the issue of gleaning is Paul de Grully's monumental doctoral dissertation for the Law Faculty of the University of Montpellier, written in 1912. The dissertation is subtitled "patrimonie des pauvres."

25 De Grully, *Glanage*, op. cit., p. 66

26 See Albert Soboul, "La Question paysanne en 1848," *La Pensée* (1948), *passim*, and Roger Price, *The French Second Republic* (Ithaca, 1972), pp. 117–18.

27 Jean Rousseau in *Le Figaro* of 1857 wrote: "Derrière ces trois glaneuses se silhouettent … les piques des émentes populaires et les échafauds de 93." Robert Herbert points out that this painting also offended the middle class, for whom Paul de Saint-Victor spoke in *La Presse*, accusing the gleaners of having "des prétentions gigantesques" and denominating them "les trois Parques du paupérisme." (*Jean François Millet (1814–1875)*, Grand Palais, Paris, 1975–76, p. 101.) Ironically, left-wing critics who admired the painting like Castagnary, defended it by saying that it was not "une harangue politique ou une thèse sociale, mais un œuvre d'art, très belle et très simple, franche de toute déclamation." Castagnary further removed the painting from the context of contemporary conflict by declaring that the motif … "s'élève au-dessus des passions de parti et reproduit … une de ces pages de la nature vraies, et grandes, comme en trouvaient Homère et Virgile." (Ibid., p. 102)

28 For Millet's refusal to accept political interpretations of his work, in contradiction to Courbet, as well as the question of a socially provocative contrast between foreground and background in the *Glaneuse*, see Chamboredon, *Actes*, op. cit., p. 24, pp. 15–16, and n. 19, p. 16.

29 This is especially true of the woman to the right. "En plaçant la ligne d'horizon au ras de cette tête, Millet, du même coup, exclu la femme du ciel et l'intègre a la grande horizontale de la moisson." *Millet*, 1975–76, op. cit., p. 102.

30 The location of the original version of the *Sarcleuses* of 1860, exhibited in the 1861 Salon, is unknown. A reduced version of the work, of 1868, is in the Metropolitan Museum in New York. See C. Sterling and M. M. Salinger, *French Paintings, a Catalogue of the Collection of the Metropolitan Museum of Art* (New York, 1966), 2, pp. 179–81. Breton himself wrote about the event that inspired the painting in the most high-flown terms, referring to "a group of weeders … crouched on their knees … their faces haloed by the pink transparency of their violet hands, as if to venerate the fecondating star." He notes the "svelte body," "long and supple" of the girl to the left. Later, he talks of the "religious tremor" the scene aroused in him: "Not one detail was bothersome, not one tone disrupted the harmony. It was," he declared, "like a natural transfiguration of the most humble of labors." Jules Breton, *Un Peintre paysan: souvenirs et impressions* (Paris, 1896), cited in *Millet's Gleaners*, The Minneapolis Institute of Arts, 1978, p. 46.

31 For contemporary 19th-century reports on the realities of life of women peasants, see E. Shorter, "Différences de classe et sentiment depuis 1750: L'example de la France", *Annales*, 29 (July/August, 1974). The observer of 1845 was one Barthélemy Chaix of Grenoble. Reports about peasant-wives serving the men at table are by Déribier-du-Châtelet, *Dictionnaire statistique … ou histoire du département de Cantal*, 2 (1853), p. 133, and *Carlo Bossi, Statistique générale de la France, département de l'Ain* (Paris, 1808), p. 311. See Shorter, *Annales*, p. 1048. There are other examples. The peasant proverbs are taken from Dr. Charles Perron, *Les Francs-Comtois: leur caractère national, leurs mœurs, leurs usages* (Besançon, 1892), p. 85. Yann Brekilien, in *La Vie quotidienne des paysans Bretagne au XIXe siècle* (Paris, 1966), remarks that the farmer's wife "n'asséy ait même pas à table, restant debout pendant tout le repas à servir les hommes. Usée par les travaux et les maternités, ignorant le repos, elle ne recevait même pas l'encouragement d'une parole affectueuse. Elle semblait réduite du rang d'esclave." (p. 69) The situation of oppression seems widespread and fairly universal. Recently, Eugen Weber has summarized the low status and hard lot of the 19th-century peasant woman in his *Peasants into Frenchmen: The Modernization of Rural France, 1870–1914* (Stanford, CA, 1976), pp. 171–74. Weber maintains that an opportunity for relative independence only arose when women could earn independent wages.

32 Vachon dates both the poem from which the first lines are taken, and the painting, a *Glaneuse*, which it accompanied, 1877. The next lines of verse are from a poem of 1890 (Marius Vachon, *Jules Breton*, Paris, 1899, p. 85). Vachon, echoing Breton, declares: "Les femmes de l'Artois sont grandes, vigoreuses et imposantes dans l'ampleur des forms auxquelles le développement par le travail des champs donne une grace fière et robuste." (p. 100)

33 *Courbet, 1977*, p. 134. Among other "oriental" elements this author finds present in the work are the high viewpoint, the monochromatic gray-and-blond color scheme, and the poses of the figures. Aside from the fact, that, as the author admits, 1854 is rather early for the presence of such elements in Courbet's art, I find no visual affirmation of such influence in the painting itself: the colors are not really *that* monochromatic, but markedly warm and bright in certain areas, like the skirt and bodice of the protagonist, or her yellow neckscarf; nor is there any sense of that decorative flattening or suave linear emphasis characteristic of the Japanese print in *Les Cribleuses*.

34 Julius Meier-Graefe, *Modern Art*, trans. F. Simmonds and G. W. Chrystal (New York, 1908), 1, p. 233.

35 Cited in *Courbet, 1977*, p. 134. He also described it as a "tableau de mœurs de paysan" when writing to Alfred Bruyas in an undated letter, probably from early 1855. See Pierre Borel, *Le Roman de Gustave Courbet*, 2nd edn (Paris, 1922), p. 61.

36 Ibid. It was also shown in Nantes in 1861, and what was perhaps a sketch for the work evidently was shown in Le Havre in 1858 and, perhaps the same sketch, in London in 1859: F. Haskell found a reference to what may have been the latter work in a London catalogue of 1859 (*Courbet, 1977*, pp. 134–35). Professor William Gerdts has informed me in personal conversation that the *Cribleuses* was exhibited in New York in 1859.

37 Weber, *Peasants*, op. cit., p. 125.

38 These are traditional identifications, reiterated by Helène Toussaint in *Courbet, 1977*, p. 134. Toussaint also hypothesizes that the boy to the right is Courbet's illegitimate son, Désiré Binet, born in 1847, hence six years old when the painting was begun. She finds the figure comparable to that of "l'enfant qui dessine dans *l'Atelier* ... dont nous disons qu'il est très vraisemblablement le petit Désiré que Courbet a toutes sortes de raisons d'introduire dans l'œuvre qui est l'histoire de sept ans de sa vie."

39 For a detailed examination of the function, structure, and history of both the *van* and the *crible*, see *Cours complet d'agriculture théorique et pratique* ..., ed. l'Abbé Rozier and M. le Baron de Morogues, et al. (Paris, 1840). For the *crible*, see vol. 7, pl. cxxcii and pp. 371–72; for the *van*, vol. 17, pp. 265–69 and pl. cccxxvii. Millet's original *Vanneur* was sold out of Ledru-Rollin's collection to an American in 1854. See Kenneth Lindsay, "Millet's Lost Winnower Rediscovered," *Burlington Magazine*, 116 (May 1974), pp. 239–45. In later versions, Millet toned down the subversive implications of the *bonnet rouge* and the *tricolor* color scheme of the original. See T. J. Clark, *The Absolute Bourgeois: Artists and Politics in France 1848–1851* (New York, 1973), p. 64 and Lindsay, pp. 240–41 and n. 12, p. 240.

40 The instrument has been denominated a *blutoir*, a closely related implement, by Suzanne Tardieu, in her important article "Un Blutoir du Berri," *Bulletin des Musées de France* (février 1947), 12:2, pp. 10–13, in which she illustrates the *blutoir* in question and points out a similar implement in Courbet's *Cribleuses*. The *blutoir*, however, is generally meant for the refining of flour (see Paul Dubreuil, *Dictionnaire populaire d'agriculture pratique*, Paris, 1895, p. 220), whereas the *tartare*, like the *van* and the *crible*, was intended more exclusively for the cleaning of grain. It was an extremely popular device during the 19th century, effecting, according to the authors of the *Cours complet d'agriculture*, "une immense économie dans le travail de main d'œuvre nécessaire pour nettoyer des rains [et] aussi le moyen d'opére ce nettoiement avec une bien plus grande perfection qu'il n'est possible de la faire par les procédés employes précédemment." (Vol. 17, p. 265)

41 See especially Hofmann, "Courbets Wirklichkeiten" in *Courbet*, Hamburger Kunsthalle, 1978, pp. 600–3.

42 The critic Edmond About evidently found the pose of the *cribleuse* not only trivial but indecent as well. See ibid., p. 600.

43 Hofmann, for example, sees the *Cribleuses* as multi-dimensional in its metaphoric implications: for example, he compares the kneeling figure of the grain sifter with her outstretched implement to that of Danae awaiting the shower of gold and connects the figure to a universal mythology of fertility embodied in the female's symbolic embrace with the male principle, a theory articulated by J. J. Bachofen in *Mutterrecht und Urreligion*, ed. V. Rudolf Marx (Leipzig, 1926). (*Courbet*, Hamburger Kunsthalle, 1978, p. 600 and n. 36, p. 613).

44 According to Andreas Pigler, *Barockthemen; Eine Auswahl von Verzeichnissen zur Ikonographie des 17. und 18. Jahrhunderts* (Budapest, 1956), 2, p. 346, Tuccia was a vestal who carried water in her sieve to demonstrate her purity. Her story is recounted in Valerius Maximus, VII, 1, 5 and Pliny, *Natural History*, XXVII, 12. She evidently served as an emblem of chastity for Ripa and appeared as a personification of virginity in works by Rubens, Coypel, and Suvée as well as in images by Mantegna, Beccafumi, Parmagianino, and Tintoretto.

45 The work, an engraving, has been attributed to François Gentil and many others. The composition has been connected to Ruggiero da Ruggieri, a mysterious artist of the Fontainebleau School, although John Schloder has told me in correspondace that Penni is a possible author. The engraving may be found at the Metropolitan Museum in the Mariette Scrapbook of Parmagianino and is mentioned in Félix Herbet, *Les Graveurs de l'Ecole de Fontainebleau*, 1896–1900, 8, p. 33, no. 10. I am grateful to Sylvie Béguin and John Schloder for this interesting information.

46 Breton's *Cribleuse de Colza* was originally shown in the 1861 Salon. A version of 1866 is now in the Corcoran Gallery, Washington, D.C.

47 This illustration has been reproduced in *Käthe Kollwitz*, Frankfurter Kunstverein, 2nd edn (Frankfurt, 1973), fig. 17.

48 De Beauvoir discusses the notion of woman as Other in great detail in the section dedicated to Myths in *Le Deuxième Sexe* (see *Le Deuxième Sexe*, Paris, 1949, pp. 185–278), pointing out that female mythic or allegorical figures can "stand for almost any quality, good or bad, as long as it, and they, are defined exclusively in relation to men" (p. 192).

49 Françoise Forster-Hahn, *Käthe Kollwitz, 1867–1945: Prints, Drawings, Sculpture*, University Art Galleries, Riverside, California, 1978, p. 6. Forster-Hahn discusses the whole series of the *Bauernkrieg* with great penetration, pp. 15–19.

50 Bebel's *Die Frau und der Sozialismus* was a most successful popularization of the essentials of Social Democracy as well as those of women's liberation. First published in 1883, it had reached over fifty editions in the original German by the time its author died in 1913. Bebel argued that women's emancipation could only take place in a Socialist society. August Bebel, *Woman under Socialism*; 33rd edn, trans. D. de Leon, introd. L. Coser (New York, 1971), p. vii and Forster-Hahn, op. cit., p. 4.

51 Otto Nagel, *Käthe Kollwitz* (Greenwich, CT, 1971), p. 35.

52 Natalie Zemon Davis, "Women on Top", in her *Society and Culture in Early Modern France* (Stanford, CA, 1975), pp. 124–51, esp. p. 129.

53 The two figures may be caricatural references to two of the most prominent feminists of the day, Jeanne Déroin and Eugenie Niboyet. Rentmeister feels that in the entire *Divorceuse* series Daumier simply bodies forth the attitude of *Charivari* and its middle-class readers (Rentmeister, *Daumier*, op. cit., pp. 69–71).

54 For a discussion of caricatures of women of the Commune, see James A. Leith, "The War of Images surrounding the Commune," *Images of the Commune*, ed. J.A. Leith (Montreal and London, 1978), pp. 135–38, and for the role of women in the Commune, see Edith Thomas, *Les Pétroleuses* (Paris, 1963).

55 For a complete analysis of the complex contemporary political and religious references contained in or implied by Brueghel's *Dulle Griet*, see Margret A. Sullivan, "Madness and Folly: Peter Bruegel the Elder's *Dulle Griet*," *Art Bulletin*, 59 (March, 1977), pp. 55–66.

56 It is significant that his own little image of the barricades of 1848, a frontispiece for *Le Salut public*, no. 2, shows a perfectly ordinary man in rather ragged contemporary dress leading the charge up the barricade; Daumier, however, contributed an allegorical half-nude figure of the Republic to a government-sponsored contest at the time. (See Bernard Lehmann, "Daumier and the Republic," *Gazette des Beaux-Arts*, 27 (1945), pp. 105–20, and Albert Boime, "The Second Republic's contest for the figure of the Republic," *Art Bulletin*, 53 (March 1971), pp. 68–83.)

Chapter 6
"In Detail: Courbet's *A Burial at Ornans*." First published in *Portfolio*, 2:5 (November/December, 1980), pp. 32–37.

Chapter 7
"The De-Politicization of Gustave Courbet: Transformation and Rehabilitation under the Third Republic." First published in *October*, 22 (Autumn 1982), pp. 64–78.

1 See Jean-Pierre Sanchez, "La Critique de Courbet et la critique du réalisme entre 1880 et 1890," *Histoire et Critique des Arts*, 4–5 (1977–78), pp. 78–79, for a summary. My interpretation of this criticism is somewhat different from that of Sanchez.
2 Théodore Duret, *Courbet* (Paris, 1917), pp. 117–18. All other citations of Duret refer to this text.
3 This strategy must, of course, be understood within the context of the more general goals of the early Third Republic, especially those of its liberal wing, dominated by the figure of Gambetta. The government was intent on maintaining a coalition among the economically dominating *haute bourgeoisie*; the more recently created, upwardly mobile middle bourgeoisie, the so-called "*nouvelles couches*"; and the peasantry through the creation of a cultural front at once aggressively secular, popular, and progressive, spiced with a certain democratic combativeness, yet at the same time bearing the promise of social and political stability to a nation recently shaken by conquest and civil strife. Both the democratic aspirations and the craving for stability and order were reinforced by nostalgia for the sturdy virtues of French provincial tradition, the vanishing strengths of the *menu peuple* of the countryside, at the very moment when this population was deserting the country for the city.
4 These studies are: Camille Lemonnier, *G. Courbet et son œuvre* (Paris, 1878); Henri d'Ideville, *Gustave Courbet, notes et documents sur sa vie et son œuvre* (Paris, 1878); and Paul Mantz, "Gustave Courbet," *Gazette des Beaux-Arts* (1878); Part I: 17, pp. 514–27; Part II: 17, pp. 17–30; Part III: 17, pp. 371–84.
5 [Jules] Castagnary, "Fragments d'un livre sur Courbet," *Gazette des Beaux-Arts* (1911): Part I (January), pp. 5–20; Part II (December), pp. 488–97; Part III (December 1912), pp. 19–30.
6 Castagnary had explicitly exonerated Courbet from all responsibility in the Vendôme Column affair in his pamphlet, *Gustave Courbet et la Colonne Vendôme. Plaidoyer pour un ami mort* (Paris, 1883).

Chapter 8
"Courbet, Oller, and a Sense of Place: The Regional, the Provincial, and the Picturesque in Nineteenth-Century Art." First published in *Horizontes*, 28:56 (1985), pp. 7–13.

1 Eudora Welty, *Place in Fiction* (a condensation of lectures prepared for the Conference on American Studies, Cambridge, England, 1954) (New York, 1957), n.p.
2 Francisco Oller, cited in the exhibition catalogue *Francisco Oller: Un Realisto del Impresionismo* (Francisco Oller: A Realist Impressionist), Museum of Art, Ponce, Puerto Rico, June–December, 1983, cat. no. 43, p. 193.
3 Ibid., cat. no. 23, p. 175.
4 Ibid.
5 Ibid., pp. 224–27.
6 Ibid., cat. no. 35, p. 185.

Chapter 9
"Courbet's *L'Origine du monde*: The Origin without an Original." First published in *October*, 37 (Summer 1986), pp. 76–86.

1 Neil Hertz, "Medusa's Head: Male Hysteria under Political Pressure," *Representations*, 4 (Fall 1983), pp. 27–54; with responses by Catherine Gallagher and Joel Fineman and a reply by Hertz, pp. 55–72.
2 Denis Hollier, "How to Not Take Pleasure in Talking about Sex," *Enclitic*, 8:1–2 (Spring-Fall 1984), pp. 84–93.
3 Gerald Zwang, *Le Sexe de la femme* (Paris, 1967).
4 Wayland Young, *Eros Denied* (London, 1968), p. 96.
5 Peter Webb, *The Erotic Arts* (London, 1975), pp. 166, 451–52, n. 67.
6 Robert Fernier, *La Vie et l'œuvre de Gustave Courbet* (Paris and Lausanne, 1977–78), 2, p. 6, no. 530.
7 Léger does not reproduce the work; I have not been able to find any reproductions of the *Origin* dating before the 1960s.
8 Charles Léger, *Courbet et son temps* (Paris, 1948), p. 116.
9 Edmond and Jules de Goncourt, *Journal: mémoires de la vie littéraire* (Paris, 1956), 3, p. 996.
10 For information about Khalil Bey, see Francis Haskell, "A Turk and his Pictures in Nineteenth-Century Paris," *Oxford Art Journal*, 5:1 (1982), pp. 40–47.
11 Ludovic Halévy, *Trois diners avec Gambetta*, ed. Daniel Halévy (Paris, 1929), pp. 86–87.
12 Maxime du Camp, *Les Convulsions de Paris*, 7th edn (Paris, 1889), 2, pp. 189–90.
13 Desmond Collins and John Onians, "The Origins of Art," *Art History*, 1:1 (March, 1978), pp. 1–25.
14 This is not the first, nor the last, time that a major artist will resort to such a gesture, needless to say; both Michelangelo in his *Creation* and David in *The Oath of the Horatii* offer memorable analogues.
15 Hertz, op. cit., p. 69.
16 Jacques Lacan, "The Insistence of the Letter in the Unconscious," in F. and R. DeGeorge, *The Structuralists: From Marx to Lévi-Strauss* (Garden City, N.Y., 1972), p. 313; see also Holly Wallace Boucher, "Metonymy in Typology and Allegory, with a consideration of Dante's *Comedy*," *Allegory, Myth and Symbol*, Harvard English Studies, 9, ed. M. M. Bloomfield (Cambridge, Mass., 1981), p. 141.

Chapter 10
"Courbet's Real Allegory: Rereading "*The Painter's Studio*." First published in *Courbet Reconsidered*, exhibition catalogue by Sarah Faunce and Linda Nochlin (New York, The Brooklyn Museum, 1988), pp. 17–41 (hereafter *Courbet Reconsidered*).

Part One
Epigraphs: Cited in *Champfleury: Le réalisme*, ed. Genevieve and Jean Lacambre (Paris, 1973), p. 190. Walter Benjamin, *The Origin of German Tragic Drama*, trans. J. Osborne (London, 1977), p. 178. Jane Gallop, *Reading Lacan* (Ithaca, 1985), p. 21.
1 The letter, cited by Héléne Toussaint in *Gustave Courbet, 1819–1877*, Grand Palais, Paris, 1977–78 (hereafter *Courbet, 1977*), pp. 260–61, was written to his friend Français to ask the latter to persuade the Exposition Universelle jury to extend the time limit for the submission of his pictures
2 For more specific information about the cast of characters, see the complete text of the letter, which is available in English translation in *Gustave Courbet, 1819–1877*, exh. cat., Royal Academy, London, 1978, pp. 254–55. All of my English translations of material from *Courbet, 1977* are taken from this source.
3 Emile Littré, *Dictionnaire de la langue française*, ed. J. Pauvert (Paris, 1936), 2:317: "Sorte de métaphore continuée, espèce de discours qui est d'abord présenté sous un sense propre et qui ne sert que de comparison pour donner l'intelligence d'un autre sense qu'on n'exprime point."
4 Angus Fletcher, *Allegory: The Theory of a Symbolic Mode* (Ithaca, 1964), p. 2. He continues: "It [allegory] destroys the normal expectation we have about language, that our words "mean what they say." When we predicate quality *x* of a person Y, Y really is what our predication says he is (or we assume so); but allegory would turn Y into something other (*allos*) than what the open and direct statement tells the reader."
5 *Courbet, 1977*, pp. 246–47.
6 See, for example, the opinions of critics and men of letters from 1855 and after – A.-H. du Pays, Champfleury, Charles Perier, Paul Mantz, Jules Buisson, and many others – gathered together as "Appréciations," in René Huyghe, Germain Bazin, and Hélène Jean Adhémar, *Courbet: L'atelier du peintre: Allégorie réelle, 1855, Monographies des peintures du Musée du Louvre*, 3 (Paris, 1944), pp. 24–28. Delacroix, who greatly admired *The Painter's Studio* when he saw it in Courbet's exhibition in 1855, referring to it as "one of the most singular works of our time," simply refused to deal with its meaning at all. *Journal*, August 3, 1855, cited in Huyghe, et al., pp. 24–25.
7 For interpretations of *The Painter's Studio* see: Werner Hofmann, *The Earthly Paradise* (New York, 1961), pp. 11–49; Pierre Georgel, "Les transformations de la peinture vers

1848, 1855, 1863," *Revue de l'Art*, 27 (1975), pp. 69–72; Alan Bowness, *Courbet's "Atelier du Peintre,"* (Newcastle upon Tyne, 1972); Benedict Nicolson, *Courbet: The Studio of the Painter* (New York, 1973); L. Nochlin, *"The Invention of the Avant-Garde: France, 1830–80," Art News Annual*, 24 (1968), pp. 13–16; Alex Seltzer, "Gustave Courbet: All the World's a Studio," *Artforum*, 16 (September 1977), pp. 44–50; James H. Rubin, *Realism and Social Vision in Courbet and Proudhon* (Princeton, 1980), esp. pp. 38–63; Margaret Armbrust Seibert, "A Political and a Pictorial Tradition Used in Gustave Courbet's *Real Allegory*," *Art Bulletin*, 65:2 (June 1983), pp. 311–16, and John F. Moffitt, "Art and Politics: An Underlying Pictorial-Political Topos in Courbet's *Real Allegory*," *Artibus et Historiae*, 8:15 (1987), pp. 183–93. This list is by no means exhaustive. See *Courbet, 1977*, p. 243, for further references.

8 This opposition between the side of the shareholders and friends on the right and the masses, "wretchedness, poverty, wealth, the exploited and the exploiters, people who live on death" (*Courbet, 1977*, p. 246), to the left, perhaps – not merely coincidentally – repeats the opposition between the blessed to the right of the Judging Christ and the damned to his left in the Christian iconography of the Last Judgment.

9 Courbet's description of this character in the letter is as follows: "A weather-beaten old man, a diehard republican (that Minister of the Interior, for instance who was in the Assembly when Louis XVI was condemned to death, the one who was still following courses at the Sorbonne last year) a man 90 years old with a begging-bag in his hand, dressed in old patched white linen and wearing a broad-brimmed hat." *Courbet, 1977*, p. 246.

10 Toussaint supported each of her specific identifications with a contemporary photograph or print of the public figure in question (*Courbet, 1977*, pp. 252–58).

11 Toussaint maintains, in considerable detail, that the crucial letter to Champfleury actually contains many hints about these hidden identities, hints available only to those who have a really idiomatic knowledge of the meaning of certain French turns-of-phrase of the period. For example, she explains, in support of her contention that the scytheman is a portrait of Kościuszko, representing insurgent Poland, that in 1855 the French term *faucheur* signified "above all, a Polish patriot." She convincingly explains the double meaning of many other phrases used by Courbet in his letter of explanation. These hints were, she feels, certainly understood by Courbet's friend and champion Castagnary, when he declared in 1881 that *The Painter's Studio* "contains a whole side of topical reference which is escaping from us through the death of almost all its audience." See Hélène Toussaint, "A propos d'une Critique," Les Amis de Gustave Courbet, *Bulletin*, 61 (1979), pp. 10–13.

12 See *Courbet, 1977*, p. 253.

13 Ibid., pp. 253–54.

14 Ibid., pp. 254–55.

15 Ibid., pp. 256–57. Toussaint originally identified the laborer representing Russian socialism as Alexander Herzen, who had worked with Proudhon in Paris until 1851. She later admitted to me, in conversation, that this figure was more likely based on a portrait of the anarchist Bakunin.

16 Ibid., pp. 257–58. Toussaint's identification of this *braconnier* or poacher-figure with Napoleon III, based on similarity of appearance and meaningful hints in accouterments – the seated figure is wearing the jackboots that often "stood for" the forbidden image of the emperor in cartoons – is extremely convincing.

17 Ibid., p. 264.

18 Klaus Herding, "Das *Atelier des Malers*," *Realismus als Widerspruch: Die Wirklichkeit in Courbets Malerei*, ed. K. Herding (Frankfurt am Main, 1978), pp. 223–47.

19 It is, of course, impossible to summarize Herding's whole article in a few sentences. I have, however, attempted to draw out the main points of his piece. I am grateful to Benjamin Buchloh for his translation of Herding's article.

20 Fletcher, *Allegory*, op. cit., pp. 304–5 and 322–23. The author cites Northrop Frye, *The Anatomy of Criticism: Four Essays* (Princeton, 1957), p. 90, to prove his case.

21 See above, the sources for the epigraphs to this chapter.

22 Fredric Jameson, *Marxism and Form* (Princeton, 1971), p. 71.

23 Angus Fletcher refers to I. A. Richards's introduction of these terms in the latter's lectures, *The Philosophy of Rhetoric*, in 1936. See Fletcher, *Allegory*, op. cit., p. 11 and n. 19.

24 Terry Eagleton, *Walter Benjamin or Towards a Revolutionary Criticism* (London, 1981), p. 19.

25 Jameson, *Marxism and Form*, op. cit., p. 72.

26 For the distinction between the work and the text, see Roland Barthes, *Le Plaisir du texte* (Paris, 1973) and "De l'Oeuvre au texte," *Revue de l'Esthétique* 24:3 (1971), esp. 230–31: "L'œuvre est ordinairement l'objet d'une consommation; … le texte demande qu'on essaye d'abolir … la distance entre l'écriture et la lecture … Le lecteur joue, lui, deux fois: il *joue au Texte* (sense ludique), il *joue le Texte;* … Le Texte est à peu près une partition; … il sollicite au lecteur une collaboration pratique.

"Ceci amène à poser … une dernière approche du Texte: celle du plaisir."

27 Hofmann, *Earthly Paradise*, op. cit., pp. 11–49, is a rare exception. Hofmann does not, however, discuss the sketchy quality of the work in relation to allegory. For a passing reference to the fact that the painting is incomplete, see Nicolson, *Courbet*, op. cit., pp. 18–20. For a first-rate analysis of the role of sketchiness, color, and brushwork in Courbet's œuvre as a whole, see Klaus Herding, "Farbe und Weltbild: Thesen zu Courbets Malerei," *Courbet und Deutschland*, ed. W. Hofmann, et al. (Hamburg, 1978), pp. 478–92.

28 He did, however, have ample time to finish it after it was shown in Paris. The work was not sold and it was shown in its present form twice during Courbet's lifetime: in Bordeaux in 1865 and in Vienna in 1873 (*Courbet, 1977*, p. 243).

29 Charles Baudelaire, "The Salon of 1845," in *The Mirror of Art*, ed. Jonathan Mayne (London, 1955), p. 29.

30 I have considered the implications of the sketch and sketchiness in both modernist and more traditional practice, as well as the issue of the privileging of the personal touch of the artist over the illusionistic representation of subject or narrative, in a lecture entitled "The Sketch, Sketchiness, and the Effect of the Aesthetic in Nineteenth-Century French Art," presented at the National Academy of Design in New York in 1987.

31 *Courbet, 1977*, p. 247. This group is presided over by the tortured and lifeless nude form of the lay figure behind it, which in turn creates further meanings, and extends the dark, "pessimistic" implications of this section as a whole.

32 Herding, *Realismus als Widerspruch*, op. cit., p. 241 and n. 81.

33 Not, it must be emphasized, within the context of art historical "influence." I am not trying to posit a specific formal or iconographic "influence" relating Dürer's *Melancolia I* to Courbet's beggar woman. Courbet scholars have, however, attempted to point out such a relationship between the figure of Proudhon, in the *Portrait of P.-J. Proudhon in 1853* and that of the Dürer engraving. See *Courbet und Deutschland*, op. cit., p. 266 and fig. 262e.

34 Benjamin, *Origin*, op. cit., p. 152.

35 Norman Bryson, *Word and Image: French Painting of the Ancien Regime* (Cambridge, 1981), p. 71.

36 Eagleton, *Benjamin*, op. cit., p. 20, and Benjamin, *Origin*, op. cit., p. 202.

37 Eagleton, *Benjamin*, op. cit., p. 20 and notes 35, 36, 37, which give his references to Benjamin's work.

38 Frye, *Anatomy*, op. cit., p. 89, Joel Fineman cites Frye in his discussion of this dimension of allegory in "The Structure of Allegorical Desire," *October*, 12 (Spring, 1980), p. 49. Also see Fredric Jameson, who, in the preface to *The Political Unconscious* (Ithaca, 1981), p. 10, declares that "interpretation is here construed as an essentially allegorical act, which consists in rewriting a given text in terms of a particular interpretive master code." Probably no critic has done more to reinstate allegory as the primary figure of interpretation than the late Paul de Man, in whose seminal essay, "The Rhetoric of Temporality," originally published in 1969 (republished in *Blindness and Insight: Essays in the Rhetoric of Contemporary Criticism*, Minneapolis, 1983, pp. 187–228), symbol is disparaged as a mystification and allegory associated with an "authentic understanding of language and temporality" (Jonathan Culler, *On Deconstruction*, Ithaca, 1985, p. 185), Indeed, de Man's study of the nature of figural language in the work of Rousseau, Nietzsche, Rilke, and Proust is entitled *Allegories of Reading* (New Haven, 1979).

39 A Barthean *punctum*? Perhaps. But even *punctum* can be unraveled. See Victor Burgin's piece, "Diderot, Barthes, *Vertigo*," in *Formations of Fantasy*, ed. V. Burgin, J. Donald, and C. Kaplan (London and New York, 1986), esp. pp. 86–101, for an interesting attempt. Virginia Woolf has commented most appositely on the male display (what Lacan calls *parade*) embodied by Courbet in his striped trousers: "Your clothes in the first place make us gape with

astonishment … every button, rosette and stripe seems to have some symbolical meaning." V. Woolf, *Three Guineas*, cited by V. Burgin, "Diderot, Barthes," p. 56.

40 Charles Baudelaire, "Puisque réalisme il y a" (1855), in *Oeuvres complètes*, ed. Y.-G. Le Dantec and C. Pichois (Paris, 1961), p. 637.

41 For the political implications of Courbet's image of Baudelaire in this painting, see the end of T. J. Clark's complex analysis locating the revolutionary context of Courbet's *c.* 1848 *Portrait of Baudelaire*, the image upon which the one in *The Painter's Studio* is based. Of the portrait Clark says: "This is an image of privacy and self-absorption, a space where one man excludes the world of public statement." T. J. Clark, *Image of the People* (Princeton, 1982; orig. publ. 1973), p. 75.

42 Charles Baudelaire, "Les Petites Vieilles," from *Tableaux Parisiens* in *Oeuvres complètes*, pp. 85–86: "Ces yeux mystérieux ont d'invincibles charmes / Pour celui que l'austère Infortune allaita!"

Chapter 10 *Part Two*

1 See L. Nochlin, "Courbet's *L'Origine du monde*: The Origin without an Original," *October*, 37 (1986), pp. 76–86 (Chapter 9 in the present volume).

2 Or of ambiguously placed branches or "bisexual spindles," which Michael Fried, in his essay, "Courbet's 'Femininity'" in *Courbet Reconsidered*, pp. 43–53, posits as signifiers of Courbet's feminine, or even protofeminist, identification with his female subjects (more accurately, perhaps, defined as "objects").

3 The phrase "representing representation" of course refers to Michael Fried's article entitled "Representing Representation: The Central Group in Courbet's *Studio*," *Art in America*, 69 (September, 1981), pp. 127–33, also published in *Allegory and Representation*, ed. Stephen J. Greenblatt (Baltimore, 1981).

4 For the relation of the ephebe, or youthful artist, to the master poet, see Harold Bloom, *The Anxiety of Influence: A Theory of Poetry* (London and New York, 1973), pp. 77–92.

5 Hélène Toussaint, and Klaus Herding following her, claim to see the portrait of Courbet's mother in the features of the nude model. See Herding, *Realismus als Widerspruch*, op. cit., p. 309, no. 13.

6 The female nude has been interpreted as an allegorical representation of Truth, Beauty, and/or Liberty by Margaret Armbrust Seibert (Seibert, op. cit.). For a complex and suggestive iconographic reading of the nude, and the central group as a whole, in relation to an eighteenth-century allegorical print of The Rights of Man, see the article by John Moffitt, op. cit.

7 Klaus Theweleit, *Male Fantasies* (Minneapolis, 1987), 1, p. 294.

8 This youthful male figure can also, of course, be read as the Bloomean ephebe. See n. 4 above.

9 See Fried in *Courbet Reconsidered*, ch. 3.

10 Ibid., *passim.*

11 Originally, he seems to have depicted himself as the postcoital lover in this painting, in the 1844 version of which he had represented himself with his current mistress.

12 For a good summary of the history of *The Wounded Man*, see *Courbet, 1977*, no, 35.

13 By the same token, one might postulate that Courbet was being proto-vegetarian in identifying, as I once suggested, with the dying trout in his poignant closeup painting of the fish. What seems important to me is not whether the artist identifies with this or that figure or element in his painting, but what such identification means, how it is to be interpreted – and by whom.

14 See Fried in *Courbet Reconsidered*, ch. 3.

15 Ibid., p. 47.

16 See Arthur Munby, *Munby: Man of Two Worlds* (London, 1972) and Liz Stanley, ed., *The Diaries of Hannah Culrick, Victorian Maid-servant* (New Brunswick, NJ, 1984) for illustrations of the powerful working-class woman. A truly androgynous – and transgressive – imagery embodying muscular masculine arms and seductive feminine face – had to wait for the twentieth century, most notably in the work of the woman collagist and member of Berlin Dada, Hannah Höch, in her provocative *Tamer* of 1930.

17 For an important discussion of the theme of sleep in Courbet's work, viewed in the context of scientific and literary investigations of the theme during the mid-nineteenth century, see Aaron Sheon, "Courbet, French Realism and the Discovery of the Unconcious," *Arts*, 55 (February 1981) pp. 114–28 .

18 Nor is the figure either fully awake or fully asleep, but rather in some intermediary state of languor, associated with sexual availability or postcoital repleteness – again, a scandalous "intermediary" state.

19 Flora Tristan [Flore Célestine Thérèse Henriette Tristan y Moscozo], *Flora Tristan's London Journal: A Survey of London Life in the 1830s* (a translation of *Promenades dans Londres*), trans. D. Palmer and G. Pincetl (London, 1980), p. 78.

20 Ibid., p. 78 and n. 1. Horrifying as this image of transgression and degradation is, it becomes even more so if we think of the "tossing of the liquids" as a euphemism for even worse – more basic acts of gendered desecration: men vomiting, urinating, or even defecating on the helpless bodies of women as a sign of ultimate contempt. Surely it is this ultimate transgressive befouling that the act – and Tristan's obsessive visual recounting of it – encodes. At the same time, the Tristan passages are interesting in the way they seem to anticipate hostile critical reaction to the bold use of pigment characteristic of Manet and the Impressionists. This critical vocabulary constantly equates synoptic brushwork with "dirt," unmodulated passages of light and dark tones as "filthy," etcetera.

21 The presence of the male hat and gloves in the boat in the background of the painting also signals a certain attempt at moral narrative here. Holman Hunt's repentant fallen woman in the *Awakening Conscience*, painted in 1852, is also wearing white lingerie – a nightdress – as a token of her moral lapse.

22 This tract was published after its author's death in 1865. See P.-J Proudhon, *La Pornocratie on les femmes dans les temps modernes*, ed. C. Bouglé and H. Moysset in *Oeuvres complètes* (Paris, 1939), pp. 303–412.

23 P.-J. Proudhon, *Du Principe de l'art et de sa destination sociale* in *Oeuvres complètes*, op. cit., pp. 1–301.

24 Ibid., p. 199.

25 Ibid., p. 201.

26 Susan Sontag, "The Pornographic Imagination," *Styles of Radical Will* (New York, 1981), p. 45.

27 Of course such practices within the realm of art need to be examined within the context of the 19th-century production of sexual discourses analyzed by Michel Foucault in the *History of Sexuality* (New York, 1980). For the classic article on the differences constituted by reading vanguard practices in 20th-century representation from a feminist perspective, see Carol Duncan, "Virility and Domination in Early Twentieth-Century Vanguard Painting," *Feminism and Art History: Questioning the Litany*, ed. Norma Broude and Mary D. Garrard (New York, 1982), pp. 293–313.

28 Susan Rubin Suleiman, "Pornography, Transgression, and the Avant-Garde: Bataille's *Story of the Eye*," *The Poetics of Gender*, ed. Nancy K. Miller (New York, 1986), pp. 117–36.

29 I have attempted to stay as close to Suleiman's original text as possible in my transposition. Here is Suleiman, discussing Bataille as a prime example of the notion of discursive transgression in pornographic texts: "What we see here is the transfer … of the notion of transgression from the realm of experience – whose equivalent, in fiction, is representation – to the realm of words, with a corresponding shift in the roles and importance accorded to the signifier and the signified. The signified becomes the vehicle of the metaphor, whose tenor … is the signifier: the sexually scandalous scenes of *Histoire de l'œil* are there to "signify" Bataille's linguistically scandalous verbal combinations, not vice versa." Suleiman, op. cit., p. 120.

30 For the complex issue of women's viewing positions as set forth in recent feminist film theory, see: Laura Mulvey, "Visual Pleasure and Narrative Cinema," *Screen*, 16:3 (Autumn 1975), pp. 6–18; Mary Ann Doane, "Film and Masquerade – Theorizing the Female Spectator," *Screen* 23:3–4 (September–October 1982), pp. 74–88; Teresa de Lauretis, "Desire in Narrative," *Alice Doesn't: Feminism, Semiotics, Cinema* (Bloomington, 1984), pp. 103–57; E. Ann Kaplan, "Is the Gaze Male?" *Women and Film: Both Sides of the Cinema* (New York, 1983), chap. 1; Annette Kuhn, *Women's Pictures: Feminism and Cinema* (London, 1982), *passim*; and esp. Mary Ann Doane, "The Desire to Desire," *The Desire to Desire: The Woman's Film of the 1940s* (Bloomington, 1987), pp. 1–37.

31 This shifty and ambiguous viewing position must be differentiated from what has been termed "oscillation" and constitutes a pleasurable subject position for women constituted in relation to an androgynous object of the gaze. I am grateful to Maud Lavin for bringing this distinction to my attention in her dissertation in progress, "Hannah Höch, Photomontage, and the Representation of the New Woman in Weimar Germany, 1918–1933," The Graduate School and University Center of the City University of New York. But this pleasurable oscillation is not possible in relation to representations that position women as closed, replete, finished, perfect natural objects; only in relation to viewing those that position "her" as a construct of disparate fragments, as in the Dada photomontages of Höch, the present-day work of Barbara Kruger, or certain vanguard feminist filmmakers.

32 Suleiman, op. cit., p. 132. The author continues: "What does appear to me certain is that there will be no renewal, either in a poetics or in a politics of gender, as long as every drama, whether textual or sexual, continues to be envisaged – as in Bataille's pornography and in Harold Bloom's theory of poetry – in terms of a confrontatiion between an all-powerful father and a traumatized son, a confrontation staged across and over the body of the mother."

33 Heterosexual of course – and middle-aged, and above all, used to wearing clothes, having names, being in authority.

34 P.-J. Proudhon, *La Pornocratie ou les femmes dans les temps modernes*, pp. 309–412. Proudhon firmly believed that women had the choice of being either housewives or harlots: nothing else. His book is the most consistent anti-feminist tract of its time, or perhaps, any other, and as such is worthy of careful study. Certainly, it raises all the main issues about woman's position in society and her sexuality with a paranoid intensity unmatched in any other text.

35 I have borrowed the words, which seem appropriate to the occasion, of Julia Kristeva in "Motherhood According to Bellini," evoking the experience of *jouissance*, Julia Kristeva, "Motherhood According to Bellini," *Desire in Language*, ed. Leon Roudiez, trans. T. Gora, et al. (New York, 1980), p. 248. The women's laughter I have borrowed from the courtroom scene in Marlene Goris's film, *A Question of Silence*. Elaine Showalter, more briefly, imagines such role reversal in her dream of a feminist literary conference at the end of "Critical Cross-Dressing: Male-Feminists and the Woman of the Year," *Men in Feminism*, ed. A. Jardine and P. Smith (New York and London, 1987), p. 132. (Showalter's article was originally published in *Raritan* [Fall], 1983.)

36 Nevertheless, my Utopian vision belongs to a well-established tradition going back to the Middle Ages, that of the "World Upside-Down." For a discussion of such role-reversing practices in early modern Europe and their relation to gender, see Natalie Zemon Davis, "Women on Top," chap. 5 in *Society and Culture in Early Modern France: Eight Essays* (Stanford, CA, 1975), pp. 124–51. The classic investigation of carnivalesque practices, including that of role reversal, is Mikhail Bakhtin's *Rabelais and His World*. trans. H Iswolsky (Bloomington, 1984). For the theme of Utopian inversion in relation to Marxism, see Gerard Raulet, "Critique of Religion and Religion as Critique: The Secularized Hope of Ernst Bloch," trans. D. Parent, ed. T. Luke, *New German Critique*, 9 (Fall 1976), pp. 76–77.

37 Carnival, as Michael Holquist points out in his prologue to Bakhtin's *Rabelais and His World*, must not, of course, be "confused ... with self-serving festivals fostered by governments, secular or theocratic" (p. xviii). My analogy between the traditional carnival and the Exposition Universelle can only go so far. Nevertheless, Courbet made of it what he could: in a sense, he transformed, for his own productive purposes, a "self-serving festival" into an irreverent carnival. See note 36 above. The theme of the ruler paying homage to the artist had a certain vogue in the earlier 19th century, in works like Ingres's *Death of Leonardo de Vinci*, in which the artist expires in the arms of François I; or Robert-Fleury's *Charles V Picking up Titian's Paint Brush*. See L. Nochlin "Gustave Courbet's *Meeting*: A Portrait of the Artist as a Wandering Jew," *Art Bulletin*, 49:3 (1967), pp. 218–19 (Chapter 2, pp. 47–48, in the present volume), and Francis Haskell, "The Old Masters in Nineteenth-Century French Painting," *Art Quarterly*, 24:1 (1971), pp. 55–80.

38 For a detailed examination of hidden political references, often of a rather "basic" or "popular" nature, in two of Courbet's paintings of the 1850s – *La Mère Grégoire* and *Le Départ des pompiers* – see H. Toussaint, "Le Réalisme de Courbet au service de la satire politque et de la propagande gouvernementale," Les Amis de Gustave Courbet, *Bulletin*, 67 (1982), pp. 5–27.

39 Fletcher, *Allegory*, op. cit., p. 328. Fletcher further defines the political grounding of allegory as follows: "The art of subterfuge par excellence, it needs to be justified as an art proper to those moments when nothing but subterfuge will work, as in a political state where dictatorial censorship prevails" (p. 345). Also see Joel Fineman: "We can note that allegory seems regularly to surface in critical or polemical atmospheres, when for political or metaphysical reasons there is something that cannot be said." "The Structure of Allegorical Desire," *October*, 12 (Spring 1980), pp. 48.

40 See, especially, Thomas Crow, "Modernism and Mass Culture in the Visual Arts," in *Modernism and Modernity: The Vancouver Conference Papers* (Halifax, Nova Scotia, 1983), pp. 215–64.

41 Ibid., p. 224. For T. J. Clark on the *Burial at Ornans*, see T. J. Clark, *Image of the People* (London and Princeton, 1982), pp. 140–49 and 153–56.

42 For information about the emperor's involvement in the Exposition Universelle, see Herding, *Realismus als Widerspruch*, op. cit., p. 238. For the most recent detailed examination of the art-politics of the 1855 Exposition, see P. Mainardi, *Art and Politics of the Second Empire* (London and New Haven, 1987), pp. 32–120.

43 Toussaint, in *Courbet, 1977*, p. 262.

44 See especially the letter from Courbet to his patron. Alfred Bruyas, describing his fateful luncheon with Nieuwerkerke, during the course of which the latter asked Courbet to do a painting for the Exhibition of 1855 which would have to be submitted to two committees for approval. Courbet proudly rejected the offer, the artist declaring to the superintendent that: "I also was a Government and that I defied his to do anything for mine that I could accept," P. Borel, *Lettres de Gustave Courbet à Alfred Bruyas* (Geneva 1951), p. 68.

45 Herding, *Realismus als Widerspruch*, op. cit., p. 22.

46 Of course, it is important to remember that Courbet by no means renounced official acceptance. He did, after all, show eleven paintings – no small number for a relatively young man of thirty-six – at the government-sponsored exhibition in the Palais des Beaux-Arts.

47 For information about the fate of the painting between the time that Courbet exhibited it in 1855 and that of its purchase for the Louvre, see "En 1920, 'L'Atelier' de Courbet entrait au Louvre," Les Amis de Gustave Courbet, *Bulletin*, 29 (1961), pp. 1–13, and p. 2, n. 1.

48 For a discussion of the depoliticization of Courbet and his work in the early years of the Third Republic, see L. Nochlin, "The De-Politicization of Gustave Courbet: Transformation and Rehabilitation under the Third Republic," *October*, 22 (1982), pp. 64–78 (Chapter 7 in the present volume). Although there were always a few people, like Jules Vallès, who saw Courbet's life and his painting as primarily political in their meaning, the repoliticization of the artist's work was not achieved until 1941, when Meyer Schapiro published his remarkable article "Courbet and Popular Imagery," *Journal of the Warburg and Courtauld Institutes*, 4 (1941), pp. 164–91, in which the author insisted on the social and political meaning of Courbet's choice of language and the impact of 1848 on the formation of his style. This reading of Courbet was the spring-board for the author's own investigation of Courbet, in both her doctoral dissertation – *Gustave Courbet: A Study of Style and Society* (New York, 1976), originally Ph.D. diss., New York University, 1963 – and articles like "Gustave Courbet's *Meeting*: A Portrait of the Artist as a Wandering Jew," *Art Bulletin*, 49 (1967), pp. 209–22 (Chapter 2 in the present volume). A full-scale revisionist reading of Courbet from the vantage point of a social history of art had to wait until 1973 and T. J. Clark's *Image of the People: Gustave Courbet and the 1848 Revolution*.

49 For a differentiation among *The Painter's Studio*, Courbet's work in general, and the project of modernism, see L. Nochlin, *"The Invention of the Avant-Garde: France, 1830–80," Art News Annual*, 24 (1968), pp. 13–16.

50 The compulsive syndrome is, as Angus Fletcher astutely points out, the proper psychoanalytic analogue to allegory. See Fletcher, *Allegory*, op. cit., p. 286. Compulsive behavior is, as Fletcher also points out, like allegory, highly orderly and above all, supersystematic (p. 291); such compulsive systematization also marks to a high degree the Utopian

theories of Charles Fourier as well as the theories and practices of his followers: the Utopian vegetarian Jupille, for instance, who proselytized for socialist salvation through a noncarnivorous diet; or the Fourietist dramatist Sardat, author of a bizarre didactic drama entitled "La Loi d'union ou nouvelle organisation sociale," in sixteen acts and a prologue, with a cast of 296 ranging in age from four to seventy, set in a "Temple de Bonheur" and setting forth the hopes, duties, pleasures, and daily life in a phalanstery of eighty families in a rhetorical structure that might well be called, for lack of a better term, a "real allegory." Courbet's allegory must, of course, be distinguished from the wilder excesses of these Utopian eccentrics described by Champfleury (*Les Excentriques*, 2nd edn, Paris, 1877, 1st pub. 1852, pp. 77–82, 149–51, and 155) but there is enough of that tradition of eccentric extremism remaining in *The Painter's Studio* to remove it from the realm of the simple, down-to-earth critique and elevate it to that of eschatological transformation. For the impact of Fourierist ideas on the iconography of *The Studio*, see Nochlin, "*The Invention of the Avant-Garde: France, 1830–80*," op. cit., esp. pp. 18–19.

51 Ernst Bloch, cited in Gerard Raulet, "Critique of Religion and Religion as Critique: The Secularized Hope of Ernst Bloch," in *New German Critique*, 9 (Fall 1976), p. 82.

Chapter 11

1 Much of this material on Courbet's *Oak* is taken from a long, unpublished lecture, "Courbet's *Oak of Flagey*: A Landscape Motif and its Meanings," presented at the NYU Institute of Fine Arts in 1978 and at Princeton University in 1979. A summary of this lecture, which was later given at the Musée d'Orsay, was published as "*Le Chêne de Flagey de Courbet*. Un motif de paysage et sa signification" in *Quarante-huit/Quatorze*, 1 (Conférences du Musée d'Orsay, 1989), pp. 15–25. It is interesting to note that an oak tree figured in one of Courbet's earliest works, a crude lithograph, "The Virgin of the Old Oak," one of a series of four illustrations for his friend Max Buchon's *Essaies poétiques*, published in Besançon in 1839.

2 See Louis Marin, *To Destroy Painting*, trans. Mette Huort (Chicago, 1995), p. 159.

3 Of course there are 19th-century tree images that assert the vulnerability of the big tree, like the oak, such as Corot's illustration of La Fontaine's fable, "The Oak and the Reed." But here we have an allegory of the small and insignificant plant, signifying the peasant, surviving when nature destroys the high and mighty lord. The message is not so much an ecological as a veiled political one.

4 Le baron (Isidore Justin) Taylor and Charles Nodier, *Voyages pittoresques et romantiques dans l'ancienne France* (25 vols, 1821–78).

5 Sir James Frazer, *The Golden Bough*, 3rd edn (London, 1922), 2, p. 363.

6 Mary Morton and Charlotte Eyerman, *Courbet and the Modern Landscape*, exh. cat., J. Paul Getty Museum, Los Angeles, 2006, p. 40.

7 Jules Etienne Joseph Quicherat, *Conclusion pour Alaise dans la Question d'Alesia* (Paris, 1858), p. 94. See also *L'Alesia de César rendue a la Franche Comté: Réfutation de tous les mémoires pour Alise* (Paris, 1857).

8 Napoléon III, *Histoire de Jules César*, 2 (Paris, 1866), *passim*.

9 I would point to exactly the opposite strategy in the landscapes of Cézanne. In a work like the *Mont Sainte Victoire* in the Metropolitan Museum, the whole vista is, as it were, distanced in terms of rejection of specific surface detail, even in the foreground, and the denial to the viewer of a point of entry into pictorial space.

10 According to Alexandra Murphy, the work may have been a commission for a great *palais* on the boulevard Beaujon built by the architect Alfred Feydeau for a Monsieur Thomas, who went under the pompous sobriquet of the "Duc de Bojano." This gives us a little hint of the pretentiousness of the whole enterprise. There is a long account of *The Gust of Wind* in Mary G. Morton, "Courbet and the Modern Landscape," *Seeing and Beyond: Essays on Eighteenth to Twenty-First Century Art in Honor of Kermit S. Champa*, ed. D. J. Johnson and D. Ogawa (New York, 2005), pp. 15–19. Also see *Courbet and the Modern Landscape*, op. cit., p. 57 and notes 9 and 10.

11 See Anne M. Wagner, "Courbet's Landscapes and Their Market," *Art History*, 4:4 (December 1981), pp. 410–31 and Klaus Herding, "Equality and Authority in Courbet's Landscape Painting," *To Venture Independence*, trans. W. Gabriel (New Haven and London, 1991), pp. 62–98.

12 Wagner, "Courbet's Landscapes," op. cit., pp. 411–12.

13 See Petra ten-Doesschate Chu, "It took Millions of Years to Compose That Picture," *Courbet Reconsidered*, exh. cat., Sarah Faunce and Linda Nochlin, The Brooklyn Museum, New York, 1988, pp. 55–65.

14 For information about *The Origin of the World*, see my "Courbet's *L'Origine du monde*: The Origin Without an Original," *October*, 37 (1986), pp. 76–86 (Chapter 9 in the present volume). More recently, Thierry Savatier has published an excellent, full-scale study of the work and its history, *L'Origine du monde: Histoire d'un tableau de Gustave Courbet* (Paris, 2006). For other interpretations of the Origin, now a prime object of Courbet scholarship, see Valérie Bajou, *Courbet* (Paris, 2003), who claims very credibly that Courbet used pornographic photographs as a source for the work; Michèle Haddad (*Khalil-Bey, un homme, une collection*, Paris, 2000) who asserts that the subject of the painting is not pornographic but rather a stigmatization of the syphilis contracted by Khalil-Bey, who commissioned the work; and Gilles Plazy, who, in a chapter dedicated to the *Origin* in *Gustave Courbet, un peintre en liberté* (Paris, 1998, pp. 179–90), argues that the model of the painting is Jo Heffernan and that the image constitutes a meditation on sexual difference that affirms Courbet's project as a realist. There is much, much more.

15 For an interesting and irreverent new take on the relation between Courbet and Duchamp, see Nicholas Lowie and Sheridan Lowrey, *Jura – L.A.* (Los Angeles, 2005), *passim*.

16 For information about sea painting in the 19th century, see Robert L. Herbert, *Monet on the Normandy Coast: Tourism and Painting, 1867–1886* (New Haven and London, 1994); also see *Manet and the Sea*, exh. cat., J. Wilson-Bareau and D. Degener, Philadelphia Museum of Art, 2003 and my *Bathers, Bodies, Beauties: The Visceral Eye*, ch. 4, "Monet's Hotel des Roches Noires: Anxiety and Perspective at the Seashore" (Cambridge, Mass., 2006).

17 There are about thirty versions of the wave motif, which fixate "on the motif of the cresting wave to suggest the ocean's raw force and its churning tides." *Courbet and the Modern Landscape*, op. cit., p. 104.

18 Guy de Maupassant, "La vie d'un paysagiste," *Gil Blas*, September 28, 1885, cited in Héléne Toussaint, exh. cat., *Gustave Courbet, 1819–1877*, Grand Palais, Paris, 1977–78, pp. 228–30, no. 147.

19 I must admit that other versions of the wave motif by Courbet come closer to my visual experience – the one in Berlin, for instance. But repeated observation never came up with anything that conformed totally to the painted image in its composition.

20 Herding, *To Venture Independence*, op. cit., pp. 91–95, *passim*.

21 For an excellent account of Charles Henry and his ideas about the psycho-physical impact of line, color, and compostion on the viewer, especially as they effected the work of the artist Georges Seurat, see Michael F. Zimmermann, *Seurat and the Art Theory of his Time* (Antwerp, 1999), *passim*.

22 The caricaturist Bertall actually satirized a Courbet landscape of cliffs and sea as a piece of cheese. The cartoon is titled "View of Roquefort, by Courbet. The slice of cheese is a real poem." From "The Salon in paint and drawing" by Bertall, *Le Journal pour rire* (November 3, 1855) in Charles Léger, *Courbet selon les caricatures et les images* (Paris, 1920).

23 There is a lot of food vocabulary connected with French "art talk." One refers to the "cuisine" of a painting, "la sauce," "la pâte," etc.

24 Joe Deal, *Between Nature and Culture: Photographs of the Getty Center* (Los Angeles, 1999).

25 Eudora Welty, "Place in Fiction," *South Atlantic Quarterly* (January 1956), pp. 57–58, 62.

Picture Credits

Ateneo Puertorriqueño, San Juan, Puerto Rico: 57; Bibliothèque d'Art et d'Archéologie, Fondation Jacques Doucet, Paris: 76; Bibliothèque Nationale, Paris: 24, 92 (formerly Alfred Armand collection); Bridgeman Art Library/Giraudon: 41; The British Museum, London: 70; Burrell Collection, Glasgow: 25; Church of San Tomé, Toledo: 51; Corbis/Bettmann: frontispiece; Detroit Institute of Arts: 39; Francis M. Naumann Fine Art, New York: 4; Courtesy Gagosian Gallery, New York. Photograph by Robert McKeever: 3; Gemäldegalerie, Dresden: pl.7; Photograph © Joe Deal: 94; Kunsthalle, Hamburg: 14; Maurauchi Art Museum, Tokyo: pls.13, 14; Metropolitan Museum of Art, New York: Gift of Harry Payne Bingham (1940) pl.4, H. O. Havemeyer Collection, Bequest of Mrs. H. O. Havemeyer (1929) 79, 87, 93; Musée des Beaux-Arts et d'Archéologie, Besançon: 6, 13, 54; Musée des Beaux-Arts, Lille: 10; Musée des Beaux-Arts, Lyon: 28, 82; Musée des Beaux-Arts, Marseille: 22; Musée des Beaux-Arts, Nantes: pl.5; Musée Fabre, Montpellier: 26, 27, 29, 31, 32, 47, 65, 69, pl.6; Musée Gustave Courbet, Ornans: 48; Musée de la Ville de Paris: 81; Musée du Louvre, Paris: 2, 5, 38, 50, 53, 67; Musée d'Orsay, Paris: 30, 72, 88, 89, pls.1, 2, 3, 9, 10, 11, 12; Musée du Petit Palais, Paris: 1, 15, 36, 74; Musées Royaux des Beaux-Arts de Belgique, Brussels: 68; Museum of Fine Arts, Boston: 85; Museum of Fine Arts, Houston, Gift of Caroline Wiess Law: 86; Museum of the University of Puerto Rico, Rio Piedras: 56; Museu Nacional d'Art de Catalunya, Barcelona: 73; Nationalgalerie, Staatliche Museen, Berlin: 55; National Gallery of Art, Washington, D.C: 63; National Gallery of Scotland, Edinburgh: 33, 90; Photograph © Neal Slavin: 52; J. Paul Getty Museum, Los Angeles: 83; Private collection: 84; Private collection, San Juan, Puerto Rico: 58; Rijksmuseum, Amsterdam: 9; Photograph © Robert Adams, courtesy Matthew Marks Gallery, New York, and Fraenkel Gallery, San Francisco: 78, 80; Smith College Museum of Art, Northampton, Massachusetts: 35, 45, pl.8 (purchased with the Drayton Hillyer Fund); State Hermitage Museum, St. Petersburg: 77; Szépmüvészeti Museum, Budapest: 66; Tate, London: 75; Trinity College, Cambridge, Munby Collection: 71

Index

Page references in *italic* refer to illustrations